Sexual Rhetoric in the
Works of Joss Whedon

D1553080

Sexual Rhetoric in the Works of Joss Whedon

New Essays

Edited by
ERIN B. WAGGONER

McFarland & Company, Inc., Publishers
Jefferson, North Carolina, and London

LIBRARY OF CONGRESS CATALOGUING-IN-PUBLICATION DATA

Sexual rhetoric in the works of Joss Whedon : new essays /
  edited by Erin B. Waggoner.
      p.   cm.
  Includes bibliographical references and index.

  ISBN 978-0-7864-4750-3
  softcover : 50# alkaline paper

    1. Whedon, Joss, 1964– —Criticism and interpretation.
  I. Waggoner, Erin B., 1983–
  PN1992.4.W49S49   2010
  791.4502'32092—dc22   2010002313

British Library cataloguing data are available

Front cover: David Boreanaz and Sarah Michelle Gellar as
Angel and Buffy Summers in *Buffy the Vampire Slayer* (1997,
WB Television/Photofest)

Manufactured in the United States of America

*McFarland & Company, Inc., Publishers
  Box 611, Jefferson, North Carolina 28640
  www.mcfarlandpub.com*

Table of Contents

Preface

I remember my mother taking me to see the original *Buffy* in theatres, beginning my love of campy vampire films. My parents always made fun of my love for *Buffy the Vampire Slayer*, believing my obsession would pass just like snowboarding or any other number of things I tried to keep my mind and body occupied. Little did they know I would become an adult who was still obsessed. Several years later, I saw full page ads in the *Tiger Beat* and *Bop* magazines I was reading at the time, announcing there was a new network, The WB, that was going to turn *Buffy* into a television show.

I remember watching the premiere, seeing how this new series was so much different than the film. Still, the show appealed to me, for reasons I wouldn't completely understand until years later as a scholar.

I watched the show religiously through the third season. After that, other things absorbed my attention and I forgot about it. Then I began watching reruns on FX during the latter years of my bachelor's degree: my obsession was reborn. How could I have missed Willow's change in sexuality? As a young lesbian myself, I felt guilty for not being aware of this shift, especially since it was Willow, the one character to whom I had connected the most. It didn't even occur to me that the show was still on. I completely missed the ending, but my membership card had been renewed.

Since the show had now ended, I tried to delve further into it, buying the DVD sets that I could (Season Six had just been released), watching all the reruns and taking notes. I was in college now, so I could take my love of the show one step further and actually study the literary and linguistic qualities. I became interested in everything, studied all the scripts, even collected memorabilia. My connection to the Whedonverse was cemented when I began winning comic book cover design contests: first for the *Angel: After the Fall* Issue Two alternative cover, then for *Angel: After the Fall* Issue Eight.

All this led me to think about all those academic essays I'd read over the years. Why couldn't I do that, too? I wrote an essay called "Buffy Gives Me Goosebumps: The Literary Effect of Music in the Buffyverse" and presented it at the 2008 Popular Culture/American Culture Association of the South conference, where I was given a chance to put the names I had read, such as Rhonda Wilcox, to faces.

As a graduate student pursuing my master's degree, I needed another 600-level course, yet nothing seemed to fit my level of interest or the requirements. That's when I remembered one of my rhetoric and composition professors had mentioned she enjoyed *Buffy*. I figured it was worth a shot, so I asked if she'd like to do an independent study on the rhetoric in *Buffy*, and she agreed.

The class began with three people, and I believe more would have taken it if it hadn't been a 600-level graduate course. At first, we started watching the show together, writing journal responses to things we noticed in each episode. As we wrote our papers, we discovered we were all focusing on some element of sex or gender in the show. Once we started to recognize patterns, we completely abandoned the journals and focused on our papers. My friend Todd and I started discussing all the safe sex subliminal messages in the background, and he mentioned connections between Buffy's forbidden love and his experience dating a man who was HIV positive. I started making notes on possible topics, and the most interesting one dealt with questions I was asking myself about Willow's love life. Why is there always a gun? Isn't a gun supposed to be a phallic symbol? Does that apply here? These questions inspired my own paper. As an added project, the class decided to apply for the Southwest/Texas Popular Culture/American Culture conference in February of 2009, where we presented an entire panel that we called "'If you're doin' it, I think you should be able to say it': Hidden and Obvious Sexual Rhetoric in *Buffy the Vampire Slayer*." As we attended other panels, we noticed that other Whedonists were discussing sexual and gender references, too. I was inspired to try a book-length work, a project that actually became a reality, right after I graduated.

There is so much to say about sexual rhetoric in *Buffy the Vampire Slayer*, *Angel*, *Firefly/Serenity*, *Dollhouse*, and even *Dr. Horrible's Sing-Along Blog*. Joss Whedon isn't writing blindly, so he's surely aware that there are sexual references in every project he's created. Yet, no book was dedicated to it until now. While there have been books dedicated to such subjects as gender representation, philosophy, aesthetics, and the family, no books have concentrated on Whedon's representation of sexuality. Lorna Jowett discusses sexuality in her book, *Sex and the Slayer*, but her emphasis is on the analysis of gender. Additionally, most of the books written have focused upon *Buffy*, with only two books on *Angel* and two books on *Firefly* and *Serenity*, while others have focused on the fandom. This book is unique in that it attempts to tackle the whole of Whedon's oeuvre in terms of one subject.

Every fan of any of the shows created by Joss Whedon knows there are sexual elements at play. The papers I received for this collection offered many great abstracts, but I eventually narrowed it down to fourteen, being sure to include two of the original panel papers from the SW/TX PCA/ACA conference: "The Symbolic Gun in Willow's Love Life," in which I investigate Willow's love life and the omnipresence of guns associated with it, and "Unthinkable Relationships: Vampire/Slayer and HIV Positive/Negative," in which Todd Parks connects his own life experiences to those of Buffy's love life with vampires. Since these were two of the three papers that started the project, and since they trod original ground, it was only fitting to include them in this collection.

Sexual rhetoric, the focus of this collection, discusses the way the mass media examines sexuality, gender, and identity. There are varying ways to see these three elements, and every person watching sees something different based on his or her own experiences. The original plan was to have three sections — gender, identity, and sexuality — but as the proposals flooded my inbox, I realized the biggest mistake would be to identify categories, since a hallmark of all of Whedon's shows is the attempt to break molds. All of the essays were carefully chosen; many worthy ones could not be included. Each contributor has something exciting to say about the shows, and I'm happy to include some of the first published essays on Whedon's latest endeavor, *Dollhouse*. At the time the essays were written, the show had just finished its first season; as publication of this book drew nearer, the final episode aired after only two seasons.

This collection includes both new and veteran contributors to the academic study of Joss Whedon's works. Those of you who are familiar with Whedon studies will recognize names from the Whedon Studies Association and *Slayage: The Online Journal of Buffy Studies*. The essays included in this collection range from exploring specific characters and love stories to more general statements about the shows as entities, showcasing how Whedon's work documents something different for everyone. I'm excited to introduce you to a new phase of the study on sexual rhetoric within the works of Joss Whedon.

Several of the papers are expanded from other panels at the 2009 SW/TX PCA/ACA conference, while other presenters at the conference decided to bring something new to the table. While at the conference, I was able to talk to others about my idea of turning this project into a book, and they were the first to get word before I even sent out an official call for papers. In a sense, the Whedonists and friends at the conference helped make this project a reality, giving me confidence that this subject would find a welcoming audience. Hélène Frohard-Dourlent and Lewis Call expand their work about the representation of sexuality in the *Buffy* Season Eight comics, focusing on Buffy's dabbling in a lesbian affair and the burgeoning relationships that involve kink throughout the series, respectively. Alyson R. Buckman surveys the romantic triangles of the Buffy/Angelverse, emphasizing one of the most popular topics in the Buffyverse: the homoerotic relationship between Spike and Angel. Tamy Burnett focuses on Anya as a positive role model for sexuality, arguing that her sexuality is more positively represented than that of the other female characters.

Sara Swain observes the process through which the three core Scoobies lose their virginity in *Buffy*, examining the rationality behind each act. Meanwhile, Kathryn Weber denotes the way sexuality is portrayed in terms of identity by exploring the sexual binaries in both *Buffy* and *Angel*, giving Willow, Xander, Spike, and Angel a ranking on the Kinsey scale of sexuality. Along those same lines, Don Tresca discusses the differing forms of paraphilia, or sexualities outside the norm, that are portrayed in several of Whedon's shows. Patricia Pender does an evaluation of the homoerotic "bring your own subtext" that revolves around Andrew's "evilness" in *Buffy*.

Of course, sexual rhetoric doesn't just mean sex, nor does Joss Whedon just mean *Buffy* and *Angel*. Jessica Price examines the role of masculinity and femininity in *Buffy*, expanding on Lorna Jowett's work. Pnina Moldovano studies the role of Faith and the other females in the verse in terms of her own femme fatale. Rachel Luria denotes the way female stereotypes, such as the damsel in distress, are shattered, but male stereotypes, like the jock and frat boy, are only reinforced in *Buffy*. Taking on the newest Whedon project, *Dollhouse*, Catherine Coker illustrates the way the characters, or dolls, are exploited not only by having perfect bodies but also by the "blank" minds they possess. Nicholas Greco combines two of Whedon's projects, *Firefly* and *Dollhouse*, to compare Inara and Echo's apparent prostitution and what roles the women play as attractive, feminine presences.

What started as a graduate school project has turned into so much more, and as Joss Whedon continues to create quality works, we continue to watch and read faithfully, both as an escape from our own realities and a need to connect something from television and film to our own lives. When David Lavery and Rhonda Wilcox established the academic study of *Buffy* and the work of Joss Whedon as not merely the study of entertainment but as educational, aesthetic moments, could they have predicted how Whedon studies would grow over the years? Such "quality television," to borrow a phrase from

Wilcox and Jowett, doesn't just entertain us; it speaks to us in a plethora of ways, and years after the shows end, they continue to speak to us beyond casual enjoyment. With the continuing success of *Buffy* Season Eight comics, *Angel's* continuation with IDW comics, as well as the occasional *Firefly*, *Dr. Horrible*, and *Dollhouse* merchandise, Whedonists continue to tune in, valuing Whedon's contributions to our intellectual and emotional lives.

Works Cited

Carstarphen, Meta G., and Susan Zavoina, ed. *Sexual Rhetoric: Media Perspectives on Sexuality, Gender, and Identity*. New York: Praeger, 1999.

Jowett, Lorna. *Sex and the Slayer: A Gender Studies Primer for the Buffy Fan*. Middletown, CT: Wesleyan University Press, 2005.

Slayage: the Online International Journal of Buffy Studies Eds. David Lavery and Rhonda V. Wilcox. Whedon Studies Association, Jan. 2001–present. <http://slayageonline.com/Numbers/slayage1.htm>.

Whedon, Joss, creat. *Angel*. Perf. David Boreanaz. 1999–2004. Fox, 2007. DVD-ROM. 30 Discs.

_____. *Buffy the Vampire Slayer*. Perf. Sarah Michelle Gellar and Alyson Hannigan. 1997–2003. Fox, 2005. DVD-ROM. 40 Discs.

_____. *Dr. Horrible's Sing-Along Blog*. Perf. Neil Patrick Harris. 2008. Mutant Enemy. DVD-ROM.

_____. *Dollhouse*. Perf. Eliza Dushku. 2009. Fox. DVD-ROM. 4 Discs.

_____. *Firefly*. Perf. Nathan Fillion. 2002. Fox. DVD-ROM. 4 Discs.

_____. *Serenity*. Perf. Nathan Fillion. 2005. Universal. DVD-ROM.

The Symbolic Gun in Willow's Love Life

ERIN B. WAGGONER

"You're my big gun, Will."— Buffy, *"The Gift"*

Introduction

In *Buffy the Vampire Slayer*, relationships tend to derive from the metaphorical and symbolic relationships that happen in real life, except with gothic and teen dramedy themes. Joss Whedon and his army of writers often used the literal and metaphoric ideas behind relationships to build a stronger show for a more academic audience. When it comes to Willow Rosenberg, relationships play around her fear of being abandoned and her fear of people leaving, and usually have something to do with a gun. During the three serious relationships that Willow embarks on during the show's seven season run, Willow's love life either starts or ends because of a gun.

To Shoot or Not to Shoot

Regarding Willow's love life, the gun plays an ongoing symbol of deadly power, life and death, and the injuries incurred representing the pain and suffering in relationships. Killing the previous identity in exchange for the next, she should be able to grow, but the gun still destroys and starts pieces of Willow's story. Not until she takes physical control of the gun is she able to take control of her own romantic/sexual identity. In the Buffyverse, whenever a gun is physically shot into a person (or demon), Willow's love life is usually in question during the episode.

The first appearance of a gun in the Buffyverse is when Darla used two guns against Buffy in the episode "Angel," the episode immediately preceding the first attempt at a relationship for Willow, "I Robot, You Jane." However, a shot only hits Angel, not even phasing him. This establishes something that is very mortal, something that can kill Buffy fast. The only other thing that is hinted that can kill or harm Buffy as fast as a bullet is Dark Willow in Season Six. In "'She's Not All Grown Yet': Willow As Hybrid/Hero...," Jes Battis mentions, "Unlike Buffy, who is the satellite around which her surrogate family of 'Scoobies' revolve, Willow has lingered on the outer edges, and proven herself to be a chaotic force more powerful than the Slayer, the Watchers, or any other instrument of authority within the show's diegesis" (Battis 2). Buffy chooses to fight with medieval weaponry (swords, stakes, crossbows) on a nightly basis, only using guns when needed to subdue another person or demon, not kill them. Guns represent a more modern replacement, a more powerful/deadly weapon, form of destruction, intended for the more mortal, humanistic elements of the show.

The first time a person is physically shot in the show is in Season Two, "What's My Line, Part 2," when Oz takes the bullet meant for Buffy, in turn saving Willow from being shot. Oz is shot just as he and Willow start to pursue a potentially serious flirtation, and continues to be shot by the tranquilizer gun (thanks to his newfound wolfiness) up until he officially leaves Willow. On his return, he is shot in *front* of Tara, in turn transferring Willow's affections from one lover to the next. Battis claims, "Willow is the only character who describes love as deficit, as lack. It is disembodying for her — she must become not abject, like Spike, but *object*" (Battis 27). Her relationship with Tara is ended by another stray bullet, and she does not even consider another relationship until a pushy potential pursues her, causing her to recreate the day Tara was shot, only this time the power of the gun is in *her* hand. She has the power to break the cycle, and Kennedy helps her by letting her work out her problems and not openly panicking at the gun Willow has pointed at her.

Both Tara and Oz pursue Willow, admitting their attraction to her, yet doing so slowly, courting her as a slow process, at times even rejecting her until they feel Willow is ready. In turn, Willow becomes the forceful power, the initiator that moves the relationship along. Only after somebody is shot does she take control, does she make the step to pursue a relationship. When Kennedy pursues Willow, the redhead feels threatened within her own identity and instead takes control of the physical gun, since Kennedy has not been shot, has no reason to be shot, and Tara's death was several months before "The Killer in Me," so Willow attempts to get rid of the problem, trying to push Kennedy away. In her article "'Is That Just a Comforting Way of Not Answering the Question?': Willow, Questions, and Affective Response...," Cynthea Masson signifies that "Kennedy acknowledges the necessity of silence

within flirting. Kennedy speaks aloud what Willow has known all along....
Willow's early concern that she can barely make vowel sounds around boys
has been completely reversed by this point in the series" (Masson 19–20).
Kennedy is able to talk her down, lets Willow grieve through the process
of aiming the gun, but still pursues a relationship. Kennedy's forcefulness
shatters Willow's safe identity, ending the cycle with the gun. Willow taking
control of the gun represents her growth from her need of power in the relationship. Masson declares, "[Kennedy] establishes her authority over Warren/
Willow, and the perlocutionary effect is literally transformative. In this scene,
more so perhaps than anywhere else thus far in the series, rhetorical mode is
inextricably linked with physical action" (Masson 21). In the Season Eight
comics, Willow is able to hold a long-distance, sexual, "on a break" type relationship with Kennedy and still be able to hold her own separate identity from
her lover. The gun is used to symbolize a weapon in her fight for emotional/
relational independence. When the gun is used by her to take away a potential love interest, she takes control of the war, and Kennedy's pushy nature
helps her take that step to end her war for independent relational autonomy.

This is perhaps why Willow has such a hard time "losing" her powers
while visiting Oz's temple in Tibet in the Season Eight comic arc, "Retreat."
At first, she seems to be excited about giving up her powers, that she could
actually have a future, but once a major problem, Twilight and his crew,
threatens to defeat the Slayer army, she begins to panic about no longer having an identity through that which makes her a weapon more powerful than
a gun: her magicks.

The irony is definitely not lost in the fact that Buffy often refers to Willow as her "big gun," first mentioned in the Season Five finale. The exchange
between Buffy and Willow informs Willow that she has the power, that she
can do what Buffy cannot. Willow's alarmed reply, "I'm your — no, I-I was
never a gun. Someone else should be the gun. I, I could be a, a cudgel. Or,
or a pointy stick" demonstrates that she's not quite ready to admit that she
has the power, that she's not ready to become the big gun in Buffy's defen-
sive arsenal.

In her article, "What Would Buffy Do?...," Shannon Craigo-Snell mentions that the Scooby gang "share a collection of symbols ... although their
understanding and use of these symbols vary ... allow[ing] themselves to be
influenced by narratives that portray life as a fight between good and evil,
their imaginations shaped by stories that valorize the struggle for good." Later
in her essay, she goes on to say that "[*BtVS*] recognizes that sexual relationships take place within a violent world and are thereby infected with violence.

Likewise, violence takes place within a sexist world, and is therefore shaped by sexual politics that oppress and victimize women" (Craigo-Snell). Instead of taking on the Freudian idea that the gun represents a phallic symbol, the gun symbolizes the troubles and warfare related to relationships, and the gun always revolves around Willow's and none of the other characters' potential serious relationships.

From One Gun to the Next

Starting off with a bang, Willow's first relationship begins when Oz jumps to protect her from a bullet that is actually meant for Buffy. Since his introduction as a character in Season Two's "Inca Mummy Girl," Oz is shown noticing Willow, often querying, "Who is that girl?" Not until the two characters are placed in a room together because of a career aptitude test do they actually meet face to face in "What's My Line, Part 1." During the two episode arc, Willow starts to recognize Oz, but not until Buffy points out that he is interested, and not until he is shot by a stray bullet, injuring his arm. For the first time, Oz is shown to have emotions (albeit pain) in his expression, making him more than a background character in the series. He states, "I, uh, I'm shot! Y'know. Wow! It's odd! And painful." His reply stands as a direct response to what relationships become, a sort of foreshadowing of the Oz and Willow relationship.

However, the relationship doesn't come to complete fruition until "Phases," later in the season. In the episode, Oz learns that he is a werewolf, and there is a hunter, Cain, equipped with silver bullets, ready to kill him. When Willow goes to confront Oz about his lack of interest in her, his wolf form goes to attack her, escaping into the wild where Cain and Buffy are both hunting the werewolf. Willow returns to the library to inform the gang not to kill the werewolf, since it is Oz, right before they go out hunting for him. While attempting to subdue the werewolf and thwart Cain from killing it, Buffy drops the gun, Willow picks it up and shoots werewolf Oz straight in the chest, near the heart. This could be interpreted as a twisted version of Cupid's bow and arrow, but the simple exchange between Giles and Willow after she shoots the tranquilizer into Ozwolf points otherwise. Giles informs Willow that she "saved [them]" by shooting Oz, which in turn gives her the strength to actually move forward and take initiative to chase an actual coupling. After shooting him, she feels guilty, and when they meet again the next day, she apologizes for shooting him, and Oz in turn apologizes for almost eating her. However, instead of turning down Oz for his newfound "wolfiness,"

Willow decides to pursue the relationship, now equipped with a newfound romantic courage.

Several times throughout the relationship, Oz has had to be shot with a tranquilizer gun, and Willow never shows fear at shooting her boyfriend. In "Wild at Heart," the beast within Oz starts to complicate his relationship with Willow. At the end of the episode, after killing Veruca, the Oz-wolf goes to attack Willow next, again thwarted by a tranquilizer gun, this time shot by Buffy. Instead of staying to work out the relationship, Oz chooses to leave Sunnydale to "tame" his wolf, in turn leaving Willow. When he returns in "New Moon Rising," Oz has supposedly achieved his goal of controlling the wolf inside. However, Willow has already started to begin a new relationship with fellow Wiccan Tara Maclay. When Oz discovers this, he transforms into a werewolf in broad daylight, running after and attacking Tara, only to be shot again with a tranquilizer dart, only this time by the Initiative and in front of Tara. Willow feels she has no control over her love life, emphasized by the fact she no longer is the one shooting the gun. Tara runs to inform Willow that Oz was shot and kidnapped, instead of just letting the Initiative take him out of the picture, positive that Oz is what Willow wants. At the end of the episode, Willow informs Oz that she has moved on, that she is happy with Tara and wants to pursue a romantic relationship with her. When Willow goes to see Tara after leaving Oz, she declares that she is with the one she loves, and again, a gun has started and transferred a serious relationship for Willow.

After her failed relationship with Oz, Willow embarks on a serious relationship with Tara, only to have a stray bullet (again meant for Buffy) take it away. In Season Six, Willow becomes addicted to the magick power she possesses, and only stops once she realizes how destructive she has become, not after Tara leaves her. After she has been "clean" for a while, Willow attempts to pursue Tara again. However, the relationship only gets a brief shot at happiness. Warren returns to exact vengeance upon Buffy, one of the first people to use a gun to attempt to kill her since the Season One episode "Angel." He successfully shoots Buffy but does not kill her. While running from the crime scene, he fires off a few more blind shots, only to have them go through the second floor window and directly through Tara's heart. "Your shirt" she responds, upon seeing the blood spattered across Willow's face and shirt. The relationship ends with a bullet right when it started again, but this time, Willow is aware of her power and status.

Willow's reaction to the death of Tara plays upon her fear of abandonment. When Oz left her, she didn't have the power she now possesses — she has since then raised somebody from the dead — but her reaction to the split remains the same: use magick. However, this time, she allows the magick to consume her. It is as though her reaction to Oz's departure was equivalent to the power of a small handgun; but her reaction to Tara's death/departure is like that of a bazooka or a battleship cannon. Battis denotes, "This radical and almost perfunctory silencing of Tara, who is denied a glorious swan-dive like Buffy, or a long, protracted moment of pain like Angel, has been the source of much audience outcry and criticism. Tara's death is further complicated by the fact that she and Willow begin the episode in bed together, after a night during which 'there was plenty of magic,' as Tara herself states wryly" (Battis 30). In "Villains," when she goes to Buffy in the hospital, Willow takes over from the doctors that are taking their time to remove the bullet, a task which only takes her a few seconds with her magick, palming the bullet like a souvenir, replying "It's so small"; slowly, Buffy gets up from the operating table and the three friends make their way to find Warren. Only after Willow destroys the Warrenbot do the others learn about Tara's death. "Guess the last shot was the charm," she tells her friends, indicating that she's allowing the magick to consume her and make *her* the deadliest weapon of all.

Willow, hell-bent on finding Warren, chases him down until she finds him in the woods, ties him to the trees, and rips his shirt open before suspending the bullet (the one extracted from Buffy) in front of his chest. Slowly, she lets the bullet rip through his skin and organs, making sure that he feels the pain tenfold instead of succumbing to an instant death by bullet. As her dark self, Willow is able to convey her feelings with more conviction, not worried about ethics and morality:

> Wanna know what a bullet feels like, Warren? A real one? I think you need to. Feel it.... First, it'll obliterate your internal organs.... When it finally hits your spine, it'll blow your central nervous system.... The pain will be unbearable, but you won't be able to move.... But the dying? It'll seem like it takes forever.... One tiny piece of metal destroys everything. It ripped her insides out ... took her light away. From me. From the world. Now the one person who should be here is gone ... and a waste like you gets to live. Tiny piece of metal. Can you feel it now? [(Dark) Willow, "Villains"].

She is quite aware the process of a bullet, only giving her more power over the gun, since she has knowledge of its power. She doesn't even bother with an actual gun anymore, as she uses her magicks to convey that she has become stronger. After she kills Warren, Willow goes on her rampage to kill the others that weren't involved in the murder; only the love of a friend could bring her back to reality, could make her deal with the fact that there is nothing she can do to bring back Tara.

After grieving for Tara, Willow pushes away the advances of Kennedy until a reenactment scene where *she* actually has the gun brings them together as an actual couple in "The Killer in Me." At first, Willow ignored and tried to resist Kennedy's flirting, but the potential's persistence finally won her over, and she succumbed to a small kiss. Thanks to the basic "Penance Malediction," or "crazy magic talk for a hex," Willow actually starts to become Warren, only to have her buying the same model gun from the same store that Warren used and recreate the scene when Tara was shot. However, this time, Kennedy has a gun pointed at her, and Willow/Warren does the aiming. Battis states, "This moment of loss, of foreclosure, results in Willow pointing a gun at Kennedy's head: case in point that Tara's death still haunts her, and will continue to delimit what she allows herself to feel, and who she lets into her life" (Battis 31). Eventually, the spell is broken and Willow drops the gun, in turn dropping her need of a physical gun ever again to control her love life. She has now acknowledged that she "doesn't know" if she's okay, but she physically and figuratively takes the steps needed, as the last image shows her walking back up the steps into the house. From there, she is able to admit she has the power and courage on her own, and she no longer needs an actual gun to control her love life, which in turn gives her the confidence to take control of her powers.

Not Your Typical Gun Symbolism

Despite popular belief on gun symbolism, Willow's gun does not represent a genuinely Freudian phallic symbol. In fact, throughout the series, Willow denies the admittance of a gun to control and penetrate her lifestyle through a male-dominated reading into a more feminine-controlling approach, as she always takes control of her relationships when a gun (phallic symbol) threatens to destroy the possibility. She takes control of the relationship, only to adapt her own identity into that of her significant other.

In Season Four, Buffy combines her essence with Willow, Giles, and Xander to fight Adam. During the battle, Adam has "upgraded" his armory (literally his arm) into a machine gun. Using the magicks that Willow brings to the table, Buffy turns Adam's bullets into doves, a remark on the naming/changing of objects, since in Judeo-Christian tradition, Adam named all the creatures. Buffy is using the magic Willow has granted her to transform/

rename Adam's bullets into peaceful entities, thus giving Willow more control over bullets and denying the penetration of a bullet into Buffy's body, in turn denying the admittance of a phallic entity to touch the gun's purpose to her own story. Willow is the most defined/signified in terms of religion, especially her Jewish upbringing, so she would understand better than any other character what the significance of the name Adam would mean.

Similarly, the dream sequence in "Restless" portrays Adam and Riley — two stereotypically chiseled male soldiers — with a gun lying on the table between them during Buffy's dream sequence. In her book *Why Buffy Matters*, Rhonda Wilcox indicates the importance of the gun in Buffy's dream sequence during the Season Four finale, "Restless," where there is a gun sitting close to Riley's hand while he explains, "Buffy, we've got important work to do. Lot of filing, giving things names" (4.22, Wilcox 53). The First Slayer has already taken what it wanted from Willow, so the redhead is nowhere near the gun in Buffy's dream. In consequence, Willow does not appear in Buffy's dream sequence, so she is unable to deny the phallic reading of the gun placed between Riley and Adam.

Buffy often refers to Willow as her "big gun," when Willow is the physical epitome of soft femininity with her gamine features and small, thin frame. Wilcox states, "At one time or another, Buffy has called both Spike and Willow her 'big gun' or best weapon. Each of these characters ... can be seen in some ways as foils and/or shadow figures for Buffy, and as completing her.... The series finale shows all of the characters working together, but Spike and Willow have special roles. As, in effect, different aspects of herself, Spike and Willow correspond to two of the emphases of the conclusion, indicated in 'saving' and 'changing' the world" (Wilcox 98). The first time Buffy says this is to Willow during the Season Five finale, "The Gift," and Willow responds by trying to deny that she was ever a gun. This indicates Willow's own unawareness, her own denial that she needs to take control of the gun in order to become independent in her relationships. When she finally takes control in Season Seven's "The Killer in Me," Willow is able to become the "big gun" in order to change the world for the better.

In Sigmund Freud's *A General Introduction to Psychoanalysis*, he claims, "For it is indeed one of the most important social tasks of education to restrain, confine, and subject to an individual control (itself identical with the demands of society) the sexual instinct when it breaks forth in the form of reproductive function. In its own interests, society would postpone the child's full development until it has attained a certain stage of intellectual maturity, since educability practically ceases with the full onset of the sexual instinct. Without this the instinct would break all bounds and the laboriously erected structure of civilization would be swept away..." (Freud 273). Willow struggles throughout the series to make an identity of her own, and when she separates herself from those she loves, she nearly destroys the world, thus ending the Freudian idea of sexual commonstance's importance to civilizations. Willow has lost her place and is determined — in a temper-tantrum revenge plot similar to those reactions of the emotionally immature — to end the world's suffering because she herself suffers.

Willow almost subconsciously appears obsessed with the gun. Freud denotes, "The obsessional neurosis takes this form: the patient's mind is occupied with thoughts that do not really interest him, he feels impulses which seem alien to him, and he is impelled to perform actions which not only afford him no pleasure but from which he is powerless to desist.... Against his will he has to worry and speculate as if it were a matter of life or death to him" (Freud 229). Willow's first serious relationship begins because Oz is shot protecting her, making her feel compelled to check on him, to force her to make the first move after a potential love interest is shot. This starts the cycle of the gun, and it only grows throughout the rest of the series until she physically takes the gun into her hands to prevent a relationship from happening instead of protecting one, as she would often do to subdue Oz. In being the one to shoot Oz, she becomes the person that controls the relationship. She knows that Oz has trouble dealing with his wolfiness and recognizes that her relationship with him would falter if something were to happen that he attacked an innocent person, so she takes control by literally drugging him into submission, taming him to her will. When Buffy (and the Initiative) is the one to shoot Oz, and Tara is shot and killed, she has no control of the gun, her subconscious obsessive act to control those around her.

The gun itself does not represent the typical phallic symbol, but rather an overcoming of the masculine order. Freud states, "With all due modifications, it is to be admitted that among the contents of the various phobias many are found which ... are specially suited by phylogenetic inheritance to become objects of dread. It is even in agreement with this that many of these dreaded things have no connection with danger, except through a *symbolic* relation to it" (Freud 356). This is manifested through Willow's fear of being left alone. What could cause aloneness more than death? What is more deadly and quicker than a gun? Whedon often connects symbolism to the real aspects, thus denying Freud's "symbolism only" response. Willow's subconsciously obsessive act with the gun represents her want to overcome her fear, yet prevents her from growing into the emotional maturity needed for such a declaration of independence. When she physically takes the gun into her hand and admits its power over her life, Willow finally overcomes her fear and is able to pursue a relationship based on her own separate identity.

The Final Shot

In the Buffyverse, there may be coincidence, or there may not be, but Whedon and his band of writers are clever enough to recognize that certain elements coincide or appear throughout the show. Wilcox denotes, "Whether or not the elements are planned beforehand or tuned afterwards, they are made to work under the guiding touch of 'perfectionist' Whedon. Both in terms of the long narrative arc and the subtle details of interconnection, no one has ever taken fuller advantage of the medium of television than third-generation television writer Joss Whedon and his creative company" (Wilcox 10). There is no proof that Whedon and crew intended for the gun to play a major role in Willow's story. However, Willow's obsessive act with the gun represents her trying to deny the patriarchal reading, a common theme with Whedon's works, by taking control of how the gun controls her love life. When she no longer has that control, her relationships end, whether through life or death.

In the Season Eight comics, we see that Willow has managed to live well into the future, though the details are sketchy. She calls upon Buffy to visit the future, where Willow plans a "dark" plot just so that she can die. When Buffy asks, "Why does it have to be me?" Willow responds, "It's a long story" (Whedon 29). We're left wondering what this long story is, but the fact that Buffy has to kill Willow with the scythe, the very scythe that Willow used during her "big gun" moment represents that everything in the Buffyverse (and even in the future Frayverse) comes back around to Willow and her subconscious obsession with the gun. It wasn't just any scythe, any slayer that could finally kill Willow after centuries; it had to be Buffy, the very person that declared that Willow was her "big gun," the first person that a gun affected in Willow's life.

Works Cited

Battis, Jes. "'She's Not All Grown Yet': Willow as Hybrid/Hero in *Buffy the Vampire Slayer*." *Slayage: The Online International Journal of Buffy Studies.* Mar. 2004. <http://slayage online.com/essays/slayage8/Battis.htm>.

Buffy the Vampire Slayer: The Chosen Collection. Creator Joss Whedon. Perf. Alyson Hannigan and Sarah Michelle Gellar. 1997–2003. DVD. Fox DVD, 2005.

Craigo-Snell, Shannon. "What Would Buffy Do? Feminist Ethics and Epistemic Violence." *JumpCut: A Review of Contemporary Media.* Winter 2006. <http://www.ejumpc ut.org/archive/jc48.2006/BuffyEthics/index.html>.

Freud, Sigmund. *A General Introduction to Psychoanalysis.* Garden City, NY: Garden City, 1943.

Masson, Cynthea. "'Is That Just a Comforting Way of Not Answering the Question?': Willow, Questions, and Affective Response in *Buffy the Vampire Slayer.*" *Slayage: The Online International Journal of Buffy Studies.* May 2006. <http://slayageonline.com/essays/ slayage20/Masson.htm>.

Whedon, Joss (w), Karl Moline (p). "Time of Your Life: Part 4." *Buffy the Vampire Slayer: Joss Whedon's Season Eight.* v1 #19 (Nov 2008). Part 4 [of 4], "Time of Your Life." v1 #16–#19 (Aug.–Nov. 2008), Dark Horse Comics.

Wilcox, Rhonda. *Why Buffy Matters: The Art of* Buffy the Vampire Slayer. New York: I.B. Tauris, 2005.

Unthinkable Relationships
Vampire / Slayer and HIV Positive / Negative

Todd Parks

Introduction

As a Slayer, Buffy Summers did a very unthinkable thing. She fell in love with a vampire: Angel. As a gay man, I fell into a similarly dangerous predicament when I found out the man I was in love with was diagnosed with HIV. As I watch episodes of *Buffy the Vampire Slayer* now, I see strict parallels between what Buffy went through with Angel and what I went through with my boyfriend,* Kenneth. The emotions are identical, as are many of the conversations, stigmas, and precautions. Buffy's relationship with Angel is directly correlative to the relationship of a couple where one person is HIV positive and one is HIV negative.

Then, as I began my research, watching Buffy, specifically noting links between Angel's character and a person with HIV, I noticed that it isn't solely Angel's storyline where Joss Whedon chooses to display stigmatizations of HIV and AIDS. The same conversations, concerns, and emotions which impacted me concerning Buffy and Angel's relationship are reinvented in the characters of Ford, Buffy's crush from Los Angeles, whose only appearance is in Season Two's "Lie to Me," and Spike, the vampire who actually replaces Angel as Buffy's love interest. Using these three characters and their interactions with Buffy, Whedon mirrors the life of a person with HIV.

Ford

I would like to start with Ford's character and his relationship to Buffy, as he is the most minor character of the show that I will discuss; but regard-

---

Names have been changed to protect privacy.

less of his brief appearance during the span of the series, his correlation to a person with HIV and AIDS proves to be just as significant. Ford enters and exits the show in only one episode, but his presence is indicative to a person coming to terms with having HIV. In "Lie to Me," viewers see Ford experience parallels of Kubler-Ross's five stages of dying: denial and isolation, anger, bargaining, depression, and finally acceptance. Ford appears in Sunnydale seemingly on a whim when he said that his dad "got the transfer" from Los Angeles, where Buffy and he were friends and former crushes. Whedon already hints at Ford's isolation by how the scene of his arrival is arranged spatially. When Buffy and he are first reunited, Buffy, Willow, and Xander are seated in the student lounge area, while Ford approaches them and remains standing. This isolation factor is further explored when the Scoobies, along with Angel, take it upon themselves to investigate Ford, thereby also isolating Buffy in keeping it a secret from her. Ford and Buffy are continuously isolated by the rest of the characters throughout the episode whether they choose to be or whether it is forced upon them. An example of their choosing to isolate themselves is when Buffy accompanies Ford out of the Bronze for a walk after Angel shows up and reacts jealously.

Bargaining is the stage of death that Joss Whedon puts into the forefront of this episode as Ford reveals his plan to offer up Buffy to Spike in exchange for Spike's promise to sire him. First time Buffy watchers do not realize that Ford is actually terminally ill as Spike and he make their deal; they only see Buffy being used as leverage. Ford tells his followers, a teen group of vampire worshippers, that they will be able to do the two things every teenager should get to do: "die young and stay pretty." The idea of dying young correlates with HIV and AIDS, at least in my own experience of living in Huntington, West Virginia, where HIV transmission is most prevalent among eighteen to twenty-nine year old gay males. In retrospect, "staying pretty" is a paradox to AIDS, as the disease causes lesions on the victim's skin and causes him or her to experience rapid weight loss while attacking the immune system. However, HIV is very deceptive, as a person with it has no defining physical characteristics.

Then, in the ending scenes of "Lie to Me," Ford's own personal stages of dying loop back to isolation, as he is the only one among the group of vampire followers who knows the sordid truth about Spike and the other vampires' deal. They have promised to change Ford, but the others in the group are merely food. His knowledge isolates him, as he knows that the vampires are not a friendly race like the other followers, Diego and Chantarelle, choose to believe. He knows that they are in fact evil but sees joining them as his only alternative to dying. Then, when Buffy foils Ford's plan, rescuing the vampire worshippers before they are eaten, Ford is left physically alone trapped in a warehouse basement with Spike's gang. Whedon leads the viewers to believe that not even Buffy can rescue him from his isolation.

Ford's physical and mental isolation becomes most evident when Buffy and he argue before Spike and his gang show up. Ford tells her, "I look good, don't I? Well, let me tell you something. I've got maybe six months left, and by then what they bury won't even look like me. It'll be bald and shriveled and it'll smell bad. No, I'm not going out that way." What he fears of his future and his impending death is the most distinctly synonymous comparison to HIV and AIDS. Ford has been unknowingly sick for a while and by the time he realizes this, the disease has already taken a powerful hold of him, and there is no cure. The lesions and severe weight loss associated with the AIDS virus transforms its victim's body into a painful visage of what the person once looked like. Ford's disease, however, is depicted as a nest of brain tumors, but the idea of vampiric blood lust and HIV and AIDS being a blood disease is a synonymous link through the episode.

In my own experience of having a boyfriend with HIV, isolation and anger played a tremendous role in our relationship. In revealing to me his condition, Kenneth was quick to tell me that he did not contract HIV from being promiscuous. He became infected with HIV during a three year relationship with his live-in boyfriend at the time. As Kenneth told me the story of how he contracted AIDS, he continuously interrupted his story by asking me to walk away from him now for my own sake, pleading with me to leave him sitting alone at the bar we were patronizing. Kenneth was intent on isolating himself, beginning with me, in keeping with Kubler-Ross's findings about the first stage of dying. It was obvious that he was even experiencing a forced form of isolation by the way some people who learned of his secret stared at him. A man I was only briefly acquainted with pulled me aside one night at a local bar to tell me of my boyfriend's disease, thinking he had not told me, and when my reaction was not of disgust or instant fear, I too became forcibly isolated, guilty by association.

Angel

In further reference to "Lie to Me," Joss Whedon seems to be using the episode as a segue to discuss HIV in two different ways, from Buffy's friend Ford dying as a teenager from a disease with no cure to a new angle of HIV, seeing it in a parallel of Buffy and Angel's romantic relationship. In this episode, Angel's jealousy of Ford is a sign of Buffy's and his growing intimacy. Ford and Angel are foil characters of one another, not only in competing for Buffy's attention and affection, but in how each one handles his own pain and guilt. The vying differences between Angel and Ford in this episode best exemplify HIV in how each character addresses the guilt factor of their unique conditions. Ford ignores any notion of guilt resulting from him offering Buffy and several other innocents to Spike and his gang in exchange for his own eternal life. His ability to suppress this guilt is a reaction of his intense anger caused by contracting his disease, much like how a person with HIV would have unprotected sex, infecting others. Angel, however, acts overly cautious in the way he treats Buffy's and his relationship.

In contrast to Ford, the way that Angel handles his condition of not only vampirism but also his curse of the restoration of his soul can best be explained in this episode ("Lie to Me") in a conversation between Buffy and himself in the graveyard during a patrol. Angel tells her, "This isn't some fairy tale. When I kiss you, you don't wake up." Buffy responds, "When you kiss me, I want to die." Viewers have obviously seen Buffy and Angel kiss various times throughout the series, but in this episode, the essence of a kiss is actually symbolically a code word for "sex." This link blends the couple's real-life conflicts of passion and romance with the fairy tale scenario of perfect love of which Angel mentions cynically. Angel warns Buffy about the danger of him infecting or feeding on her; this is comparable to HIV and its spread through sexual intercourse. Buffy's reaction is one of classical romanticism: better to die early in life and to have had a love than to live a long life and never have a love. Having this conversation in a cemetery only reiterates the futility of life, along with the physical danger of their love. Buffy sees love as overruling all, but Angel, plagued by his guilt, cannot see past himself infecting her.

Then, Joss Whedon further steps up the parallel between guilt and intimacy in "Surprise" just a few episodes later in Season Two. Buffy and Angel's relationship is becoming much more physical, and the theme of sex is now cast into the foreground. In this episode, sexual intimacy is addressed in conversations between Buffy and her mother Joyce, Buffy and Willow, and Jenny Calendar and her gypsy uncle, Enyos. The dialogue between these characters not only relates to a loss of virginity but also to HIV and AIDS and guilt.

Twice in "Surprise," Buffy's mom asks her, "Do you think you're really ready, Buffy?" The first time occurs in a dream where Buffy is walking around the Bronze in her pajamas, vulnerable. Then, Buffy's attention is directed toward Angel, who reaches out to her before he is staked from behind Drusilla. As he turns to dust, Drusilla casually wishes her a happy birthday. Then, later in the episode, Joyce asks Buffy again if she is really ready this time, concerning getting her driver's license. These two warnings are a blend of reality and sub reality referring to Buffy's internal battle of whether or not to lose her virginity to Angel. The driver's license issue refers to her coming of age — her adulthood. The instance where Angel gets staked is a reference to the supernatural influence existing in their relationship. Fans of the show are reminded in every episode that Angel is different; he carries with himself a burden, a blood-related contagious disease in many ways synonymous with HIV and AIDS. His burden is further amplified by his immense guilt and fear of getting "too" close.

Then, when Buffy and Willow are discussing sex in the courtyard of the school, both girls seem to be ignoring any reservations of the negative repercussions of sex. "I think we're ready to seize it ... the moment," Buffy tells Willow. Willow agrees and is excited at the development of her best friend's relationship. The way they act with each other and the levity of their conversation is referential to typical teenage girlhood. This is in direct contrast to the serious and negative tone of Buffy's dreamlike premonition predicting Angel's death and depicting Buffy's frailty.

It is not until fans hear the conversation between Jenny Calendar and her uncle Enyos, a gypsy elder, that there is a big reveal, and the consequences of Buffy and Angel's consummation comes into the foreground of the show. Viewers learn that Angel's vampirism and the restoration of his soul are connected to a gypsy curse. As a vampire, Angel fed on a gypsy girl and was soon after cursed by her tribe in which his soul was restored. His malady, therefore, is not actually his vampirism but the curse of being able to remember his sinful past and being unable to ever experience a moment of pure happiness. The curse insinuates that he will live forever in the world but not actually be part of it, as the guilt from his transgressions as a soulless vampire consumes him. He is plagued to remember all the innocents he murdered. It is important to note that the gypsy elder who placed the curse could have actually just restored his soul, making him no longer evil, but the elder woman's goal was to actually fulfill a vendetta and seek justice. A gypsy man tells Angel as the transformation takes place:

> It hurts, yes? Good. It will hurt more. You don't remember ... everything you've done for a hundred years. In a moment, you will. The face of everyone you killed.... Our daughter's face ... they will haunt you, and you will know what true suffering is.

This is further reprised in the episode "Surprise," as Jenny Calendar vouches for all of Angel's heroic efforts and good deeds to her uncle, a descendant of the gypsy elder woman. Enyos reminds Jenny that it is not enough for him to be chivalrous and goodhearted now. He reprimands her:

> So you just forget that he destroyed the most beloved daughter of your tribe ... that he killed every man, woman, and child that touches her life. Vengeance demands that his pain be eternal as ours is. If this girl gives him one minute of happiness it is one minute too much.

Angel is never able to be whole again as there is part of him infected — his ability to feel joy or love or, more abstractly, his ability to feel forgiven. Like HIV and AIDS, Angel's guilt spreads throughout all facets of his life.

When Angel and Buffy do finally have sex, Angel again loses his soul, a consequence neither he nor Buffy anticipated. Sex actually becomes synonymous with death. As sex is the dominant vehicle for HIV transmission, it is not a stretch to link what happens between Buffy and Angel with what happened to my ex-boyfriend Kenneth. "I know I'm going to live to be old," he told me one night. Like Angel's immense guilt of his past, Kenneth too felt guilty for his past. He told me it was on his mind all the time that he felt that he deserved getting HIV for some reason but did not know why.

Similarly, like Angel's constant warnings to Buffy about how their relationship cannot get too close, Kenneth too warned me about our proximity, and it was not just concerning sex. He compared it to electrical synapses firing. When he would come over for one of our dates and I would greet him with a kiss, a synapse would fire. When I would place my hand on top of his, a synapse would fire. Even after something as simple as me drinking after him, a synapse would fire. He knew I could not get the disease from him in any of these ways, but still he thought "what if?" The facts and statistics of HIV and AIDS transmission did not matter. Only the guilt of being HIV positive and the possibility of giving it to me mattered to him. As Angel and Buffy's sex resulted in a metaphorical death of Angel's soul, Kenneth's diagnosis of HIV too resulted in a metaphorical death of his ability to be completely happy.

Finally, when Angel returns in the third season after his stint as the villainous Angelus, there is yet another spectrum of HIV and AIDS contraction that Angel represents. It concerns the guilt of being a burden to friends and family. This is best depicted in Season Three's prom episode, when Angel speaks with Joyce regarding Buffy's future. Joyce, worried about Buffy's fate with Angel, knowing that his vampirism on very serious levels hinders their relationship, seeks him out at his mansion. She tells him that she trusts he will do what is in Buffy's best interest. As Joyce outright addresses this truth, she confirms what Angel has been fearing and denying throughout the series. He feels like her dependent, like he is always in some sense holding her back.

A dream that Angel has concerning Buffy and himself after his conversation with Joyce depicts this. Buffy and he are standing at the altar of a beautiful Catholic church in front of a priest. He looks at her in an elegant white wedding dress and places a ring on her finger. She stares at him in his tuxedo and places a ring on his finger. The two are married after a kiss, and they begin to walk down the church aisle toward a large open church door brightened by sunlight. Angel's face shows tremendous trepidation as Buffy and he near the sunlight. When they reach the sunlight outside on the church steps, his worry turns to relief because he has not caught fire, but then his attention is drawn to Buffy. She is consumed by fire in one of the most tragic scenes of the series, and as she reaches for him, her body begins to turn to ashes and the wedding ring falls to the ground.

The significance of this dream directly refers to how Angel fears not only infecting Buffy but also fears holding her back—in a sense, taking her forever out of the sunlight. Instead of Angel dying, he is forced to stand by her side and watch her die. The guilt bestowed by his curse that overtakes him has now, in his dream, spread to her.

In my own experience with Kenneth, he too felt that his affliction, the HIV, put us into two different worlds. He referred to my "fast track" of being in college, aspiring to have different careers, and having an active social life. Kenneth, however, shared none of these things with me, as not only his realization of HIV brought him down, but the side effects of his daily medications also made him frequently weak and dizzy. He considered these things to be a barrier between us, and it could not be helped. Similar to how Angel felt, Kenneth felt that he was holding me back and would continue to do so. He also did not want me to be around during the dizzy and vomiting spells; he did not want me to be part of that life.

In my opinion, Angel reaches his greatest character arc in Season Three's Christmas episode, "Amends." The First Evil targets Angel's darkened past and uses it to amplify his guilt. This omniscient demon latches onto him, plaguing him with memories of his past life where he savagely killed innocents, but in this warped reality, his victims are able to talk to him again, making accusations and declaring their unforgiveness. The most extensive scene where viewers witness this is when Angel is being stalked and tormented by a representation of Jenny Calendar, Giles's lover and Buffy's teacher that he murdered in Season Two after losing his soul. In both Angel's mentality, as well as the opinions of viewers, her death is still fresh and holds the most emotional significance. As Angel is cornered by her and crying, he asks her why she is back and what does she want. She replies:

> I wanna die in bed surrounded by fat grandchildren.... You're sorry? For me? Don't bother. I'm dead. If you wanna feel sorry for someone you should feel sorry for yourself. Oh, but guess you already have that covered.

Her words have Angel weak and cowering as she looms over him. She tells him, "I don't wanna make you feel bad. I just wanna show you who you are." In the middle of the last statement, Jenny transforms into Daniel, another of Angel's past victims.

The First Evil represented by manifestations of Jenny Calendar and Daniel taps into Angel's fear that he is nothing more than his affliction. He is unable to transcend from the role of vampire no matter how he tries. Then, actually seeing Jenny reminds him of how he has negatively and outwardly affected others. In his mind frame, the guilt of being confronted by her and his other victims becomes unbearable, and he decides to commit suicide by waiting for the sun to rise and turn him to dust.

In choosing to kill himself, Angel feels like it gives him strength. By dying, Angel feels that he is facing a punishment and no longer trying to avoid his fate. Buffy finds him by the end of the episode on top of a hill overlooking Sunnydale. She pleads with him to come with her and he says, "Buffy, please. Just this once ... let me be strong." He is sobbing, emotionally beaten, and is simply looking for a way out. Buffy tells him, "Strong is fighting. It's hard, and it's painful, and it's every day. It's what we have to do. And we can do it together." Then, it begins to snow which, according to Joss Whedon's commentary, represents "redemption, hope, and purpose." The thick blanket of clouds and the large snowfall cover and prohibit the sunlight from penetrating him. From here through the rest of the season and then in his own spinoff series, Angel is granted a new beginning and outlook. Though he still suffers from guilt, he is spared from having it consume him.

Like Angel, Kenneth too went through a period of weakness where he ironically thought strength was synonymous with giving up. The night that he confessed his HIV to me, Kenneth went home later, drunkenly deciding to take a knife to his wrists. I remember begging him to not drive home. He told me that it would be best for me to just go on and forget about him, that it would be easier on the both of us.

I must have called him fifty times that night in a span of just a few hours, but he was not answering. When he finally did, we were on the phone for twenty or thirty seconds. He told me he found a way to take care of it all before hanging up.

I had no idea what to do. It was nearly five o' clock in the morning, and I didn't know where he lived exactly, only having been to his house one time before. I drove around piecing together partial directions to get to his place. Surprisingly, I was able to find it with only minor difficulty. I pounded my fist loudly on the door and stopped breathing for a moment when he actually answered the door.

Kenneth's eyes were droopy and his face was flushed. He stepped aside as I walked in, and we sat beside each other on his couch. He showed me the shallow horizontal cuts on both his wrists; they more resembled burns. In his drunkenness, he could find nothing more than a butter knife and had tried rubbing it horizontally across his wrists. He apologized and we cried together as he told me, it was all just too much and he had to make it stop.

Sadly, this was not Kenneth's last suicide attempt. While his first attempt was explicit and seemingly rapid, in the second he again vowed strength in choosing death by refusing to take his medication. In trying to get me to understand his reasoning, Kenneth said that he just couldn't see himself taking his meds for years in the future. They made him weak: dizzy or nauseated. Kenneth saw strength in choosing his exit under his own terms. He was being controlled by his medicine, just as Angel was being controlled by his guilt. However, it was not snow cover that gave Kenneth redemption or hope. It was a much needed reconciliation with his mother. When she told Kenneth just how much he meant to her and how much she needed him, he was instilled with purpose and given new strength in fighting his HIV.

Spike

A final character (again a vampire) that personifies a struggle with HIV and AIDS is Spike. An evil character in the series' second season when he makes his first appearance, Spike loses his ability to bite innocents when he is captured by a government organization known as the Initiative in Season Four. Before he is able to make an escape, this group of scientists and demon hunters implant a chip into his head that impedes his predatory nature when he attempts to bite someone, triggering an intense pain in his brain. Spike's character becomes ruled by this medical entity.

Two episodes, in my opinion, that convey this best are Season Four's

"Pangs" and "Hush." In "Pangs," Spike is comically kicked out of his crypt by his girlfriend, Harmony, for being weak and pathetic. He is usurped by her as she begins to form her own gang. Having nowhere else to turn, he arrives pale and frail on Giles's, Buffy's Watcher, doorstep. They reluctantly take him in, and this episode begins a new dynamic in Spike's relationship with the Scooby gang. He becomes dependent of them — an obligation — as they protect him, investigate his chip, and even bring him animal blood to feed on. In a way, this could compare to how an AIDS victim feels like a burden on their family and friends that take care of him as the disease progresses to its ultimate end.

"Hush" further exemplifies a link between Spike's character and living with HIV. As a mysterious spell has been cast upon the Sunnydale residents, making them lose their voices, the scene is set for misunderstandings. In one instance, Anya is keeping tabs on Spike, and she falls asleep on Giles's couch. Meanwhile, Spike is drinking animal blood from a mug and some of it is running out of the sides of his mouth. Spike spills his mug beside where Anya is laying, and as he is cleaning it up, Xander walks through the door. With Anya unconscious on the couch and Spike with blood-stained lips beside her, Xander thinks he has fed on her and pounces on him.

This scene, although comical, makes a good point concerning HIV and AIDS, which was already previously addressed on some level with Angel's character. Despite him knowing that Spike cannot feed, Xander assumes that Anya has been infected or preyed upon by Spike. Like my boyfriend Kenneth felt with cold stares at the local gay bar, or like how I was received with similar looks at times, there is a certain fear and guilt by association that comes with having HIV or being in a relationship with a person who has it. There is an unreasonable fear of infection.

Spike's character undertakes a much more serious tone and storyline by Season Six of *Buffy the Vampire Slayer*. In Season Five, Joss Whedon writes in an obvious romantic tie between Buffy and Spike. Spike spends Season Five completely fawning over Buffy, living in Angel's and Riley's shadows. Buffy's infatuation with him is much more subtle. Spike goes from being the next best person to protect her mother and sister aside from herself in Season Five to being the person she is most able to confide in by the start of Season Six to them actually having a sexual relationship by the middle of Season Six. Then, when Buffy tries to end things with him out of both fear and ridicule from the other Scoobies, a drunken Spike reverts back to being aggressive and predatory. It is here in his dialogue that Buffy researchers can draw a connection between HIV and AIDS.

In "Seeing Red," Buffy has tried yet again to end the pattern of sexual trysts with Spike, and he obviously refuses to let things go. In one shocking scene in particular, Buffy is dressed in a gray bathrobe getting ready to take a shower when she realizes that Spike is standing in the doorway watching her. The fact that she appears as an object of voyeurism and is almost nude seemingly strips her of her slayer prowess and draws attention to her vulnerability. Spike refuses to leave when she asks him to go and instead approaches her, touching her underneath her robe. He ignores her protests and shrugs off her attempts to push him away. He tells her, "I know you feel like I do. You don't have to hide it anymore…. Let yourself feel it…. I know you felt it when I was inside you…. You'll feel it again…. I'm gonna make you feel it."

Spike does not succeed in raping Buffy, as she is finally able to harness her slayer strength, and Xander appears, hearing the struggle. But it is what Spike says that targets a guttural, animalistic lust and violence that I attribute in a way to a person suffering from HIV and AIDS. The word "feel" can be interpreted in a more abstract sense. Instead of "feel" meaning "as to touch," "feel" can represent an internal struggle of emotions and fears. The same can be said for when Spike says, "I was inside you," meaning Buffy's feelings and vulnerability were penetrated. Though he is obviously committing a violent, heinous act, it is Spike's twisted way of showing Buffy how torn up he is over her on the inside.

Kenneth revealed a deep resentment to me one night, that I previously touched upon in mentioning Ford's struggle. Kenneth said that part of him wants to sleep around and infect others just so they would "feel" how he feels. He attributed it to the proverb, "Misery loves company." He and I both knew he would never do such a thing, never prey upon an innocent no matter how un-innocent his prey seemed to be on the dance floor on a Saturday night. This anger stage was just part of him coping with his own affliction and future.

I would like to end with Spike's succession in *Buffy the Vampire Slayer*, relating it in a link to those living with HIV and AIDS. According to Kubler-Ross's stages of dying, Spike is the only character I have mentioned that reaches the last stage — the acceptance stage. This can be seen in Season Seven's episode "Touched." In trying to inspire Buffy to be confident as she faces her biggest adversary yet, the First Evil and his army of ubervamps, Spike gives a monologue that best summarizes his character arc during the series:

> I've been alive a bit longer than you, and dead a lot longer than that. I've seen things you couldn't imagine, and done things I prefer you didn't…. I follow my blood which doesn't exactly rush in the direction of my brain.

So I make a lot of mistakes.... In 100+ years, there's only one thing I've been sure of: you ... when I say "I love you," it's not because I want you or because I can't have you.... I love what you are, what you do, how you try [Spike, "Touched"].

I will argue that this is the first time the fans see Spike as completely selfless. Whereas Buffy usually provides inspirational speeches, he now fills that role. He also has no alternative motive in saying these things: not to beat the girl or get the girl but rather to just be beside the girl. It is also important to note that while Ford proved to be villainous despite having a soul and Angel was granted his soul only as a precursor to a gypsy curse, Spike earns his soul by enduring trials. He crosses the line several times between villain and hero, but in the end does ascend and has acceptance of his life as a whole. This is best depicted in the final episode of the series, "Chosen." Spike, wearing a mystical amulet, is credited for rescuing Buffy and the world and for closing Sunnydale's Hellmouth. After telling Buffy again that he loves her, he glows from the inward out incinerating what was left of the demon war before crumbling into ashes. In the last episode, his character represents a savior figure.

People living with HIV and AIDS usually seem to find their acceptance stage in spreading awareness and education. This does not have to be in a large format but rather with those individuals around them — those that see them from day to day facing the hardships that come with their disease. Acceptance is not reached by everyone, but like Spike and those AIDS victims that spread communication, true acceptance is achieved by leaving a legacy.

Throughout my years of being a fan of *Buffy the Vampire Slayer*, I found that I watched the show for various reasons. I had a hard day and needed a laugh. I was lonely and wanted a sense of romance. A boy broke my heart and I needed Buffy to slay something so that I would feel better. But then when I fell for Kenneth, a loving man with HIV suffering hardship and trying to cope, I found a new reason to watch *Buffy the Vampire Slayer*. I was seeking an outlet that understood what I was going through, and *Buffy*, despite all of its sub-reality, did that.

The relationship Kenneth and I shared unfortunately didn't last. Like Angel with Buffy, he left me as his means of protecting me. However, we still talk. Kenneth still battles guilt and isolation, but with each passing day, the struggle seems to get a little easier for him. I feel lucky to have been the shoulder for him to cry on, the ear that got to listen, because I learned so much from him. I will probably always in some sense love him, but like Buffy, I have learned that sometimes the best things in life cannot simply last forever.

Works Cited

"Amends." *Buffy the Vampire Slayer*. Writer, Director Joss Whedon. WB. 15 December 1998.
"Chosen." *Buffy the Vampire Slayer*. Writer, Director Joss Whedon. WB. 20 May 2003.
"Hush." *Buffy the Vampire Slayer*. Writer, Director Joss Whedon. WB. 14 December 1999.
"Lie to Me." *Buffy the Vampire Slayer*. Writer, Director Joss Whedon. WB. 3 November 1997.
"Pangs." *Buffy the Vampire Slayer*. Writer, Director Joss Whedon. WB. 23 November 1999.
Perring, Christian. "Death, Dying and the Quality of Life." *Philosophy 350*. University of Kentucky. 16 Dec. 2008 <http://www.uky.edu/Classes/PHI/350/phi350.htm>.
"The Prom." *Buffy the Vampire Slayer*. Writer, Director Joss Whedon. WB. 11 May 1999.
"Seeing Red." *Buffy the Vampire Slayer*. Writer, Director Joss Whedon. WB. 7 May 2002.
"Surprise." *Buffy the Vampire Slayer*. Writer, Director Joss Whedon. WB. 18 January 1998.
"Touched." *Buffy the Vampire Slayer*. Writer, Director Joss Whedon. WB. 6 May 2003.

"Lez-faux" Representations

How *Buffy* Season Eight Navigates the Politics of Female Heteroflexibility

HÉLÈNE FROHARD-DOURLENT

Introduction

In issue 12 of the *Buffy* Season Eight comic books, a full-page panel reveals that Buffy is in bed with Satsu, a fellow Slayer who has confessed to loving her. This is no great romance beginning between the two women. Buffy does not love Satsu back, and the affair ends a couple of issues later, with the pair sleeping together a second and ultimate time.

Joss Whedon might claim that Buffy sleeping with another woman (twice) is "just something that happens" (Gustines), but the volume of discussion generated in reaction to this plot twist is an indication that this is not just another creative decision. In a social context where non-heterosexuality remains contentious, a story that touches on our understanding of sexuality and same-sex desire necessarily fuels passions and engages subjectivities. Buffy and Satsu's story also cannot be separated from the larger cultural narrative about female sexuality that it is part of. Indeed, Buffy is hardly the first straight female character to dabble in same-sex pleasure. In the last two decades, mainstream popular culture has generated numerous fictional women who are allowed to be intimate with other women and still retain the label "heterosexual." This trend of behavior, described by Laurie Essig as "heteroflexibility," simultaneously exemplifies a normalization of same-sex intimacy and raises concerns over the reification of heteronormative standards in our modern imaginary.

A number of anthologies, such as Steven Capsuto's *Alternate Channels*, Vito Russo's *The Celluloid Closet*, or Suzanna Walters' *All the Rage*, have already extensively mapped past gay and lesbian[1] representations in film, television and popular culture at large. These works demonstrate that these images have been unsupportive, especially when "sexual deviance" was portrayed overtly (Russo 156): LGBT people, and non-heterosexual women in particular, have a history of being portrayed as dangerous psychopaths, social deviants who can only be redeemed through a return to conventional heterosexual values. Today, explicit images of non-heterosexuality have become commonplace, and although negative portrayals of homosexuality as unnatural persist, they are outnumbered by images that offer much more ambiguous readings, so that nowadays whether an image is evaluated as positive or not by the gay and lesbian community has become more tightly dependent on one's epistemological stance. Rebecca Beirne sums up the debate as opposing assimilationists, who celebrate normalizing images of gays and lesbians, and liberationists, who argue these same images maintain the heteronormative status quo rather than emancipate the LGBT community (*Lesbians* 21). Willow and Tara's relationship provides a good example in the Buffyverse of an image that has been both celebrated as groundbreaking progress towards more positive representations of lesbian couples (Wilts) and criticized as perpetuating a narrow social norm (Beirne, "Queering").

Although it is important to recognize this context as it highlights the multiple and contradictory ways in which representations of sexual minorities are read, my primary aim is not to weigh into this debate. I do not attempt to classify Buffy and Satsu's story as a positive or negative portrayal of lesbianism, let alone an authentic one. This stems from an awareness that value judgments are themselves steeped in normalizing schemas (who gets to be a positive image?), an understanding that trying to classify any intimacy between women as authentic or inauthentic lesbianism essentializes these experiences, and an acknowledgment that all viewers bring their own subjectivities onto the text, which in turn influences what is considered a positive, and truthful, representation. I am more concerned in this paper with examining how various (sometimes conflicting) discourses are reified, resisted and destabilized in the course of the storyline. In order to do this, I first offer an analytical framework for representations of heteroflexibility in popular culture, then look at the ways in which Buffy and Satsu's story reinforces but also disrupts this framework. Finally, I consider how multiple voices are included and how this impacts the representation of sexual minorities in the Buffyverse. Although I recognize the importance of symbolism, my primary preoccupation is in Season Eight as a text that explicitly deals with issues of sexuality and sexual identity. While subtext is fertile for queer readings (Mendlesohn), I am interested in this narrative precisely because it does not deal with subtext but instead wrestles in the open with its cultural context and our modern assumptions around sexuality, sexual identity, and desire. In other words, the questions that guide this paper are: How does Buffy, both as a character and as a show, do heteroflexibility? How do they navigate discourses of identity politics in conjunction with the growingly popular idea that sexual fluidity is emancipatory? And more importantly, is Buffy gay now?

Lesbians, Heteroflexibility, and Popular Culture

Representations of non–heterosexual characters have evolved remarkably over the past couple of decades. The change from "polluted homosexual" to "normal gay" that Seidman describes for gay men is certainly emblematic of a broader trend in the representation of sexual minorities. Moving away from traditional representations of lesbians as psychotic and predatory (Capsuto 4, Russo 154), analyses of more recent representations point out contemporary trends that tend to center lesbian storylines around marriage and motherhood (Warn, "Baby Boom"; Beirne, *Lesbians* 66–75). Rebecca Beirne notes that this trend is accompanied of a growing saturation in the mainstream media of images of lesbians as "expressive of an idealized and excessive femininity,"[2] which hypersexualizes them for the male gaze (*Lesbians* 46). As irreconcilable as they might seem, these new representations all find their foundations in a new imaginary around sexual identity that emphasizes that gays and lesbians are "just like everybody else" (Britzman 86; Walters 125) and frames sexuality as a matter of individual desire (Diamond 106). The prototype of the heteroflexible storyline that interests me here is at the crossroads of these contemporary impulses and changing ideas around sexuality.

Laurie Essig coined the term "heteroflexibility" in a 2000 *Salon* article to refer to people who are open to same-sex encounters but maintain "a primarily heterosexual lifestyle, with a primary sexual and emotional attachment to someone of the opposite sex" (1). Heteroflexibility has become a topos of popular culture. Movies, and teen movies in particular, are certainly part of the trend (Jenkins), but it is the world of television, maybe because its serialized form requires constant renewal, that has most often been the site for portraying heterosexual females who, for the length of a kiss or a night, engage in same-sex intimacy. The 1992 episode of *L.A. Law* that is often acclaimed for being the first TV episode to feature a same-sex kiss follows a heteroflexible structure, as do episodes of numerous popular TV shows that have shown women kissing. This is the case of *Sex and the City* (1999), *Ally McBeal* (1999),

Friends (2001), *Gilmore Girls* (2004), *Smallville* (2004), *One Tree Hill* (2005) and *The O.C.* (2005). The point is that these kisses are all, in Hefferman's words, "reversible" because the women will not be starting a relationship (see also Warn, "Straight Women").[3] This plot twist was so frequent at one point that it earned its own name, "lesbian sweeps," for the tendency of TV shows to schedule these kisses during sweeps period, in the hopes of drawing larger audiences when ratings are recorded (Lo). Indeed, featuring a female same-sex kiss became popular at least partly because it had the advantage of bringing on temporary controversy that could bring up ratings without the risk serious economic consequences (Becker 131; Walters 114).

At first glance, this trend may seem like a positive change compared to a time where homosexual intimacy could not be shown (Hantzis and Lehr). However, these homoerotic moments do little to challenge dominant heterosexuality. As Sarah Warn points out, they actually contribute to "the increasingly popular belief in American culture that most women are secretly attracted to other women, but (almost) always in addition to — and subjugated to — their attraction to men" (*Ally McBeal* 1). This is a safe display of homosexuality, one that doesn't threaten the participants' sexual availability in the "conventional heterosexual marketplace" (Diamond 105). To the extent that these kisses have increased homosexual visibility, they have done so within strict *heterosexual* parameters. One can even argue that this type of homoeroticism has taken away from the portrayal fully fleshed out, long-term same-sex relationships. Under the cover of portraying sexual diversity, TV continues to incorporate few regular gay, lesbian, or bisexual characters (Warn, "Jumping").

Another consequence of these heteroflexible storylines is that they naturalize the social and cultural dominance of heterosexuality by depicting sexual identity as solely a matter of individual practice. Lisa Diamond explains:

> [These women] are portrayed as having rejected the possibility of lesbianism or bisexuality not because they are closed-minded and sexually repressed, but because it is simply not natural for them, which they know for a fact because they tried it. In a cultural context that prizes self-exploration and open-mindedness, *this is a more appealing and legitimate way to establish one's heterosexual credentials* than to reject the idea of same-sex sexuality out of hand [106, emphasis mine].

The assumption here is that heterosexuality — and implicitly, homosexuality — is something that one is or is not, at an individual level. It is conceived as a fixed state, thereby obscuring how sexual identities are social constructions partly shaped by cultural expectations and narratives. Following this logic, the fact that these open-minded women in popular culture are systematically found to be heterosexual ends up being a mere coincidence: they could have been gay, it just so happens that they are not. This, in turn, further overlooks notions of institutional power by ignoring the role that heteronormativity and the expectation of heterosexuality plays into cultural representations. This also ignores the fact that TV does not exist in a vacuum, but rather is embedded in a cultural context that promotes heterosexuality almost exclusively and thus one instance of heteroflexibility, while appearing inconsequential by itself, actually bolsters well-oiled structural inequalities.

As a consequence, I prefer the term "heteroflexible" to other words that point to similar behavior, such as weekend lesbianism or bicuriosity, because it makes clear that what is at stake is a modern recentering of *hetero*sexuality that, unwittingly or not, trivializes same-sex sexuality (Wilkinson). By positing that engaging in homosexual behavior can be *just* about fun, heteroflexible behavior ignores the stigma and systemic difficulties that come with renouncing conventional heterosexuality (Branner 2). Homosexual behavior only comes at little price to one's status if one has a socially heterosexual identity to fall back on. Additionally, in a heteronormative universe, equating homosexual behavior with light-hearted fun while heterosexuality remains the avenue for forming significant relationships cannot but have powerful implications regarding what is considered the more meaningful sexuality. I argue that heteroflexibility is one of the processes by which heteronormativity adapts to a changing social context. By appropriating rather than rejecting non-normative sexualities, heteroflexibility neutralizes their power of disruption and maintains a status quo that privileges heterosexuality.

Now, what of Buffy and Satsu? On the surface, their story follows a traditional heteroflexible pattern. The lead character is, by Whedon's own account, an open-minded heterosexual woman to whom intimacy with another woman "just happens" (Gustines). Following the conventions of the heteroflexible model, Buffy does not appear ashamed of having enjoyed her night with Satsu, but she is equally unabashed about not wanting a relationship: "tomorrow I'm gonna blush, then I'm gonna smile ... but I'm not sure if it goes any further than that" (8.12). The power differential in this story is undoubtedly in Buffy's favor: as the heterosexual woman and the partner who is not in love, but also as Satsu's military leader, Buffy has the privilege of drawing the limits of the relationship in private as well as in public. She effectively makes use of this authority in both realms, first by making it clear to Satsu that she is not looking for a relationship, and later in front of everyone at their headquarters when she puts Satsu in her place after Satsu expresses unwelcome doubt (8.13). This is not to deny that Satsu has agency — while we do not know for sure who initiated the first night, Satsu is the one who initiated the second, even once the limits of the relationship have been reiterated, thus demonstrating if necessary that she is a willing agent. But it is important to keep in mind that Satsu is not only in a more vulnerable position in every respect, her choices are also intrinsically contained within the limits that Buffy has set *on her own*. This is by no means a relationship of equals, and in a heteronormative context, the fact that it is the heterosexual partner whose agency dominates cannot be taken lightly.

Disrupting the Heterosexual

Despite this problematic framework, I argue that Season Eight also undermines the heterocentricity of this set-up in a number of ways. Because heteroflexible storylines ultimately serve to bolster the heterosexual norm, the first element that I want to consider is how Buffy's heterosexuality is dealt with in the comics. Of course, Buffy is not a blank state when Season Eight begins. Her hyper-femininity, in compliance with Hollywood standards of beauty, has worked in conjunction with heterosexual identity to make her the quintessential modern straight woman in the series: she represents an ideal that has managed to combine strength and independence with femininity. She attracts and is attracted to men,[4] and primarily to the men that Lorna Jowett calls the "tough guys" (95), who embody a more traditional version of masculinity. Buffy might never openly deny the possibility of being attracted to someone of the same sex, but her continuous interest in hyper-masculine males and reliance on men for approval (Mendlesohn) make her an unlikely candidate for an homoerotic experience at first glance. The Season Eight comics unsurprisingly build on this heterosexualized identity that the audience has come to expect of Buffy: for example, she fantasizes about men (8.03 and 8.10), she dresses up to meet an ex-boyfriend (8.16) and she enthuses over a male actor's attractiveness (8.23).

The three of Buffy's fantasies that we are privy to constitute the most significant, as well as the most explicit, expressions of heterosexualized desire because they all visually stage Buffy with men talking about or engaging in intimate behavior. Two of these daydreams are narrated by Buffy to Willow (8.10). In the first one, she imagines herself at the beach with a very brawny Daniel Craig who would like her to spread sunscreen on him, to her delight; the second one features her in 19th century setting in the company of two Christian Bales, planning for an escape that will conveniently require her to "waltz obscenely close in plain view" with one of them. Both these narratives are set up in unoriginal settings with traditional clues of heterosexual romance, and by depicting a *Little Women* and a *Reign of Fire* version of Christian Bale, that tale even manages to combine two ideal types of traditional protective masculinity. In other words, these fantasies are conventionally straight, a fact that Willow does not hesitate to point out and even mock — she calls the Craig fantasy "generic" and comments sarcastically on the beauty of the double Bale scenario. So we can only imagine the kind of remarks that she would make about the last of Buffy's fantasy that is disclosed to the reader. This time it is not a narration, but a peek into Buffy's "dreamspace," a collection of all the dreams that are "part of [her]" (8.03). A full-page panel, all in shades of rose and red, depicts Buffy, dressed up in a nurse uniform and chained in a sandwich between Spike and Angel, who are both naked. Cupids float around, and in the background, two trains are entering opposite ends of a tunnel, which itself is about to explode. Even more than the fantasies featuring Craig and Bale, this dream plays on the accumulation of commonplace hyper-heterosexualized images to the point of self-parody.

These images do not challenge Buffy's established heterosexuality. On the contrary, they bolster it by over-representing her (male) object of desire and making plain her desire for these men in multifarious forms. Additionally, they undermine the idea that Buffy's heterosexuality is a default assumption. By making Buffy's own subjectivity deeply embedded in these images through her own narration and the engagement of her subconscious, these depictions are clearly marked not as passive but rather as representative of a (hetero)sexuality that Buffy has appropriated and embraced. The disruption thus does not come from the heterosexual framework, which is untouched and even reinforced, but from the kind of heterosexuality that is represented here. The dream panel in particular — which one could argue is likely the closer to Buffy's most intimate fantasies than the ones that she is willing to share — depicts a number of non-normative elements: the pairing up of one woman with multiple male partners, the resulting homo-erotic subtext and the presence of chains are not traditional, but they are also not unusual in the Buffyverse. Buffy has explicitly engaged in BDSM sexuality in the past (Call), and this is an unsurprising continuation of this development. These hints at Buffy's non-normative heterosexual desire, along with the burlesque caricature of hetero-romance, effectively unsettle heterosexuality's hegemonic position as the respectable and natural sexuality. This, I argue, implies that despite the overwhelming heterosexuality of these images, the normality of heterosexuality is destabilized.

There are other ways in which Buffy and Satsu's story disrupts the heterosexual center of traditional heteronormative narratives. There is substance to Whedon's claim that he "tried not to [...] spend months going 'Wait for the Buffy kiss so she can figure out how heterosexual she is!'" Unlike most heteroflexible storylines, there is little emphasis in Season Eight on reasserting Buffy's straightness once she has slept with Satsu. As she lies in bed with Satsu after the event, Buffy is certainly more concerned with her "gay performance" than with defending her heterosexuality. She almost takes offense at Satsu's assumption that she is still straight, because she is afraid this may mean Satsu was not impressed. Her ensuing analogy with a school test — she argues that she has not read the lesbian sex manuals and did not have a lot of prep time, which "should be taken in consideration before final grades are given" (8.12) — posits that sex with another woman is something that she wants to be good at (and that one should be proud to be good at). Additionally, she worries that she "didn't do enough things" (8.12), compared to Satsu, rather than take it as a relieving sign that she is not as gay as Satsu. These anxieties, when coupled with the absence of heterosexual reinforcement in the scene, accomplish an almost complete reversal of roles from the heteroflexible norm. Non-penetrative sex (what we think of as "lesbian sex") is usually constructed as lesser, less complete and less "real" than (heterosexual) penetration (Braun et al. 243). But here it is the *heterosexual* character who has to prove herself worthy and equally expert, and the homosexual character who has the power to find the performance wanting, instead of Buffy being able to diminish the sexual relationship as incomplete or inconsequential against the normative yardstick of heterosexuality.

Another feature of the heteroflexible narrative that recenters the heterosexual subject, the voyeuristic heterosexual male gaze, is also subverted in the comics. Traditionally this voyeuristic gaze is established through stylistic devices, but it can also be literal, such as Ally and Ling kissing in front of a male coworker in *Ally McBeal*. Although Jane Garrity has challenged the default assumption of a male viewer, processes that commodify lesbian intimacy for the pleasure of heterosexual males are well-documented (Jenkins 495–500, Diamond 105). In Season Eight, this topos is turned on its head when two of the (small) male cast stumble on Buffy and Satsu naked in bed. Although Andrew's indifference could be discounted on the basis that he is generally coded gay, Xander's reaction is particularly noteworthy, as he has embodied the typical male aroused by girl-on-girl action in the past (Willow and ex-girlfriend Tara in 4.22, and the Slayers-in-Training Gone Wild in 7.18). In contrast, this time when Xander stumbles on Buffy and Satsu, he smacks a hand to his eye and promises, "I didn't see anything!" (8.12). He goes on to lament "Oh, my eye, my burning, beautiful eye" as if he had been struck by a horrible sight rather than what is supposedly the fantasy of every heterosexual male. A few panels later, when he does mention dreaming about the scene, the effect is burlesque rather than sexy since the scene itself has become absurd, with every main character walking in on the two naked women one after the other. Both elements undermine the traditional lens of the male gaze by downplaying the sensuality of the scene once the girls are not alone anymore. As for the role of the reader as voyeur, it is also tempered by the depictions of the girls in bed, who remain covered from their shoulders up throughout the scene instead of the sultry images that have tended to characterize lesbian intimacy in mainstream comics. It is not until later, when they sleep together for a second time, that they are actually shown kissing naked in a single panel that symbolizes the warmth and comfort that human beings can find in each other rather than hypersexualizing them.

By poking fun at the normalized image of heterosexual desire, undermining the power of heterosexuality to judge homosexual sex by its normative standards, and playing against the trend of voyeuristic commodification, Season Eight succeeds in unsettling certain mechanisms of dominant heterosexuality. While the problematic elements discussed earlier are not challenged directly, heterosexuality's power over minority sexuality is repeatedly displaced, and gives readers a glimpse into an alternative heteroflexibility that need not shore up an heterosexual ideal.

Establishing Identity Politics

Beyond the internal dynamics of the story, one of the most striking features of the Buffyverse version of a heteroflexible storyline is that the inevitable recentering of heterosexuality is counter-balanced by a renewed focus on lesbianism. A by-product of the traditional heteroflexible narrative is that, because the straight character is always the primary character, the sexual minority character ends up reduced to a minor role or written out of the story altogether. In mainstream popular culture, where full-fledged same-sex relationships are still rare, this often means returning the focus of the story to an all-straight cast. In other words, heteroflexible twists ensure that the depiction of sexual minorities will be kept to a minimum, while the illusion of presenting a moment of non-heterosexuality allows the creative and producing forces behind the TV show to make a claim of inclusivity.

The Buffyverse is in a different position because the primary cast includes a lesbian character (Willow) who is in a long-term relationship with another woman (Kennedy). This established lesbian presence alone acts as a signifier that sexual diversity is not *just* heterosexually-centered, but Willow and Kennedy are not simply useful decorum. Their lesbian subjectivities are actively implicated in the storyline when they express concern and skepticism over Buffy and Satsu's fling. This explicitly gives voice within the narrative to some of the common complaints that heteroflexible behavior raises: when Willow refers to Buffy's "little experiment" (8.15) or Kennedy calls Buffy "lez-faux" (8.16), they are effectively verbalizing discomfort at the heteroflexible narrative and what it represents — i.e., the threat of the appropriation of homosexuality by heterosexuals for pleasure. These utterances also challenge the depoliticization of a narrative that usually assumes that there are no political implications to a straight woman engaging in lesbian sex for fun before returning to men for long-term commitment

At the same time, these critiques also reveal a certain disapproval of fluid sexual boundaries, and defend a "true" lesbian identity to which they believe Buffy has no claim. In the comics there is a clear line drawn between the lesbian community (composed of Willow, Kennedy, and Satsu) on one side, and Buffy on the other. This sense of community amongst the lesbians is perhaps most explicit when Willow tells Buffy she has to "look out for [her] sisters" (8.15), but it is constituted by a variety of discursive elements. The private talks that Willow and Kennedy both have with Satsu (8.13 and 8.22) contrast with Buffy's silence on the topic (she only briefly discusses the event with Willow in 8.15), and the language used by the three lesbians continually sets Buffy apart from the cohesion of their social group. Willow never questions whether Buffy should be included in "her sisters."

This represents a major shift from *Buffy*'s previous engagement with the question of lesbian identity. In the past, *Buffy* has been acclaimed for its portrayal of lesbianism (Warn, "Buffy"; Wilts), but Willow, Tara, and their relationship have been criticized by scholars (Beirne, "Queering") for embodying what Steven Seidman calls "the normal gay," which is the idea that lesbians can only access representation as normal and acceptable if they abide by narrow social norms of heteronormative standards.[5] For example, Davis and Needham note that it is typical for LGBT characters to see the gay aspects of their lives elided post–coming out (7), and this very much applies to the treatment of Willow's sexuality in the series. In discussing Willow's ambiguity to her lesbianism, Cochran notes that the word "lesbian" is only used by Willow once (52–53). Considering the negative connotation remains attached to the term (Beirne, *Lesbians* 8, 185), it is not surprising that most characters also prefer to use the more neutral "gay."[6] Although there is unquestionable evolution from the layers of unsaid that characterized Willow and Tara's relationship in Season Four (Willow's coming out to Buffy in "New Moon Rising" is a perfect illustration — see Beirne, "Queering") to the forthright utterances of later seasons (such as Willow's "Hello? Gay now!" in 5.11, or Buffy's "Willow, you're a gay woman" in 7.06), non-heterosexuality remained something that was rarely discussed on the TV show. By the end of the series when Kennedy asks "how long have you known? That you were gay," this fairly innocuous question is still enough to cause Willow to become flustered and try to dodge answering. As far as the audience is aware, this is actually the first time, Tara aside, that Willow is interacting with someone else who identifies as non-heterosexual. Over her two years of relationship with Tara, and the extra year spent alone, Willow has never been depicted going to, or talking about a community event nor has she ever made explicit mention of any non-heterosexual acquaintances. In comparison, Kennedy's unabashed embracing of her non-heterosexual identity is unusual indeed, and it is a first gesture towards a different depiction of lesbianism, one where community has and should have a place.

This is the conception that seems to have prevailed by the time Buffy and Satsu sleep together in Season Eight. Willow might still be hesitant to use the term dyke and lesbian, unlike Satsu and Kennedy, but the repeated use of the term "sister" in her mouth does point to the existence of a bond with other lesbians that she had never before referred to. The use of the word "dyke" by Satsu (8.13), but also "hetero" by Kennedy (8.22), emphasizes this at the linguistic level. Dyke in its non-pejorative form points to a process of reclaiming that has occurred within the LGBT community as a response to prejudice in the heteronormative majority: it is by nature a political term that contrasts with assimilationist streaks that look to minimize differences between straight and non-straight citizens. Similarly, the word "hetero" is a term that, in either its playful or pejorative usage, is used to refer to the heterosexual majority in sexual minority communities rather by heterosexuals themselves. In the comics, Buffy herself validates this community: when Willow tells her she has to look out for her sisters, Buffy does not question that statement. She simply accepts it by replying, "I know" (8.15).

Season Eight thus offers a version of lesbianism that is no longer isolated and completely apolitical. Sexual identities and lesbian desire are no longer simply mentioned in passing, but rather they are at the center of several conversations that serve the purpose of establishing sexual orientation as innate rather than socially constructed, a staple of identity politics. This message is in continuity with the TV series, which has depicted gayness with essentialist undertones.[7] Willow is regularly named as unequivocally gay, both by herself and by other characters, and in addition to this performativity, the phrase "I think I'm kinda gay" has been used twice to suggest that Willow's homosexuality is intrinsic to who she is. This essentializing tradition is perpetuated here by the lesbian characters that treat sexuality as fixed. The possibility that Buffy might be *something else* than heterosexual is denied via a variety of speech acts. Immediately after sex, Satsu already has no doubts that Buffy "didn't just turn gay" (8.12); later, Willow unambiguously informs Satsu that Buffy is not gay (8.13), and Kennedy does not hesitate to tell Satsu that she should "face the hetero" (8.22). When accompanied, as I have discussed above, by the lesbian community defining itself against Buffy, these reaffirmations of Buffy's heterosexuality, always in the declarative mood, make it clear that the Slayer cannot, according to the lesbian characters, make a claim to a nonheterosexual identity.

Queering Via Heteroflexibility

"Nothing seems to make sense tonight" (8.13) is one of Willow's first reactions after discovering Buffy and Satsu in bed. Indeed, the binary prism that the lesbian characters are using — that one has to be straight *or* gay — makes Buffy's behavior rather incomprehensible. Bisexuality, an obvious way to reconcile Buffy's fling with Satsu with her continuing interest in men, is never considered, which may seem strange until one realizes that this is actually a common feature of both heteroflexible storylines (Diamond 106) and mainstream cultural products that attempt to promote "positive" images of lesbianism (Beirne *Televising* 3). This emphasizes the way in which gay identity being played up against straight identity, a strict binary that leaves little room for fluidity. Yet, it is precisely because of this inflexible understanding of sexual identity that an interesting space opens in the comics.

Buffy herself seems to disregard bisexuality as an option; however, there is no indication that she does so because she believes that she neatly fits in the homo/hetero binary. Unlike the lesbian characters who constantly reify this binary and unambiguously identify her as straight (and themselves as lesbians), there is little evidence that Buffy identifies with *any* sexual orientation. Even when others are defining her categorically, such as when Satsu uses declarative statements to define her ("but you're not gay" and "I know you didn't just ... turn gay"), Buffy responds either with ambiguity ("not so you'd notice") or with a mix of worry and challenge (*"how* do you know that?"). In other words, Buffy never challenges the lesbians' assumption that she is straight, but she also does very little to confirm it. This absence of clear-cut identification with an heterosexual identity is particularly stark when contrasted with the emotional boundaries that Buffy is not afraid to reaffirm (8.12, 8.15): identity label is really the only thing about which she remains ambiguous.

Of course, the primacy of heterosexual identity in our culture means that heterosexuality does not need to name itself; it simply *is*. Yet Stevi Jackson reminds us that heterosexuality does name itself when it is under threat (23), and a sexual encounter with someone of the same-sex could certainly be perceived as a threat to heterosexual identity. Buffy's lack of interest in reaffirming her heterosexuality is not only unusual; it suggests that she might be purposefully avoiding terms that would stick a specific sexual label on her. Although her silence makes it difficult to discuss intent, this absence of definition certainly allows for the reading that the sexual categories we traditionally use are inadequate to describe Buffy's experience. These inflexible labels not only fail to encompass the complexity and diversity of sexual experiences, but they render them unintelligible. If Buffy never responds to Willow's "nothing seems to make sense tonight," it may be because Willow is right: Buffy's experience does *not* make sense through the prism of essentialist identity politics with which we are familiar. Buffy's silence hints at a delineated space between heteroflexibility and identity politics that we don't know how to speak of, because it is neither heterocentrist enough, nor gay enough.

A number of scholars have made convincing arguments regarding queer readings and queer impulses in *Buffy*, with the figure of the vampire being a perfect candidate for embodying sexual taboos. Most of these discussions find queerness in the subtext, rather than moments where the show openly tackles issues of sexuality and sexual identity. Buffy and Satsu's storyline brings a different kind of queer to the surface. "Queer" here is not about pushing the envelope of sexual taboos, nor is it only an umbrella term that embraces all types of non-normative sexualities. Rather, this is the queerness that Alexander Doty discusses, a queerness that "should challenge and confuse our understanding and uses of sexual and gender categories" (xvii). By not making a claim on heterosexuality *or* non-heterosexuality, Buffy opens a space that messes with this constantly shored up binary. It is a productive space because it is incomprehensible; it works to point to the cracks in identity politics, to the moments where our categories fail to recognize the reality of these complex experiences. It is not a space of political force nor is it a vocal rejection of our system of sexual hierarchies; but it is a reminder of its imperfection and a rejection of its capacity to give us words to define ourselves.

Heterorigid Meta Text

Most heteroflexible storylines shore up heterosexual primacy and buttress modern conceptions of sexuality as personal and apolitical. But the way that Buffy and Satsu's adventure is tackled in Season Eight opens a much more paradoxical approach to sexual identity. On the one hand, the story allows the Buffyverse to establish itself as a text that champions a mainstream liberal understanding of sexual identity as innate and fixed. By giving lesbian characters the primacy in discussing the storyline, it marks a new stage in *Buffy*'s handling of sexuality as a source of community and identity rather than a solely individual experience. On the other hand, this affirmation of sexual minorities, combined with an absence of heterosexual reinforcement, carves out a space in which subjects can live out fluid sexuality by navigating the hetero-homo continuum rather than having to find a fixed point on it based on predetermined identities. Although these two movements may seem contradictory, their coexistence allows us to suggest a flexible understanding of sexuality that does not reaffirm heterosexuality as the one stable and primordial identity, because the importance of identity and community for sexual minorities is bolstered rather than negated.

Season Eight thus weaves discourses of identity politics and queer possibilities into a complex plait. The comics allow sexual minority characters — who are not in a position of institutional power — to affirm their identity and the importance of their community while dominant sexuality is regularly destabilized, and ultimately queered by Buffy's refusal to label herself. That is not to say that there are not more problematic aspects to the storyline: the complete erasure of bisexuality remains highly questionable, and it is not an accident that sexual complexity would be explored through female rather than male characters. Still, the acknowledgment of identity politics in the context of a plot twist that usually denies it, and its hint at a more complex understanding of human sexuality, give the comics rare subtlety in its treatment of heteroflexible possibilities.

The final irony, then, comes from the meta-text. In an interview with the *New York Times,* Whedon defended the storyline by assuring that Buffy was still straight and that she was simply "young and experimenting," thereby reifying the crutches of stable identity and individualized desire that the comics as a text destabilizes. By establishing the one thing that Buffy herself is very careful *not* to say, Whedon undermined the queer possibilities of his own text. While this does not prevent the comics from being read against this grain, it does speak to the difficulty of walking the tight rope that the story-line does in a cultural space where we have few words to talk about complex sexual identities and a failure to do so is always at risk of reinforcing the heterosexual center. But while it may be true that Buffy is not turning gay — she is certainly not turning straight, either.

Notes

1. Although the use of LGBT — the acronym for Lesbian, Gay, Bisexual and Transgender — has become standard when writing about sexual minorities, its use often obscures the power dynamics within the LGBT community. Thus I prefer to use "gay and lesbian" when I feel it would be misleading to imply bisexual and trans voices are adequately included.

2. If these lesbians are to be attractive, anyway. In the same section, Beirne rightly points out those stereotypes of lesbians as mannish and unrefined.

3. Showing a kiss (and other displays of affection) between two women who are actually involved in a romantic relationship was still cause for censorship from networks in the late nineties, as Whedon found out for himself (Walters 116).

4. Over the course of the show, Buffy has sex with four men and dates a fifth one, Scott. She is the lead character on the show that has had the most partners, to the audience's knowledge.

5. As Suzanna Walters puts it, "This brave gay world is white, bourgeois, coupled, familial, and familiar" (125).

6. Anya, who is the more candid and blunt character likely to use language that others would not, is the only character to refer to Willow as a "lesbian" over the course of the series.

7. This is despite the numerous queer elements that can be found in the show (see Call). Beirne in "Queering the Slayer-Text" speaks specifically to the loss of queer possibilities that occurs when the subtext becomes text.

Works Cited

Becker, Ron. *Gay TV and Straight America.* New Brunswick, NJ: Rutgers University Press, 2006.

Beirne, Rebecca. *Lesbians in Television and Text after the Millenium.* New York: Palgrave Macmillan, 2008.

_____. "Introduction: A History of Lesbian Television Criticism." In Rebecca Beirne, ed., *Televising Queer Women: A Reader.* New York: Palgrave Macmillan, 2007. 1–15.

_____. "Queering the Slayer-Text: Reading Possibilities in Buffy the Vampire Slayer." *Refractory: A Journal of Entertainment Media* 5 (2004). 10 Oct 2004. <http://blogs.ar ts.unimelb.edu.au/refractory/2004/02/03/queering-the-slayer-text-reading-possibilit ies-in-buffy-the-vampire-slayer-rebecca-beirne/>

Branner, Amy C. "Weekend lesbians: Enticing or insulting?" *Off Our Backs* (July 1994). 14 Sept 2008. <http://findarticles.com/p/articles/mi_qa3693/is_199407/ai_n8725907>

Braun, Virginia, Nicola Gavey and Kathryn McPhilips. "'The 'Fair Deal'? Unpacking Accounts of Reciprocity in Heterosex." *Sexualities 6* (2003): 237–261.

Britzman, Deborah. *Lost Subjects, Contested Objects.* Albany: State University of New York Press, 1998.

Call, Lewis. "'Sounds Like Kinky Business to Me': Subtextual and Textual Representations of Erotic Power in the Buffyverse." *Slayage: The Online International Journal of Buffy Studies* 6.4 (2007). 13 July 2009 <http://slayageonline.com/essays/slayage24/Call.htm>

Capsuto, Steven. *Alternate Channels: The Uncensored Story of Gay and Lesbian Images on Radio and Television: 1930s to the Present.* New York: Ballantine Books, 2000.

Cochran, Tanya R. "Complicating the Open Closet: The Visual Rhetoric of *Buffy the Vampire Slayer*'s Sapphic Lovers." In Rebecca Beirne, ed., *Televising Queer Women: A Reader.* New York: Palgrave Macmillan, 2007. 49–63.

Davis, Glyn, and Gary Needham. "Introduction: The Pleasures of the Tube." In Glyn Davis and Gary Needham, eds., *Queer TV: Theories, Histories, Politics.* New York: Routledge, 2009.

Diamond, Lisa M. "'I'm straight, but I kissed a girl': The Trouble with American Media Representations of Female-Female Sexuality." *Feminism and Psychology*, 15 (2005): 104–110.

Doty, Alexander. *Making Things Perfectly Queer.* Minneapolis: University of Minneapolis Press, 1993.

Essig, Laurie. "Heteroflexibility." Salon.com 15 Nov. 2000. 12 Oct. 2008 <http://archive.salon.com/mwt/feature/2000/11/15/heteroflexibility/index.html>

Garrity, Jane. "Mediating the Taboo: The Straight Lesbian Gaze." In Calvin Thomas, ed., *Straight with a Twist.* Urbana: University of Illinois Press, 2001. 191–231.

Gustines, George G. "Experimenting in Bed When Not After Vampires." *New York Times* March 5 2008. 12 Oct. 2008.<http://www.nytimes.com/2008/03/05/books/05buffy.html>

Hantzis, Darlene M., and Valerie Lehr. "Whose Desire? Lesbian (Non)Sexuality and Television's Perpetuation of Hetero/Sexism." In Jeff Ringer, ed., *Queer Words, Queer Images: Communication and the Construction of Homosexuality.* New York: New York University Press, 1994.

Hefferman, Virginia. "It's February; Pucker Up, TV Actresses." *The New York Times* February 2005. July 2, 2009. <http://www.nytimes.com/2005/02/10/arts/television/10heff.html>

Jackson, Stevi. "Sexuality, Heterosexuality, and Gender Hierarchy." In Chrys Ingraham, ed., *Thinking Straight: The Power, Promise and Paradox of Heterosexuality.* New York: Routledge, 2004. 15–37.

Jenkins, Tricia. "'Potential Lesbians at Two O'Clock': The Heterosexualization of Lesbianism in the Recent Teen Film." *The Journal of Popular Culture 38* (2005): 491–504.

Jowett, Lorna. *Sex and the Slayer: A Gender Studies Primer for the Buffy Fan.* Middletown, CT: Wesleyan University Press, 2005.

Lo, Malinda. "Sweeps Lesbianism a Mixed Bag." *AfterEllen.com* 23 Feb 2005. 16 Oct 2008 <http://www.afterellen.com/archive/ellen/TV/2005/2/sweeps.html>

Mendlesohn, Farah. "Surpassing the Love of Vampires; or, Why (and How) a Queer Reading of the Buffy/Willow Relationship is Denied." In Rhonda V. Wilcox and David Lavery, eds., *Fighting the Forces: What's at Stake in* Buffy the Vampire Slayer. Lanham, MD: Rowman and Littlefield, 2002. 45–60.

Moore, Candace. "Getting Wet: The Heteroflexibility of Showtime's *L Word*." In Merri Lisa Johnston, ed., *Third Wave Feminism and Television*. New York: I.B.Tauris, 2007.

Russo, Vito. *The Celluloid Closet: Homosexuality in the Movies*. Rev. ed. New York: Harper, 1981.

Seidman, Steven. "From Polluted Homosexual to the Normal Gay: Changing Patterns of Sexual Regulation in America." In Chrys Ingraham, ed., *Thinking Straight: The Power, Promise and Paradox of Heterosexuality*. New York: Routledge, 2004. 39–62.

Walters, Suzanna D. *All The Rage: The Story of Gay Visibility in America*. Chicago: University of Chicago Press, 2001.

Warn, Sarah. "How *Buffy* Changed the World of Lesbians on Television."*AfterEllen.com* 6 June 2006 16 Oct 2008 <http://www.afterellen.com/TV/buffy-end.html>

_____. "Jumping the Lesbian Shark: Network TV." AfterEllen.com 18 May 2006. 16 Oct 2008 <http://www.afterellen.com/ column/2006/5/shark-networkTV.html>

_____. "More Lesbian Kisses on TV — Between Straight Women." *AfterEllen.com* 26 Oct 2004. 16 Oct 2008 <http://www.afterellen.com/TV/102004/lesbiankisses.html>

_____. "TV's Lesbian Baby Boom." *AfterEllen.com* 3 Jan 2003. 16 Oct 2008 <http://www.afterellen.com/TV/lesbianbabyboom.html>

_____. "*Ally McBeal*, Heteroflexibility, and Lesbian Visibility on TV." *AfterEllen.com* 7 Aug 2003. 16 Oct 2008 <http://www.afterellen.com/TV/allymcbeal.html>

Wilts, Alyssa. "Evil, Skaky, and Kinda Gay: Lesbian Images and Issues." In Lynne Y. Edwards, Elizabeth L. Rambo and James B. South, eds., *Buffy Goes Dark: Essays on the Final Two Seasons of* Buffy the Vampire Slayer *on Television*. Jefferson, NC: McFarland, 2009. 14–56.

Whedon, Joss. Interview with Sheerly Avni. *The MoJo Interview: Joss Whedon*. November/December 2008. <http://www.motherjones.com/media/2008/11/mojo-interview-joss-whedon>

Triangulated Desire in
Angel *and* Buffy

Alyson R. Buckman

"If we make it through, does one of us get to be a real boy?"—Angel, *"Not
Fade Away," 5.22*[1]

Introduction

Since I originally wrote this essay for a conference presentation almost five
years ago, a great deal of work has been done on the construction of sexuality
in *Buffy the Vampire Slayer* and its spinoff, *Angel*. The original essay focused on
the construction of masculinity and sexuality, especially pertaining to the relationship between Buffy's two immortal loves: Angel and Spike. Since then,
scholars such as Stacey Abbott, Cynthea Masson, Marni Stanley, Lewis Call,
Roz Kaveney, Rhonda Wilcox, David Lavery, Dee Amy-Chinn, and Allison
McCracken have written in depth about this very subject, continuing the work
of Arwen Spicer, Stevie Simkin, Lorna Jowett, A. Susan Owen, Laura Diehl,
and Victoria Spah upon which I had relied. Gender and genre transgression
and conservation, camp, and kink have all been discussed in fascinating ways.
However, no essay has focused predominantly on the function of the erotic
triangle in these two series. This is surprising, since there is a multitude of
triangles present. In analyzing these triangles, I have come to discover the primary generic *modus operandi* of each show is responsible for the expression of
the erotic triangle and its concomitant expression of masculinity and sexuality.

* * *

Lorna Jowett and Stacey Abbott have written a great deal about the
influence of genre upon the construction of *Buffy* and *Angel*. Jowett writes
that, while *Buffy* utilizes feminized forms, such as soap opera, romance, and
melodrama, it partakes of more masculinized forms as well, such as the superhero and horror text (9). Whedon has repeatedly talked about it being about
high school and the horrific aspects of being a teen (see, for instance, Whe-

don). However, Whedon does not merely mindlessly recapitulate the conventions of the genres; he actively and critically engages with them, upending function through the forms (both narrative and visual) he creates.[2] For instance, *Buffy* simultaneously uses what Jowett refers to as "resolvable" and "open-ended" plotting; this, in turn, enables the text's resistance to the marriage plot[3] and construction of a traditional nuclear family, both of which are a part of our patriarchal system.[4] Staking patriarchy is at the heart of the text;[5] although it utilizes masculinized and feminized forms, the content is feminist.[6] As A. Susan Owen puts it, *Buffy* is concerned with the destabilization of "masculinist metanarratives" (24), including the codes of the horror genre. The narrative construction of young men who worship demons in order to gain financial returns, men who treat women like toilet seats, the Initiative, and the Watcher's Council are only some of the more obvious and frequent textual sallies against the forces of patriarchy. However, such sallies are not simply the retaliation against patriarchy that a vengeance demon such as Anya wields: you hurt a woman, I torture you, you die (sometimes simultaneously).[7] The stories are more complex and layered than that generally — although sometimes such flawed men *are* simply hit over the head with a stick.

I bring up the question of form and function in *Buffy* because it is intimately related to the ways in which triangles are formed and treated in this show and in *Angel*. While, as Judith Butler would argue, gender can't be separated from sexuality (a point which Dee Amy-Chinn also makes [316]), one might also make the argument that the representation of gender and sexuality cannot be separated from genre. Gender, genre, sexuality, and power are interdependent, and this is illustrated in *Buffy*. This doesn't mean, however, that the three are essentialistic or inflexible. As Jowett writes, for instance, "the tough-guy model of masculinity is consistently shown to be redundant, partly because the old-style action hero is replaced by Buffy in a genre and gender reversal, but also because these characters refuse to adopt the new behaviors required to deal with powerful females" (15). Such new behaviors include the construction of desire within the text. So although genre, gender, sexuality, and the representation of power are interdependent, the *ways* in which these are articulated in the text is essential to the analysis as well. Since other scholars have focused on the construction of gender within the series, I would like to look specifically at its use of the homoerotic triangle. Gender, genre, and sexuality will be discussed in more depth in *Angel*, since less scholarly work has been done on this series.[8]

* * *

As both Michael Kimmel and Suzanne Pharr write, sexuality can never be proven; as a result, we simultaneously fight to prove our sexuality and consistently fail to achieve (an unachievable) hegemonic ideal. Kimmel argues that homosocial competition, in which masculinity must be "proved ... and proved again — constant, relentless, unachievable," is the basis for constructing a masculine identity; "ultimately, the quest for proof becomes ... meaningless..." (Rothenberg 83). He goes on to argue that this masculinity is proven, in part, through the maintenance of white, middle class, early middle-aged, heterosexuality as the standard from which Others — other masculinities, other classes, other sexualities, other races, other genders — are judged. Thus, Kimmel's discussion of manhood is built upon the repudiation of those who do not "fit the bill." "The hegemonic definition of manhood," he goes on to state, "is a man *in* power, a man *with* power, and a man *of* power. We equate manhood with being strong, successful, capable, reliable, in control" (85, original emphasis). Masculinity becomes a social construction built upon sand and reliant upon the control of power. Although masculinity becomes tied up with hierarchy, all men are assumed to have and exert more power than all women.

Eve Sedgwick contemplates the erotic triangle to discuss homosocial competition. Citing Rene Girard's *Deceit, Desire, and the Novel*, she discusses the connections between rivals and lovers, writing:

> What is most interesting ... [is that] in any erotic rivalry, the bond that links the two rivals is as intense and potent as the bond that links either of the two rivals to the beloved: that the bonds of 'rivalry' and 'love,' differently as they are experienced, are equally powerful and in many senses equivalent.... [There are many examples] in which the choice of the beloved is determined in the first place, not by the qualities of the beloved, but by the beloved's already being the choice of the person who has been chosen as a rival [21].

This bond between the rivals may, in fact, be even more important than that between the rivals and their object of affection in determining "actions and choices" (21), with the object of affection becoming a conduit for the expression and assertion of male heterosexuality as well as male bonding and/or competition. The female body may become the grounds upon which men may prove their masculinity and sexuality through the exchange of women and the penetration of the female body (21).

Buffy

The cast of *Buffy* is more gender-balanced than that of *Angel*: the most central core contains two women and two men: Buffy, Willow, Giles, and Xander. The last episode of the television series re-establishes this core by having the four Scoobies walk together down the hall, discussing what they will do the day after the big battle. Throughout the series as a whole, there are generally 3–4 main female and 3–4 main male characters. Jowett provides one possible rationale for this when she states that the characters are placed in heterosocial groupings, in part to deflect the idea that the "new men" of the show are gay: Spike, Xander, Oz, and Giles, for instance, are all heterosocial, primarily socializing with women (119, 128, 135, 161).

The issue of appearing gay is an important one even for texts which question traditional conceptions of masculinity (and perhaps even more so than texts which espouse traditional masculinity), as arguably do both *Buffy* and *Angel*, through the construction of what Jowett terms feminized "new men": "passive, sensitive, weak, and emotional ... repressing their 'real' masculinity ... they too work hard to construct and reconstruct postfeminist gendered identities" (119). The constant boogeyman of gay baiting for the nonpatriarchal male surfaces humorously in both series, as main male characters have their sexuality questioned by others within the series. This will be important to the construction of homoerotic triangles, especially in *Angel*, which is much more influenced by masculinized genres.

*   *   *

Part of the argument here is that the more feminized genres of *Buffy* (teen romance, melodrama, and soap opera), lead to an increased number of romantic triangles in *Buffy* than in *Angel*. However, even though there are more triangles, there are nearly the same number of triangles in which two men are fighting over one woman (there is one more in *Buffy*); the formation of the triangle as two women and one man (rather than two men and one woman) is more common in *Buffy*. By my estimate, *Buffy* is three times more likely than *Angel* to have two women in the triangle and one man. This will be a significant point and, again, ties into the genre and mission of the show.

The homoerotic triangle works differently in the two shows, especially if there are two women and one man rather than the opposite. One might assume that the former would be an inverted replay of Sedgwick's homoerotic triangle in which the use of the man maintained the safe heterosexuality of the female characters, dispersing fears that they might engage in homoerotic behavior; alternately, given American society's fixation on lesbian relationships as erotic for men — especially those unions including a man (i.e., a threesome) — one might suppose the triangle would work differently. The relationship between the two women is not, however, always the focus;

instead, this version of the triangle may still work to emphasize the desirability and heterosexuality of the male in the middle.

In *Buffy,* while some of the two woman-one man (W-M-W) triangles do provide the potential for titillation (in part through the potential for the problematically termed and eros-laden "cat fight"), these triangles generally are used to develop dramatic tension and to deepen characterization. For example, in the Willow-Oz-Veruca triangle, the introduction of Veruca reveals another side to Oz's werewolf character, one usually not seen or only hinted at. Oz is generally depicted as a gentle, laconic young man, but Veruca literally brings out the wolf inside him. Similarly, in the one episode Buffy-Riley-Faith triangle, Faith's seduction of Riley (while in Buffy's body) underscores not just what Lewis Call might deem the vanilla aspect of Riley and Buffy but also Faith's character and her desire and inability to *have* Buffy's life. Additionally, it underscores Riley's emotional commitment to Buffy in that he will not play games with her or treat her roughly; this confounds Faith, who has no known history of emotional intimacy. Riley's refusal of not only Faith's games, but also of Professor Maggie Walsh in favor of Buffy, alerts us that his character is a good and decent one, and one not interested in the patriarchal control represented by the Initiative and Walsh's incestuous pseudo-mother role.

The Buffy-Angel-Darla and the Drusilla/Harmony-Spike-Buffy triangles also work to deepen characterization and further emplotment. The former (which will be discussed further in the section on *Angel*) illustrates for a new audience the potential dangers of Angel, provides Buffy with important knowledge, and tests Angel's rejection of his vampiric nature and his commitment to Buffy, thus foregrounding Angel's change from demon to champion.[9] Buffy and Darla, while rivals, function as two different choices Angel can make, significantly split in terms of the women's physical and metaphorical attributes between the light and the dark. The Drusilla/Harmony-Spike-Buffy triangle[10] serves as a comedic attempt by Spike at illustrating his love for and commitment to Buffy when he threatens to stake Dru. Similarly, Harmony's engagement in role-playing games with Spike illustrates his obsession when he asks Harmony to dress as the slayer. Although Harmony also attempts to kill the slayer, this, too, is comedic and seems to be done not out of Harmony's inherent evil or jealousy but because it's expected — it's what a vampire *does.*

The Buffy-Angel-Cordelia triangle is one example of a W-M-W triangle that does work in part to emphasize the heterosexual desirability of Buffy as well as working as a critique of Cordelia's self-centered and manipulative behavior. The ice queen, though she is the center of the Sunnydale universe (at least as she sees it), cannot have that which Buffy possesses, suggesting a reward for Buffy's sacrifices as the Chosen One. One might also see Cordelia as Roz Kaveney does, which is as a former model of Buffy, i.e., what Buffy's character was before she became a slayer, and thus illustrating Buffy's superior character as the Chosen One ("'She Saved...'" 9). Coded as butch in "The Wish," an episode in which she and Angel never had a relationship because she had never come to Sunnydale, with combat boots, dark eye makeup, unstyled hair, and combat-ready clothing, the subtext of the Buffy-Angel-Cordelia triangle is that her heterosexual relationship with Angel "saved" her from becoming butch; it also maintains Angel's fragile heteromasculinity (we shall discuss this further in a little while) in that both women desire him.[11] The triangle additionally is used for humor and to forecast Cordelia's inclusion in the Scoobies, working ultimately as a bridge to Cordelia's presence in *Angel*.

Another important triangle of this sort is that of Buffy-Xander-Willow (B-X-W). Although Buffy is the Slayer, the chosen one who "alone will stand against the vampires, the demons, and the forces of darkness," she is also the love interest of Spike, Angel, and Riley and is desired by Xander. She is set up as an object of desire in the very first episode of *Buffy*, when Xander sees her and subsequently crashes his skateboard.[12] Xander's repeated difficulties in his pursuit of Buffy as well as his tendency to get involved with demon women is a source of humor in the show: "Dammit! You know what? I'm sick of this crap. I'm sick of being the guy who eats insects and gets the funny syphilis. As of this moment, it's over. I'm finished being everybody's butt-monkey!" (*Buffy*, "Buffy v. Dracula"). He is not beefcake but zeppo and "butt-monkey," an interesting choice of slang in this context. He does not live up fully to the mandates of heterosexuality[13]; he is never fully portrayed as a "manly man" in the mold of Angel, Riley, or Spike[14]— all of whom are sexually successful with Buffy — unless we count "The Pack," in which he is possessed by the spirit of a hyena and becomes aggressively sexual.[15] He even riffs on this in Season Seven when he announces to Willow, "I'm going gay. I've decided I'm turning gay. Willow, gay me up. Come on, let's gay." Willow responds, "What if you just start attracting male demons?" ("First Date"). A. Susan Owen writes that "Xander and Willow play *les femmes* to Buffy's butch performance, each yearning for the super-heroine from a related, yet different, position in the gender matrix of the narrative" (26). Although there are regular indications of Xander's possible gay subtext, Jowett notes, he has always coupled with women (138), anchoring the character against a full exploration of his homoeroticism (outside of slash fanfic).

Like the triangle featuring Cordelia, above, Jowett argues that this (B-X-W) triangle works to secure Xander's desirability, buttressing the heteronormativity of a character that has a clear homoerotic subtext (Jowett 137–138; Owen 26; Simkin para 28; Kaveney, "'She Saved...'" 10).

This triangle works similarly for Willow. In the light of the possible identification of Willow as "kinda gay" in "The Wish" and "Dopplegangland," (3.9 and 3.16, respectively) her heterosexuality is temporarily anchored through prior episodes which have established the blossoming of desire between Xander and Willow even as they are in relationships with Cordelia and Oz. Had the eroticism of her dalliance with Xander not been established, Willow may have been more firmly identified as lesbian, potentially making "Hush" less effective as an episode in which Willow becomes attracted to Tara. Additionally, the fact that gay Willow is a vampire also muddles sexual identification, since vampires are known to be polymorphously perverse both within and without the Whedonverse, although Angel hints that non-vampire Willow has a basic psychological connection with Vamp Willow.

The introduction of Tara in "Hush" (4.10) nine months and sixteen episodes later engages with this earlier exploration and creates another of the W-M-W triangles; however, here the triangle doesn't work against Willow's incipient lesbian identity.[16] When Willow is forced by Oz to choose between himself and Tara in "New Moon Rising" (4.19) — with Oz accusing Tara, "You smell like her. She's all over you, do you know that?" suggesting that there's been more physical contact between the two than we have seen on screen — information is revealed about Willow's character and her connection to Tara. Of course, the fact that Oz loses control (after working hard and traveling the world to gain it) and almost kills Tara illustrates and critiques his own hypermasculinity (as represented by the wolf within and the jealous lover without) as well. The man is not used to anchor female heterosexuality or to act as a conduit between the two women; instead, the triangle here critiques heteronormativity and what we will discuss as hypermasculinity in the *Angel* section in addition to providing character growth and narrative depth.

While the B-X-W triangle potentially works to reassure us of Xander, Willow, and Buffy's heteronormativity (whether this falls apart later on or not), it also reveals a deepening of characterization through the growth of both Xander and Willow away from the object of their original fancies (at least the fully textual ones) and, hence, the original triangle: Xander gradually relinquishes Buffy as a possible lover, eventually growing into a caring relationship with Anya, and Willow ultimately chooses Oz over an erotic relationship with Xander. Finally, she discovers her lesbian identity, entering into a mature relationship with Tara. Rather than working against the close ties of the women in the triangle through homosocial competition, the women in these triangles are emotionally intimate and do not need a male as conduit for their desire for each other (again, slash fanfic aside), although he may work to anchor their sexuality as heterosexual, at least temporarily.

*   *   *

The struggle of two women over a man is a very traditional and conservative pattern in general, working to support myths of women as more interested in men than in preserving female friendships and thus promoting heteronormativity. Such struggles in the Buffyverse may be used to destabilize such patterns, however, through critiquing them.[17] While Cordelia maintains this paradigm (of interest in men over emotional intimacy with women), her behavior is regularly critiqued as superficial and emotionally immature. One example of the critique of heteronormativity is in "Bewitched, Bothered, and Bewildered" (*Buffy*, 2.16), an episode in which Xander attempts to regain Cordelia's affections (tarnished by her rejection from her clique) by casting a love spell on her; the spell goes horribly awry and nearly gets him killed when all women (except Cordelia) find him irresistible. Xander is clearly depicted as objectifying women through his attempt at control over one and must experience such objectification himself. He also temporarily quashes his female friendships, including that with Willow. The homosocial competition that occurs between women in this episode as a result of the spell is depicted as violent, savage, mindless, and wrong. Xander, rather than the competing women in this episode, is the object of the gaze and the narrative center, thus emphasizing Xander's position and role and, hence, the critique.[18] In another episode, Xander is nearly raped and killed by Faith, although he is ironically saved by Angel, providing him with the same lesson and forcing his character to experience feminization as he steps into the role usually reserved for women; this latter reversal of roles (between traditionally masculine and feminine behavior) occurs as well in "Inca Mummy Girl," "Teacher's Pet," "Buffy versus Dracula," and "First Date," for example, as Xander is repeatedly objectified and pursued as victim of romance. The irony of these reversals illustrates the hurtful and unhealthy aspects of such heteronormative dynamics even as they fit the shoe on the male gender's foot. This reversal is also part of Xander's homoerotic subtext: he's not a manly man.

Heteronormativity is supported as well by the two men-one woman (M-W-M) triangle discussed by Sedgwick. Women's bodies are used as objects of exchange to assert masculinity — often through violent struggle or the threat of such between the men in the triangle — and dissipate the fear of homosexual behavior between the two men. In this triangle, the female is often a background player, never as interesting as the relationship between the men.[19] As we will later discuss, this sort of construction is maintained in several of the main triangles in *Angel*, since it is a show very much concerned with the construction of masculinity.[20] However, masculinity is contained within *Buffy*, since it is a show which rejects traditional constructions of masculinity, and therefore such triangles are illustrated as problematic. As stated earlier, there are far fewer triangles involving two men and one woman in *Buffy* than in *Angel*; these triangles generally revolve around Buffy, although this is not always the case.[21]

One example of an M-W-M triangle that works against patriarchal formations while simultaneously asserting a homoerotic subtext of the sort above is that of Riley-Buffy-Forrest.[22] Forrest quickly becomes jealous of Riley's interest in Buffy, encouraging Riley to play the field instead of "mooning over some freshman for the next three months" ("The Initiative"). One of the first comments the revivified Forrest makes when he sees Riley is "Really looking forward to trying out your girl again" ("Primeval"). He replies to Adam's order to kill Buffy with, "I thought you'd never ask"; he then enjoins Riley to watch him kill Buffy. Forrest gets killed, of course, and is represented unsympathetically for his hatred of Buffy and his desire to pull Riley back into a patriarchal institution that works against collective (female) power (even though a woman is at its head). Like the Watcher's Council, the Initiative (and, hence, Forrest) wants Buffy to sit back and take orders, to "toe the line" as she puts it in "Primeval," to be a good little girl.[23]

The more normatively masculine the representation of a male character, the less he requires such anchoring by the triangle and vice versa (even as such normative masculinity is critiqued). Thus it is that we have several triangles revolving around Xander and two women (Faith, Buffy, Willow, Cordelia, Anya — I'm not counting the number of demon women with whom he dallies) and Xander and another man and woman (Riley, Spike, Angel, Oz) yet we only have two of the former with Riley (Buffy, Faith, and Maggie Walsh) and three of the latter (Angel, Spike, and Forrest).[24] The use of Faith within the triangles is largely to test the devotion of the beloved while also exploring the possible dark side of the slayer and her slaying: just as Cordelia is one possible incarnation of Buffy (were she not Chosen), so, too, is Faith a possible incarnation were Buffy to lose all support. The threat of the loss of desire is important within the genre of the teen romance as it is for the character of Buffy, since she is so grounded within heterosexual relationships. When Riley loses his superhuman abilities due to his break with the Initiative and the death of Walsh, he significantly creates another triangle as he engages with vampire prostitutes. Riley also forms triangles with Angel, Spike, Dracula, and, possibly, Xander, although by this point Xander has matured past his constant need for posturing over Buffy. Additionally, Xander seems to worship Riley as an exemplar of traditional masculinity[25] more than he resents him for being with Buffy, creating one of the homoerotic subtexts to his character. Xander and Angel, like Riley, take their relationships with Buffy as a means to prove their masculinity. Angel succeeds, Xander becomes comic fodder,[26] and Riley is unable to accept his allegedly reduced masculinity and thus leaves.

The Riley-Buffy-Angel (R-B-A) and Riley-Buffy-Spike (R-B-S) triangles serve as anchors for the masculinity of all three men in addition to providing dramatic tension, deepening characterization and furthering emplotment. The R-B-A triangle illustrates that Angel is still a part of Buffy's life, even as she has moved on. Additionally, it is used to bridge *Buffy* and *Angel*, attempting to solidify the audience for the latter in its first year. It serves as well to illustrate a lack of trust in the Riley-Buffy relationship (and hence one of the fatal flaws of the relationship), when, for example, Buffy fails to tell Riley that Angel lost his soul through intercourse with her and when Riley assumes she has slept with Angel again during a trip to L.A. (and during their relationship) in "The Yoko Factor." This episode constructs the homosocial competition between Riley and Angel as "testosterone poisoning" and as childish: Riley refuses to leave so that Angel can have a private discussion with Buffy, and Angel and Riley both threaten violence to the other. Additionally, this triangle, like those discussed earlier, constructs Buffy as desirable and heterosexual; it also potentially provides wish fulfillment to the audience since, allegedly, every woman wants men to fight over her.[27]

Angel and Spike reveal the point that I am making about the difference in functions of the W-M-W and the M-W-M triangulations. When Angel and Spike are involved in the former, it develops their characterization; when they are involved in the latter, it's all about the testosterone and establishing the female body as their territory. They are interesting cases in that there are fewer triangles in which they are involved than Xander, and yet they are simultaneously masculinized and feminized. Their vampire identities enable some resistance to normative masculinity in terms of sexuality even as they create a clear connection to other aspects of normative male behavior, such as violence. This resistance is limited in that they are generally depicted as heterosexual; it is only with each other that the homoerotic subtext becomes textual, albeit elliptically. The possible homoeroticism of vampire sexuality is only hinted at, even as the potential for kink is highlighted in Season Six of *Buffy*, as Lewis Call argues ("Sounds"). They are aggressively masculine in a way Xander is not.

Normative masculinity is defined in part by violence and (heterosexual) virility. Over the course of seven seasons, *Buffy* suggests that masculinity can be both non-normative and positive, although Lorna Jowett does argue convincingly that the construction of these "new men" remains problematic. Violent, hierarchical masculinity remains critiqued with the show, however, as shown through the construction of Angel(us), Spike, and Riley.

Let us take a brief but useful detour and discuss the representation of Angel and Spike's bodies in *Buffy*. The detour is useful because it both illustrates the containment of masculinity in *Buffy* as a result of its form and function as well as setting up the construction of the Angel-Buffy-Spike triangle we will discuss later on.

While Angel is aggressively masculine, Jowett, Owen, and McCracken have successfully argued that Angel's body is feminized through its objectification in *Buffy*: according to McCracken, he "function[s] as a masochistic object of teen girls' erotic pleasure" (118), taking on the role of object and of supporting character usually played by women (119–121). Through repeated eroticization (for instance, the number of shirtless scenes) and penetration of his body by female characters and viewers (ex. through Drusilla's torturing of him in "What's My Line, Part 2") as well as his construction within a feminist text, a queer space is formed for the deconstruction of traditional patriarchal gender and sexual relations. While he is the "most powerful male," McCracken writes, Angel is also the show's "most deviant" due to his vampirism (117).

Spike's body later took on these functions, perhaps more masochistically (McCracken 130). According to Jowett, not only is Spike's body there to be looked at as the object of the gaze, but it is also presented as that of a "feminized, passive victim" (163–4). Several authors have examined the role of Spike, depicting him as everything from a courtly lover (Spah) to a code-switching queer character (Amy-Chinn) to an avatar of kink (Call, "Sounds"). Dee Amy-Chinn argues that he does not feel the need to constantly reassert his masculinity in the way that Angel does (320), and yet Simkin makes the observation that, for Spike, violence equates with masculinity: the chip the Initiative implants in his brain to prevent him from attacking humans doesn't only interfere with his vampire attacks on humans, it also provides a metaphor for sexual impotency, as we see when he attempts to attack Willow in the same episode ("The Initiative") ("'Who Died..."para 32–35).[28] Both Angelus and

Spike see themselves as emasculated by the elements that control their violence (the gypsy curse and the chip, respectively) (Jowett 157).

Ultimately, *Buffy*, while repeatedly using triangles, utilizes them in such a way that they function as critiques of heteronormative behaviors, including homosocial competition and the control of women's bodies as objects of exchange. The homoerotic triangle is utilized for reasons of development (both plot and character) and dramatic tension in addition to reasserting the heterosexual desirability of main characters. Although Buffy is enmeshed within heteronormative behavior[29] which, one might argue, is itself critiqued in the first episodes of Season Four, she is not backgrounded as a conduit for the expression of desire between men — at least, not in her own show. (This is an important clarification as we approach our *Angel* section.) However, the patriarchal underpinnings of the exchange of female bodies is brought from subtext to text, and they are critiqued, as in Buffy telling Riley and Angel that, "I see one more display of testosterone poisoning and I will personally put you both in the hospital!" ("The Yoko Factor"). Buffy identifies the construction of masculinity as the root of the conflict between Angel and Riley in this scene. *Angel*, however, has quite a different approach, and this is, in large part, due to the generic differences between this show and *Buffy*, as well as the show's function.

Angel

In *Angel*, Angel advances from being background boyfriend with a tortured past to protagonist of the show. Both shows veer away from the purity (if one might call it that) of the vampire text in that they engage with a host of other demon figures who interact with gender and sexuality in ways that are not transgressive at heart and are often, in fact, conservative. While the most obviously sexist characters are quickly dispatched (as in "She," "I Fall to Pieces," and "Expecting," to name a few from the first season), the subtext of a great deal of the show often is more problematic in terms of its representation of gender and sexuality,[30] including the construction of the homoerotic triangle.

Angel, like *Buffy*, is an amalgam of genres: detective, neo-noir, action/adventure, superhero, buddy film, vampire, and chivalric romance (see Abbott, "Walking" and "Kicking"; Jacob; Stoy; Comeford; McCracken). Romance and melodrama are included, as they are in *Buffy*, but the former elements are foregrounded, especially the neo-noir and superhero conventions. The hybridity of the generic treatment conjoined with a generally playful approach to sexuality in the series has the potential to work against easy categorization and binary oppositions. However, the generic elements as well as the core cast construction work to create a much more masculine show than *Buffy* and one that is more ambivalent in its treatment of gender and sexuality. While we begin the show with a central cast of two men and one woman (Angel, Doyle, and Cordelia), eventually there are four main male characters in the core of the group (Angel, Wesley, Gunn, and Lorne) and two female (Cordelia and Fred). On the opposing team of Wolfram and Hart, female Lilah is balanced by male Lindsey as the main villains.

Ultimately, the homoerotic triangle within this show overall is conservatively produced, meaning that women's bodies are exchanged between the men in a show of homosocial competition and displacement of the threat of homosexuality. Although this is made most textual in the final season — and this is the vital season for the most analyzed homoerotic triangle, that of Angel and Spike — the subtextual elements earlier on in the series combined with the treatment of the triangle in the end work to maintain such conservative constructions of gender and sexuality even as the text and subtext are playfully rendered.

*   *   *

Although mediated by the construction of the film noir hero — another of the genres we will discuss presently — as debased and alienated, the character of Angel also functions as a superhero: high angle shots of the city from the perspective of Angel looking down are used to convey Angel's character as a champion (Abbott, "Kicking" 8–9). His billowing coat shot in slow motion signifies doubly in that it is simultaneously reminiscent of the detective's traditional raincoat, while also evoking a cape as the wind blows his coat upward. Although "dark avenger" is quickly discarded as a title for Angel by Cordelia and Doyle, Angel embodies a "celibate dark superhero" (Jowett 158); Stoy agrees: "the superhero ethos has triumphed over the noir ethos" (163). While Jowett and Stoy have chosen one form over the other as dominant, Janet Halfyard sees no contradiction in the genres, especially when one analyzes contemporary superheroes such as Batman (Tim Burton's 1989 version) and Spider-man (Sam Raimi's 2002 depiction): the need for the superhero to separate himself from the law, often in an oppositional stance as above and beyond the law, and the moral ambiguity of these more contemporary versions of beloved superheroes forge a connection with the world of film noir (Halfyard 150–153). Additionally, the world of the superhero is often a homosocial world in which human females can't catch up with the men and superhero women are few and far between.

Angel is also inflected with elements of the buddy film. As Stacey Abbott argues in *Angel: TV Milestones*, aspects of the buddy/odd-couple genre are clear in the relationship between Angel and Spike. This includes the repudiation in each other of that which they see in themselves: "what they deny in each other is that which they have in common, namely their past" (78). This past then becomes the means to their bonding as allies. This genre includes within itself a homosocial and homosexual subtext which is often denied. The fight between Angel and Spike over the cup of Eternal Torment in "Destiny," Abbott writes, is, as in other buddy film examples like *Butch Cassidy and the Sundance Kid*, "used to channel all of the unacknowledged sexual tension through an acceptable masculine outlet." However, "here [such tension is] made transgressive when the fight literally climaxes with Spike stabbing Angel in the shoulder with a wooden stake, a moment that is consciously replete with sexual and phallic symbolism" (79).

The buddy-film element also provides, I would argue, a link to the chivalric romance. What are King Arthur and Lancelot in *Le Morte d'Arthur,* by Sir Thomas Mallory, but an early incarnation of buddies? The homoerotic element is there as well. For instance, Sir Thomas Mallory's King Arthur states at the beginning of the conflict with Lancelot that, "I regret less the loss of my queen, for of queens I had my choice, than of our fellowship, which was surely without equal in all Christendom. Alas! That Sir Aggravayne and Sir Modred, led by the evil in their hearts, should have brought us to this" (Mallory, Graves and Baines 480). Queens are a dime a dozen, but male fellowship is a true reward. Women in this text connive and cheat, but men are stalwart and true (with the exception of Modred)— unless you happen to have killed members of their family. Then they go medieval.

Benjamin Jacob additionally sees a connection between the chivalric romance and *Angel* in theme, setting, and characterization (81–85); although he doesn't discuss the homosociality of the show specifically, he does point out the "'Round Table' of fellow champions, the Gothic façade of Angel's first office, the Hyperion Hotel's castle-like halls, towers, ramparts and arches, not to mention the various *damsels in distress*, swords and battle axes, wizards and warriors, magic and monsters of Los Angelus" (81, emphasis mine). While Buffy does rescue women from demons, they are not treated as damsels in distress; however, they are treated as such by Angel, who, as part of his mission from the Powers That Be, must reject his self-isolation and interact with humans more. These rescued women then become potential romantic liaisons. While Buffy romancing those whom she rescues would work against the (heterosexual) teen romance and gender expectations about romance and chivalry,

Angel's romancing of the women he rescues (or the possibility of it) is in keeping with the various genres at the heart of the series as well as its cast and male lead.[31]

*   *   *

The vampire text has consonances with the romance as well, since vampires speak to forbidden and transgressive desire as well as heightened emotions which often leave logic behind. Scholars too numerous to name here have discussed the sexual freedom presented by the vampire due to its status as a liminal figure (for a few of the most notable and/or specifically from the Whedonverse, see Auerbach; Wilcox, "Every Night"; Amy-Chinn; Hill and Williams; Owen; Wisker; Djikstra; Diehl; and Craft). The homoeroticism of the vampire is clear at least as early as Byron's 1816 *Varney the Vampire* (Auerbach 1). When Bram Stoker's titular Dracula declares to the weird sisters that Jonathan Harker belongs to him, the command is charged with both violence and desire. While the subtext of the vampire's desire may change over time, the desire of the vampire, writes Laura Diehl, "is ungendered and free-floating, a force that has no sense of man/woman, in/out, top/bottom binarisms"; further, she argues, "what [is a] more appropriate association than the vampire for distilling the perversions of queer sexualities?" (para 41). A. Susan Owen puts it this way: "Vampires are cartoonish figures standing in for the failed grand narratives of middle America: stable family life, equanimity, justice, rule of law, and the conquest of nature" (30). Potentially, then, the vampire text more easily confronts heteronormativity and the exchange of women's bodies. However, the other generic aspects of *Angel* pull it away from the transgressive possibility inherent in the vampire text.

Like the vampire, the noir detective is a liminal figure; the genre itself suggests the instability of sacred institutions such as those of family, justice, and law. There is no firm moral ground within film noir and this includes the characterization of the detective: he is a morally ambiguous character, and it is never certain whether he will come down on the side of justice or not.[32] There are no certainties in the world of film noir, and *Angel* uses this theme repeatedly as we wonder whether Angel is still a champion rather than being assured of his character. Roz Kaveney writes, "If the last moments of the show take place in darkness and rain, this is not just noir gesturing — it is because Angel has always inhabited the moral borderland of great cities.... Angel has always been morally ambiguous" ("A Sense" 71).

Kaveney's comment references the visual construction of *Angel* as well, in that darkness, rain, and low key interior lighting is central to *Angel*. Benjamin Jacobs' double signification of place and protagonist — Los Angeles and Los Angelus — is a meaningful pun; Jacobs not only shows the consonances between Angel and the city in which he resides but also the resonances between genre and setting. "'American' noir," he writes, "was originally a 'Los Angelian' genre that represented Los Angeles steeped in literal and metaphorical darkness" (80). Part of the playfulness of *Angel* comes in the self-awareness of the characters in regard to their roles in a noir drama. In "Somnambulist" (1.11), for instance, Cordelia parodies a gumshoe monologue on the hard city: "So, you've discovered the seamy underbelly of the candy-coated America, have you?" In "Hero," she fantasizes a commercial for Angel Investigations straight out of a promo for a noir film: "Okay, we fade up on an aerial shot, downtown, skyscrapers, lights, yada, yada, yada. We hear a narrator, preferably famous ... and he says: 'it's a big, bad city out there.' Cut to a woman walking down a dark, spooky street, alone." The aerial shot, which Cordelia pictures, is the same shot often used in the series, including the beginning of the pilot, in which Angel's voice-over is a dead-on reproduction of noir: "Los Angeles. You see it at night and it shines. A beacon. People are drawn to it. People and other things. They come for all sorts of reasons. My reason? No surprise there. It started with a girl" ("City Of").

Importantly for this essay, film noir also is a genre about masculinity and the relationships between men (Abbott, "Kicking" 8) as well as the containment of women. The genre arose in reaction to the changing role of women as well as the experience of men during World War II.[33] The need for containment of female sexuality and agency as well as of male homosocial relationships crept into the cultural imagination. For women, this meant the development of the femme fatale figure, a woman who was dangerous, sexual, and assertive: she represented the fear of those women who had gone out to labor in the paid workforce in numbers larger than ever during World War II, and who had to return to domesticity to make room for returning servicemen. The femme fatale must be punished through death or imprisonment by the end of the film, making clear the punishment that awaits women who suddenly knew what they wanted and how to get it.

Steven Cohan, in his study of masculinity in 1950s movies, cites George Chauncey, who links prewar performances of masculinity with working class culture. Film noir depends upon working class ideals of masculinity, ideals which survive in contemporary culture as signs of normative masculinity: the wielding of "physical, sexual, mental" violence in its construction of a "hierarchy of men outlining homosocial power relations among hegemonic, conservative, and subordinated masculinities within its diegesis"

(84). Weaker (read: effeminate and thus coded homosexual) men descend to the bottom of the hierarchy, and the hero rises in all his violent glory, secure in his performance of masculinity.[34] However, all men are joined together — even the weak — and validated in their difference from the feminine. Female agency is seen as taking control away from men, creating angst and dependency upon bonding with other men. During the war, homosociality was a given, but this becomes cause for unease in the postwar era; "militant, aggressive, and latent homosexual masculinity" (84–85) becomes a reason for apprehension. Even as virility became a marker of strong heterosexuality, the emphasis on the male body within the context of the war — its bonding with other male bodies and its display among other men — encouraged male sexual bonding without denying heteronormativity ... as long as getting one's kicks with other men was only a substitute for "normal" sexual relationships (85–86). To a postwar culture worrying about wartime buddy relationships, male homosociality became worrisome and emotional bonds between men needed to be clearly transferred to women. The veteran, writes Cohan, needed to make a "successful transition from male bonding to heterosexual romance" (88). Domesticity became a means to pacifying male aggression (96–97).

For neo-noir fictions, which surfaced in the 1970s, anxiety over masculinity continued. While the anxiety of politics separated from ethics (ex. Watergate) and a growing sense of moral ambivalence in the world is at the heart of this style, it is also a conservative reaction to the feminist movement. Although the transgressive women of neo-noir might not be punished with death or imprisonment,[35] the movement of the genre continued to attempt the containment of women in its imaging. Since it is also about the containment of masculinity, the shaping of masculinity into proper channels, noir also often has a queer subtext in its construction of, and emphasis on, homosocial behavior.[36] As Cohan writes, "Homosociality has as much to do with power (*over* women as well as other men) as it does with desire (*for* other men as well as women), which is why it so readily takes the form of one man's domination of another, emphasizing independence, competition, and aggression as the hallmark features of virility, and usually going even further to manifest fear of alternate male behavior — such as effeminacy — in homophobic violence" (84).

Brooding masculinity is often in evidence in noir, and perhaps this is due to the existentialism within it (Abbott, "Walking" para 7), a philosophical approach that connects with contemporary vampire fictions as well in that these more contemporary vampires often brood over the state of their existence and see little or no meaning in the world beyond their own action.[37] Cynthea Masson's excellent essay on "The Girl in Question" sees existentialist dilemma at the heart of this episode; though roundly criticized both for its placement within the series and for its alleged meaninglessness within the larger story arc, Masson argues that the episode is more important and complex within the drama than previously acknowledged. She posits Angel and Spike as stuck, needing to move forward and yet failing to do so in a *Waiting for Godot*-type stasis. Their existentialist dilemma in this episode is the result of both their repeated history with the Immortal and their own failures to progress, although this dilemma is present elsewhere in the series. Stacey Abbott brings together existentialism, noir, and chivalric romance in arguing that "[w]hile Angel both protects the lost and needy from the city's demons, he is often presented as being adrift and under threat himself, instigating the crisis of the Noir protagonist unable to control the events of his life" ("Walking" para 7).

One might easily add the standard representation of homosexuality within cinema to this list of cinematic influences on *Angel*. The alienation, loneliness, and violence of film noir work well with the traditional representation of gays within American culture and film; the homosocial competition between men and the homophobia within film noir makes this connection even firmer.[38] Additionally, while scholars such as Benjamin Jacob, have linked the episode "Are You Now, Or Have You Ever Been" to noir in both the visuals of the episode and the emphasis upon the paranoia and alienation of the McCarthy hearings (80), this episode is also linked to the representation of gays in our culture, although this is subtextual. McCarthyism is responsible for gays becoming Cold War scapegoats, with McCarthy alleging there was a "homosexual underground" and that gays had penetrated President Harry Truman's State Department. Intolerance is diffusely represented in the episode, as Sara Upstone notes, in that racism is targeted as well as communism (105–106). Homophobia easily could be included as well. This textual connection will be important to the later argument.

The delineation of the genres and influences involved in the construction of *Angel* is meant to illustrate some of the commonalities between these forms that, in turn, impact upon the construction of the erotic triangle so that it functions more conservatively than in *Buffy*. For instance, entering the world of film noir means entering a homosocial world (as is also true of the buddy film, the superhero genre, and the chivalric romance). A brooding masculinity dependent upon aggression, strength, and virility as signs of masculinity is also an overlapping element between many of these genres as well as the backgrounding of women to a supporting role. There are visual and narrative consequences to this.

*   *   *

Analyses of the construction of masculinity in the show vary in their interpretations. Wilcox and Lavery argue, as do many, that the representation of gender in the series is complex, and they cite several examples as support: for instance, Connor calls his dad a "girl" for his good penmanship; Cordelia compliments Angel's cooking, and Angel is represented as a nurturing, caring person as well as the strong male lead. In comparing *Buffy* with *Angel*, Wilcox and Lavery go on to state that they "both use the extreme feminine and masculine gender stances," seeing the two as reflections or shadows of each other even as the two shows illuminate the constructedness of gender (227). For Jowett, the possibility of hypermasculinity in relation to Angel first arises on *Buffy*. The role of the "action hero, the Romantic hero, the older boyfriend, the dangerous lover, and the mysterious stranger" lends itself to an exaggeration of masculinity (152). Angel represses Angelus' trove of "physical and sexual power" and ultimately is feminized in his role as love and backgrounded to Buffy as action hero (152–153) — again, the genre and mission of the show have consequences for the representation of character. This is in keeping with Abbott's contention that, while *Buffy* made a clear delineation between Angel and Angelus (Angel's demonic self), *Angel* is more ambiguous in its treatment of the two. Often, Angel enacts a combination of both the heroic, brooding, romantic Angel and the darker Angelus, providing a more ambiguous characterization in keeping with the tenor of noir ("Walking" para 20–27) as well as one which is more normatively masculine. Thus, while Angel and Angelus — Jowett's new man and the hypermasculine male, respectively — are separate on *Buffy*, they merge on *Angel*, thus forming a more masculinized version of the character than heretofore.

*   *   *

Over the course of *Angel*, a more traditional masculinity is asserted; as the show gets darker and more uncertain in relation to Angel's (and other male characters') moral center, a masculinity dependent upon stoicism, hierarchies of power, violence, aggression and heterosexuality becomes more and more dominant. While Wilcox and Lavery and Abbott rightfully argue that there is humor interlaced with this darkness, keeping the show from being unremittingly noir ("Afterword" 227–228 and "Nobody" 189–201, respectively), this darkness is important to the construction of the homoerotic triangle and the construction of masculinity. Look, for instance, at the construction of the male vampire as a result of crises of masculinity.

While we learned first in *Buffy* that Angel had turned on and killed his family as soon as he became a vampire, we are given more insight to Angel's past in his show. In "The Prodigal," we learn that Liam has internalized all of the negative criticism his father has spewed upon him for years and become that which his father saw in him: a drunken, lazy lout. Before killing him, he says to his father, "You told me I wasn't a man. You told me I was nothing. And I believed you. You said I'd never amount to anything. Well, you were wrong." His face then contorts into that of the vampire, and he continues, "You see, father? I have made something out of myself, after all." This exchange and the one that follows between Darla and Angelus suggest that Angelus — the Angelus that, as we first learned in *Buffy*, was one of the most vicious of vampires, cutting a swathe of destruction across Europe — becomes one of the most notable vampires because of his human rejection by his father. Darla asks, "This contest is ended, is it?" to which Angelus replies, "Now I've won.... I proved who had the power here." Darla continues, "You think? Your victory over him took but moments ... but his defeat of you will last lifetimes.... Nor can he ever approve of you — in this world, or any other. What we once were informs all that we have become." Liam's rejection by his father creates his yearning for escape and is transformed into success of a sort: he succeeds by being the monster his father identified in him while he was a human. Placed in this light, Angelus' monstrosity becomes linked to masculinity and the desire to please the father.

Spike, who will enter *Angel* in its fifth season, also became a vampire out of a crisis in masculinity. Rejected by the woman he worships and ridiculed by the society around him, William is constructed as effeminate and a "bloody awful" poet; when asked for his reaction to disappearances in town, he replies in a haughty tone: "I prefer not to think of such dark, ugly business at all. That's what the police are for. I prefer placing my energies into creating things of beauty." The woman he worships, Cecily, sees him as "beneath" herself. After being humiliated by the aristocratic circle, William meets and is turned by Drusilla. He then chooses to turn his mother (who seems to be dying of tuberculosis), as well. When she becomes a vampire, she reviles his poetry and their connection and accuses him of incestuous love for her. After he stakes her in an embrace, he perverts the comment by a fellow aristocrat about his poetry that "I'd rather have a railroad spike through my head than listen to that awful stuff!" ("Fool for Love," *Buffy*) Not only does he torture his victims with railroad spikes, but he also takes the spike as his name. Like Angel, his humiliation as a man leads to his seduction by a female vampire who seems to offer an escape to a world in which he is validated and in which he can become and be seen as hypermasculine, the antithesis to his human self with all its weaknesses. In *Buffy*, Angel's hypermasculinity will be limited to background action and to a strict division between the more hypermasculine Angelus and the soulful Angel. Spike will be allowed to maintain his hyper-masculinity, but it will never truly threaten the slayer's life or ability. When he becomes a regular on the show, he is quickly castrated (metaphorically) and becomes one of the slayer's minions. The moment at which his hyper-masculinity most expresses itself— his attempted rape of Buffy — is the moment at which he must choose to give Buffy "what she deserves." He then fulfills the role of the chivalric lover, sacrificing himself for her and for the world in the last episode. However, in *Angel*, both Spike and Angel are enabled in their hypermasculinity.

The return of the father occurs multiple times in the series, not only for Angel but also for Wesley. Jowett marks the role of the father as part of the continuing contestation over Angel's masculinity when she writes that he "assum[es] a more obvious patriarchal role. He even manages to become a father, simultaneously the ultimate 'proof' of masculinity and of his new-man status" (158); McCracken also cites Angel's paternity as contributing to a more normative representation of masculinity in the show (139–140). One might argue that he has become a father far previous to the conception of Connor, having sired multiple vampires, including not only Drusilla — who calls him "daddy" repeatedly — but also a few vampires featured on *Angel*. Significantly, we rarely see these fruits of his vampirism on *Buffy*, other than Drusilla and Spike, since the moments at which we are forced to acknowl-edge his reproductive activity are moments of horrific recognition of his vam-piric past, ones which distance the character from his soulful romanticism as Angel.[39] He is responsible not only for the murder of innocents but also for the creation of monsters who themselves slew innocents, thus unleashing hor-ror upon the world. Angel was Spike's real sire, Roz Kaveney argues, "into the ways of atrocity": "while it was Drusilla that turned him, it was Angelus who made him a monster" ("A Sense" 63). Spike alludes to this in "School Hard" (*Buffy*) when he rebukes Angel for being "housebroken": "You were my sire, man! You were my ... Yoda!"[40] In addition to the presence of Drusilla and Spike in *Angel*, several other victims of Angelus' monstrous paternity are featured: the serial killer-like Penn in "Somnambulist," due to whom Kate recognizes the monster within Angel and reviles him; the child vampire, Sara, who is used by Angelus to torture her father, Holtz; and Lawson, the only person Angel turned after he regained his soul. Whole episodes are devoted to the results of Angel(us)' vampiric reproduction, adding to Angel's liminality and the darkness of the show. The conception of Connor adds to Angel's hypermasculinity. Vampires should not be able to conceive a child, so his child with Darla comes replete not only with his own mythology but also with a sense that Angel is more masculine than other vampires: he's able to conceive a child where no other vampire can.

The hypermasculinity of the noir hero is reflected in the characters of Wes and Gunn, as well; like Angel, each becomes more morally ambiguous — and more normatively masculine — as the series continues. Wesley starts out as a clumsy and effeminate character in *Buffy* and returns as such in the first season of *Angel*. His relationship with his father — and his sense of failure — becomes part of the text just as it does for Angel. Unlike Angel and, eventually, Spike, who can carry off the leather look easily, Wes uses leather as a signifier of his masculinity — and then, notably, begins walking funny: "These pants ... they tend to chafe one's ... legs" ("Parting Gifts"). He is unable to walk the walk of hypermasculinity. He is frequently marked as gay, providing humorous relief to dramatic moments, and often needs rescuing by Angel, whether physically or economically (gaining employment). As scholar, Wes represents an effeminate character; for instance, Cordelia states, in "Untouched," "All evidence to the contrary, Wes, you're not a woman." The triangle between Wes — Fred — Gunn begins Wesley's descent into darkness, one which is furthered when Wes makes the choice to take Connor from his father out of fear for his safety. He is cast out from the group, Angel attempts to suffocate him, and he begins his kinky and questionable relationship with Lilah. The loss of Fred to Illyria sends him further into darkness, although he returns somewhat. His suffering has deepened his characterization and made him a tragic and lovely figure, but one which is also much more normatively masculine than when he started. As we will discuss, this relates to the construction of the erotic triangle.

Gunn is yet another tragic figure.[41] Like Wes, his increasingly normative male behavior (with all the attendant difficulties in his racial characterization) is related to the Wes — Fred — Gunn triangle. In attempting to "save" the damsel, Fred, from losing her innocence[42] through the murder of the professor who relegated her to slavery and near death on Pylea, he corrupts himself and thus ironically still loses her; in the process, he once again is blackened from his previously color-blind narrative status (Meyer 182). Afterwards, his need to enhance himself intellectually and become more like Wes (see below) results in the loss and metaphoric rape of Fred, since he unwittingly signs the sheet for customs to release Illyria's sarcophagus.

The role of Gunn is very important in his construction as brute black male who must have an intellectual upgrade in order to compete with the white men who surround him. Gunn, one of the only recurring black characters, is constructed with racist overtones at least. His street mentality, his name, his relationship with Fred and participation in her revenge on the professor that sent her to a hell dimension, the artificial reconstruction of his mental capacities and his quest to keep them, his function as the brawn for a major portion of the series, and his particular physical embodiment of the Wolfram and Hart partners are part of the problematic construction of his character. He functions in ways that shore up the white middle class masculinity of Angel, Spike, and Wesley, especially providing contrast to the white, middle class, feminized Wes.[43]

Wes and Gunn are rendered tragic — there's a lot of sympathy evoked for Wes' decision to take Connor and all that follows, for his thwarted romance with Fred, and for his loss of Fred at the very beginning of their relationship. So, too, is Gunn's involuntary consignment of Fred to death sympathetically treated (if still problematic in its construction of lower class black masculinity). None of these tragic paths are treated lightly, nor is the normativization of the masculinity of the characters unremittingly depicted as good. McCracken argues that normative masculinity is derided on *Angel*, in part by arguing for the polysemic nature of the text: "critical and queer positions remain equally valid and narratively independent — they are not used to buttress normative masculinity but to provide valid, often preferable, alternatives to it" (132). However, simultaneously some of the narrative underpinnings of the show reinforce those normative male positions. This includes the homoerotic triangles forged over the course of the show. While deepened characterization is a result of many of these triangles, as is the case in *Buffy*, these triangles, unlike those of *Buffy*, serve to reinforce normative masculine behavior and depend upon the exchange of female bodies.

*   *   *

As is appropriate to a noir text — and, indeed, I contend that the noir genre motivates this treatment — women (Darla, Lilah, Fred, and Cordelia) play integral roles in the construction of triangles around the rejection and containment of the feminine and the bolstering of hypermasculinity. Powerful female characters, such as Jasmine and Illyria, are ultimately monstrous and must be destroyed or domesticated; containment is constantly an issue in the treatment of Illyria, although, to be fair, the men consistently fail to contain her. To begin with the example used above of Angel's fatherhood, it is significant that Darla, who shares a triangle with Angel and Lindsey, must die in order for Connor to live. She must stake herself in an alley so that her son may come forth. This action creates resonances with the treatment of monstrous female figures; for instance, in their seminal study of 19th century literature, Sandra Gilbert and Susan Gubar discuss the punishment of women who failed to be angels in the house and who were, instead, transgressive. Poor Darla just can't catch a break, having been turned by the Master as a prostitute dying of syphilis, dusted by Angel in favor of Buffy, brought back to life by Wolfram and Hart, pursued romantically by Lindsey in a tug of war with Angel, set on fire by Angel, impregnated in violence, and forced to share Connor's soul so that she chooses the ultimate in maternal devotion over her own life. In "Lullaby," she says to Angel:

> We did so many terrible things together. So much destruction, so much pain. We can't make up for any of it. You know that, don't you? This child ... Angel, it's the one good thing we ever did together. The only good thing. You make sure to tell him that.

Motherhood comes to define her sense of self, and her tragic end becomes a small penance for her monstrous self-assertion.

The Lindsey — Darla — Angel triangle clearly works as a power struggle between two men over a woman, as well as a displacement of Lindsey's potential desire for Angel, which Roz Kaveney also notes, citing Darla's comment to Lindsey: "It's not me you want to screw — it's him.[44] You all think you can use me to get to Angel" ("Darla") ("A Sense" 66). This desire is made textually manifest again in "Not Fade Away," when Angel says to Lindsey, "I want you, Lindsey." He pauses and then follows this with "I'm thinking about rephrasing that," to which Lindsey replies, "Yeah, I think I'd be more comfortable if you did."[45] These are two men who have struggled repeatedly over power, and the conquest of Darla is just one more example of their homoerotic competition with each other. Lindsey will use Eve, a woman with whom both eventually become "groin buddies" (*Angel*, "You're Welcome"), in the same way: as a means to get at Angel.[46]

*   *   *

The rejection and containment of women goes beyond the use and abuse of Darla. Cordelia is raped and impregnated several times, her body functioning as a means for the men to demonstrate their ability to rescue her; she does not rescue herself, as would Buffy. Neither would Buffy castigate herself as deserving punishment for her unfeminine behavior, as does Cordy. One might argue that Cordy's behavior is all too feminine from the perspective of negative stereotypes of female behavior. In framing herself as Queen C, Cordy is a powerful figure at Sunnydale High School who ultimately is taken down several pegs through her ostracization by other popular women, Xander's affair with Willow, and her father's financially criminal behavior. She moves to L.A. to begin an acting career, but she fails at this. She sees this failure and her attempted murder by a ghost as punishment for her behavior as a "queen." The visions she endures as Doyle's surrogate form a sort of rape as well, but one which she endures as a means of penance and redemption for her previous "bitchy" persona. Like Angel, she feels a need for redemption, but, unlike Angel, her redemption takes the form of the passive repeated violations of her body by visions that are killing her. Her final demonic pregnancy is a rape as well, as Cordy's body is involuntarily used as a vessel for the rebirth of Jasmine. Angel verbally makes this connection clear when he says to Spike that, "I lost Cordelia because some thing violated her. It crawled inside and used her up" ("Shells"). As Hill and Williams write, "More so than any other character on *BtVS* or *Angel*, Cordelia has suffered and been threatened with bodily invasion and rape, either symbolically or literally" (206).

She also provides the first potential triangle of the show, working as a bridge between *Angel* and *Buffy*. Her desire for Angel having been established in *Buffy*, her employment by Angel provides some brief moments of dramatic tension at the beginning (as Doyle fears Angel may have designs on Cordelia), as well as enabling Cordelia in her comic commentaries on Angel's patterns of desire. Later on, Cordelia will participate in a triangle with Fred and Angel, as Fred, having been recently rescued by Angel and company, will desire him as the damsel in distress often desires her rescuer. This triangle will serve to reinforce Angel's desirability and heteronormativity and the possibility of Cordelia's interest in him, which is quickly displaced for a time (an entire season) through the Groosalugg, for reasons of narrative sexual tension. It takes Lorne and Groosalugg — two men — to make it clear to Angel and Cordy, respectively, that they love each other.

More importantly, Cordelia is also involved in one of the more disturbing triangles in *Angel*: that between she, Angel, and Connor. Milking the drama of Oedipal tragedy,[47] Cordy seemingly betrays her love for the father by having sex with the son. That this involves the involuntary use of her body by a fascistic goddess isn't made fully clear to the audience or other characters until eleven episodes after they begin their tryst. Although the audience is given clues that something is odd (and evil) about Cordelia, we don't know what it is, and the Oedipal triangle is maintained until the "birth" of Jasmine. Thus, while this particular triangle is not about the displacement of a homo-erotic relationship between father and son, it does involve their homosocial competition and the exchange of the female body between them; it is through his sexual relationship with Cordelia that Connor becomes a man. The rape of Cordy as part of this process makes it even more disturbing, although the audience isn't aware until much later that Cordy as we knew her was not a willing participant in sex with and seeming impregnation by the son, thus concealing her rape and making it less overtly distasteful. Like Fred, her body has been violated; she, too, eventually will die as a result of this violation.

One might think these violations of the female body stop there ... but then we look at the figure of Fred. She begins her life in the series as the mon-strous madwoman, making little sense and eventually riffing on Charlotte Perkins Gilman's "The Yellow Wallpaper" by writing all over the walls of her room in the Hyperion Hotel. Eventually, she becomes the brains of the group and yet she simultaneously functions often as a damsel in distress and an object of exchange between Wes and Gunn. Wesley and Gunn "share" Fred serially, and their relationships with her help to define their manhood and their relationship with each other. The end of her life functions as a rape as well, as the demon Illyria forcibly and involuntarily penetrated her body and took it from her. Gunn's desire for Wesley's status, knowledge, and, one might argue, his whiteness,[48] leads him to eventually (though inadvertently) betray Fred and make her vulnerable to Illyria. The black man becomes responsible for the rape and death of the innocent white female.[49] It is significant as well that Gunn then takes on Wesley's previous identity as betrayer and is stabbed by Wesley with a phallic weapon. Wes has a shotgun but doesn't use it; instead, he picks up and uses a scalpel, a signifier of the procedures Gunn was will-ing to sacrifice others for, as well as a signifier of the phallus. Gunn then resigns himself to suffering torture in a hell dimension in order to aid the group and attempt redemption. In hell, his nuclear "family" of wife and child are white and middle-class, representatives of what he was trying to attain through his betrayal.[50] His stoicism in suffering through his torment is a marker of his hypermasculinity, as well.

Lilah presents us with yet another problematic image of women, as Jen-nifer Stoy has written, as well as yet another triangle laden with the detritus of hypermasculinity and noir influence. Discussing the role of Lilah as femme fatale in *Angel*, she concludes that "[o]n the surface, we have a straight-for-ward tale of the detective and the femme fatale, straight out of 1948, where —

after the threat of the dangerous woman is removed — the world returns to placid normality" (174). While she concludes that "Lilah and Wesley were not just a reproduction of [*The Maltese Falcon's*] Sam Spade and Bridget O'Shaughnessy, or even [*The Big Sleep's*] Vivian Rutledge and Philip Marlowe" (174), still there are provocative similarities for the thesis of this paper, which, in part, is that women continue to function as objects of exchange in the homoerotic triangles of *Angel* and do so in large part as a result of its generic influences. Lilah first begins a sexual relationship with Wesley after he has been cut off from the group, including his object of desire, Fred. Lilah pretends to *be* Fred in a little role playing fantasy during sex games with Wes. While Lewis Call finds the relationship between Lilah and Wes to be "part of *Angel's* ambitious, ongoing project to normalize kink," and while he sees a mutual exchange of power between Lilah and Wes (para 48), her death still works as a containment of female transgressive power: it is "[a] predictable, poignant, but not particularly progressive or feminist ending for Lilah the moral agent" (Stoy 170). The triangle of Lilah-Wesley-Fred serves to illustrate Wes' desire for Fred, as well as cement the hypermasculinization of Wesley. While it deepens characterization, it does so through the dark development of Lilah; we may have suspected already that she would be kinky, but she demeans herself through her pursuit of Wes, being willing to take crumbs of affection from him. Although this relationship gains complexity and a measure of compassion, if not respect, Lilah's body is used as replacement for intimacy with Fred and to illustrate how low Wes has sunk as a character or, more positively, how complex he has become. The fact that Lilah continues to betray Wes for the good of Wolfram and Hart works simply to subdue her complexity: she's all about the evil. While her body is not exchanged between two men, she continues to function as a means to prove Wes' hypermasculinity.

Spike and Angel

It is in a discussion of the queering of Angel and Spike, as well as of the Angel-Buffy-Spike triangle, that these threads most clearly and overtly come together: the hypermasculinity, the use of the female body, the construction of genre, and the homoeroticism. The encoding of the male body is most evident in this relationship as is the play in this encoding. This triangle first surfaces in *Angel*, not *Buffy*, and it surfaces in terms of Spike's homoerotic relationship with Angel rather than his desire for Buffy. A great deal of humor comes through in this relationship, as well.

In the second episode of Season One, "In the Dark," as one of several

crossovers that will be used to establish an audience for *Angel*, Spike visits
L.A. to regain the gem of Amara, which will make a vampire invulnerable.
Buffy has sent the gem to Angel via Oz, and Angel has hidden it away. We
are first made aware of Spike's presence after Angel saves a young woman
from an abusive lover. Spike, in the best *Mystery Science Theater* style, falsely
narrates a wonderfully wicked exchange between Angel and the damsel:

> No, helping those in need is my job, and working up a load of sexual
> tension and prancing away like a magnificent poof is truly thanks enough!
> "I understand. I have a nephew who is gay, so..." Say no more. Evil's still
> afoot! And I'm almost out of that Nancy-boy hair gel I like so much.
> Quickly, to the Angel-mobile, away!

Even as Angel is attempting to intercede in domestic violence, Spike is
considering his own (domestic) violence against Angel in order to gain the
gem of Amara: desire, death, violence, and revenge — all elements of a classic tragic triangle — are evoked. Significantly, Spike codes Angel as gay in this
mock dialogue. Later, he will be the agent of Angel's body becoming a site
of delectation and torture with, again, phallic objects (ex. hot pokers) as Angel
is chained to a ceiling, objectified, and tortured by another male vampire,
Marcus. In this scene, he simultaneously is object of the vampire and the
audience's gaze, as well as the object of penetration.[51] "He's known love,"
comments Marcus, and Spike replies, "Yeah, and with a Slayer no less. How's
that for a perversion?" When Spike claims that Marcus will not betray him
for the ring, he states:

> It's called addiction, Angel.... I believe yours is named "Slutty the Vam-
> pire Slayer." ... I ran into her recently. Your name didn't come up.
> Although she has been awful busy jumping the bones of the very first
> lunkhead who came along.... Used her shamelessly. She is cute when she
> is hurtin', isn't she?

Angel retorts, "I think she's cuter when she's kicking your ass." Each
tries to "outman" the other through a façade of toughness and violence but
also through their virility, an exchange not uncommon to noir, buddy, and
superhero genres. Buffy is used as an object of exchange, eliciting desire and
humiliation in the homosocial competition between Spike and Angel. This
will set up a triangulation of desire within both shows, although it is primarily evidenced in *Angel's* fifth season.

The text is queered through the emphasis of "In the Dark" on penetration, perversion, homoeroticism and reversal of the gaze, just as it is in multiple other episodes.[52] Power is part of the formula as well, and Roz Kaveney

argues that the power dynamic between Spike and Angel is part of their homo-eroticism ("A Sense" 63). The queering of the text is noted by Wilcox and Lavery, as well; they write that *Angel* uses "the queer text method of frequent textual games with the characters' sexual and gender roles — especially for Angel himself..." ("Afterword" 228). Genre is part of this textual play, as noted above and in McCracken, who comments that "*Angel* exposes and celebrates the queer subtext of the noir genre" (134). This is in part due to *Angel* making manifest the hypermasculinity and homoeroticism beneath the surface of noir. While never textually sexual with each other, Laura Diehl argues, the costuming of Angel and Spike in leather pants and Goth style visually marks them as homoerotic (para 43), and she sees this as transgressive and freeing of the American bind between gender and sexuality (para 47). Part of the play and transgression of *Angel* is verbal; the more Spike remarks upon the masculinity of Angel and other men, the more he makes clear his own performance of masculinity (Masson and Stanley para 18).

*   *   *

Feminizations of each character — often a coding for homosexuality — occur fairly frequently. In *Angel*, feminizations of Spike[53] might include his status as a noncorporeal entity in the first several episodes of Season Five, his relationship with Fred and dependence upon her to become corporeal again, and his physical subordination to Illyria in an episode such as "Origin," in which Spike is testing Illyria's strengths and weaknesses: Illyria images Spike as frail, while Spike asserts a concern with appearance and emotion. This scene might be read as part of the flipping of binaries — in this case, a female acting out a traditionally male role — in which Whedon often engages. Spike's concern with physical appearance ("no more punching me in the face") helps to cement this reading of the scene as engaging with a feminized Spike.[54]

Such queering of Angel occurs in the first episode of Season Five ("Conviction"), as well. Angel visits the apartment of Spanky, a mystic who also enjoys S&M. While Spanky insists that he has "nothing against people doing their thing," he also states that he doesn't spank men. Angel, after being attacked by Spanky, states, "There's something else you should know about me ... I have no problem spanking men." Later, when Angel confronts a member of Wolfram and Hart's special ops, the agent argues that Angel and his group "lack conviction"; they're too "conflicted" in their moral dilemmas, and Angel is a "pathetic little fairy." Angel replies, "Hey, I'm not little." Although this is read humorously, it is part of a larger framework which questions the stability of Angel and Spike's sexual categorization, hinting at the possibilities of polymorphously perverse sexuality or, at least, the defiance of contemporary constructions of male sexuality, especially one which works within an opposition of the homosocial and the homosexual. Additionally, here is a moment at which intense heteromasculinity is critiqued as the special ops officer wields homophobia and the threat of violence in an attempt to deflate Angel's masculinity. He is in for a rude awakening in that regard, as Angel asserts his own violence.

The episode "Hellbound" makes clear the buddy nature of Spike and Angel's relationship, as well as the construction of masculinity and sexuality. While Spike asserts that Angel's "mystique" is that of a "brooding block of wood," Angel retorts that Spike is far too chatty and his hair is "radioactive." In fact, their conversation resembles odd couple bickering at its finest. Each asserts that he never cared for the other, but then comes the moment of truth: Angel admits, "There was one thing about you ... I never told anyone about this, but I — I liked your poems." Spike is unimpressed and dryly responds, "You like Barry Manilow." Once again, Angel's penchant for poems, "power ballads" (as Faith calls them), and Barry Manilow mark him as queer. While the queering of the text is full of transgressive possibility, the construction of the erotic triangle limits its expression.

*   *   *

The rivalry in Season Five between Spike and Angel over the love object allegedly proves the masculinity and heterosexuality of each to the other and to the viewing audience in the context of playful banter, and yet we also have the reification of traditional models of masculinity, which generally work to exclude and displace evocations of homoerotic desire. Masculinity — through the guise of becoming a champion and a "real boy" — is proven through the exercise of power and violence, as well as through the body of the Slayer, even as such masculinity is critiqued in its most overt forms. However, Buffy not only functions, in Season Five, as a means to reiterate masculinity and heterosexuality but also acts as a conduit for Spike and Angel's feelings for each other. Significantly, we never see Buffy (although we see the back of a double for her in one episode); she is only cited verbally.[55] Lewis Call writes, "By the end of *Angel*, Spike and Angel can almost be honest about what they are: two longstanding members of a kinky vampire community who have always shared power and pain and who, despite their constant textual sniping, clearly need each other and clearly satisfy one another' s mutual erotic needs" (para 41). Like Call, I would note that it is not until Season Five that the kinkiness of the series reaches full throttle, and this is in Angel's relationship with Spike, another vampire who can most easily bring out the homoeroticism and who plays a comic figure.[56]

One might argue that this triangle (Angel-Buffy-Spike) enables a continuum of sexuality in which men can be both/and rather than either/or, i.e., in love with both the Slayer and each other, in the mode of Kinsey's continuum of sexuality or Adrienne Rich's lesbian continuum.[57] Alfred Kinsey wrote, "Males do not represent two discrete populations, heterosexual and homosexual. The world is not to be divided into sheep and goats. It is a fundamental of taxonomy that nature rarely deals with discrete categories.... The living world is a continuum in each and every one of its aspects" (639). Rich's work also argues that sexuality goes beyond erotic interactions to include nurturing ties and intimacy; sexuality is not simply about penetration but about other richer and more emotionally satisfying connections. Each work reveals the difficulty of a dualistic approach to sexuality, an approach that denies the possibility, for instance, of bisexuality, although Sedgwick argues that bisexuality cannot exist within American culture for men since such a continuum is vehemently at odds with notions of masculinity and homophobia: homosociality is placed in opposition to homosexuality due to homophobia.

So does this leave Angel and Spike as champions of a free play between heterosexuality and homosexuality? Perhaps they are merely polymorphously perverse. Even if this is so, the way in which women are used as conduits for the expression of male sexuality and masculinity is problematic in *Angel*. The homosocial paradigm remains, excluding the characters of Cordelia, Fred, Eve, and Harmony from participating in the same sort of egalitarian community which is in place in Buffy at the end of Season Seven — or even a version of female autonomy that is free of stereotypical gender constructions. They function, as does Gunn, I would argue, as means to prove the masculinity and sexuality of Angel and Spike. Buffy's absence in Season Five — and yet her continuing presence as object of allusion — makes clear the fabrication of the triangle, its falsity, its function as subterfuge. Buffy is not physically present in Season Five and not a candidate for actualized romance with either character. However, references to Buffy actually become more frequent. Their pursuit of an absent Buffy in "The Girl in Question," as well as their continued bickering over which one of them is the real champion, which one has been more heroic, which one of them should be the "real boy," and who had a real relationship with Buffy (and whether sex can define a relationship) — and Buffy's absence from this conflict — makes it clear that their relationship with each other is far more important than their relationship with her at this point. Lewis Call argues that "quite obviously [Angel and Spike go to Italy in "The Girl in Question"] for the real purpose of permitting the homoerotic relationship between the two male vampires to eclipse their mutual obsession with Buffy" (para 2); while this may be so, they end where they began.[58] Their dialogue is typical of homosocial behavior once again; each one is trying to prove his heteromasculinity through use of the female body. In "Destiny," Spike argues that he is the true champion because he chose it rather than having it thrust upon him by a gypsy curse. Angel states, "Really? I heard it was just to get into a girl's pants." Later, in the same episode, they continue their cockfight, with Spike yelling, "Take a long look, hero. I'm nothing like you!" Angel replies, "No. You're less. That's why Buffy never really loved you: because you weren't me." Throwing Angel against a wall, Spike retorts, "Guess that means she was thinking about you ... all those times I was puttin' it to her." In this last line, the connection between Angel and Spike is made evident. Here we again have the mixture of sexuality, homosociality, homoeroticism, violence, and sexism at work concurrently in the construction of gender. Buffy-as-person is no longer important; Buffy-as-vagina/conduit is cited. She is fragmented, reduced to her "pants" and proof of one man's virility over another. This is a very traditional representation of masculinity and of the heroic quest: woman as reward for the hero.[59]

Perhaps this is one reason why Angelus is so fascinating: he is not a part of this triangle and yet is highly queered. Angelus seems to be more polymorphously perverse than Angel, although he simultaneously sees himself as stronger than Angel, whom he perceives as weak and spineless. The simultaneous defiance of traditional heterosexuality and maintenance of masculinity is most clearly constructed through Angelus and Spike's relationship.[60] A flashback from Season Five ("Destiny") to the "good ole' days" shows Drusilla bringing the newly sired William home to "daddy" Angelus and asking if he approves; Angelus answers that he is tired of traveling with women all the time and would enjoy a male companion in his destruction, even though "some would call that deviant," the word "deviant" acting as a code for the alleged deviance of homosexuality. He and William share an S&M moment as Angelus thrusts William's hand into the sun, then his own after William jerks his hand back; William then pleases Angelus by thrusting his hand out himself. They are sharing a moment of male bonding laced with pleasure and pain, pain being something for which Angelus is well known. In this flashback, the bodies of Darla and Drusilla are available as sites for Angelus and Spike to exercise their heterosexuality simultaneous to the exercise of both homosociality and, potentially, homosexuality; the threat of homosexuality is kept in check through the presence of the women. In a flashback later in the episode, we see Angelus having intercourse with Drusilla, reminding William that he is the Alpha male; William has declared Dru his "destiny," and Angelus will have none of it. He is also using Dru as a conduit to William for both pleasure and pain. Dru is literally a conduit between Angelus and William in that Angelus sired Drusilla, who, in turn, sired William.[61] While Angelus characterizes himself as potentially "deviant," he does so in a context that emphasizes pain and destruction, hallmarks of an aggressive masculinity.

It is also notable that the most obviously textual references to homoeroticism occur in relation to Spike and his history with Angelus. While playful sexual banter continues to occur between Spike and Angel, the effect is mitigated by the emphasis on a *past* homoeroticism between *Angelus* and Spike. So while Shapiro, for instance, writes that Angel is far more likely than Spike to bite other men and thus is more fully coded as homoerotic, his research reflects upon *Angelus*, not Angel. As far as the canon of the series goes, Angel only bites two people while he has a soul: the submarine officer and Buffy. While the submarine officer brings a sixty-one year history into the present, Angel rejects his history with the officer, who also brings the threat of death to his friends. He turned this officer not out of homoeroticism but out of patriotic need[62]: Lawson is the only one who can fix a damaged propulsion system, and he has been mortally wounded. Angel bites Buffy at her insistence when he has been poisoned by Faith; the blood of a slayer is all that will save him, and Faith has escaped. The Buffy bite is far more erotic than that of Lawson, replete with orgasmic imagery. Angelus is, indeed, much more textually sexually adventurous than Angel; however, while his construction provides for a great deal of play, Angelus is past, a persona that Angel has rejected even as it continues to live within him. One might even argue that the repression of this demon includes the repression of his sexual and erotic past. Angel's eros is carefully aimed at women: Buffy, Kate, and Cordelia to name the most important.

In addition to a reliance on continued hypermasculinity, on the past, and on Angelus in relation to the most obvious citations of homoeroticism, the use of humor is important as well in considering the power of the homoerotic triangle. While, yet again, opening up a play of sexuality and the possibility for polymorphously perverse behavior, the emphasis on humorous references to possible homoerotic behavior and desire cuts the potential power of this representation. The gay lifestyle remains a joke, part of a buddy/sibling type banter. McCracken argues this point as well, writing, "Gay references abound in later episodes of *Angel,* but they are not developed, nor do they act as critiques. In fact, such references more often function in the later episodes of *Angel* as the type of ambiguously homoerotic and/or phobic jokes found in more conventional action texts, the kind used to deflect, rather than develop, homoerotic relationships" (McCracken 140). While Spike is treated as a camp[63] figure in *Buffy*, Masson and Stanley assert that he becomes less campy in *Angel* (para 22); perhaps this is because Lorne is already a clear camp figure[64] and the show is unable or unwilling to include an increased emphasis on camp. Stan Beeler writes that "[camp] is a strategy for allowing the representation of the marginal to appear in mainstream forms of discourse; forms which would not normally tolerate the representation of gay men without recourse to camp humour" (89); thus, Lorne is permissible in that he *is* a camp figure rather than simply a gay person. Notably and noticeably, he also is an alien figure with his green skin and horns and thus is less easily identified with than Angel or Spike, who, while demons, are in human guise a majority of the time. The gay lifestyle remains at a distance even as it is referenced both sub-textually and textually. Lorne is also the figure who most often, most force-fully, and most accurately critiques Angel for his hypermasculine and heteronormative behavior (see note on this, above).

Although Spike is more easily queered and feminized, Angel remains a character for whom true manhood[65] remains a defining element of his char-acter. He is clearly the hero of this show, and he is a very different type of hero than Buffy. As a result of the change in genre, the romantic triangle functions more conservatively than it does in *Buffy,* and the women in *Angel* are much less self-actualized than those in Buffy. Even Fred, the scientific brain of the group, is rendered as giggly and hysterical at times, as when she writes notes all over the room trying to solve the problem of Spike's corpo-reality; here she references her behavior in her room at the Hyperion: "I'm not crazy. Again" ("Hellbound"). In addition, the female body often func-tions as a site for demonic intrusion in addition to being represented as requir-ing rescuing. The men of the group, although often ultimately unable to do so, feel the need to protect the women, as in "Lineage" (*Angel* 5.7) in which Fred is wounded on a mission with Wesley. Perhaps this failure to protect the women offers yet another critique of the hypermasculinity of the show in that it often fails; if this is so, however, the critique is a diffuse and subtextual one. Although community is important, and this is a community in which power is somewhat diffused (i.e., all members of the community play valu-able roles and share — to a degree — in the decision making), the exchange of women to shore up masculinity is an important part of the show as is the male bonding which occurs. The show's debt to film noir, superhero, buddy,

and romance genres ultimately is paid back through a conservative representation of the erotic triangle and of masculinity and femininity.

*   *   *

Three of Joss Whedon's now defunct series have made their way into
comic books: *Buffy*, *Angel*, and *Firefly*. I was curious to see whether the playful approach to sexuality continued in the comics for *Angel*; others, such as
Hélène Frohard-Dourlent and Lewis Call ("Slaying") have analyzed Buffy's
Season Eight comics and found their representation of sexuality, while beyond
the usual normative representation of sexuality in mainstream fiction, less
than fully transgressive. *Angel: After the Fall* is keeping with the tone of the
final season of the *Angel* television series in that it is more serious and less
comic. The series, in keeping with the stereotype of comic book series, loses
some of its noir style, although the backgrounds continue often to be dark
and the preoccupations continue to be isolation, alienation, betrayal, paranoia, and masculinity. One might argue that genre continues to determine
the construction of gender and sexuality; although there are far less homoerotic triangles, especially since our protagonists are spread out over hellish
Los Angeles, there continue to be a few, and the representation of women continues to be problematic.

Gone, however, is a large measure of the playful banter between Angel
and Spike; they are separated for a large portion of the comic issues, as are
the other members of team Angel. Illyria is with Spike, who seems, at first,
to be running a harem; it turns out that the highly sexualized women around
him are, in fact, protecting both him and Illyria. As the series continues, the
men group around her, attempting to protect her in honor of Fred. Ultimately,
however, she is the biggest of the Big Bads for this segment, and, in a replaying of Willow's situation in *Buffy*'s Season Six, she must be talked out of
destroying the world in order to cease the pain of the humans around her.

Women continue to be utilized as objects of exchange, although their
agency is increased. The minor triangle of Angel-Gwen-Gunn in the TV
series has become a triangle of Gunn-Gwen-Connor, with Gwen betraying
Connor in favor of Gunn; this underscores Gunn's hypermasculinity, already
enhanced due to his being turned into a vampire during the apocalyptic Season Five fight. Gwen, who is a monstrous female in her own right (unable to
touch others due to the electricity in her body), desires only that she be made
"normal" so that she can consummate heterosexual relationships; Gunn has
the ability to make her "normal," and so she follows his orders. Gunn continues to be haunted by the specter of whiteness; he holds Angel responsible

for not protecting him from being made a vampire, and he believes that he can be the heroic vampire with a soul, replaying the homosocial competition between Angel and Spike. His desire to be *the* hero is critiqued as highly problematic due to his ensuing behaviors, including the betrayal of his friends and his killing of several women.[66] Finally, due to a time loop, Angel is able to save Gunn and prevent this disaster.

Before this time loop, however, Angel is made human by the Senior Partners of Wolfram and Hart; he continues to play the role of vampire through magics possessed by Wesley, brought back in ghost form in a replay of Lilah's situation. Angel is made human in the worst possible world to be a human: that of hell. Angel's isolation is critiqued, as it is during the TV show; he continues to attempt hypermasculinity when he is biologically less able to do so: he no longer has demon strength, and his bravado becomes dangerous to his continued survival as he makes more and more enemies of demons. All of the men attempt to protect Illyria/Fred, and their inability to fully do so is clear as well. They also suffer from a lack of growth, the existentialist dilemma posed by Masson in regards to Season Five, in that all of them must deal with the detritus of their constructions of masculinity from before the Fall. Wesley is most cruelly represented; the Senior Partners return him to his guise from Season One, removing all the growth he has experienced in the last six years (at least externally). Lynch, the scriptwriter of the comic writes: "As for Wesley's return to suit-and-tie? Well, Lorne explained it best in issue 4: Wolfram & Hart is cruel. They know Wesley's evolved beyond the person he was when he sported this look, so they slap him back down and force him to wear it 24/7." Wes is dressed once more in apparel from his first appearance in *Buffy* in what Cordelia refers to as his "Men's Warehouse" suit, thus leaving behind his earned look of rugged (hyper)masculinity, and he is once again ineffectual (since noncorporeal) and reserved. This is depicted as a hellish end for him.

In the end, the series validates the power of emotion once more, just as it did with Willow, by convincing Illyria that she should not end the world. The male characters remind her of who Fred once was and how these men felt about her. Illyria is given access to Fred's emotions through the men around her, once again suggesting, problematically, that women are not able to understand themselves properly; they require male surrogates (see the Angel-Cordelia-Groosalugg triangle, above). However, emotion is validated as a useful way of perceiving the world, working against the ethos of rationality and logic as a superior and male-identified world view. It also works against the hypermasculinity both celebrated and critiqued in the comics.

Unfortunately, most of the women have been lost along the way. The angel in the house, Cordelia, visits Angel in his near-death state but is ineffectual in changing the course of events. She is in the most passive of positions in relation to team Angel, unable to act at all until Angel almost dies; at that moment, she is able only to talk to and comfort him. The few women who are left mostly continue to be passed between the men as a means for maintaining a masculine identity.

Notes

1. Thank you to the person(s) behind the Buffyverse Dialogue Database (http://vrya. net/bdb/) for their immensely helpful labor of love as well as to the California State University, Sacramento for a much earlier sabbatical that allowed me to update my research in Whedon studies.

2. As Joss Whedon has noted in countless interviews and commentaries, the show began with the idea to reverse the usual treatment of the cute little blonde girl in the alley who gets terrorized in a horror film.

3. The marriage plot is the traditional emphasis upon the marriage of the female characters in (especially feminized forms of). Authors and films as varied as Jane Austen and *You've Got Mail* utilize the marriage plot.

4. See Suzanne Pharr, for instance. She analyzes the ways in which heteronormativity — the social and institutional pressure on people to give signs that they are heterosexual rather than homosexual through such actions as marriage and gay baiting — is tied to homophobia. Heteronormativity is tied to gender and power as well; for instance, progressive feminist organizations such as Planned Parenthood and NOW are regularly accused of being gay institutions (i.e., gay baited). Women and men who would like to work with and/or for such institutions — regardless of gender or sexuality — are pressured not to based on this gay baiting tactic.

5. See, for instance, not only Jowett on this but also Rhonda Wilcox's *Why Buffy Matters* and Wilcox and David Lavery's introduction to *Fighting the Forces* as just three examples of scholarship on the anti-patriarchal stance of *Buffy*. I spend far less time on this issue in *Buffy* than I do in *Angel*, since so much has already been written about the construction of the female hero and the feminism of the show in the scholarship on *Buffy*.

6. Some would dispute this claim. Scholarship which does so generally predicates itself upon the appearance of the lead actress, Sarah Michelle Gellar, including her clothing and Buffy's heteronormative behavior. Certainly, *Buffy* is a commercial product that sold itself to a teen audience, though the WB quickly learned that more than just teens were watching it. Jowett especially does a wonderful job of analyzing the contradictions within *Buffy* as a feminist text while simultaneously discussing its transgressive properties. As Lorna Jowett notes, in *Sex and the Slayer: A Gender Studies Primer for the* Buffy *Fan*, the series is polysemic in its representations of gender and sexuality; she cites Joss Whedon's comment that "'Part of the attraction of the Buffyverse' is that it 'lends itself to polymorphously perverse subtext. It encourages it.... I love all the characters, so I say B.Y.O. Subtext!'" noting that "resistant readings are in some sense 'authorized' and celebrated" (12–13).

7. See, for instance, Rhonda Wilcox's nuanced discussion of the treatment of patriarchy in "Hush" (*Why Buffy Matters* 146–161).

8 This essays is indebted to the work of both Stacey Abbott and Lorna Jowett in their discussion of these issues.

9. This triangle will provide humor later in *Angel* as well as illustrate the danger represented by stasis for Angel, as Cynthea Masson argues in her essay on "The Girl in Question." Masson quotes Cordelia's witticism about the type of woman to which Angel is attracted in order to illustrate the potential for Angel to be static: "One thing you can say about Angel at least he's consistent. It's always some little blonde driving him over the edge" (*Angel,* "Redefinition," 2.11). Additionally, this triangle will set the stage for Angel's attempt to help the newly revived (by Wolfram and Hart) Darla, providing sympathy for Darla and her tragedies. Angel's relationship to Darla will also function as part of his descent into isolation and cruelty in Season Two of *Angel*.

10. I don't delineate Harmony from Drusilla, since they are both female vampires and they play, in part, the same role in this triangle, although Drusilla is far more threatening.

11. Jowett argues that Buffy is masculinized by her role in general, but that this is recuperated by her feminine appearance, including her emphasis on clothing. Masculine and feminine are allowed ironic free play within Buffy's characterization (21–23).

12. It is significant that, immediately after his first glimpse of Buffy, Xander crashes into a stair railing, hurting his groin. This scene works to: situate Buffy as an object of desire, characterize Xander as desirous of her as said object, construct Xander's alleged lack of masculinity as a fumbling teenage boy, and sexualize Xander's alleged lack.

13. Michael Kimmel argues that no man can live up to the ideals of hegemonic masculinity, although they consistently try to do so.

14. Significantly, the three other men are all characterized as much more proficient at violence. In addition to his past as one of the most vicious vampires ever, Angelus, Angel is comfortable with a variety of weapons and can more than hold his own in a demonic battle. Similarly, Spike received his nickname from the spikes he used to torture victims prior to his residency in Sunnydale. Riley, while a human, is a covert military operative working for The Initiative. Unlike Spike or Angel, he cannot hold his own with Buffy, especially once his biological conditioning by The Initiative ceases. Significantly, the loss of the conditioning causes him to feel less a man since a woman — albeit the slayer — is stronger than he.

15. "The Pack" and "Beauty and the Beasts" are two episodes which are critical of aggressive masculinity; in "The Pack," Buffy is nearly raped by Xander. In "Beauty and the Beasts," a male student's concoction of a potion to make him more virile instead creates a Dr. Jekyll and Mr. Hyde situation. Under the influence of the potion, he physically and verbally abuses his girlfriend. These episodes implicitly critique male domination, rape, and domestic abuse. The contrast between the clear critique of aggressive male sexuality and implicit acceptance of it in the construction of Buffy's relationships is part of the polysemic nature of the text; one might also discuss it as part of the show as hegemonic product: while obvious abuse of women, for instance, is frowned upon on the surface, the conditions for its maintenance are maintained within our culture. For more on this point, see Jhally's *Dreamworlds II* and Katz's *Tough Guise* (both of which were produced and directed by Sut Jhally).

16. It does suggest Willow's ability to choose, however, although Farah Mendlesohn suggests, in *Fighting the Forces*, that Oz refuses Willow agency and choice when he disappears after "New Moon Rising" (55).

17. Farah Mendlesohn argues that the relationship between Buffy and Willow is marked by Buffy's preference for her relationships with men over her emotional intimacy with Willow; Willow, on the other hand, works against this paradigm (52–56).

18. Xander's desire for Cordelia and the ensuing madness of homosocial competition is set against Angelus' competition with Spike for Drusilla's affections: while Spike, like Xander, plans to give his love a heart necklace, Angelus skips to the chase and gives Dru an actual heart, creating an ironic metonymic reversal of the symbolism of Valentine's Day. However, here the competition IS homosocial and homoerotic; it is undercut by Drusilla being overcome by Xander's spell as well, humorously saving him from an attack by Angelus.

19. For a non–Whedonverse example, *L.A. Confidential* comes to mind. In this film, the female of the triangle explicitly states that one man is sleeping with her because it's his way of sleeping with the other man.

20. This includes the triangles of Lindsay-Darla-Angel, Gunn-Fred-Wes, Gunn-Gwen-Angel, and Spike-Buffy-Angel.

21. The W-M-W dynamic may also work to bolster and yet contain masculinity as we have discussed, just as it is also in keeping with the genres used in and challenged by the show.

22. See Simkin on this as well.

23. The character of Forrest Gates is problematic, as is the characterization of many characters of color within the Buffy and Angelverses. As Meyer argues re: Charles Gunn in *Angel*, Forrest is styled as a character who seeks white approval and connection and, having come to stand in for those institutions, is punished for this. Forrest Gates represents the possible wilderness — the gates of the forest — into which someone with grrl power can fall when she chooses patriarchal institutions — even those that might be highly seductive, as is the organized and armed Initiative that *seems* to be doing work similar to Buffy's own — over collective feminist work.

24. Riley's lower number of triangles may be due to his one season on the show versus seven seasons for Xander, three for Angel and more than four for Spike (as a regular).

25. Xander's lack of hostility to Riley (and his attempt to fix the break between Buffy and Riley at the end of the relationship) might be attributed to the ways in which Riley meets Xander's ideals of masculinity. Xander seems to have some appreciation for the highly heteronormative and homosocial military. Xander had a brief and limited encounter with the military ("Halloween," 2.6) and has maintained his knowledge of that fantasy. He also is shown in "Restless" to have an appreciation for *Apocalypse Now*.

26. His inability to deal constructively with his jealousy of Angel is critiqued as well. For instance, Xander's homosocial competition with Angel is crucial to his betrayal of Willow and Buffy in "Becoming, Part II" (2.21).

27. It is interesting that Riley will marry a woman named "Sam" while he is away from Buffy — her name works as a double signifier, enabling a subtextual reading that supports a homoerotic subtext.

28. Of course, Buffy and Faith also connect violence to sexuality in a masculinizing move for them. This connection often is depicted with reservations — Buffy loses Riley

when he can't perform masculinity to his and her standards, Faith almost kills Xander, and Buffy has kinky sex with Spike. The latter example creates embarrassment and self loathing for Buffy.

29. See Helene Frohard-Dourlent on the Season Eight *Buffy* comic books, which, she argues, perpetuate heteronormative expectations even as Buffy dabbles in a lesbian affair.

30. The representation of race is also a concern. For more on this, see, for instance, Mendlesohn.

31. Victoria Spah discusses Spike's characterization as courtly lover as well, although her analysis focuses on his treatment in *Buffy*.

32. For instance, in *The Maltese Falcon*, Sam Spade tells the femme fatale, Brigid, why he's going to turn her in to the police; in doing so, he verbally sets up a balance sheet, one which is neither implicitly nor explicitly about morals. He purrs, "Don't be too sure I'm as crooked as I'm supposed to be. That sort of reputation might be good business, bringing high-priced jobs and making it easier to deal with the enemy, but a lot more money would have been one more item on your side of the scale." Even though he asserts a detective code, in which "[w]hen a man's partner's killed, he's supposed to do something about it," loyalty to his partner doesn't seem paramount: he had a casual affair with his partner's wife.

33. Early noir dates to the late 1930s; however, its heyday is in the '40s.

34. See, for instance, the scene in which Humphrey Bogart's Sam Spade knocks Peter Lorre's Joel Cairo unconscious. Cairo has been coded as gay from his lilac-scented business card, his scented handkerchief, and the size of his gun as well as his personal mannerisms.

35. For instance, at the end of *Body Heat* (1981) we see Matty Walker on a beach sipping an exotic drink while her lover, Ned Racine, languishes in jail for the murder of her rich husband. The fate of the women in *Chinatown* (1974), however, is much gloomier as one is killed and her daughter left in the care of her incestuous grandfather/father.

36. See, for instance, not only the more recent the neo-noir *L.A. Confidential* (1997) for this queer subtext but *The Usual Suspects* (1995), in which multiple references are made to homosexual behavior.

37. See, for instance, Anne Rice's *Interview with a Vampire* series, Charlaine Harris' Sookie Stackhouse novels, and Laurel K. Hamilton's Anita Blake books.

38. See, for example, *The Celluloid Closet* on the history of cinematic representations of homosexuals.

39. Stacey Abbott notes that Angel's vampirism is emphasized more in *Angel* as well, although she links it to the visual style, increased occurrence of seeing Angel drinking blood, and references in dialogue to Angel's liquid diet. She attributes this change in emphasis to the missions of the two shows and how Angel's vampirism is used: in *BtVS* it is used as romantic obstacle while in *Angel* is a constant battle within him ("Kicking" 4).

40. Kaveney also connects this power dynamic to the homoeroticism between the two (63), which will be discussed further later in the essay.

41. For more on the racial dimensions of Charles Gunn, see Meyer.

42. Meyer argues that Gunn is also saving her whiteness (182). Were Gunn not to act on behalf of Fred, he fears she would turn to Wesley instead; this would, in turn, threaten his manhood.

43. Meyers makes many of these same points in her essay on Gunn.

44. This line is very similar to one in the neo-noir film *L.A. Confidential* (1997), in which the prostitute, Lynn Bracken, says to Bud White's shadow figure, Ed Exley, "Fucking me and fucking Bud aren't the same thing, you know."

45. The backtracking of each here simultaneously serves to underscore the sexual undertones of the previous line and distance Angel from homosexual attraction: he gets to have his cake and eat it, too.

46. When she has sex with Angel, Eve is, admittedly, under a spell. The tension between the two was present before this, however.

47. Although Cordelia is not literally Connor's mother, she functions in that role until he is stolen by Holtz. She then quickly becomes object of desire when he returns as a fully grown male in conflict with his father.

48. See Meyer for more on this since she makes a similar point.

49. I am purposely alluding here to the relationship between the portrayal of Fred and Gunn's relationship and the history of black male representation.

50. Gunn's experience in hell forms a not-so subtextual critique of this lifestyle and his desire: "Do you know what the worst part of that place was? Wasn't the basement. At least there, you knew where you stood. Demon was gonna cut your heart out and show it to you. Nah. It was the fake life they gave you upstairs. The wife, kids, all the icing on the family cake. But somewhere underneath it, there was the nagging certainty that it was all lies, that all the smiles and the birthday candles and the homework were just there to hide the horror. Is that all we're doing here — just hiding the horror?" ("Timbomb" 5.19).

51. See earlier discussion of Angel's body in *Buffy* and the work of Jowett and Owen.

52. Since Lorne, the queerest and campiest figure in the series, is not involved in these erotic triangles, I am not exploring his representation, although it is one potential site in which hypermasculinity is critiqued. Lorne repeatedly attempts to control or redirect Angel's hypermasculinity, and his nickname for Angel, "Angelcakes," is one example of this since it simultaneously plays with Angel's body as beefcake and as effeminate. His refusal to stay with Team Angel after Angel requests that he kill Lindsay is a mark of his satiety in dealing with hypermasculinity. It is significant as well that, when L.A. goes to hell in the comics, Lorne has created one of the only peaceful abodes.

53. In "'Love's Bitch but Man Enough to Admit It': Spike's Hybridized Gender," Spicer argues that Spike's engendering defies conventional categorizations and that Spike is often either feminized by others or feminizes himself in *Buffy*. Instances of Spike's feminization in *Buffy* include: his wounding and placement in a wheelchair, his relegation to dependency on Drusilla, the implantation of the chip which is referred to as a neutering or emasculation of him, his subordinate role to Buffy, and his strong and multiple emotional relationships with women (Spicer). We might also discuss the conversation over onion blossoms and his enjoyment of them in Season Seven, episode 19, of *Buffy*, "Empty Places," when he is riding on a motorcycle with Andrew, a highly feminized character who is much more explicitly and firmly coded as gay. Spike's past as a poet emasculated by the object of his affection also feminizes him.

54. See Dee Amy-Chinn on Spike as a queer character; she argues that his sexuality is presented as fluid rather than monolithic.

55. This is later explained in the Season Eight comics, when we learn that the slayer in Italy was not Buffy but a double for her. The replacement of the real Buffy by a dou-

ble without the knowledge of Spike and Angel creates a dynamic at odds with the usual representation of romance: they do not know their beloved is not their beloved — how could they not if she was truly their beloved? Perhaps the answer is that she is not their "forever love" but only a substitute for the other male.

56. See Cynthea Masson and Marni Stanley on Spike as a camp figure.

57. Alfred Kinsey found, in his 1948 research, that approximately 90 percent of adults existed along a continuum from fully heterosexual to fully homosexual.

58. See the note on Cynthea Masson's essay on "The Girl in Question," above.

59. In addition to the Angel-Buffy-Spike triangle, Angel's intercourse with Eve, discussed above, and Cordelia's reappearance in Season Five also function to reiterate Angel's heteromasculinity.

60. Tania, a slash fiction writer, also notes in her list of reasons why she has paired Angel and Spike that "Angel has a fabulous habit of Bending [sic] Spike over by throwing him onto a table (*Fool for Love*), or counter (*Lover's Walk*), or car hood, or up against a fence (*In the Dark*) whenever they fight."

61. The Oedipal issues of the show are of interest as well; they impact, of course, upon the construction of both masculinity and sexuality. Connor is not the only one who must kill or attempt to kill the father, either literally or symbolically, in order to shore up his own sexuality: Angel, Wes, Spike, and even Fred (through Gunn) kill fathers or father figures in order to come into their own as individuals. This is touched upon earlier.

62. The episode also signifies upon the homosociality and homoeroticism of military personnel during World War II (see Cohan, above). Steven S. DeKnight and Drew Goddard, the writers for this episode, link this World War II history with patriotism and doing what is necessary — however unsavory — to protect one's country. Ironically, during the McCarthy era which followed, homosexuality would be aligned with the perceived Communist threat.

63. While not synonymous with gay representation, the two often overlap; were we to image both in a Venn diagram, we would find the two occupying separate but overlapping circles. Camp is about humor and transgression and shares much in common with the carnivalesque.

64. For more on Lorne's function and construction within *Angel*, see Beeler.

65. See Kimmel and Katz on the construction of masculinity.

66. One might critique the representation of race here yet again, in that the man of color becomes one of the big bads due to his usurpation of the white protagonist's role.

Works Cited

Abbott, Stacey. Angel: *TV Milestones.* Detroit: Wayne State University Press, 2009.

_____. "Kicking Ass and Singing 'Mandy': A Vampire in LA." Abbott, *Reading.* 1–13.

_____. "'Nobody Scream ... or Touch My Arms': The Comic Stylings of Wesley Wyndham-Price." Abbott, *Reading.* 189–202.

_____. "Walking the Fine Line Between Angel and Angelus." *Slayage: The Online International Journal of Buffy Studies* 9/3.1 (Aug. 2003): 27 para. <http://slayageonline.com/essays/slayage9/Abbott.htm>. Accessed 8 July 2009.

_____, ed. *Reading* Angel: *The TV Spin-Off with a Soul.* London and New York: I.B. Tauris, 2005.

Amy-Chinn, Dee. "Queering the Bitch: Spike, Transgression and Erotic Empowerment." *European Journal of Cultural Studies* 8.3(Aug. 2005): 313–328.

Auerbach, Nina. *Our Vampires, Ourselves.* Chicago: University Chicago Press, 1995.

Beeler, Stan. "Outing Lorne: Performance for the Performers." Abbott, *Reading.* 88–100.

Buckman, Alyson R. "Real Boys and Longtime Companions: Angel, Spike, and the Homosocial Network." Southwest/Texas Popular Culture/American Culture Association (SW/TX PCA/ACA), Albuquerque, NM, February 2005.

Butler, Judith. *Bodies that Matter: On the Discursive Limits of Sex.* New York: Routledge, 1993.

Call, Lewis. "Slaying the Heteronormative: Representations of Alternative Sexuality in *Buffy*'s Season Eight Comics." SW/TX PCA/ACA, Albuquerque, NM, February 2009.

_____. "'Sounds Like Kinky Business to Me': Subtextual and Textual Representations of Erotic Power in the Buffyverse." *Slayage: The Online International Journal of Buffy Studies* 24/6.4(Summer 2007): 63 para. <http://www.slayageonline.com/essays/slayage24/Call.htm>. Accessed 24 June 2009.

The Celluloid Closet. Dir. Rob Epstein and Jeffrey Friedman. Sony Pictures Classics, 1996.

Cohan, Steven. *Masked Men: Masculinity and Movies in the Fifties.* Bloomington: Indiana University Press, 1997.

Comeford, Ami. "Knights, Dragons, and Maidens vs. Champions, Demons, and the Helpless: Medieval Romance and Chivalry in *Angel.*" SW/TX PCA/ACA, Albuquerque, NM, February 2009.

Craft, Christopher. "'Kiss Me with Those Red Lips': Gender and Inversion in Bram Stoker's *Dracula.*" *Dracula*, by Bram Stoker. Norton Critical Edition. Ed. Nina Auerbach and David J. Skal. New York: Norton, 1997: 444–459.

Diehl, Laura. "Why Drusilla's More Interesting Than Buffy." *Slayage: The Online International Journal of Buffy Studies* 13–14/4.1–2(Oct. 2004): 49 para. <http://www.slayageonline.com/essays/slayage13_14/Diehl.htm>. Accessed 24 June 2009.

Djikstra, Bram. "[*Dracula*'s Backlash]." *Dracula*, by Bram Stoker. Norton Critical Edition. Ed. Nina Auerbach and David J. Skal. New York: Norton, 1997: 460–461.

Frohard-Dourlent, Hélène. "'Tomorrow I'm gonna blush, then I'm gonna smile ... but I'm not sure if it goes any further than that'": Heteroflexibility and Buffy's Dabble Outside of Heterosexuality." SW/TX PCA/ACA, Albuquerque, NM, February 2009.

Gilbert, Sandra, and Susan Gubar. *The Madwoman in the Attic: The Woman Writer and the Nineteenth-Century Literary Imagination.* New Haven: Yale University Press, 1979.

Halfyard, Janet K. "The Dark Avenger: Angel and the Cinematic Superhero." Abbott, *Reading.* 149–162.

Hill, Matt, and Rebecca Williams. "*Angel*'s Monstrous Mothers and Vampires with Souls: Investigating the Abject in 'Television Horror.'" Abbott, *Reading.* 203–220.

Jacob, Benjamin. "Los Angeles: The City of Angel." Abbott, *Reading.* 75–87.

Jhally, Sut. *Dreamworlds II: Desire, Sex, and Power in Music Video.* Media Education Foundation, 1995.

Katz, Jackson, and Jeremy Earp. *Tough Guise: Violence, Media, and the Crisis in Masculinity.* Dir. Sut Jhally. Media Education Foundation, 1999.

Kaveney, Roz. "A Sense of the Ending: Schrodinger's *Angel.*" Abbott, *Reading.* 57–72.

_____. "'She Saved the World. A lot': An Introduction to the Themes and Structures of

Buffy and *Angel.*" *Reading the Vampire Slayer: An Unofficial Critical Companion to* Buffy *and* Angel. Ed. Roz Kaveney. London, New York: Tauris Parke, 2002. 1–36.

Kimmel, Michael. "Masculinity as Homophobia: Fear, Shame and Silence in the Construction of Gender Identity." *Race, Class and Gender in the United States: An Integrated Study.* 7th ed. Ed. Paula Rothenberg. New York: Worth, 2006. 80–92.

Lynch, Brian. *Angel: After the Fall: Director's Cut.* May 2008. IDW Publishing.

Mallory, Thomas. *Le Morte d'Arthur: King Arthur and the Legends of the Round Table.* 1485. Trans. Robert Graves. New York: Signet, 2001.

Masson, Cynthea. "What the Hell?—*Angel*'s 'The Girl in Question.'" SC 3: The Slayage Conference on the Whedonverses, Arkadelphia, AK, June 2008.

_____, and Marni Stanley. "Queer Eye of That Vampire Guy: Spike and the Aesthetics of Camp." *Slayage: The Online International Journal of Buffy Studies* 22/6.2(Winter 2006): 23 para. <http://www.slayageonline.com/essays/slayage22/Masson_Stanley.htm>. Accessed 24 June 2009.

McCracken, Allison. "At Stake: Angel's Body, Fantasy Masculinity, and Queer Desire in Teen Television." *Undead TV: Essays on* Buffy the Vampire Slayer. Durham: Duke University Press, 2007. 117–144.

Mendlesohn, Farah. "Surpassing the Love of Vampires; or, Why (and How) a Queer Reading of the Buffy/Willow Relationship is Denied." Wilcox and Lavery, *Fighting.* 45–60.

Meyer, Michaela D.E. "From Rogue in the 'Hood to Suave in a Suit: Black Masculinity and the Transformation of Charles Gunn." Abbott, *Reading.* 176–188.

Owen, A. Susan. "Vampires, Postmodernity, and Postfeminism: *Buffy the Vampire Slayer.*" *Journal of Popular Film & Television* 27.2(Summer 1999): 24–31.

Pharr, Suzanne. "Homophobia: A Weapon of Sexism." *Making Sense of Women's Lives: An Introduction to Women's Studies.* Ed. Lauri Umansky and Michelle Plott. Lanham, MD: Rowman and Littlefield, 2000. 424–437.

Rich, Adrienne. "Compulsory Heterosexuality and Lesbian Existence." *Blood, Bread, and Poetry: Selected Prose, 1979–1985.* New York: Norton, 1986. 23–75.

Sedgwick, Eve. *Between Men: English Literature and Male Homosocial Desire* New York: Columbia University Press, 1986.

Shapiro, Paul D. "Someone to Sink Your Teeth Into: Gendered Biting Patterns on *Buffy the Vampire Slayer*— a Quantitative Analysis." *Slayage: The Online International Journal of Buffy Studies* 26/7.2(Spring 2008): 29 para. <http://www.slayageonline.com/essays/slayage26/Shapiro.htm>. Accessed 24 June 2009.

Simkin, Stevie. "'Who died and made you John Wayne?': Anxious Masculinity in *Buffy the Vampire Slayer.*" *Slayage* 11&12 (April 2004): NP. Accessed 9 June 2009. <http://www.slayageonline.com/essays/slayage11_12/Simkin_Wayne.htm>.

Spah, Victoria. "'Ain't Love Grand?': Spike and Courtly Love." *Slayage: The Online International Journal of Buffy Studies* 5/2.1 (May 2002): 18 para. <http://www.slayageonline.com/Numbers/slayage5.htm>. Accessed 24 June 2009.

Spicer, Arwen. "Love's Bitch But Man Enough to Admit It: Spike's Hybridized Gender." *Slayage* 7 (December 2002): 24 para.

Stoy, Jennifer. "'And Her Tears Flowed Like Wine': Wesley/Lilah and the Complicated(?) Role of the Female Agent on *Angel.*" Abbott, *Reading.* 163–175.

Tania the Webgirl. "Why Slash Angel and Spike?" http://www.fangedfour.com/deadboy/whyspikeangel.htm. Accessed 27 May 2006.

Upstone, Sara. "'L.A.'s Got It All': Hybridity and Otherness in *Angel*'s Postmodern City." Abbott, *Reading*. 101–113.

Whedon, Joss. Interview. "Welcome to the Hellmouth/The Harvest." DVD special features, season one. 20th Century Fox, 1998.

Wilcox, Rhonda V. "'Every Night I Save You': Buffy, Spike, Sex, and Redemption." *Slayage: The Online International Journal of Buffy Studies* 5/2.1(May 2002): 18 para. <http://www.slayageonline.com/essays/slayage5/wilcox.htm>. Accessed 24 June 2009.

_____, and David Lavery. "Afterword: The Depths of *Angel* and the Birth of *Angel* Studies." Abbott, *Reading*. 221–229.

_____, eds. *Fighting the Forces: What's at Stake in* Buffy the Vampire Slayer. Lanham, MD: Rowman and Littlefield, 2002.

Wisker, Gina. "Vampires and School Girls: High School Hijinks on the Hellmouth in *Buffy the Vampire Slayer*." *Slayage: The Online International Journal of Buffy Studies* 2/1.2 (March 2001): 43 para. <http://slayageonline.com/PDF/wisker.pdf>. Accessed 9 September 2009.

Andrew and the
Homoerotics of Evil

PATRICIA PENDER

While the compelling, histrionic heterosexual rhetorics of *Buffy the Vampire Slayer* have been energetically analyzed, and the overtly lesbian narratives have begun to attract increasing attention, the flawed and often foiled homoerotic desires of the series' ostensibly straight male characters call out for further attention.[1] This paper attempts to queer the character Andrew in *Buffy's* Season Seven — a queering that may or may not be superfluous depending on your favored viewing positions and pleasures. Indeed, it is questionable whether it is even possible, let alone worthwhile, to "queer" Andrew because Andrew already seems to queer himself. If Andrew's queerness was written largely at the level of narrative (as Willow and Tara's is, for instance), rather than suggested (no matter how broadly) at the level of subtext, this endeavor would be, as Buffy suggests Andrew's archival project is in "Storyteller," "pretty pointless." In a series that demonstrates such delight in the slippage between text and subtext, moreover, upholding distinctions between them might seem counterintuitive. But, equally, it seems to me that even if Andrew's queerness is highly legible and the source, for many viewers, of much of the humor in the season, the *meanings* of that queerness are not always so obvious and, in fact, could be conceived as considerable cause for contention. How do Andrew's desires change between Seasons Six and Seven? Does he offer a positive or negative image of homoerotic desire? And does the fact that Andrew's primary erotic attachment is to Warren — and, through him, to evil more generally — mean that the representation of this desire is *ipso facto* homophobic and misogynist, or could it be interpreted in other less straightforward and formulaic ways? This essay considers Andrew's desire for evil, and by extension Warren and Jonathan, in order to consider how a queer reading of these relationships might affect prevailing understandings of the operations of gender and sexuality in a series so invested in both.

First broadcast in 1997, following the film version of 1992, *Buffy the Vampire Slayer* went to air in the decade that gave birth to the New Queer Cinema and shares with it several key characteristics. In her 1992 essay, "New Queer Cinema," B. Ruby Rich characterizes the queer films of the 90s, which included Jennie Livingston's *Paris is Burning* (1990), Todd Haynes's *Poison* (1991), and Tom Kalin's *Swoon* (1992) among many others, as "Homo Pomo," and saw them as invested in "appropriation," "pastiche," and "irony."[2] New queer girl films (later additions to the canon) that bear a closer relationship to *Buffy*'s content include *The Incredibly True Adventures of Two Girls in Love* (Maria Maggenti, 1995), *All Over Me* (Alex Sichel, 1997), and *But I'm a Cheerleader* (Jamie Babbit, 2000). In her 2004 reevaluation of the movement, Michele Aaron argues that the films of the New Queer Cinema share a strategy of "defiance" (3): they tend to "eschew positive imagery" and "defy the sanctity of the past, especially the homophobic past." They defy cinematic convention "in terms of form, content and genre" (4) and they also, tellingly, defy "death" (4). In its pastiche and irony, complex characterization, and defiance of the conventions of content and genre, *Buffy* shares many formal features with the new queer cinema. In its revision of historical narratives, fascination with death, and play with positive and negative imagery, it shares significant ground in content as well.

Queer is an appropriate lens through which to look at both the world represented in *Buffy* and the text that is *Buffy*. Aaron speaks to the "theoretically lucrative" valence of the term when she writes that queer represents "the resistance to, primarily, the normative codes of gender and sexual expression — that masculine men sleep with feminine women — but also the restrictive potential of gay and lesbian sexuality — that only men sleep with men and, women sleep with women" (5). In this way, queer, as a critical concept, "encompasses the non-fixity of gender expression and the non-fixity of both straight and gay sexuality." At its most expansive and utopian, Aaron argues, "queer contests (hetero- *and* homo-) normality" (5, emphasis added). In its theoretical applications, then, "queer is not just about gender and sexuality, but the restrictiveness of the rules governing them and their intersection with other aspects of identity" (7). Furthermore, Aaron makes clear that it is not just cultural production which demands queering, but also the analysis of those productions: "the queering of contemporary western culture is not just about the products alone, but about their theorization" (10).

Buffy is a queer text at both the narrative and meta-narrative levels; indeed there is reason to suggest that the series is most queer when it is not directly addressing explicitly homosexual content. Farah Mendelsohn has argued that representations of Willow's overtly "gay" (the term preferred by the characters) relationships overshadow the homoerotic undercurrents of Willow's potentially queer relationship with Buffy. Alison McCracken has recently argued convincingly for a queering of Angel's ostensibly straight male body, and she extends this queering to the viewing practices of *Buffy*'s legion of young female fans. She writes that the program's serial structure "permits girls' desires to shift and complicate over time, promoting the idea of sexual desire not as a fixed identity or goal-oriented pursuit (ending in a "solid" relationship), but as a queer continuum of erotic possibilities, opportunities and challenges" (118). Significantly expanding the horizon of queer readings of *Buffy*, McCracken argues that the term queer "acknowledges, as other descriptors cannot, the way in which *Buffy*'s feminist focus works to queerly recode a relationship between a pretty blonde and a hunky male that could otherwise be read as 'straight.' Sexual norms are always set atremble when a female is on top," McCracken writes, "and *Buffy*'s feminism enables queer readings in a way that distinguishes the program from other instances of queerness on television" (118–19).

Andrew presents a rich test case for queer readings of *Buffy* because his representation evolves over time and invokes several of the more misogynist, homophobic stereotypes of homosexuality as well as more open-ended or potentially progressive readings of homoerotic desire. I would argue that the series does so wittingly, that is, self-consciously and deliberately, so that homophobia and misogyny are actually thematized at the level of narrative, and are not merely, or perhaps not *only*, residual subtextual echoes. In Season Six, for instance, Andrew is represented variously as the "invisible" queer ("Who are you?"), as a clueless queer member of a tight homosocial unit ("I like Timothy Dalton!"), and as the closeted gay man acting out homophobia through the sexual objectification of women ("Free cable porn!"). In Season Seven, these resonances reach their highest pitch when Andrew is portrayed as a version of the "homosexual as killer." At the same time, Andrew's characterization is more complex than these examples would suggest. His development in Season Seven takes him on a bumpy, sometimes reluctant journey of remorse and redemption, and, as I have argued elsewhere, "Storyteller" in particular portrays Andrew simultaneously as a figure of the fan and of the author (or auteur), opening possibilities for queer readings of spectatorship and cultural production that retrospectively reverberate across the series.[3]

It is useful to examine Andrew's early incarnations in order to assess how his character evolves. In "Flooded," we are introduced to Andrew and his buddies, Warren and Jonathan, who have banded together to form the "Evil

Trio." In a flashback whose very inarticulateness bears eloquent testimony to the group's dynamics and to their lame aspirations, Warren asks, "You guys wanna team up and take over Sunnydale?" One month later, they have devised a bullet-pointed, white-boarded master plan: "Shrink rays, trained gorillas, and Chicks! Chicks! Chicks!" Egregiously puerile and often unwittingly hilarious in their nerdly pursuits ("We can do anything! We can stay up all night if we want!"), the Trio, in the early episodes of Season Six, sometimes function as an object of gentle satire and sometimes as an emblem of the darker sides of adolescent male posturing and competition. Perennial infighting and squabbling among the Trio make them the butt of obvious humor ("You're still sulking because I wouldn't make you a Christina Ricci robot"), but their initial portrayal also comes across as a rather tender homage to "geek love" from a creator who has identified himself as the fanboy extraordinaire. Whedon is, after all, on record as saying that Buffy is "a show made for losers, by losers."[4] "Flooded" provides a telling counterpoint between main plot and subplot, when Buffy's voice over, "I know, they're so cute you could die," seems to offer an analysis of the Trio but instead (or as well) refers to the childhood bed linen she offers Giles in the following scene. In one of those proleptic plantings that the Whedon team is famous for, this almost throw-away line will quickly acquire poignancy: there are many ways in which the Trio are not cute at all, and as their tests of Buffy over subsequent episodes indicates, she *could* very well die, and ultimately, someone does.

Throughout Season Six, the Trio functions as a homosocial unit that has decidedly queer overtones. The "horn" of their surveillance vehicle plays the *Star Wars* theme song and the language they use to describe their exploits is broadly metaphorical: Jonathan's jubilant "Crime is our wormhole!" is followed by Andrew's extended meditation on the depth of this "cavity" which is in turn foreclosed by Warren's "Dude, don't be a geek!" ("Flooded"). They regularly address each other with sexualized monikers, "Penis" and "Spanky," or evoke intertextual references to potentially queer popular texts: "Shut up Frodo!" ("Gone"). A less obvious example of this strategy occurs when Andrew invokes queer modernist writer E. M. Forster by lamenting that they do not have "a lair with a view" ("Dead Things"). Andrew summons demons through various phallic-shaped musical instruments — a small delicate flute in "Life Serial" escalating to a honking great didgeridoo in "Normal Again." The demons themselves are seen as phallic extensions: in "Normal Again," Warren instructs Andrew to "deploy your little friend." There is not a lot of subtlety involved in these representations, but then I don't think subtlety is intended. In their early presentation of the Trio, Whedon and Co. relish the art of turning a double entendre into a single entendre: "Give me my bone!" "Stop touching my magic bone!" If these guys are closeted, they are so only to themselves; the Trio inhabits a sort of Emperor's New Closet, which frames and amplifies the homoerotic subtext they are at pains to repress.

Stevie Simkin sees the Trio as "a group of anxious males who have retreated into, or never emerged from, a state of perpetual adolescence and fantasy" ("Who Died" par. 12) and he notes that, "an homoerotic subtext is clearly traceable in their relationships" ("Who Died" fn. 5). As rabid fans of *Star Wars*, *Star Trek*, and various competing versions of James Bond, the Trio's ostensibly grandiose schemes are regularly undercut by the one of the series' signature rhetorical strategies — bathos: "I think Timothy Dalton should get an Oscar and beat Sean Connery over the head with it!" Andrew rages in "Life Serial." Simkin points to "the paltry nature of [the Trio's] ambitions, in comparison with the considerable powers they have developed magically and technologically" ("Who Died" par. 12) and draws attention to Andrew's lament in "Gone": "But we had so many plans. Naked women, and all ... well, all-all the naked women!" Andrew's faltering regret registers a distinct lack of detail — he hasn't gone further than "naked women" because this is probably not where his own fantasies lie — and despite what Simkin calls the queer "trainspotting" pleasures ("Who Died" par. 28) that his ellipses provide, at this stage in the narrative he is certainly complicit with the group's overarching game plan of female objectification: "We can make [Buffy] our willing sex bunny!" ("Flooded").

Lorna Jowett sees the Trio as the "real-world" villains of Season Six, "a homosocial group viewing women primarily as sexual objects" (26). At various points in the series the group resembles, as Buffy's doctor tells her in "Normal Again," "just three pathetic little men ... who like playing with toys." Warren evokes the specter of homosexuality in a coercive fashion: "When you girls have stopped playing with each other...." And it is notable that it is Warren again, emerging as the leader of the group, who disciplines the others through the threat of exposure: "Well you know what homophobia really means about you, don't you?" At a certain level, this construction of the Trio seems to be a clear case of what Ron Becker identifies as homosociality presented in a "simple, typically homophobic opposition to homosexuality — through a shared exploitation of women or cooperative violence against fags" (132). Warren's toxic misogyny sounds the dominant note of Trio. His experiments on a former girlfriend, Katrina, take the form of rape, and it pays to remember that it is Warren who literally kills off the only "out" "gay" relationship in series, when he shoots Tara whilst aiming for the Slayer. But while

Warren's manipulations of the Trio's homoerotics are dastardly and ultimately deadly, Andrew's negotiation of this desire is portrayed with an overlay of pathos, and eventually, empathy, that make his character less straightforward.

Andrew's queer credentials are flagged in "Entropy" when the Trio unexpectedly stumbles across live action footage of Spike having sex with Anya in the Magic Box (pun probably intended). Initially unsure about what he is watching ("What are they ... ? Ooh!"), Andrew becomes transfixed by Spike and murmurs reverently, "He is so cool." Abashed by the raised eyebrows of his friends, he quickly compensates: "And I mean, the girl is hot too." The desire to be Spike and to have Spike is conflated in this scene. These tendencies are made explicit in "Seeing Red," where the Trio acquires the Orbs of Nezzla'khan. As Simkin notes, "It is difficult not to interpret the orbs as phallic — or, more precisely, testicular: Warren even has a pouch, slung on his belt, designed to hold them" ("You hold" par. 21). The testicular metaphor is played broadly for laughs. Watching an enhanced Warren overturn a security van, Andrew sighs, "Man, I can't wait to get my hands on his orbs." However, when abandoned by Warren later in the episode, Andrew is genuinely devastated. As Simkin notes, "Andrew's despair has an overt romantic theme" ("You Hold" par. 21): "How could he do that to me? He promised me we'd be together. He was just using me. He never really loved —(catching himself)— hanging out with us." Trapped in jail, Jonathan is somewhat salaciously but also phobically obsessed by the thought that a fellow prisoner wants to make him his "butt monkey" (fn. 20), but Andrew's grief raises his longing for Warren to another level. Butt monkey jokes can no longer adequately assuage or express his desires.

By the time we get to Season Seven's "Storyteller," Andrew is in the process of switching his fannish allegiance from evil to good, although this "switch" is still performed through the male homosocial rhetoric favored by classic film narratives in the buddy and outlaw genres: "We gotta make it right!" "We're outlaws with hearts of gold!" In "Storyteller," Andrew's romanticized recollections of successful super-villainy bump jarringly against his position as a hostage, or in his preferred terminology, "guestage," of the Scooby household. Retreating from one of Buffy's pep talks to address the camera directly, Andrew offers us a glorified, revisionist narrative of his "personal journey":

> Honestly, gentle viewers, these motivating speeches of hers tend to get a little long. I'll take you back in there in — in a little while, but in the in-between time, I thought you might want to know a little about me, your humble host. You see — I am a man with a burden, a man with a dark past. You see — I was once a *super villain*.

There follows a flashback to the "Evil Workshop" in which an ultra-suave Andrew, in a black suit, shirt, and tie, informs the geeky Jonathan and Warren (wearing jeans, t-shirts, and protective eye goggles) of his latest invention. Stepping into the big shoes of Timothy Dalton, Andrew has, in his own imagination, acquired the masculine mastery to succeed his hero. Clearly attached to his experiment, he has anthropomorphized it in a distinctly virile, even kinky fashion. The "kinda sweaty" smell of Andrew's prized concoction leaves the audience curious about its mixture of ingredients. The scene continues to show Jonathan and Warren fascinated and almost worshipping Andrew. The innocent pleasure Andrew takes in the (fabricated) adulation of his friends is fairly endearing. It is not the least of Tom Lenk's admirable acting skills that he manages to make Andrew so accessible at the same time that he is so despicable. The Trio's beltlessness is a delectable, if late-breaking, detail (admirably analyzed by Linda Rust) and it is interesting to note that even in his own fantasy depiction, Andrew retains an essential gormlessness and immaturity that might seem to make him seem less culpable than he actually is. Andrew, as "Storyteller" demonstrates explicitly, is far from innocent, and he must learn to take responsibility for the effects of his actions.

In the final season of *Buffy*, the Scooby gang battles an unseen "big bad" whose signature calling card is the motto: "From beneath you it devours." Hiding in Mexico after the eviscerating effects of their last attack on the Scoobies, the remaining members of the Trio, Andrew and Jonathan, are plagued in dreams by a voice that intones *"Desde abajo te devora."* Translating this warning as "It eats you starting with your bottom," Andrew enacts a queering of Evil that, if not unexpected, is at least surprisingly and explicitly sexual: to Andrew, the dead Warren has become the embodiment of The First and he offers, quite literally, a consummation devoutly to be wished. In Andrew's breathless, titillated translation, the big kahuna has become a master rimmer.

We are introduced to Andrew's recollections of his "Mehico" sojourn because Buffy and the Scoobies are trying to shut the Seal of Danzalthar, an opening in the earth that Andrew activates when he kills Jonathan on Warren's orders. The trip to Mexico is presented as a sort of white washed *Y tu mamá también* fantasy for nerdlings (although rather than being triangulated by an attractive older woman as in Alfonso Cuarón's 2001 film, the relationship between Andrew and Warren is triangulated by a younger, rounder man — Jonathan, aka "the shortcake"). The "Seal" is itself another instance of the series' indulgence in anal humor, a giant orifice complete with interlocking, tooth-like panels, it resembles nothing so much as a sphincter dentata. Andrew is enlisted by the Scoobies to "speak to it in its own language. "Give it commands and stuff," an exercise that positions him as an expert "analinguist."

Andrew's role as translator positions him between the real-time solidarity of Scoobies' community and the severed remains of the Trio's homoerotic triangle. Flashbacks to "Somewhere in Mexico, 2002" in "Storyteller" juxtapose the "bromance" of Andrew's relationship with Jonathan with the more insidious and sexually charged depiction of his yearning for Warren. Thrashing and heaving in their shared double bed, Andrew and Jonathan erupt simultaneously from their joint nightmare: Though the Scoobies are less than impressed with his blow-by-blow recollection of this *tête-à-tête*, it is significant that, at this stage, Andrew is still wedded to his infatuation with evil. Reassuring Jonathan about his evil performance anxiety, Andrew invokes the automated language of management consulting, adding a laughable corporate gloss to their joint enterprise.

When, in the present-time of the episode, Willow interrupts with "Whoa, I think we're getting a little off topic here," Andrew responds with, "Shh, it's gonna get interesting. Jonathan's going to go to the bathroom." And sure enough, Warren enters. Andrew is pathetically grateful for Warren's presence, and Warren is able to manipulate his willing tool by flattering his fantasies. In a flirtatious scene (from Andrew's perspective) of reassurance, Warren allays Andrew's fears of "pillow creases" by insisting on his legible masculinity, again registered through the homosocial codes of classic narrative cinema. When it comes to the point, however, of Warren's visit, Andrew stalls. Effectively talking to Jonathan's penis, whose "shy" functions he is clearly familiar with, Andrew exploits his physical intimacy with Jonathan to buy more time with Warren.

It would be reductive to say that Andrew's desire for Warren is portrayed negatively *simply* because Warren is evil incarnate. The fact that Warren = Evil does not necessarily mean that this representation = homophobia. But *Buffy* certainly treads a fine line in this respect. There are ways in which the series' depictions of Andrew produce an ostensibly queer version of the homosexual as murderer that bears disturbing similarities with the more overtly homophobic portrayals of mainstream cinema.[5] As Ron Becker notes, "[f]or what might be called post-closet TV, gay men who are *not* out — who fail to identify with the label waiting for them, who refuse to accept the straight world's tolerance, who expose the gaping hole in the post–civil-rights logic — are a real problem" (127). One reading of Andrew's capitulation to Warren's insistence "Stab him! You have to! If you fail, you'll die a lost soul, and I'll hate you forever!" would be to see Andrew's closeted state as the cause for his moral failure: "Got it. If I kill him with this knife, we live as gods."

Andrew's own musical "break away hit," "We Live as Gods," represents a comic apex in his portrayal, one of the scenes in which he is most clearly "gay," and a potentially disturbing comment on the self deception to which his desires lead him — a comment that may or may not relate to his closeted state. Andrew's fantasy of a life joined to Warren and Jonathan takes the form of an idealized pastoral with overtones of *The Sound of Music* (a text that has been successfully queered by gay culture, as its frequent dress-up, sing-a-long reprisals attest). Set in what the script refers to as the "Fantastic Fields," Andrew, Warren, and Jonathan are dressed in togas, playing harps, and frolicking in fields of daisies. Butterflies flit around and bars of gold lie around in piles. A unicorn (suggestively phallic but also mythically innocent) runs by them as they dance and sing "We Are as Gods."

In his analysis of straight reception of queer mainstream film, Harry M. Benshoff outlines a typology of constructions of queer male identity in which, in addition to being "psychologically and socially out of the closet" or "both unconsciously queer and socially closeted," that is, firmly in or out, other intermediary positions are available. Benshoff identifies one of these as being "psychologically in the closet but socially out, a seemingly rare situation in which friends and family recognize queerness in an individual before he does" (174). Andrew occupies this "seemingly rare" position in Season Seven. While he may be still psychologically closeted, he is at least socially out to Warren, who manipulates Andrew's patent desire for him to his own nefarious ends. As Ellis Hanson has argued, "To be in the closet is not necessarily to be sexually out of sight, since discretion and secrecy are curiously readable modes of self-articulation" (17). In "Storyteller," Andrew is arguably out to the Scoobies as well, who are the reluctant audience to his fantasy's repetition, and whose disapproval stems not so much from his object choice ("gay" is OK) as from his choice of object: Warren. Indeed it could be argued that Andrew's redemptive arc in Season Seven does not so much require him to renounce his queer desires as to find more a worthy object for them: Xander and, ongoingly, Spike.[6]

How, then, do we critically assess Season Seven's queer representation of Andrew? Discussing the proliferation of queer images in contemporary popular culture and expressing concern about the possible dilution of queer's oppositional stance that such proliferation entails, Thomas Peele argues that in popular primetime shows such as *Friends*, "same-sex desire between men is regularly invoked to propel the action of the series, but it is never allowed to achieve sexual expression. Queer desire is tolerated and made use of, but it is never presented as a desirable state, at least among the men of the series" (2). The fact that Andrew's sexual desires never receive overt expression (in fulfillment) in the series might seem to support this critique. The fact that Andrew's queerness is largely played for laughs also jeopardizes the progressive potential of his portrayal. As Jes Battis has argued in his careful analysis of Xander, while male characters' negotiations with dominant forms of masculinity "are meant to be funny and gentle":

> [I]t remains the case that, for queer audiences, every ironic jab at hypothetical queerness is a violent intrusion on someone's living queer reality. Jokes about turning gay, about the prospect of "gaying" or being "gayed up," are funny to straight audiences because *being gay* is funny to them; and they are funny to queer audiences because most queers experience this sort of humor as a kind of laughable irony, a playful self-criticism that is part of their tactics of survival in a predominantly heterosexual world. But for those whose living space is threatened by legislated homophobic violence, for those who are looking for representations of themselves in popular television and finding nothing, and for those who look up to *Buffy* as a show that rhetoricizes tolerance and inclusion, these ironic asides can appear patronizing at best, and insulting at worst [54].

The "funny" here is part of the problem.

Joss Whedon and Co. have developed an unusually intimate relationship with their loyal fan base, and as several critics have noted, the series makes several opportunities to respond to fan feedback.[7] Whedon relates that some fans were disappointed with the "vanilla" nature of Willow and Tara's lesbian relationship: "Well, they're obviously gay. Why aren't they gay enough? They're not gay enough. You need to make them more gay."[8] However Whedon also reserves the right to subvert expectation, insisting that he has learnt that one of his main responsibilities as a storyteller is "to be irresponsible": "If I made *Buffy the Lesbian Separatist*, a series of lectures on PBS on why there should be feminism, no one [would] be coming to the party and it would be boring."[9] The "positive images" debate, whether focused on queer representation or feminist messages, can certainly be overly simplistic. Hanson notes that queer theory is valuable as "a mode of deconstruction and analysis of sexual rhetoric" (5) but that "dogma inevitably produces insight at the expense of a certain level of blindness.... Our critical vocabulary seems to render palpable only those pleasures it is destined to describe, such that our dogmas result in an impoverishment of language that masquerades as sophistication" (10).

In the case of Andrew, any account that assesses his portrayal simply as a character risks overlooking the important point that in his fannish procliv- ities he also functions as a figure for the audience; his desires therefore queer serial spectatorship in important ways. Andrew's purported "effeminacy" is not even the issue here. One would hope that in a series so committed to the positive portrayal of female power and so critical of hegemonic masculinities, Andrew's femininity need not register as pejorative. As McCracken has argued, in the Buffyverse, "the wounded, masochistic man is the ideal man, the man for all seasons" (125). As the world-turned-upside-down carnival of "Story- teller" demonstrates, and regardless of the viewer's sexual identity and identifications, the queer, feminized fan Andrew = us. To some extent, this is a generic predisposition. Alexander Doty notes that the central conventions of horror and melodrama "actually encourage queer positioning as they exploit the spectacle of heterosexual romance, straight domesticity, and traditional gender roles gone awry." In this sense, he argues, "*everyone's* pleasure in these genres is 'perverse,' is queer, as much of it takes place within the space of the contra-heterosexual and the contra-straight" (15). Andrew's homoerotic view- ing position, however, makes this position queerer. Doty contends that queer positions, readings, and pleasures "suggest that what happens in cultural recep- tion goes beyond the traditional opposition between homo and hetero, as queer reception is often a place beyond the audience's conscious 'real-life' definitions of their sexual identities and cultural positions — often, but not always, beyond such sexual identities and identity politics, that is" (15). Cross- identifying with Andrew as fan, audiences from a range of sexual identities, both hetero and homo, can partake of his queer viewing pleasure.

Andrew's representation as a character in Season Seven is curious, com- plex and multivalent, employing a mix of homophobic stereotypes, more pro- gressive depictions, and overblown camp musical. At the narrative level, he is a decidedly queer character whose trajectory remains open-ended:

> Here's the thing. I killed my best friend. There's a big fight coming, and I don't know what's going to happen. I don't even think I'm going to live through it. That's, uh, probably the way it should be. I guess I'm...

Instead of finishing his sentence, Andrew looks at the camera, sighs, points the remote control, and turns it off. At the end of "Storyteller," Andrew is unable or unwilling to identify exactly what he is. However, the episode does not ultimately code this inability as failure. The closing credits reprise Andrew's fantasy "We Are as Gods" in place of the regular Mutant Enemy animation, "Grrr ... Argh." Andrew retains the last word and his queer desires set the seal on this episode. Moreover, Andrew's role at the meta-narrative level, as a figure of the fan and thus the audience, queers the text of *Buffy* in a more comprehensive fashion, offering an endearingly queer celebration of the "perverse" pleasures of serial spectatorship that cuts across sexual identity politics. Andrew, after all, returns, in *Angel* Season Five, as a junior "Watcher," a role that formalizes, and grants unexpected authority and distinction to, his position as queer spectator.

Notes

1. On Willow and Tara, see Mendelsohn, Battis, Beirne and McAvan. For other studies which analyze ostensibly straight male characters see Simkin, Battis, Jowett, Camron, McCracken, and Masson and Stanley.
2. Rich, reprinted in Aaron, 16.
3. Patricia Pender, "Why Can't You Just Masturbate Like the Rest of Us?"
4. Quoted in "The Wit and Wisdom of Joss Whedon."
5. See Aaron, "Introduction."
6. The larger project from which this paper draws queers Andrew in the context of these relationships as well.
7. See in particular Larbalestier (*"Buffy*'s Mary Sue") and Saxey.
8. Quoted in "The Wit and Wisdom of Joss Whedon."
9. Quoted in "The Wit and Wisdom of Joss Whedon."

Works Cited

Aaron Michele. "New Queer Cinema: An Introduction." *New Queer Cinema: A Critical Reader*. Ed. Michele Aaron. Edinburgh: Edinburgh University Press, 2004. 3–14.

Battis, Jes. *Blood Relations: Chosen Families in* Buffy the Vampire Slayer *and* Angel. Jefferson, NC: McFarland, 2005.

Becker, Ron. "Guy Love: A Queer Straight Masculinity for a Post-Closet Era?" *Queer TV: Theories, Histories, Politics*. Eds. Glyn Davis and Gary Needham. Oxon: Routledge, 2009. 121–140.

Beirne, Rebecca. "Queering the Slayer-text: Reading possibilities in *Buffy the Vampire Slayer*." *Refractory: A Journal of Entertainment Media* 5 (2004). Ed. Angela Ndalianis. http://blogs.arts.unimelb.edu.au/refractory/category/browse-past-volumes/volume-5/

Benshoff, Harry M. "Reception of a Queer Mainstream Film." *New Queer Cinema: A Critical Reader*. Ed. Michele Aaron. Edinburgh: Edinburgh University Press, 2004. 172–186.

Call, Lewis. "'Sounds Like Kinky Business to Me': Subtextual and Textual Representations of Erotic Power in the Buffyverse. *Slayage: The Online International Journal of Buffy Studies* 24 (2007). http://slayageonline.com/Numbers/slayage24.htm

Camron, Marc. "The Importance of Being the Zeppo: Xander, Gender Identity and Hybridity in *Buffy the Vampire Slayer*." *Slayage: The Online International Journal of Buffy Studies* 23 (2007). http://slayageonline.com/Numbers/slayage23.htm

Davis, Glyn, and Gary Needham, eds. *Queer TV: Theories, Histories, Politics*. New York: Routledge, 2009.

Doty, Alexander. *Making Things Perfectly Queer: Interpreting Mass Culture.* Minneapolis: University of Minnesota Press, 1993.

Hanson, Ellis. "Introduction: Out Takes." *Out Takes: Essays on Queer Theory and Film.* Ed. Ellis Hanson. Durham: Duke University Press, 1999. 1–19.

Jowett, Lorna. *Sex and the Slayer: A Gender Studies Primer for the Buffy Fan.* Middletown, CT: Wesleyan University Press, 2005.

Larbalestier, Justine. "*Buffy*'s Mary Sue is Jonathan: *Buffy* Acknowledges the Fans. *Fighting the Forces: What's at Stake in* Buffy the Vampire Slayer? Eds. Rhonda Wilcox and David Lavery. 227–238.

_____. "The Only Thing Better Than Killing a Slayer: Heterosexuality and Sex in Buffy the Vampire Slayer." *Reading the Vampire Slayer: An Unofficial Critical Companion to* Buffy *and* Angel. Ed. Roz Kaveney. 2d ed. New York: Tauris Parke, 2004. 195–219.

Masson, Cynthea, and Marni Stanley. "Queer Eye of that Vampire Guy: Spike and the Aesthetics of Camp." *Slayage: The Online International Journal of Buffy Studies* 22 (2006). http://slayageonline.com/Numbers/slayage_22.htm

McAvan, Em. "'I Think I'm Kinda Gay': Willow Rosenberg and the Absent/Present Bisexual in Buffy the Vampire Slayer." *Slayage: The Online International Journal of Buffy Studies* 24 (2007). http://slayageonline.com/Numbers/slayage24.htm

McCracken, Allison. "A Stake: Angel's Body, Fantasy Masculinity, and Queer Desire in Teen Television." *Undead TV: Essays on* Buffy the Vampire Slayer. Eds. Elana Levine and Lisa Parks. Durham: Duke University Press, 2007. 116–144.

Mendelsohn, Farah. "Surpassing the Love of Vampires; or Why (and How) a Queer Reading of Buffy/Willow is Denied." *Fighting the Forces: What's at Stake in* Buffy the Vampire Slayer? Eds. Rhonda Wilcox and David Lavery. 45–60.

Peele, Thomas. "Introduction: Popular Culture, Queer Culture." *Queer Popular Culture: Literature, Media, Film, and Television.* Ed. Thomas Peele. London: Palgrave Macmillan, 2007. 1–8.

Pender, Patricia. "'Why Can't You Just Masturbate Like the Rest of Us?': Andrew and the Erotics of Fandom in *Storyteller.*" Paper presented at the *Slayage* Conference on the Whedonverses, Gordon College, Georgia, 26–28 May 2006.

Rust, Linda. "'In my plan, we are belt-less': Andrew's Fannish Practices in 'Storyteller.'" Paper presented at the Slayage Conference on *Buffy the Vampire Slayer.* Nashville, Tennessee, May 28–30, 2004.

Saxey, Esther. "Staking a Claim: The Series and Slash Fan-Fiction." *Reading the Vampire Slayer: An Unofficial Critical Companion to* Buffy *and* Angel. Ed. Roz Kaveney. 2d ed. New York: Tauris Parke, 2001. 187–210.

Simkin, Stevie. "'You Hold your Gun Like a Sissy Girl:' Firearms and Anxious Masculinity in *Buffy the Vampire Slayer.*" *Slayage: The Online International Journal of Buffy Studies* 11–12 (2004). http://slayageonline.com/Numbers/slayage11_12.htm

_____. "'Who died and made you John Wayne?': Anxious Masculinity in Buffy the Vampire Slayer." *Slayage: The Online International Journal of Buffy Studies* 11–12 (2004). http://slayageonline.com/Numbers/slayage11_12.htm

"The Wit and Wisdom of Joss Whedon." PDF link at *Slayage: The Online International Journal of Buffy Studies.* http://www.slayageonline.com/pages/Wit_Wisdom_Joss_Whedon.pdf

Slaying the Heteronormative

Representations of Alternative Sexuality in *Buffy* Season Eight Comics

LEWIS CALL

In a 2007 *Slayage* article, I observed that the *Buffy* and *Angel* television shows offer strikingly positive representations of erotic power exchange, also known as kink. I argued that these representations were largely subtextual in the early seasons of the two shows; as the plots progressed, however, these depictions became increasingly open and textual. In this essay, I want to argue that kink remains highly textual and very visible in *Buffy* Season Eight comic books. Indeed, I maintain that *Buffy* comics offer us images of kink which are more explicit and more radical than those of the televised Buffy-verse. Comics feature a rich visual vocabulary, a limitless special effects budget, and an extremely relaxed censorship regime. They thus provide the ideal medium for provocative, positive meditations on alternative sexuality. While *Buffy* television did present a serious challenge to heteronormativity, *Buffy* comics go further. The comics abandon all concept of a normative sexuality. These comic books offer us a model of sexuality which is diverse, tolerant, and inclusive. They continue the process of "mainstreaming" which began in the televised Buffyverse.[1] The comics take kink out of the closet and present it as part of everyday life. "Hey, I likes me some kink," says Faith in a casual way (#6, p. 15).[2] Of course, Faith has always accepted kink as natural, but by Season Eight, everyone in the Buffyverse has come to share her remarkable attitude. Mainstreaming allows *Buffy* comics to develop a powerful ethics of kink. Sex in the Buffyverse is never vanilla. But it is usually consensual and loving; when it is not, all hell breaks loose. Within this strangely beautiful system of sexual ethics, no consensual sexuality is privileged over any other, but all non-consensual acts are soundly rejected. The

Buffyverse consistently authorizes erotic relationships between humans and those who are inhuman, transhuman, or superhuman. Those relationships may be gay, lesbian, bisexual, or straight. Sex in the Buffyverse remains relentlessly queer and kinky; thanks to the unique characteristics of the comics medium, the Buffyverse's representations of sexuality are more subversive than ever.

People like Douglas Wolk, Scott McLeod, and Robert C. Harvey have shown us that we don't read comics the same way we read novels or other prose: comics are visual. The visual element of comics is central to the medium: words and pictures act together to produce something which exceeds both. This raises questions about the role which visual pleasures might play in comics. In his groundbreaking study, *Reading Comics*, Douglas Wolk views comics through the lens of Immaneul Kant's famous aesthetic theory. For Wolk, the "default style" of mainstream superhero comics is what Kant would call "agreeable": it gives pleasure with interest, and gratifies desires (55). Kant doesn't much care for the "agreeable"; he prefers the "beautiful," which gives pleasure without interest or gratification of desire. Personally, I'm with Nietzsche: Kant's aesthetic theory contains "a fat worm of error" (Nietzsche 104). Why *shouldn't* art satisfy our desires? The default style, as Wolk observes, gives a sense that everyday actions are "charged with sex, power, and beauty" (50). For Kant, this would be a bad thing, but Kant needs to get out more. The Buffyverse has always been about power and beauty. *Buffy* comics are definitely drawn in Wolk's "default style," with one important difference: since the default style is designed to promote a somatic response, characters are often drawn to be as sexy as possible, with the women sporting wasp waists, big breasts, and flowing hair (50). Joss Whedon, on the other hand, promotes a very different visual aesthetic: "All the people I work with draw actual women" (Rudolph). So *Buffy* comics proudly provide pleasure *with* interest; they gratify our desires, but without descending into reactionary and damaging representations of women. If anything, the pleasures of *Buffy* comics are even more radically feminist than those of the show. Televised images are transitory, but George Jeanty's powerful cover for #5 ruled the shelves of comic book stores for a month. Jeanty put a frightened high school girl in the lower right corner of his cover. He drew a larger than life poster of Buffy behind the girl, and this image dominates the cover. Buffy points her finger directly at the poster's viewers, like Lord Kitchener or Uncle Sam. The poster's caption reads, "I Want You to be Strong." So Buffy is organizing schoolgirls everywhere into an unstoppable girl power army, taking back the night in force. But Buffy is not pointing at the anonymous schoolgirl in this illustration. She is pointing out of the picture, at the legions of real girls and women who are invading the traditionally male preserve of the comic book store to buy Season Eight comics.

The most privileged category in the Kantian aesthetic is the sublime: "that by comparison with which all else is small." As Wolk observes, comics literalize that idea (56). Case in point: a gigantic Dawn Summers, rampaging through the streets of downtown Tokyo (covers for #14). Dawn begins Season Eight as a giantess, and long-time Buffy fans will not be surprised to learn that this unfortunate situation is the result of a sexual indiscretion on Dawn's part. After all, sex is dangerous business in the Buffyverse: if you have sex, your boyfriend might lose his soul. Dawn recognizes the nature of her predicament: "This is about sex, isn't it?" (#7, pg. 8). Here Georges Jeanty uses page layout and panel composition very effectively, to illustrate Dawn's incredible size: the massive Scottish castle occupies a small panel on the left, while Dawn takes up an entire page-length panel on the right. Initially Dawn perceives her plight in purely negative terms. However, Xander provides a very interesting alternative viewpoint. Prior to Season Eight, Xander typically played the role of "big brother" to Buffy's little sister Dawn. But Season Eight Dawn is in no way little, and Xander's feelings begin to change. Xander finds himself swimming in Dawn's gigantic undergarments (#10, p. 10). As he begins to feel desire for a forbidden erotic object, Xander experiences a corresponding sexual anxiety. This is illustrated visually with anxiety lines, and textually with a typical Xanderism: "Lord of Hosts, I'm in the frilly!"

Dawn's not thrilled to be gigantic, but when a magical attempt to shrink her backfires, she is transformed into a centaur. She likes her new form even less. A full page illustration conveys her frustration very nicely: here is half-human Dawn, naked, glaring, uttering an utterly unconvincing "Neigh" (#16, p. 8). However, Dawn's interpretation of her own condition is clearly at odds with the representations provided by the book's artists. In Jo Chen's striking cover for #18, Dawn is clearly meant to be beautiful, powerful, and sexual. (This effect could probably not have been achieved on television; in the comics, it simply involves hiring a talented painter.) Dawn holds one hoof aloft; she seems to be prancing playfully. Her human half is having a good stretch: her upper back is arched. Her hair provides strategic cover for her naked breasts. The smile on her face is perhaps still shy, but also seductive. And this is really the first time Dawn has been portrayed as an authentically sexual being. She actually becomes *more* sexual as she becomes *less* human. She can't recognize this herself, but again, Xander's response makes the argument very clear. His desire for Dawn is inversely proportional to her humanity: as she moves further from the human norm, he finds her increasingly attractive. Dawn still describes herself in terms typical for a teenage girl with body-image issues: "my ass is huge" (#16, p. 15). Xander replies tenderly, "Are you kidding? Dawn ... you really don't know how awesome you look?" Dawn's open-mouthed facial expression shows that Xander's desire has had a powerful impact on her.

Unfortunately, things get too serious too quickly (as often happens in the Buffyverse). Dawn and Xander are cut off from the rest of the team during a demon attack. Dawn tells Xander that "you're gonna have to ... ride me..." (#17, p. 12). We get a panel of total confusion. Then Xander, who suddenly looks about twelve years old, gets it: "Ah! Ride you!" The scene is played for laughs, and Xander's sexual anxiety *is* funny, but something deeper is happening here, and they both know it. After a brisk gallop through the forest, Dawn feels like she was "ridden hard and put away wet" (#18, p. 5). As usual, Xander freaks out at the innuendo, but he quickly gets ahold of himself and realizes "it's just true." Here he's trying to relate to Dawn as a real, flesh and blood person, rather than a forbidden fantasy. Xander realizes that a new Dawn is rising. She is strong, powerful, and very attractive, not despite her inhuman status but *because of it.* She can even take a little friendly hair-pulling; when she complains about this, as she thunders through a battlefield full of glowing green demons, it's hard to take her protests too seriously (#17, p. 13). Not since John Varley's *Titan* books has the centaur been depicted in such playfully erotic terms. There is no fear of bestiality here. The Xander/Dawn relationship confirms the fact that in the Buffyverse, relations between the human and the inhuman are entirely legitimate.

Xander's attraction to Dawn is part of his ongoing project to find a place for himself in this world of powerful women. He eventually works up the courage to court Slayer Renée. When you date Slayers, things are automatically kinky. Renée summarizes their first date as follows: Xander dressed her up like a schoolgirl, used her as bait on the streets of Japan, lit a vampire on fire, then geared up to go into battle with several hundred other girls (#14, p. 15). By this point, Xander has had a number of erotic relationships, some more serious, some less so, but all of them thoroughly kinky: giant praying mantis woman, Inca mummy girl, Faith, and of course, Anya. Xander's been around long enough to pick up the language and the culture of kink. He tells Renée that "nobody's babysitting anyone here ... if anything, that fantasy comes much later and only if we both agree to it and have a safeword" (#12, p. 3). So Xander wants to be safe, sane, and consensual. This sequence also reveals that the writers expect a fairly high level of sophistication on the part of the book's audience. Xander never explains the importance of consent or safewords; the audience is simply expected to understand these things. Since most of that audience has already received seven seasons of kink-positive education on *Buffy* and another five on *Angel*, it's probably a reasonable assumption.

Xander identifies as a straight male: he's clearly attracted to Dawn, and definitely interested in Renée. Yet, his most significant Season Eight relationship is homoerotic, and this relationship is rife with erotic power. Season Eight features the return of the notorious Dracula. Xander's reunion with Dracula gets a full page (#12, p. 22). The largest panel shows Dracula re-asserting his dominance over Xander: "Hello, manservant." Xander makes no attempt to resist this move. He replies, "Hey, how's it going..." Then, utterly powerless, with his single eye cast down, he acknowledges Dracula's dominance: "Master." But we need to be clear about the precise nature of this Master-manservant relationship. It's definitely mutual, in the sense that Dracula and Xander both get important benefits from the relationship. Andrew reprises his role as the "Geek chorus" of Buffy: he informs an audience of Slayers (and the real world audience, which is us) that Dracula is "fond of Xander. They have a ... unique relationship. Xander taught him to ride a motorbike" (#13, p. 7). Naturally, it's difficult for outsiders to understand this "unique relationship." Dracula anticipates that Xander will change into his "manservant bloomers" before attending to his Master; Xander tries to assure Renée that he has never worn manservant bloomers (#13, p. 5). She replies, "I don't even know what that means." But Renée's troubles are only beginning. Nothing has prepared her for the homoerotic, vampire-human love fest which ensues: Drac notes that Xander has lost weight, Xander assures Drac that he looks good, too (#13, p. 11). Dracula, who can't see himself in mirrors, needs more reassurance, and Xander provides it: "No — you're more handsome than ever." Renée can only hang her head in disbelief and despair.

Some would say that Dracula has brainwashed Xander with his vampire magic, but there's clearly something more going on here. (Anyway, Drac's powers are "nothing but showy Gypsy stuff," as Spike observed in "Buffy vs. Dracula.") Xander may be Dracula's submissive, but he's not a doormat. He can stand up for himself and negotiate on his own behalf. Xander eventually rejects the "manservant" label, promising to kill Dracula in his sleep if he uses it again. Xander also refuses "lackey," "minion," and especially "houseboy": "still getting killed" (#15, p. 23). He's right to reject these terms, all of which suggest an economic master-servant relationship. The proper term here is *slave*, specifically erotic slave, and although Xander and Dracula don't use such terminology themselves, the reader can get there through process of elimination.

Meanwhile, Willow is also eight seasons away from any kind of cultural or sexual norm. Season Eight finds our self-proclaimed "gay wiccan jewess" (#7, p. 9) hanging out with a beautiful otherworldly snake goddess. Punchline: Willow can only enter the realm of this goddess during orgasm. Things really start to heat up in the story arc "Time of Your Life," written by Joss himself. Willow enters the presence of the goddess once again. Artist Karl Moline puts naked Willow front and center, in a sumptuous central panel which bleeds out into the book's margins (#18, p. 14). Willow's red hair contrasts nicely with the green fog, and the goddess's tentacular snake tail is startlingly prominent in the foreground. You won't see this on television (nor would you have seen it in comics, prior to the rise of "direct market" comic books in the 1990s, and the corresponding decline of the Comics Code Authority). Here's an erotic dalliance between a human woman and a female nonhuman: it's kinky and queer, thus perfectly acceptable in the ethical system of the Buffyverse. In fact, the writers carefully use the reactions of other characters to emphasize that there is nothing wrong or even strange about Willow's choice of partners. Her sexuality may be as far from the heteronormative as you can get, but it's still legitimate. Buffy is the first to learn about Will's snake goddess lover. Buffy's been living off tepid fantasies, and she reacts with jealousy: "Wow. Your bad is way better than mine" (#10, p. 17). Xander's reaction is even better. As a straight male human, he is the most nominally normal member of the team, and yet every word that comes out of his mouth legitimizes kink: "I need to know everything about the demon lover with the snake body and don't shield me from anything deviant or ... I don't want to say kinky —" (#16, p. 6). This joke works brilliantly, because he clearly *does* want to say kinky, and these days he *can* say it. The Scoobies have grown up. Kink is part of their everyday lives now. It doesn't have to hide in the subtext as it did in early season *Buffy*; it's open, textual, and honest.

When it's dishonest, as usual, everything goes to hell. In this way, the writers make an unmistakable argument in favor of full and open negotiation. Willow has kept her liaison with the snake goddess hidden from the one person who needs to know about it more than anyone else: her girlfriend, Kennedy. Alert readers may remember a similar moment in Season Seven, when Willow ran off to the City of *Angel* for a weekend, wound up doing some pony play with young Winifred Burkle ("Orpheus," *Angel* 4.15), and never told Kennedy about it. Willow and Kennedy were just getting started back then, and Will never had sex with Fred, so that behavior was tolerably ethical, as I've argued previously. This new deceit, however, is clearly not OK. Willow has always had issues with commitment, and no wonder: in the Buffy-verse, commitment is more serious than it is in our world. It's not enough to *say* you'd die for someone, you actually have to *do* it, as Kennedy has apparently done for Willow: "it was mystical, and kind of mellow" (#10, p. 20). Kennedy's a Slayer, so she can take it. Still, "headline: death!" As usual, Willow has trouble matching Kennedy's level of commitment. It's clear she loves Kennedy. "Ken-doll" has to be the cutest nickname ever, and it looks like they watch *Battlestar Galactica* together, which is geek love at its finest (#18, p. 4). The problem, of course, is that Willow can't manage full disclosure. It turns out she is using her girlfriend sexually. Sex with Kennedy has become a means to an end for Willow, her entry into the realm of the goddess, and Kennedy doesn't know a thing about it. That gets us to the saddest panel in the book, a panel way too sad for dialogue: Kennedy beams, thinking she's just given Willow the time of her life, while Willow, who wasn't even there when it happened, buttons up her blouse, awash in guilt and shame (#18, p. 17). It's hard to imagine a more powerful argument in favor of honesty, negotiation, and consent.

But it's Buffy's experience that tests the limits of kink in Season Eight, as in Seasons Six and Seven before. It's been a slow year for the Buffster, and her fantasies are becoming a bit more exotic (albeit in the safe, wholesome, "bunny cuffs" way that is Buffy's ironic trademark). In issue #3, Georges Jeanty dedicated about two-thirds of a page to a gorgeous full-bleed panel of nurse Buffy, chained up with naked Angel and Spike (#3, p. 3). The forest of stakes which hovers menacingly around the threesome puts Buffy firmly on top, and the cartoon cherubs keep it cute (though not cute enough for television, one suspects: a good example of the easy visual subversion which is possible in a direct market comic.)

Ever since Spike, Buffy has been resolutely kinky, but she has always been completely straight. Yet Buffy never reckoned with Satsu, a beautiful Asian Slayer with a crush on the boss lady. Buffy thinks it's the sweetest thing ever. She tells Satsu "you're hot, you have great taste, you're a hell of a Slayer and you smell good" (#11, p. 12). Very sweet, but Satsu's no fool: "But you're not gay," she replies. "Not so you'd notice," Buffy admits. Season Eight is very much like Season Six, however, in that it forces Buffy to experiment sexually. She is always reluctant, but she always benefits from the experience. Respect: *Buffy* always pushed the limits of queer representation on network television. Willow's romance with Tara was the longest running lesbian relationship on the networks, while Willow and Kennedy gave those networks their first lesbian sex scene. *Buffy* TV mainstreamed lesbianism, in part by portraying "femme" lesbians who fit into regular society (Wilts 54). But here's something we certainly wouldn't see on the WB, or even UPN: our straight heroine naked in bed with her same-sex lover, spending one well-earned page-length panel saying "wow" (#12, p. 4). As we know from his commentary on "Once More with Feeling," Joss Whedon sometimes likes to hint at lesbian porn, but it always seems to be in the service of some bigger message. "Wolves at the Gate" author Drew Goddard learned from the master; Goddard moves us immediately from "wow" to "how do we handle tomorrow?" (#12, p. 8). Satsu knows that Buffy didn't just "turn gay all of a sudden." There's a brief interlude in which Buffy experiences straight girl performance anxiety about her ability to have lesbian sex. Then the famous line: "tomorrow, I'm gonna think about what we did. And I'm gonna blush. And then I'm gonna smile" (#12, p. 9). Buffy thinks that's as far as it goes, but the truth is that she has shared a very meaningful experience with Satsu, and she's afraid of what that might mean. She asks Satsu not to tell anyone what they have done (#12, p. 10). Then, Jeanty gives us a beautiful, tight close-up on Buffy, showing her completely boxed in, absolutely trapped by the situation. "It's not that I'm ashamed or anything," Buffy insists. (Some of her best friends are gay.) Buffy quickly retreats into a kind of passive, unconscious homophobia. It's just "better," for no particular reason, if they keep it between themselves. Jeanty places the close facial shot in the middle of a three-panel top tier; the other tiers on this page consist of single panels. This page layout strategy draws the eye to the upper tier's crucial central panel, which provides the moral anchor for this sequence.

The passive homophobia that Buffy exhibits here is entirely common in our world, but it is anathema in the Buffyverse. That 'verse enforces a radical toleration of sexual difference. And so Buffy must face the agonizing yet oddly hilarious consequences of her phobia. Xander walks in, and nearly loses his other eye to spontaneous blindness when he sees the Slayers in bed together. Then, Jeanty does something that television hasn't really done since Rod Serling's *Twilight Zone*. It works flawlessly in a comic: we see giant Dawnie, the omnipresent kid sister, her horrified eyes and lips framed tightly by the window as Satsu and Buffy struggle to get their clothes on (#12, p. 12). There are never any secrets in the Buffyverse, and just to make sure everybody gets the point, Willow crashes through the roof to report a demon attack and (more importantly) to ask Buffy why she's in bed with Satsu (#12, p. 13). The Buffyverse's straightest character has been experimenting, and no one's quite sure what to make of it. Satsu understands that Buffy is not like the other Slayers: she's the general, they're the army (#13, p. 19). Also, as Willow kindly points out, she's not — "A dyke?" Satsu interjects. Willow was going to say "friend of Sappho," but she's hip with whatever the kids are saying these days.

Buffy may not be gay, but she and Satsu clearly have *something* going on: Buffy finds it sexy when Satsu calls her "ma'am" (#14, p. 13). The two of them are exchanging power, if nothing else. Buffy quickly runs afoul of Kennedy. Listening to Willow lecture, Kennedy is understandably "hot for teacher" (#16, p. 15). Buffy offers some seemingly harmless, nostalgic reminiscences about "her" Will, and gets this: "Hey, grubby paws *off*, lez-faux." Kennedy is the deceived, vulnerable girlfriend of Buffy's best friend. That gives her enough moral authority to pull *this* off: "I love that you're in your experimental phase — 'cause I really kinda thought you were a 'phobe — but you put the moves on red and I'll kill you like a chicken." Confronted with a newly bi-curious straight girl, Kennedy performs a common lesbian reaction. Kennedy will respect Buffy's right to experiment and even encourage it, to the extent that it might mitigate her latent homophobia. But bi-curious Buffy will not be accepted as a friend of Sappho, and she will certainly not be allowed to interfere with established relationships. Kennedy's reaction may seem a bit excessive, until we realize what is actually at stake here. Buffy's bisexuality, like all bisexuality, threatens to undermine the possibility of identity politics. As David Allyn has observed, "To conceptualize the notion of bisexuality, one has to step outside the entire framework of sexual identity and step into the framework of sexual self-invention" (219). Buffy's project of self-invention challenges Kennedy's identity politics, although this entire process occurs outside of Buffy's consciousness: she can only reply, "Hamnoo?"

Clearly, Buffy's Satsu problem is not going away. Then again, who said Satsu was a problem? And why *should* she go away? At the end of "Wolves at the Gate," the two Slayers are positively glowing, almost radiant (#15, p. 25). Colorist Michelle Madsen uses a palette much lighter and more brilliant than anything you'd find in Sunnydale. The two women agree, once more, that it was one of the best nights of their lives. Then comes the typical Buffy refrain: "What do we do now?" (If this were the musical episode, she'd sing, "Where do we go from here?") Satsu decides that they could always save goodbye for tomorrow. What does Buffy think? Jeanty's panel composition is always clean and careful; here it is particularly precise. Satsu's sitting on the bed. Buffy's on the floor beneath her, looking up into her eyes. The power configuration has switched; Buffy has now assumed a submissive posture. When Satsu makes her play, we get a tight shot on the two faces, already joined together through composition. We can hardly be surprised when Buffy and Satsu find what warmth they can, as Willow does with her demon lover, in an intercut sex scene of the kind which typically precedes an apocalypse in the Buffyverse (#15, p. 26). Scenes like this confirm Em McAvan's point that the Buffyverse associates bisexuality with kink (paragraph 15). McAvan's reading suggests that these sexualities are usually allied in a way which is excessive or even evil (paragraph 16), but I wish to challenge that view. Buffy and Satsu offer a positive image of a caring, consensual bi-sexual relationship. This relationship is mutual and flexible in its approach to power sharing. Buffy and Satsu confirm the erotic ethics of the Buffyverse by endorsing both bisexuality and kink as legitimate options.

In *Comic Book Nation*, Bradford Wright argues compellingly that American comics have always reflected the cultural concerns and anxieties of the age which produced them: Superman was a child of the Depression, Captain America was born to fight fascism in World War Two, and the O'Neil/Adams *Green Lantern/Green Arrow* books of the early 70s addressed issues of poverty, social justice, and drug addiction. Following Wright, I argue that *Buffy* Season Eight comics reflect the concerns of the remarkable historical moment which we currently occupy. In *Buffy* comics, as in the real world of the new millennium, sexuality is flexible, diverse, and generally life-affirming. The Buffyverse provides a rigorous system of sexual ethics which will be extremely useful to the ravenous real world audience of Buffy comics. Under that system, no consensual sexuality is privileged over any other, but all consensual sexualities are privileged over the non-consensual. The Buffyverse categorically rejects the latter. As for all the rest, the message is clear: ethical beings should find what warmth they can, by sharing love and desire in any of the infinite configurations that make up what we call sexuality.

Notes

1. On HBO's excellent vampire drama *True Blood*, some vampires choose to come "out of the coffin," forsaking the traditional secretive existence of the undead to "live" among humans. This process is known as "mainstreaming." *Buffy* mainstreams kink in a way which is analogous to the mainstreaming of vampirism depicted on *True Blood*.

2. *Buffy* Season Eight comic books are not paginated. I have counted pages in order to provide citations, counting only story pages (not advertisements).

Works Cited

Allyn, David. *Make Love, Not War. The Sexual Revolution: An Unfettered History.* New York: Routledge, 2001.

Buffy the Vampire Slayer Season Eight. Milwaukee, OR: Dark Horse Comics, 2007–2009.

Call, Lewis. "'Sounds Like Kinky Business to Me': Subtextual and Textual Representations of Erotic Power in the Buffyverse." *Slayage: The Online International Journal of Buffy Studies* 6.4 (Summer 2007), <http://slayageonline.com/>

Harvey, Robert C. *The Art of the Comic Book: An Aesthetic History.* Jackson: University Press of Mississippi, 1996.

McAvan, Em. "'I Think I'm Kinda Gay': Willow Rosenberg and the Absent/Present Bisexual in *Buffy the Vampire Slayer.*" *Slayage: The Online International Journal of Buffy Studies* 6.4 (Summer 2007), <http://slayageonline.com/>

McCloud, Scott. *Understanding Comics: The Invisible Art.* New York: HarperCollins, 1994.

Nietzsche, Friedrich. *On the Genealogy of Morals and Ecce Homo.* Trans. Walter Kaufmann. New York: Vintage Books, 1969 [1967].

Rudolph, Ileane. "*Buffy the Vampire Slayer* Is Back: The Complete Joss Whedon Q&A." <http://www.tvguide.com/news/Buffy-Vampire-Slayer-35722.aspx> Posted 7 December 2006. Accessed 30 January 2009.

Varley, John. *Titan.* New York: Berkley Books, 1984 [1979].

Wilts, Alissa. "Evil, Skanky, and Kinda Gay: Lesbian Images and Issues." in *Buffy Goes Dark: Essays on the Final Two Seasons of* Buffy the Vampire Slayer *on Television.* Ed. Lynne Y. Edwards, Elizabeth L. Rambo and James B. South, 41–56. Jefferson, NC: McFarland, 2009.

Wolk, Douglas. *Reading Comics: How Graphic Novels Work and What They Mean.* Philadelphia: Da Capo Press, 2007.

Wright, Bradford W. *Comic Book Nation: The Transformation of Youth Culture in America.* Baltimore: The Johns Hopkins University Press, 2001.

Anya as Feminist Model of Positive Female Sexuality

Tamy Burnett

"I like you. You're funny, and you're nicely shaped. And frankly, it's ludicrous to have these interlocking bodies and not ... interlock. Please remove your clothing now."

— Anya to Xander, "The Harsh Light of Day"

Introduction

"Why can't you just masturbate like the rest of us?" is the shocking question Anya demands in exasperation — and complete seriousness — of geeky Andrew when she discovers him using the one bathroom in an overcrowded household to film his Masterpiece Theater-style documentary in the *Buffy the Vampire Slayer* episode "Storyteller." Anya's question highlights a central tenant of Anya's character — her frank and completely unashamed attitude toward human sexuality (her own and others') — and her assumption that this attitude is the norm.[1] While Anya's revealing, and oftentimes outrageous, comments provide comic relief, they also mark her as a unique amongst *Buffy*'s other female characters. Many varied forms of female strength and feminist characteristics are portrayed in the series, but ultimately women of the Buffyverse represent a fairly similar strong woman archetype, focused on physical and/or mental strength and the ability and willingness to fight to protect self and others. While physical and mental strength are powerful attributes and alone pose no problem to viewers' engagement with the narrative or the characters, women of the Buffyverse also tend to stay within a rather narrowly defined concept of femininity and performance of female gender identity — that is to say, Buffy and her female friends tend to be "girly girls." While one might wish for a more complicated depiction of possible performances of femininity,[2] the portrayal of individual female characters as choosing a more traditionally feminine gender performance does not invite criticism in and of itself. However, when these two patterns are combined, viewers are offered a restricted construction of idealized womanhood: strength accompanied by traditional femininity. Unfortunately, such a narrow, singular construction of ideal womanhood tends to lead to an equally narrow — and problematic — conceptualization of feminism and other possible aspects of femaleness, especially sexuality.

Particularly, in this essay, I wish to question Joss Whedon and his creative team's consistently problematic representations of female sexuality in *Buffy the Vampire Slayer*, an element which undermines the otherwise multifaceted and complex collection of feminist figures in the series. In order to consider the ways that the show rhetorically constructs female sexuality, we must consider both how sex is talked about and also the series' larger meta-narrative rhetoric about the pursuit of female sexual pleasure. In other words, we must ask: which vocal expressions of sexuality are acceptable and which are taboo, and what happens to women who pursue sexual desire or physically express their female sexuality? The sad answer is that *Buffy* exhibits a pattern wherein women who step outside of traditional "good girl" engagement with their own sexuality or pleasure — in word or action — are nearly always punished for transgressing boundaries of traditional feminine gender performance because "sexual relationships are almost always depicted as dangerous and deceptive and create an atmosphere of horror" (Heinecken 103). The answer is that, by and large, women of the Buffyverse are taught, in Cordelia's words, that "sex is bad" ("Expecting" *Angel*).[3] The one notable exception to this problematic pattern is found in Anya, the (mostly) ex-demon struggling to understand the subtleties of human behaviors and interactions, especially when it comes to expressions of sexuality.

In order to demonstrate the series' pattern of punishing transgressive female sexuality and highlight Anya' s defiance of this pattern, this chapter will directly compare the ways in which four key female figures — Buffy, Willow, Faith, and Anya — talk about sex, as well as the narrative rhetoric revealed by the trajectories of each woman's romantic and sexual relationships. Although other women in the Buffyverse could provide a suitable contrast to Anya, Buffy offers the most developed example of traditional (restricted) feminine expressions of desire and is the most often and overtly punished by the larger narrative rhetoric for pursuing her own desire, making her an ideal point of contrast. As Lorna Jowett notes, "Buffy's sexual activity is inflected by gendered constructions, especially of blame and shame" (62). While Willow's characterization allows for more complex constructions of female sexual expression than Buffy's, she ultimately conforms to the model established by Buffy. After all, as the title character, it is ultimately Buffy's story that viewers witness. In contrast, Faith is just as outspoken and unfettered as Anya about her sexual desires (although her enactment of sexuality is sometimes problematic, such as when she attempts to strangle Xander while mimicking their previous sexual encounter), but Faith never achieves the acceptance within the group that Anya does, limiting her ability to provide a suitable model of positive female sexuality. In contrast, Anya's eventual integration into the core heroic group legitimizes her perspective such that she stands alone as the only woman of the Buffyverse to remain unashamed and unpunished for her expressions of sexuality.

While much critical attention has been paid to *Buffy*'s representations of sexuality, particularly Buffy's relationships (Cocca, Jowett, Symonds), especially her sexual relationship with Spike (Call, Burns, Burr); Willow's lesbianism (Jowett, Masson, McAvan, Tabron); and Faith's use of sexuality as a weapon (Helford, Jowett, Tjardes); critics who discuss Anya tend to focus on her positioning as outsider or the redemptive aspects of her character development (Jowett, Riess). Yet, nowhere in the breadth of available scholarship has the intersection of sexual rhetoric and the larger metanarrative response to expressions of female desire been explored in depth, especially in relation to Anya's unique positioning among women of the Buffyverse. Anya's irrepressible approach to sexuality is a feminist model of positive female sexuality that breaks the otherwise troubling pattern in *Buffy the Vampire Slayer* of women being punished for transgressing traditional expressions of female desire and sexuality.

I have deliberately chosen the term "feminist model of positive female sexuality" to both evoke sex-positive feminism and separate my argument from that movement, in an effort to avoid creating unfair connections between Anya or *Buffy* and some of the more extreme aspects of the movement. Sex-positive feminism originates in the early 1980s when many feminists split into oppositional camps on specific topics related to sex and expressions of women's sexuality. Sex-positive feminists, such as Gayle Rubin, Carol Queen, and Betty Dodson,[4] argue that sexual freedom is a crucial factor for achieving gender equity in society. Two of the most hot-button issues championed by this movement are pornography and sex work. Sex-positive feminists argue that pornography can (and should) be enjoyed by women, rather than condemned as an exclusively male entertainment genre and tool of patriarchal oppression. Further, sex-positive feminists argue that women who choose to perform sex work — such as acting in pornography or engaging in prostitution — should have the right and ability to do so without shame or censure. In contrast, those opposed to the sex-positive movement, such as Andrea Dworkin, Catharine MacKinnon, Robin Morgan, and Dorchen Leidhodlt,[5] argue that sex-based industries and entertainment are among the most culpable for building and sustaining a culture of oppression and violence for women. In the wake of these debates, 1990s and early 2000s culture emerged, which is even more split in terms of representing women's sexuality. Ariel Levy, for example, in *Female Chauvinist Pigs* calls the current cultural atmosphere — wherein women's participation in exploitative media enterprises like *Girls Gone Wild* is an accepted rite of passage — "raunch culture." According to Levy, whose book is partially a critique of sex-positive feminism, raunch culture presents itself as empowering to women's sexuality, yet it actually encourages young women to embody and perform their sexuality for a heterosexual male gaze, in a manner that is ultimately disempowering because it reinforces their status as object rather than subject. While there is no clear evidence that the women of the Buffyverse inhabit either a full-blown raunch culture world or that the characters can conclusively be identified for or against movements like sex-positive feminism, elements of these cultural moments are clear, especially in Anya's attitudes towards and expressions of her own sexuality. Specifically, I wish to contemplate Anya's alignment with these movements and cultural moments, alluding to sex-positive feminism and its cultural influence in my consideration of her character. Although, for example, there is no overt textual evidence that Anya would either decry or embrace pornography for her own pleasure, her demonstrated characteristics, especially her comfort with her own sexual desire — as highlighted by her question to Andrew — suggest she would not be opposed to pornography. At times, her performance of sexuality and her verbal sexual expression even seem to mimic pornographic tropes of female sexuality. Likewise, her history as a vengeance demon is clearly set up as allegorical to prostitution (Francis), and it is an enterprise in which Anya finds empowerment and success rather than the expected degradation and abuse (even if her empowerment is in the service of evil). These elements of her character and backstory align her with sex-positive feminism. However, it is a stretch to say her character is exclusively representative of that movement; in order to evoke those ideas without unfairly tying Anya to them, their multi-faceted history, and their larger socio-political contexts, I use the label "feminist model of positive female sexuality." In using this term, I hope to establish a middle ground between the extremes of sex-positive feminism, sex-negative feminists, and Levy's raunch culture, one which offers a new, positive conceptualization of women's sexuality as demonstrated by Anya.

Buffy

The show's title character, Buffy, is one of the most traditional when it comes to the rhetorical constructions of her sexuality. Buffy is so traditional in this way, in fact, that she displays a reluctance to talk about her sexual desire or choices, even with herself. Notably, when first considering sleeping with (and losing her virginity to) her first love Angel, Buffy's dream that brings the question into her conscious mind does so only obliquely. During the dream sequence in "Surprise," Buffy walks through the local nightclub, The Bronze. Buffy's encounter with her mother in this scene, a location representative of the shift from adolescence to adulthood that Joyce visits at no other time, highlights Buffy's desire for guidance. Joyce's question "Are you ready?" followed by the dropping and shattering of the saucer she holds is equally significant. Although the saucer is not an unusual item in a club that serves coffee in deference to its underage crowd, it also represents traditional domestic femininity and that tradition's accompanying emphasis on virginity and limited or non-existent female sexuality. The scene suggests that if Buffy chooses to sleep with Angel, she breaks both her virginity (in a literal sense) and her connection to that model of a woman's lack of expression of female desire. Just as threatening is the sequence's conclusion where Buffy moves toward Angel, seemingly haven chosen him, but before she can reach Angel, Drusilla stakes him. Angel's death in the scene is all the more significant for coming at the hands of Drusilla, a woman whose innocence Angel's evil alter ego Angelus purposefully destroyed through psychological torture and — although the series never explicitly says so — likely sexual assault before turning the woman into a vampire. She is the most obvious legacy of Angel's evil history at this point in the series, and her position as his executioner here is significant, something viewers familiar with the subsequent events well know.[6] In the dream, Buffy cannot articulate the central question "Am I ready to have sex?" any further than the first three words (translated into the second person perspective as they come from Joyce), demonstrating her inability to talk about sex frankly and openly.

This pattern is repeated throughout the series, ranging from Buffy's choices to hide sexual or potential sexual relationships from her family and friends to her indirect ways of talking (or not talking) about sex. Even with her sexual partners, Buffy is reluctant to talk about sex directly. When she sleeps with Angel, and he suggests that maybe they should not proceed past making out, Buffy's verbal response is "Don't. Just kiss me" ("Surprise"). Likewise, when she sleeps with Parker, her one-night-stand in college, he asks,

"Is this okay? Because I can stop if you wanna. It's your choice" ("The Harsh Light of Day"). Buffy's response is to pull him closer (action not words), and when he asks for clarification — "What are you doing?" — she responds, "Making a choice." She never articulates verbally what that choice is. The one time that viewers see her being most directly articulate about her sexual desire is when in bed with Riley in "Where the Wild Things Are," and she says, "Don't stop. Never stop touching me." This last scene is perhaps an unfair representation, however, given that Buffy and Riley's sexual desire is super-charged in the episode due to supernatural influence. Buffy, especially, uncharacteristically ignores cues that something is amiss (like Willow screaming), insisting on continuing the sexual encounter, suggesting her vocalization here is also somewhat uncharacteristic. Continuing the pattern is the language Buffy chooses when talking with Spike about their sexual encounters during the sixth season. In an uncharacteristic (for that relationship) tender moment, when Spike compliments her by saying, "You were amazing," Buffy can offer no more direct a response than "You got the job done yourself." Her inability to directly or unashamedly talk about sexual desire or pleasure is reflected in this awkward response that is unequal to the compliment paid her by Spike, even though in the same conversation she acknowledges her body is still recovering from the intensity of the sexual experience to the point that she physically cannot yet engage in her normal pattern of, in Spike's unique phrasing, "kick[ing] me in the head and run[ing] out, virtue fluttering" (Dead Things"). Further, as Heinecken notes, several episodes in the sixth season which detail Buffy and Spike's sexual encounters position Buffy as "the 'good girl,' denying her true desires.... She continually tells him she will never do it again, but, invariably, she returns to him.... Spike, able to speak his desire, is the verbal aggressor in the relationship as a whole. Buffy's desire remains unspoken" (116).

While Buffy does (mostly) acknowledge the existence of her own sexual desire to some degree with her sexual partners, she is still hesitant to talk about sex directly with her family and friends. When she is forced to acknowledge her sexual involvement in Angel's transformation into Angelus, the other characters guess the nature of that involvement without Buffy outright stating it. In fact, when Giles, hesitatingly asks, "Wh — How do you know you were responsible for —" Buffy answers his question with a significant look, never actually verbalizing the message she conveys to him ("Innocence"). Similarly, when talking to Willow after sleeping with Parker early in Season Four, Buffy's response to Willow's inquiry for "details. I mean not details. I don't need a diagram. But, you know, like maybe a blurry watercolor" is simply "It

was nice" ("The Harsh Light of Day"). Although Buffy does verbally acknowledge her sexual desire and behavior here, "It was nice" is barely an outline
sketch, let alone the blurry watercolor Willow suggests would be a comfortable and acceptable level of detailed talk about sex between the two friends.
Buffy's vocalizations about the intense sexual experience she shares with Riley
in "Where the Wild Things Are" deny any pleasure (given the influence
of poltergeists on Buffy and Riley's behavior), and she classifies the experience to Willow as her and Riley being "wrapped up in each other." Moreover, coming full circle, even when Buffy finally acknowledges/confesses the
nature of her relationship with Spike during the sixth season to Tara, the
other woman initially thinks Buffy's questions, "Why do I feel like this? Why
do I let Spike do those things to me?" are about Spike's ability to physically
harm Buffy when he cannot harm other humans ("Dead Things"). Again,
Buffy conveys her true meaning through a significant look rather than verbal
clarification.

In addition to the words Buffy uses — or does not use — to articulate the
realities of her sexual behavior, the courses her various relationships take contribute to the construction of a metanarrative rhetoric of punished female
sexuality in *Buffy*. Sadly, the series often "depict[s] [Buffy's] sexual desires as
destructive and linked to darkness" (Heinecken 112). Buffy's sexual relationships are characterized by a failure of the relationship due to her transgression of some expectation of female sexuality. The most obvious is the drastic
personality change Angel undergoes when he loses his soul and capacity for
goodness as a result of their sexual encounter ("Surprise" and "Innocence").
In one of the most oft-cited metaphors of the series, the teenage Buffy engages
in sex — notably for the first time — and her boyfriend turns into a completely
different person, a monster who would hurt and abuse her for sadistic pleasure. This storyline echoes the classic partner abuse cycle, where the abuser
first gains his victim's trust and affection and then becomes a manipulative,
hurtful, inescapable presence that dominates her life,[7] making the narrative
arc an invaluable, realistic representation of teenage sexuality. Yet, the larger,
inescapable message here is that Buffy is punished for choosing to have sex,
a lesson that suggests expressions of female sexuality are inappropriate in many
situations: for a teenager, outside of marriage, etc.— in short, whenever the
act is one of a woman's own agency and transgresses socially approved conventions. Ultimately, the inability for Buffy and Angel to express sexual intimacy makes their relationship untenable, leaving them with the choice
between a physically unfulfilled love or ending their relationship. Angel recognizes the position this choice puts Buffy in, demanding she become a sex-

less warrior, a position that would further separate her from the "normal" life she strives to balance with her calling. He leaves Buffy because, as a feminist, as a man who supports gender equity, he cannot contribute to a life of sexual repression for another, let alone for someone he loves.

Unfortunately for Buffy, the pattern established by her night with Angel is reinforced when essentially the same thing happens with Parker, the first man she sleeps with following Angel's departure from her life. While Parker initially seems to offer potential for a positive relationship, he ultimately treats her in the same manner as Angelus, albeit somewhat milder because he poses no threat of physical violence. Parker first gives Buffy the brush-off, indicating that their time together was nothing more than "fun" ("The Harsh Light of Day"). Later, though, Parker reveals his true self (his "evil" persona released after sexual conquest over Buffy) when he describes Buffy to another man by saying, "You know the difference between a freshman girl and a toilet seat? A toilet seat doesn't follow you around after you use it" ("The Initiative"). Parker provides a non-supernatural version of Angel's abandonment of Buffy after sex, once again contributing to a narrative rhetoric that marks her physical expression of sexual desire as something to be punished.

Of Buffy's other sexual relationships, her involvement with Riley is perhaps the least problematic expression of her sexuality. And yet, Riley's insecurities over his place in Buffy's life lead him to cheat on her, metaphorically expressed through the pleasure he finds in paying — notably female — vampires to feed on him because "they made me feel something.... Something I didn't even know I was missing" ("Into the Woods"). These insecurities also ultimately prompt his decision to leave her. While most viewers can agree Riley's unease with Buffy's superior physical strength and her corresponding habit of exhibiting mental and emotional strength (notably traditionally masculine characteristics) is at the heart of the conflict in their relationship, the fact that the incident which signals the end of their involvement is tied up in images of prostitution and Riley seeking a base physical pleasure elsewhere means that viewers cannot ignore the suggestion of sexual dissatisfaction. This suggestion of sexual dissatisfaction — and Riley's framing of that issue as Buffy's fault because "they [the female vampires] needed me" ("Into the Woods") in a way Buffy never did — contributes to the larger narrative rhetoric of punishing a woman because her expressions of sexuality are inappropriate in some way.

Buffy's sexual relationship with Spike also contributes to this pattern. In fact, Justine Larbalestier suggests that "in some respects, Spike is a mixture of elements from all Buffy's previous love interests. He's Angel: the brooding demon lover with a soul; he's Parker Abrams: callous and mean to women; he's Riley: consumed by unrequited love" (195). In addition to the specifics of her involvement with Angel, the fact that Buffy engages in sex with these two characters, who are both vampires and evil at different times in the series, is itself a transgression, offering allegory for sexual pairings that violate norms of race, class, or sexuality (the latter is a point which the show explicitly addresses and one to which I will return later). In regards to Buffy's relationship with Spike, specifically, while many viewers and critics have explored (and celebrated) the show's normalizing of the kinkier sexual behaviors to which Buffy and Spike's relationship alludes,[8] the relationship is ultimately unhealthy with Buffy taking on the role of abuser and Spike as victim. Buffy clearly manipulates Spike's affections for her, even going so far as to take out her frustrations on him physically by harshly beating him in "Dead Things." Notably, the physical markers of this beating take a significant amount of time to heal and are still present in the following episode "Older and Farther Away," even given the vampire's supernaturally-accelerated healing and the show's practice of generally healing damage to characters' bodies by the next episode, unless the damage is exceptionally severe. While Buffy's choice to engage sexually with Spike is problematic to begin with (given her reasons for being with him are about self-punishment),[9] the fact that the climax of this troubled relationship is Spike's attempt to rape Buffy in order to "make you feel it [love]" ("Seeing Red") is clearly constructed as a punishment for Buffy's previous expressions of sexual desire, regardless of the complex ethical questions the trajectory of their relationship raises.[10]

In contrast to her sexual encounters with men is Buffy's affair with the slayer Satsu in the Season Eight comics. Initially, this encounter seems like a positive exploration for Buffy of her sexuality as she explores her "heteroflexibility" (Frohard-Dourlent).[11] While *Buffy* does articulate a clear pattern of punishing expressions of female desire, one distinct positive engagement with female sexuality is found in the series' foregrounding of positive and supported images of lesbian relationships (often an easy target in other (con)texts when chastising transgressive female sexuality) as demonstrated through Willow's relationships with Tara and Kennedy (discussed below), as well as Buffy's affair with Satsu. However, what is most significant (and familiar) is how quick Buffy and her peers, especially Willow, are to point out the lack of significance of Buffy and Satsu's involvement. Buffy breaks her pattern to a degree in "Wolves at the Gate, Part One" by being more articulate about her enjoyment of her time with Satsu, saying, "I had a wonderful night. And ... it's been a while since I said that. So ... tomorrow, I'm gonna think about what we did. And I'm gonna blush. And then I'm gonna smile."[12] However, Buffy follows her admission of enjoyment with, "But I'm not sure it goes any further than that." Further, Willow, as the voice of lesbian authority in the series, later pulls Satsu aside to explicitly name Buffy as heterosexual; specifically, she identifies Buffy as "not a ... friend of Sappho" ("Wolves at the Gate, Part Two"), reinforcing euphemistic rhetoric. Both of these rhetorical maneuvers work to make abundantly clear, to Satsu and the reader, that Buffy's dalliance with the younger slayer is non-normative (for Buffy), that she has, to some degree, taken advantage of Satsu's feelings for her to explore her own sexuality. While this encounter may be a positive expression for Buffy of her sexuality and Buffy does not directly suffer negative consequences, this storyline inverts past narrative moments, positioning Satsu where Buffy once was — as the woman who expresses her sexuality freely and whose lover wants nothing more than one night of pleasure in spite of the woman's desire to transform that carnal experience into an emotional relationship.

Willow

The series' other constant main female character, Willow, also contributes to the Buffyverse pattern of female sexuality constructed in problematic and often punitive ways, although representations of Willow's sexuality offer more complex constructions of the possibilities for female sexualities. Further, they demonstrate how Willow grows in her ability to talk about sex openly during the course of the series, both with her sexual partners and with her friends. Willow's first lover is Oz, her high school boyfriend who is also a werewolf— another relationship like Buffy's with either Angel or Spike that can be read as analogous to relationships that are socially taboo due to either partner's racial/ethnic identity, gender, etc. Significantly, Willow is only slightly more articulate about her sexual desire at this point than Buffy's action-based communication. When Willow first attempts to communicate to Oz her desire to sleep with him, she explains the cliché scene she has set up (candles, a fire, Barry White playing in the background) by saying, "We're alone, and we're both mature younger people, and, and so ... w–we could ... I–I'm ready to ... w–with you" ("Amends"). Willow's obvious discomfort, indicated by her stuttering and inability to actually say what she means, is reinforced when she continues in a whisper, "We could do that thing." Although Oz turns down Willow's offer, recognizing it as a misguided attempt to apologize rather than a true reflection of her readiness to change the nature of their relationship, this moment is part of a larger pattern for the two when it comes to talking about their relationship. When they are first dating, Oz attempts to offer Willow the opportunity to break off their relationship after he becomes a werewolf, and Willow's response is "I'd still if you'd still" ("Phases"), a sentence that leaves out specifically what Willow would still do (date Oz) rather than explicitly articulating her desire. When the two do sleep together for the first time, Willow's contributions to the conversation leading up to the act are not about sex at all; rather she is worried about an upcoming battle she fears she and her friends may not survive and is mad at the laid-back Oz for not obviously panicking alongside her. When he kisses her, she only says, "What are you doing?" ("Graduation Day, Part 1"). Oz's reply of "panicking" is enough talk for the two. The construction of the sexual rhetoric in this moment is not entirely unexpected, given, as Cynthea Masson points out, Willow's ongoing "rhetorical strategy of questioning" during the course of the series "most acute in conversations between Willow and her [romantic] partners," although Willow also communicates through questions in many varied situations with different conversational partners.

Willow's second sexual partner is Tara, whom Willow meets in her first year of college. Initially Willow follows Buffy's example of hiding the relationship from her friends, although her motivation is that Tara is a woman (rather than being a supernatural creature like a vampire). For the first few months of their relationship, Willow explains away time spent with Tara in innocuous terms, such as claiming that she was in "the chem lab, by myself" ("A New Man"). When she does introduce Tara to her friends, Willow only identifies Tara as a "friend," rather than as her "girlfriend." To be fair, the series is unclear about when exactly Willow acknowledges Tara's position in her life to herself, which makes the significance of the label Willow chooses at this point debatable in terms of whether it reflects hiding from her friends or unawareness of her changing sexual identity. However, Willow is forced to come out — both internally and externally — when Oz returns from his journey to find a way to control his previously uncontrollable werewolf side. When he frankly and directly indicates that he returned for Willow, and says that he asked one of her friends if she had a new guy, she replies, "No. No new ... guy" ("New Moon Rising"), giving enough pause to indicate to viewers that she is both telling the truth and not being fully honest with Oz. When she finally comes out to Buffy later in the episode, her actions are prompted by Buffy's concern with Willow's lack of enthusiastic reaction to Oz's return. Buffy says, "Okay, I'm all with the woo-hoo here, and you're not." Willow's response is fairly direct and starts to break the pattern of women who cannot talk about their sexual desire, especially nonheteronormative desires like lesbianism: "No, there's 'woo' and, and 'hoo,' But there's 'uh-oh,' and 'why now?' And it's complicated." At Buffy's prompting she elaborates, "It's complicated because of Tara," a statement which Buffy does not understand at first, even though Willow is being more direct here than is standard for the two friends. But at the episode's end, when Willow goes to tell Tara that she has chosen her over Oz, Willow reverts back to indirect language. Tara expects Willow to break up with her, and Tara attempts to ease the situation by saying "You have to be with the person you love." Willow's response of "I am," prompts Tara to ask "You mean?" and Willow to respond simply "I mean," again avoiding direct articulation of what exactly Willow means or desires. Instead, Willow promises to make up to Tara for the distress she put the other woman through while figuring out how to respond to Oz's return. As a suggestion of love and sexual desire, but an unspoken and unseen one, Tara blows out the candle she is holding, leaving the women in the dark and hidden from the viewer's gaze.

Likewise, Willow's lesbianism is an important contribution to expanding the bounds of female sexuality outside traditional, narrow parameters connected to ideas about femininity, which construct female sexuality as a component of male sexual pleasure rather than an end in itself. *Buffy* generally represented Willow and Tara's sexuality by displacing it onto images of them practicing magic together (Jowett 50). Partially, this displacement can be attributed to network censors and the ground that characters like Willow and Tara broke in terms of gaining equal representation access for gay, lesbian, or otherwise non-heteronormative characters on network television. The careful construction of lesbian sexuality in which *Buffy* engages as a result of challenging social conventions is important to recognize, but it ultimately contributes to the larger pattern of not talking about (or visually representing) positive expressions of female sexuality in both heteronormative and nonheteronoramtive contexts.

Both *Buffy's* and Willow's increasingly complex representations of female sexuality through the construction of lesbian sexuality continues in the seventh season. Following Tara's death at the end of the sixth season, Willow meets her third sexual and romantic partner in the series, the potential slayer Kennedy. In "The Killer in Me," when Kennedy tricks Willow into going on a date, she bluntly asks Willow, "How long have you known? That you're gay." Willow's lack of comfort with talking about her own sexuality resurfaces when she responds, "You just assume that I'm ... I'm gay. I mean, presume much?" Kennedy, undeterred, clarifies her question more bluntly: "Okay. How long have you enjoyed having sex with women?" Willow is even more taken aback, but eventually answers the question by saying, "Three years ago. That's when I knew. And it wasn't women, it was woman. Just one." Willow's insistence on clarifying her sexuality in terms of her relationship with Tara as unique suggests she still lacks a level of comfort with talking about her sexual desires, even in the abstract. Further, it implies that Willow's understanding of her own sexuality is still constrained by traditional notions of sexuality as polarized along heterosexual or homosexual boundaries, rather than being fluid.[13] While she will not deny her relationship with Tara, she also is not yet prepared to fully and publicly identify herself with the label "gay" when she starts dating Kennedy, although she does identify herself as gay privately with statements such as "Hello? Gay now!" ("Triangle") and "I think I'm kinda gay" ("Tabula Rasa"). Further, Willow's private identification as gay is emphasized in her assurances to Tara that, although she has not "establish[ed] [her] lesbo street cred" by engaging in a previous lesbian relationship, her homosexuality is not "a college thing, just a, a little experimentation before [she] get[s] over the thrill and head[s] back to boys' town" ("Tough Love"). While these examples all represent Willow's ability to privately identify as gay, throughout the course of her relationship with Kennedy, Willow grows more comfortable with this identity, to the point where she can joke in a semi-public space — a room full of potential slayers (rather than just her closest friends) — about performing an important spell by saying, "It's a total loss of control, and not in a nice, wholesome, my-girlfriend-has-a-pierced-tongue kind of way" ("Chosen").

In addition to the ways that Willow talks about sex, the metanarrative rhetoric — what happens to her in connected with her relationships — reinforces the pattern established in Buffy's relationships of punishing female sexuality, while still offering a more complicated construction of women's possible sexuality. Willow and Oz's relationship is unique in that it can be read as metaphorical for the kind of relationship shared between two people when one partner has a contagious, potentially deadly, sexually transmittable disease. Oz's lycanthropy (werewolf-ness) is a disease transmittable through a bite, analogous to an exchange of fluids. The fact that his blood-based illness could kill Willow (while he is in wolf form) has obvious parallels for incurable STDs like HIV/AIDS and diseases that are deadly if left untreated. Willow chooses to remain with Oz and the two take precautions (locking Oz in a cage during his transformation is analogous to using condoms and/or avoiding sexual contact during visible outbreaks of a disease), and this choice sets a positive model for a woman and her sexual partner exerting agency over their own sexuality and sexual behavior. Yet, in the end, regardless of the sacrifices Willow is prepared to make, Oz leaves her behind when he sets off on his quest to control the wolf. While he ultimately does this for her, he makes the decision without her, denying her agency over her sex life, as Jowett and other critics have observed.

Also, of course, one cannot ignore the punitive aspect of Tara's death. Although she is killed by a stray bullet from an attack not remotely connected to Willow and Tara's sexuality (except in that the man wielding the gun is a misogynist of the highest order), it is impossible to dismiss the fact that Tara dies the morning after making up with Willow and engaging in a night of unrestrained — and therefore transgressive — female sexuality. As Heinecken observes, "Tara's death immediately after reunion sex with Willow recall[s] a homophobic cliché" (104) of "the dead evil lesbian" (Tabron). While *Buffy*'s writers' choice to kill Tara as an impetus for Willow's grief-stricken descent into evil at the end of the sixth season raises question about representations of lesbians and other queer characters on television, especially network television, I agree with readings like Roz Kaveney's that suggest the accidental nature of Tara's death subverts the stereotype to a significant degree (35). For the purposes of this discussion, however, what is important is that Tara dies, punishing Willow for her sexual behaviors by taking away her love(r).

In fact, Willow's guilt over her response to Tara's death manifests itself to punish her yet again when she first starts to entertain romantic and sexual feelings for Kennedy in "The Killer in Me." In this episode, when Willow and Kennedy first kiss, Willow's guilt, aided by a spell, transforms her into Warren, the man she tortured and murdered in revenge for killing Tara. Willow's remorse over killing Warren is directly connected to her sexuality and socially "taboo" relationship with Tara. That guilt, in combination with her guilt about having and acting on feelings for another woman, serve to punish Willow for both her past violent deeds and her current sexual desires. Significantly, Willow names the pattern of punishing female sexuality when explaining what is happening to her: "I'm being punished.... I kissed you [Kennedy] just, just for a second, but it was enough. I let her go. I didn't mean to." Ultimately, Willow and Kennedy's relationship survives and flourishes, suggesting that Willow's growth towards understanding and openly expressing her own sexuality may be pushing her to break the model established by the series. However, the many ways in which she has difficulties talking about sex and through which the metanarrative rhetoric constructs her moments of expressed sexuality reinforce a history of constrained and punished female sexuality that follows the precedent set by Buffy.

Faith

In contrast to *Buffy*'s "good girls"—Buffy and Willow—the series' resident "bad girl," Faith, comes the closest of all the women of *Buffy*, aside from Anya, to breaking the pattern of punished female sexuality. Faith is comfortable with her sexual desires and freely talks about her sexuality, both when she is consciously playing up her "bad girl" persona and later in the series when she is reformed from her earlier approach to life. For example, in "The Zeppo," Faith seduces Xander. While she is not so direct as Anya will later be—notably, Xander will call Anya's directness "still more romantic than Faith" ("The Harsh Light of Day")—Faith is direct in expressing her desires, instructing Xander to "just relax. And take off your pants," promising to "steer [him] around the curves" ("The Zeppo"). She also demonstrates her comfort with sexual talk and her knowledge of the power such ease can give her when she is masquerading as Buffy (having switched bodies with Buffy). Faith-as-Buffy approaches Spike, now incapable of harming humans due to the behavior modification chip in his brain, and uses her security with her own sexuality to torment the vampire: "I could have anything. Anyone," she says seductively as she slides her hands up Spike's chest, continuing, "Even you, Spike. I could ride you at a gallop until your legs buckled and your eyes rolled up. I've got muscles you've never even dreamed of. I could squeeze you until you popped like warm champagne, and you'd beg me to hurt you just a little bit more" ("Who Are You?"). Faith's actions here represent her conflation of sources of power—she wields her sexuality as easily as the stake she uses to slay vampires—summed up in her assertion that slaying stimulates her appetites, both hunger and sexual arousal. Faith's speech to Spike recalls an earlier scene, and both scenes reinforce Faith's opposition to Buffy. Following Faith's pronouncement that "slaying leaves [her] hungry and horny" ("Faith, Hope, and Trick"), Buffy's friends turn to look at Buffy in surprise, seeking confirmation of Faith's claim. Buffy's "good girl" positioning, and conversely, Faith's as "bad girl," are reaffirmed when Buffy, wide-eyed and uncomfortable, admits, "Well, sometimes I crave a nonfat yogurt afterwards" ("Faith, Hope, and Trick").

Although both of the above incidents occur prior to Faith's choice to reform herself by voluntarily ceasing to use her slayer powers for personal gain and by atoning for the crimes she committed, her ability to talk about sex comfortably is not lost after she reforms. When she returns to help Buffy and the others in the final televised season, Faith and Spike have a conversation where they bond over their shared dark pasts. Faith comments that "this one guy I ran with, he liked me to dress up like a school girl and take this friggin' bullwhip..." before later joking that given the length of her incarceration, she's "thinking about looking up the guy with the bullwhip" ("Dirty Girls"). The conversation continues with Faith revealing to Spike that she was the person in Buffy's body a few years previous when "Buffy" taunted him about her sexual prowess. When Faith suggests that Spike should have realized she wasn't Buffy, implying that such comfort with one's sexuality is not Buffy's style, Spike chuckles and says, "Oh, you have been away," referring to his sexual relationship with Buffy during the previous year. The fact that this conversation occurs in the episode named "Dirty Girls" is significant because the suggestion of "dirtiness" or "badness" is not in reference to Faith or Buffy's past sexual behaviors. Rather, it is the perspective of the villain-du-jour, an evil, misogynistic preacher who believes women to be the root of all sin, especially strong women like Buffy and Faith who pose a credible threat to the patriarchal oppression he believes to be the "natural" order of humanity. The opposition of Faith's dialogue with Spike in this episode to the preacher's views reinforces the acceptability of Faith's sexual vocalizations; the preacher's vision of Faith and the other women is so twisted and perverted that all their actions — including Faith's jokes about sexual role playing and bondage — are thrust into an acceptable light.

While Faith succeeds at presenting a woman who can talk about sex comfortably, the metanarrative development of her character fails to follow through on the promise her ability to talk about sex suggests in terms of her ability to function as a model of positive and unpunished female sexuality. Her clearly troubled conflation of love and sexual intimacy repeatedly present her model of physical sexual expressions as a cautionary tale. While she is not necessarily punished by narrative plot points, she punishes herself, contributing to the larger pattern. Like Willow, Faith is motivated at times by guilt and anger. Elyce Rae Helford notes that "intense guilt and self-loathing that she cloaks as anger begin to dominate Faith's personality after she and Buffy grow apart" (31). This conflation of guilt and anger are illustrated by her attempt to strangle Xander after sleeping with him ("Consequences"); her negative reaction to Riley's whispered "I love you" and the implied intimacy of the moment when in bed with him (while disguised as Buffy) ("Who Are You?"); and her self-destructive attempt to get first Buffy and then Angel to kill her following her sexual encounter with Riley. While beating on her own body (with Buffy in it), Faith screams at herself, "You're nothing! Disgusting, murderous bitch! You're nothing! You're disgusting!" ("Who Are You?"). After Buffy switches their bodies back, but refuses to kill the other slayer, Faith flees to

Los Angeles (where Angel lives); there she captures and tortures one of Angel's friends and her former Watcher, a man who was supposed to protect and guide her, before throwing herself at Angel and pleading, "I'm evil. I'm bad! I'm evil.... Please just do it. Just kill me. Just kill me" ("Five by Five" *Angel*). While Faith's choice to torture her former Watcher, Wesley, plays heavily into her desire to escape her guilt through death, we cannot overlook the fact that the sequence of events starts because of her reaction to Riley's whispered endearment while making love to her. Granted, in that scenario, Faith's sexual behavior is tantamount to rape — given that Riley would not have engaged in sex with her had he known she was not Buffy — but it is still significant that her self-punishment is tied up in her experience of what should be a positive sexual encounter. However, Faith's character is constructed in such a way that her physical expressions of sexuality use, abuse, and hurt others; because Faith is a "bad girl," she is not positioned so that she can have a positive sexual encounter or express her sexuality in a healthy manner. She is, as Jowett argues, an example of "the uncontrollable nature of female power on *Buffy*" (84), which is significant because of the way that something uncontrollable is a threat. Because Faith is set up as such, her struggle towards absolute redemption, which would allow her to fully break the pattern of punished female sexuality, is hampered by her oppositional positioning to Buffy.

What ultimately discounts Faith from providing a positive model of female sexuality is her ongoing positioning as an outsider who will never be fully accepted. While Buffy and her friends do utilize Faith's help during the seventh season, after she has reformed, she remains forever on the margins of that group, a consequence of her past actions that pitted her so obviously in contrast to Buffy. Sue Tjardes argues that "Faith is presented as not what Buffy might be, but as what she is *not* and never will be" (70), suggesting that Faith's initial construction as an oppositional image of Buffy means that the metanarrative is incapable of allowing Faith full redemption and welcome as an ally to Buffy. In fact, the progress she makes towards being accepted by the group is erased in the Season Eight comics where she once again finds herself on the outside, first chosen by Giles for an assassination mission because he wants to protect Buffy, both from the woman who wants her dead and from killing a human ("No Future for You, Part One"). One of the strongest tenants underlying the series' mythology is the emphasis on slayers not killing humans. Faith, in contrast to Buffy, can be called upon to complete the mission as she has already killed a human and is therefore not as heroically pure as Buffy. Faith's marginal position is further reinforced when Buffy misreads the situation mid-mission (not knowing of Faith's involvement) and assumes Faith to be in collaboration with the villainous woman, disbelieving Faith's assurances that she is on Buffy's side ("No Future for You, Part Three"). While Faith is able to talk openly about sex, her marginal position which leaves her forever outside the group means that she can never be a fully representative model of positive female sexuality.

Anya

In contrast to the models Buffy, Willow, and Faith provide, Anya stands alone in the series as a woman whose sexuality is not limited, restricted, or otherwise punished. Although other characters repeatedly try to suppress her forthright way of speaking about sex and chastise her for expressing too overt an enjoyment of her sexuality, Anya is never truly quieted on this subject. Jowett argues that "Anya's frank discussion of sex makes her an object of ridicule because she cannot distinguish what is 'appropriate' to air in public" (35). However, I disagree with this reading; while she is not initially liked by Buffy and Willow, as she becomes a more central member of the group, the other women come to find amusement in Anya's "inappropriate" comments rather than seeing them only as a reason to ridicule her. Further, the fact that Anya cannot understand the others' conservative rhetoric of female sexuality serves to set Anya apart from the rest of the Buffyverse women in an advantageous way; in her rejection of their perspective, she establishes a missing model of positive female sexuality in the Buffyverse, one that is not punitive, but instead celebrates and encourages the open and direct expression of a woman's sexual desires, in both word and deed.

Unquestionably, Anya refuses to feel the shame that the others believe should censor her expressions of and about sexuality. From the beginning of her relationship with Xander in Season Four, Anya is clearly comfortable with sex and views it as a natural part of humanity, claiming that "it's ludicrous to have these interlocking bodies and not ... interlock" ("The Harsh Light of Day"). She initiates her relationship with Xander, when she shows up in Xander's living area and drops her dress before explaining her plan for getting Xander out of her mind (after their one date the previous season). Xander, used to a world where women do not talk about sex much, let alone stand in front of him naked while propositioning him, cannot immediately process Anya's offer. In an attempt to get a handle on the situation he says, "So, the crux of the plan is —" before Anya cuts him off impatiently with the bluntly stated "sexual intercourse. I've said it like a dozen times" ("The Harsh Light of Day"). While Xander does not yet possess the maturity to express his desire verbally, the show employs visual rhetoric — Xander's juicebox squirting — to make clear to viewers his reaction to her proposal. Xander reinforces the world he is accustomed to by claiming "hysterical deafness" in the face of such una-bashed expressions of Anya's desire, but Anya remains undeterred and con-tinues her business-like explanation by clarifying, "I think it's the secret to getting you out of my mind. Putting you behind me." Her comfort with talk-ing about sex is reinforced when she further clarifies the specifics of her vision for their proposed sexual union: "Behind me figuratively. I'm thinking face to face for the actual event itself." Here Anya's ability to stand naked and frankly negotiate for the sexual experience she desires locates her in direct opposition to Buffy and Willow, who so often speak in short, euphemistic phrases or convey meaning solely through action (and usually while still mostly clothed).

The series contains many other examples of Anya verbally expressing her sexual desire. In "Pangs," as she, Buffy, and Willow watch a presentation ded-icating a new cultural center for the University, a ceremony at which Xander will be digging as part of his construction worker job, Anya's interest is cen-tered on the physical appeal and potential sexual fantasy Xander-as-manual-laborer represents. She says, "Look at him. Have you ever seen anything so masculine? ... I'm imagining having sex with him right now." Whereas Buffy and Willow's conversation shifts to a more philosophical discussion about Thanksgiving and America's history of colonialism, Anya's focus remains on Xander, especially when he begins to dig: "Look at him.... Soon he'll be sweat-ing. I'm imagining having sex with him again." Anya's repetition of the phrase "look at him" directs and invites the other women to share her sexualized gaze, foregrounding not only the idea of sexual fantasy, but Anya's specific fantasy image. In this instance, Buffy and Willow exchange amused grins at Anya's transgression of the social norm, and Buffy even quips, "Imaginary Xander is quite the machine," allowing Anya's sex talk to exist as a quirk of her per-sonality. Likewise, in "Hell's Bells," when Anya expresses a desire to see (her fiancé) Xander before the wedding, Willow reminds the other woman that "it's bad luck for the groom to see the bride in her dress, remember?" Anya agrees, "Right. I can't keep all these ridiculous traditions straight," before coming up with a solution that fulfills both her desire and — she believes — conforms to the letter, if not the spirit, of matrimonial custom: "What if I'm not wearing my dress when I see him?" Here, Willow and Tara are Anya's audience, and they giggle indulgently, knowing that while Anya is joking, the comment is also quintessentially Anya, due to the woman's established ways of talking about sex.

However, Anya's frank approach to talking about sex is not accepted by all characters. Giles, the parental and patriarchal authority of the group, most often and overtly chastises her verbal expressions of sexuality. Even though he helps Buffy to subvert other patriarchal structures such as the Watcher's Council who view the Slayer as a tool for their use rather than as a person with her own agency, Giles still tends to take on a paternal role within the circle of Buffy's family and friends, especially in the absence of her own father. Simultaneously, Giles's British sensibilities and older generation set him apart from the young Americans; whereas they can grin at Anya's forthrightness even if they themselves would not act similarly, Giles is often taken aback by the young woman's vocalizations. In "Hush," Giles asks Xander to watch Spike (whose recent implantation with a computer chip makes him unable to harm humans and in need of the group's protection). Giles explains, "I have a friend who's coming to town, and I'd like us to be alone." Anya attempts to clarify the situation in — to her perspective — a perfectly rational way by asking, "Oh, you mean an orgasm friend?" Giles, uncomfortable with Anya's forthright ways of speaking about sex, censures the woman by saying "Yes, that's exactly the most appalling thing you could have said." Likewise, in "The Replacement," when Xander is split into two selves representing his strengths and his weaknesses — scruffy Xander and suave Xander — Anya sees sexual potential in the situation and suggests, "Well, maybe we shouldn't do this reintegration thing right away. See, I can take the boys home, and we can all have sex together, and, you know, just slap 'em back together in the morning." Although Giles's own history as something of a wild child in the 60s means the suggestion of a three-way sexual encounter should not be completely foreign to him, even when two participants are halves of the same person, his reaction is again one that makes clear he believes Anya's sexual rhetoric is out of line: "Uh, uh, we just need to light the candles," he says, referring to the spell to reintegrate Xander's two halves, before clarifying, "Also, we should continue to pretend we heard none of the disturbing sex talk."

In contrast to Giles's reactions are Xander's. While Xander does at times try to teach Anya social conventions that distinguish between public and private spaces as a means of restricting her "sex talk," his involvement with Anya parallels growth in Xander's rhetorical abilities. Whereas upon their first encounter, the series was forced to employ the visual rhetoric of Xander's juice box squirting to answer Anya's sexual proposition, his comfort and ability to talk about sex evolves long before Buffy and Willow's abilities do. In fact, only a few episodes after the juice box scene, Willow asks Xander for advice regarding her relationship with Oz. She initially talks in hypotheticals and euphemism: "What does it mean when a girl wants to ... you know" ("Wild at Heart"). Xander's response in the conversation demonstrates his greater comfort with talking about sexual desire when he first says, "If you're doing it, I think you should be able to say it," and then later teases, "Will, I've deciphered your ingenious code." Both of these conversational moves by Xander force Willow to be more direct, to name both the act to which she refers and her sexual partner. That Xander's comfort with sexual talk, in the abstract, develops so quickly suggests that the juice box moment should be read more as a comic visual than a reflection of his true ability to talk about sexual behaviors and his own desires. By and large, men in the Buffyverse are more able to openly and freely talk about sexuality, a double standard that has deep roots in Western culture. But, Xander's abilities in this area — as opposed to the parental Giles — situate him as an equally matched partner for Anya, one who is comfortable referring to their sex life as "Tales of Anya and Xander's sexcapades" ("Into the Woods"), even as he explains to Anya that the current moment is not the time for such tales.

Anya clearly recognizes and understands that how she talks and acts can affect others' perceptions of her. And yet, she never represses the sexual part of her personality and outlook on the world, a positive and unusual characteristic among the women of her social circle. Although Anya sometimes misses the mark in her attempts to fit into human society, she never visibly limits or represses her comments or attitudes toward sex. Unlike Buffy or other women of the Buffyverse, who are punished by the larger narrative rhetoric for expressions of sexuality, the implosion of Anya and Xander's relationship is not presented as being about sexuality, either as a consequence of Xander's response to Anya's sexual desire or as a punishment of the woman for acting upon her sexual desire. The false visions of their married future Xander witnesses in "Hell's Bells" — an effort of a man Anya cursed during her demon days to extract revenge on the woman — do suggest an unhappy marriage where lack of sex is a problem and one of their children is clearly part-demon (implying sexual unfaithfulness on Anya's part). However, the ultimate deterioration of their marriage is presented in the false vision as a reenactment of the abusive, miserable cycle Xander's own parents are locked in and which he grew up witnessing ("Hell's Bells"). Xander leaves Anya at the altar because of his own fears of not being the kind of husband he wants her to have, not because he is a jerk like Parker, subject to a mystical curse like Angel, must leave her due to death like Tara, because of Anya's position within the group, or in reaction to how her own (sexual) behavior has influenced his decision (as Buffy experiences with Riley and Spike). While all the main characters suffer some kind of personal implosion during the sixth season of *Buffy*, Anya's loss of Xander is clearly not constructed as a punishment for her expression of sexual desire the way that the endings of Buffy and Willow's relationships so often are over the course of the series. In fact, Xander's action of leaving Anya is a punishment, but it is a punishment that comes as "a direct consequence of her previous power: one of her victims comes back for his revenge" (Jowett 36). Here, Anya's past actions as an evil demon are punished rather than her human actions of talking about or enacting her female sexuality.

The one possible exception to the pattern-breaking example Anya offers is found in her Season Six sexual liaison with Spike, following the break-up of each of their respective relationships (Anya with Xander and Spike with Buffy). While this moment contributes to the larger sense of implosion for the season, as the potential for reconciliation of either couple spirals further away, it cannot be read in the same way as Buffy's many disastrous relationships. For both Anya and Spike, the sex act is less about expressing pure sexual desire than about attempting to reaffirm their own sexual and romantic desirability.[14] Likewise, while Xander's reaction to learning of Anya's act is initially anger and betrayal, the two eventually reconcile, suggesting that ultimately Anya is not punished by the larger narrative rhetoric here the way that Buffy and other women are throughout the series. However, even if one reads this moment in line with the larger pattern of punished women in *Buffy*, the rest of Anya's behavior clearly breaks the expectations of that pattern.

Arguably, in her refusal to repress her sexuality Anya is the most human of the group, a depiction that is ironic, given her struggles to understand human society and her shifts between human and demon status. She refuses to bow to convention and the dictates of polite society when it comes to taboo issues like sex, modeling a healthy, forthright recognition of her desires and breaking the pattern established by the other women of the Buffyverse. Because *Buffy* is so often recognized and lauded for being a progressive, feminist text, it is especially important to recognize where the limits of the series' feminism lie and what spaces for critique exist within the text, especially in terms of the ways female characters are constructed. Buffy and Willow, as the two central female characters throughout the course of the series, hold the most narrative authority. As such, it is discouraging that their sexual rhetoric — spoken and embodied through the trajectory of their relationships on a metanarrative level — is so often constrained and punished. Similarly, Faith's inability to escape the "bad girl" label and achieve full legitimization in the core group only reinforces the metanarrative construction of her forthright

performance of sexuality as a negative characteristic. In contrast, Anya's attitude toward sexual desire marks her as transgressing traditional forms of female
sexuality, a significant break to the pattern by which other women on the show
are constrained. Her death in the television finale positions Anya as failing to
achieve the ultimate narrative legitimacy that could have been granted her in
the Season Eight comics. Nevertheless, the ways in which Anya explodes the
pattern of punished female sexuality in *Buffy the Vampire Slayer* allow her to
set an example of positive female sexuality that is feminist, refreshing, and
necessary.

Notes

1. In fact, gender theorist Michael Kimmel observes in *Michael Kimmel: On Gender:
Mars, Venus or Planet Earth? Men and Women in a New Millennium* that "masturbation
[is] the best behavior measure of your entitlement to pleasure you can possibly come up
with. 'I'm so entitled to pleasure, I'll do it myself.'" As proof of his claim that masturbation rates reflect social attitudes about sexuality, Kimmel cites statistics from 1954 and 1996.
In the two studies, which measured the percentage of American women over the age of
twenty-five that have practiced masturbation, the rates jump from 41 percent to 90 percent; Kimmel argues that such a large change in a relatively small historical time period
reflects shifting attitudes towards sexual expression, particularly female sexuality. In contrast, data from the same surveys show that in 1954, 96 percent of American men had
engaged in masturbation; by 1996 that number had only increased one percentage point.

2. This is especially true given the depiction in the Season Eight comics of Simone, a
slayer with a traditionally "butch" gender performance. Simone turns out to be something
of an "evil" slayer, who attempts to kidnap Andrew and wishes to challenge Buffy for the
position of head slayer rather than working within a larger community of slayers.

3. While Cordelia's observation comes from her time on *Angel*, the fact that she is
speaking to Angel (and alluding to his troubled sexual history with Buffy as well as her
own history) makes this moment applicable to the other women of the Buffyverse. Women
who exist exclusively on *Angel* do provide more complicated images of female sexuality;
for example, Fred's loss when transformed into Illyria is especially tragic because it comes
on the heels of the realization of her romance with Wesley (within the pattern established
on *Buffy*, he is punished more so than she is, for he must live on having lost her), and her
relationship with Gunn is not specifically punished, in defiance of the cultural stereotype
against interracial couples. Cordelia, on the other hand, is less sexually complicated on
Buffy, but her time on *Angel* is rife with direct sexual activity resulting in disaster (i.e.:
her impregnation by demon in "Expecting," the threat of losing her vision-powers if
she engages in sexual activity with Groo in Season Three, and the Oedipal nature of her
sexual relationship with Connor that results in the birth of a demon-god bent on world
domination in Season Four). Likewise, Cordelia is subject to (metaphorical) rape on
several occasions, evoking the — disturbing and ridiculous — old defense of rapists that
women who have previously exhibited or engaged in sexual behaviors are "asking for it,"
that her expressions of sexuality opens her up to these attacks. For more on Cordelia's

metaphorical sexual abuse, see AmiJo Comeford's "Cordelia Chase as Failed Feminist Gesture."

4. For further information, see Rubin's "Thinking Sex: Notes for a Radical Theory of the Politics of Sexuality" (1984 in *Pleasure and Danger*, ed. Carole S. Vance); Queen's *Real Live Nude Girl: Chronicles of Sex-Positive Culture* (1997); and Dodson's *Sex for One: The Joy of Self-Loving* (originally published 1974 as *Liberating Masturbation*). Dodson, in particular, argues that women's sexual pleasure and masturbation are essential for the realization of feminist goals.

5. For more information, see Dworkin's *Pornography — Men Possessing Women* (1981); MacKinnon and Dworkin's *In Harm's Way: The Pornography Civil Rights Hearings* (1998); and Leidholdt's *The Sexual Liberals and the Attack on Feminism* (1990, co-authored with Janice G. Raymond).

6. Given how Angel "dies" when he is transformed into Angelus, the dream obviously contains an element of prophecy, a result of Buffy's slayer gift of prophetic dreams. However, as so often happens with prophecy, Buffy only sees the image of Drusilla killing Angel as a literal threat, rather than reading Drusilla as representative of Angel's past, as viewers recognize her to be. Further, Drusilla is a highly sexualized character in the series, adding another layer to the sexual implications of her positioning as Angel's executioner. Because Buffy does not correctly interpret the prophetic warning in the dream, viewers understand that she reads the portion of the dream questioning her readiness for sexual activity as a manifestation of her subconscious rather than a warning of Angel's forthcoming transformation.

7. While partner abuse is most often found in heterosexual couples with men as abusers and women as victims, as reflected by the pronoun choice in this example, such abuse also occurs with women abusing men and between same-sex romantic partners.

8. See Lewis Call's "Sounds Like Kinky Business to Me."

9. Gregory Stevenson argues that the problematic nature of Buffy and Spike's sexual relationship is clear in the visual images that accompany their first sexual encounter, namely the abandoned house they are in falling down around them as metaphor for Buffy's life imploding due to her inability to adjust to life post-resurrection (199). Likewise, Heinecken observes that this episode, "Smashed" (BtVS), "juxtaposes images of a building smashing ... around them as they make love ... suggesting the destructive nature of the relationship" (108).

10. As Heinecken notes, the attempted rape scene's construction is exceedingly complex and morally ambiguous: "It [the scene] is disturbing primarily because it is easy to see the assault from both sides. It is quite clear that his actions are bad — Spike himself recognizes the depth of his transgression and is guilt-ridden. But Spike's point of view is also poignantly apparent.... Moreover, given the context of their relationship all season, in which Buffy says no but means yes and in which fighting is foreplay, it is easy to believe, as Spike does, that she is simply denying her feelings ... politically it [the scene] walks a very thin line in dealing with a real social problem in that it urges the viewer to sympathize with the attacker's point of view" (117).

11. Frohard-Dourlent's essay in this collection is an expansion of the conference paper she originally presented on this topic.

12. Lewis Call, in a 2008 conference paper titled "Slaying the Heteronormative: Representations of Alternative Sexualities in *Buffy* Season Eight Comics," asserted that the genre

change to comic form allows the characters to exhibit more sexuality. Call's contribution to this volume is an extended version of that paper. Indeed, Buffy's ability to talk about sexuality seems to increase in Season Eight, with an image of a dream-fantasy wherein "Nurse Buffy" is trapped between the naked bodies of Angel and Spike and all three are chained together while surrounded by obviously Freudian metaphors for heterosexual intercourse (*The Long Way Home, Part Three*). Further, in *Anywhere But Here*, Buffy and Willow play a game of the same name, wherein they share fantasies of where else they would rather be. While the version of this game they play during their high school years is much tamer, both women's fantasies in *Anywhere But Here* clearly contain sexual elements.

13. In an interview concerning the (then forthcoming) first season of *Dollhouse*, Joss Whedon said, "I think people's sexuality is much more fluid and interesting than most of them admit" (qtd. in Jensen), a comment reflective of his oft-stated view of human sexuality as fluid rather than fixed.

14. The categorization of Anya and Spike's liaison as being about their own insecurities rather that sexual desire is illustrated when Anya says, "You know I'm only doing this 'cause I'm, I'm lonely and drunk and you smell really good" ("Entropy"). Spike's reply is to reinforce her candidness by saying, "See? Forthright," referring to earlier in the conversation when his chief complaint was his inability to determine what Buffy really wanted of him due to her inability to talk about her sexual desires in a direct manner. Both Anya and Spike want to escape the hurt they feel due to rejection by their previous romantic partners. Their encounter reflects that emotional state rather than being a reflection of sexual desire for one another. As such, an evaluation of this moment using the same standard as other sexual relationships in the Buffyverse creates an unfair comparison.

Works Cited

"Amends." *Buffy the Vampire Slayer.* Writer, Director Joss Whedon. 1998. 20th Century Fox, 2003. DVD.

"Anywhere But Here." Executive Producer and Script Joss Whedon. Pencils Cliff Richards. Inks Andy Owens. Colors Dave Stewart. Letters Richard Starkings and Comicraft's Jimmy. Milwaukie, OR: Dark Horse, Jan. 2008. Print. Vol. 10 of *Buffy the Vampire Slayer Season Eight.*

Burns, Angie. "Passion, Pain and 'Bad Kissing Decisions': Learning about Intimate Relationships from *Buffy* Season Six." *Slayage: The Online International Journal of Buffy Studies* 6.1 (2006): n. pag. Web. 5 Sept. 2009.

Burr, Vivien. "Ambiguity and Sexuality in *Buffy the Vampire Slayer:* A Sartrean Analysis." *Sexualities* 6.3–4 (2003): 343–360. Web. 8 Sept. 2009.

Call, Lewis. "Slaying the Heteronormative: Representations of Alternative Sexuality in *Buffy* Season Eight Comics." Southwest/Texas Popular Culture/American Culture Associations Annual Conference. Hyatt Regency, Albuquerque, NM. 28 Feb. 2009. Address.

_____. "'Sounds Like Kinky Business to Me': Textual and Subtextual Representations of Erotic Power in the Buffyverse." *Slayage: The Online International Journal of Buffy Studies* 6.4 (2007): n. pag. Web. 8 Sept. 2009.

"Chosen." *Buffy the Vampire Slayer.* Writer, Director Joss Whedon. 2003. 20th Century Fox, 2004. DVD.

Cocca, Carolyn. "'First Word "Jail," Second Word "Bait"': Adolescent Sexuality, Feminist Theories, and *Buffy the Vampire Slayer.*" *Slayage: The Online International Journal of Buffy Studies* 3.2 (2003): n. pag. Web. 8 Sept. 2009.

Comeford, AmiJo. "Cordelia Chase as Failed Feminist Gesture." *Buffy Meets the Academy: Essays on the Episodes and Scripts as Texts.* Ed. Kevin K. Durand. Jefferson, NC: McFarland, 2009. 150–160. Print.

"Consequences." *Buffy the Vampire Slayer.* Director Michael Gershman. Writer Marti Noxon. 1999. 20th Century Fox, 2003. DVD.

"Dead Things." *Buffy the Vampire Slayer.* Director James A. Contner. Writer Steven S. DeKnight. 2002. 20th Century Fox, 2004. DVD.

"Dirty Girls." *Buffy the Vampire Slayer.* Director Michael Gershman. Writer Jane Drew Goddard. 2003. 20th Century Fox, 2004. DVD.

Dodson, Betty. *Sex for One: The Joy of Self-Loving.* 1974 as *Liberating Masturbation.* New York: Three Rivers, 1996. Print.

Dworkin, Andrea. *Pornography—Men Possessing Women.* 1981. New York: Plume, 1991. Print.

"Entropy." *Buffy the Vampire Slayer.* Director James A. Contner. Writer Drew Z. Greenberg. 2002. 20th Century Fox, 2004. DVD.

"Expecting." *Angel.* Director David Semel. Writer Howard Gordon. 2000. 20th Century Fox, 2003. DVD.

"Faith, Hope, and Trick." *Buffy the Vampire Slayer.* Director James A. Contner. Writer David Greenwalt. 1998. 20th Century Fox, 2003. DVD.

"Five by Five." *Angel.* Director James A. Contner. Writer Jim Kouf. 2000. 20th Century Fox, 2003. DVD.

Francis, James, Jr. "'Selfless': Locating Female Identity in Anya/Anyanka Through Prostitution." The Slayage Conference on *Buffy the Vampire Slayer.* Renaissance Hotel, Nashville, TN. 29 May 2004. Address.

Frohard-Dourlent, Hélène. "'Tomorrow I'm Gonna Blush, Then I'm Gonna Smile ... But I'm Not Sure It Goes Any Further than That': Heteroflexibility and Buffy's Dabble Outside of Heterosexuality." Southwest/Texas Popular Culture/American Culture Associations Annual Conference. Hyatt Regency, Albuquerque, NM. 28 Feb. 2009. Address.

"Graduation Day, Part 1." *Buffy the Vampire Slayer.* Writer, Director Joss Whedon. 1999. 20th Century Fox, 2003. DVD.

"The Harsh Light of Day." *Buffy the Vampire Slayer.* Director James A. Contner. Writer Jane Espenson. 1999.20th Century Fox, 2004. DVD.

Heinecken, Dawn. *The Warrior Women of Television: A Feminist Cultural Analysis of the New Female Body in Popular Media.* New York: Peter Lang, 2003. Print.

Helford, Elyce Rae. "'My Emotions Give Me Power': The Containment of Girls' Anger in *Buffy.*" *Fighting the Forces: What's at Stake in* Buffy the Vampire Slayer. Ed. Rhonda V. Wilcox and David Lavery. New York: Rowman & Littlefield, 2002. 18–34. Print.

"Hell's Bells." *Buffy the Vampire Slayer.* Director David Solomon. Writer Rebecca Rand Kirshner. 2002. 20th Century Fox, 2004. DVD.

"Hush." *Buffy the Vampire Slayer.* Writer, Director Joss Whedon. 1999. 20th Century Fox, 2003. DVD.

"The Initiative." *Buffy the Vampire Slayer.* Director James A. Contner. Writer Douglas Petrie. 1999. 20th Century Fox, 2003. DVD.

"Innocence." *Buffy the Vampire Slayer*. Writer, Director Joss Whedon. 1998. 20th Century Fox, 2002. DVD.

"Into the Woods." *Buffy the Vampire Slayer*. *Buffy the Vampire Slayer*. Writer, Director Marti Noxon. 2000. 20th Century Fox, 2003. DVD.

Jensen, Michael. "Joss Whedon's 'Dollhouse' Has Room for the Gays ... Sort Of." *AfterElton.com*. N.p. 25 July 2008. Web. 15 Sept. 2009.

Jowett, Lorna. *Sex and the Slayer: A Gender Studies Primer for the Buffy Fan*. Middletown, CT: Wesleyan University Press, 2005. Print.

Kaveney, Roz. "'She Saved the World. A Lot.': An Introduction the Themes and Structures of *Buffy* and *Angel*." *Reading the Vampire Slayer*. 2d ed. Ed. Roz Kaveney. London: Tarius Parke, 2004. 1–82. Print.

"The Killer in Me." *Buffy the Vampire Slayer*. Director David Solomon. Writer Drew Z. Greenburg. 2003. 20th Century Fox, 2004. DVD.

Kimmel, Michael. *Michael Kimmel: On Gender: Mars, Venus or Planet Earth? Men and Women in a New Millennium*. Media Education Foundation, 2008. DVD.

Larbalestier, Justine. "The Only Thing Better Than Killing a Slayer: Heterosexuality and Sex in *Buffy the Vampire Slayer*." *Reading the Vampire Slayer*. 2d ed. Ed. Roz Kaveney. London: Tarius Parke, 2004. 195–219. Print.

Leidholdt, Dorchen, and Janice G. Raymond. *The Sexual Liberals and the Attack on Feminism*. Oxford: Pergamon, 1990. Print.

Levy, Ariel. *Female Chauvanist Pigs: Women and the Rise of Raunch Culture*. New York: Free Press, 2006. Print.

"The Long Way Home, Part Three." Executive Producer and Script Joss Whedon. Pencils Georges Jeanty. Inks Andy Owens. Colors Dave Stewart. Letters Richard Starkings and Comicraft's Jimmy. Milwaukie, OR: Dark Horse, May. 2007. Print. Vol. 3 of *Buffy the Vampire Slayer Season Eight*.

MacKinnon, Catharine A., and Andrea Dworkin, eds. *In Harm's Way: The Pornography Civil Rights Hearings*. Cambridge: Harvard University Press, 1998. Print.

Masson, Cynthea. "'Is that Just a Comforting Way of Not Answering the Question?': Willow, Questions, and Affective Response in *Buffy the Vampire Slayer*." *Slayage: The Online International Journal of Buffy Studies* 5.4 (2006): n. pag. Web. 19 Sept. 2009.

McAvan, Em. "'I Think I'm Kinda Gay': Willow Rosenberg and the Absent/Present Bisexual in *Buffy the Vampire Slayer*." *Slayage: The Online International Journal of Buffy Studies* 6.4 (2007): n. pag. Web. 19 Sept. 2009.

"A New Man." *Buffy the Vampire Slayer*. Director Michael Gershman. Writer Jane Espenson. 2000. 20th Century Fox, 2003. DVD.

"New Moon Rising." *Buffy the Vampire Slayer*. Director James A. Contner. Writer Marti Noxon. 2000. 20th Century Fox, 2003. DVD.

"No Future for You, Part One." Executive Producer Joss Whedon. Script Brian K. Vaughan. Pencils Georges Jeanty. Inks Andy Owens. Colors Dave Stewart. Letters Richard Starkings and Comicraft's Jimmy. Milwaukie, OR: Dark Horse, Sept. 2007. Print. Vol. 6 of *Buffy the Vampire Slayer Season Eight*.

"No Future for You, Part Three." Executive Producer Joss Whedon. Script Brian K. Vaughan. Pencils Georges Jeanty. Inks Andy Owens. Colors Dave Stewart. Letters Richard Starkings and Comicraft's Jimmy. Milwaukie, OR: Dark Horse, Nov. 2007. Print. Vol. 8 of *Buffy the Vampire Slayer Season Eight*.

"Older and Farther Away." *Buffy the Vampire Slayer*. Director Michael E. Gershman. Writer Drew Z. Greenberg. 2002. 20th Century Fox, 2004. DVD.

"Pangs." *Buffy the Vampire Slayer*. Director Michael Lang. Writer Jane Espenson. 1999. 20th Century Fox, 2003. DVD.

"Phases." *Buffy the Vampire Slayer*. Director Bruce Seth Green. Writer Rob Des Hotel and Dean Batali. 1998. 20th Century Fox, 2002. DVD.

Queen, Carol. *Real Live Nude Girl: Chronicles of Sex-Positive Culture*. San Francisco: Cleis, 1997. Print.

"The Replacement." *Buffy the Vampire Slayer*. Director James A. Contner. Writer Jane Espenson. 2000. 20th Century Fox, 2003. DVD.

Riess, Jana. *What Would Buffy Do?: The Vampire Slayer as Spiritual Guide*. San Francisco: Jossey-Bass, 2004. Print.

Rubin, Gayle. "Thinking Sex: Notes for a Radical Theory of the Politics of Sexuality." *Pleasure and Danger: Exploring Female Sexuality*. 1984. Ed. Carole S. Vance. New York: Harper Collins, 1993. 267–319. Print.

"Seeing Red." *Buffy the Vampire Slayer*. Director Michael Gershman. Writer Steven S. DeKnight. 2002. 20th Century Fox, 2004. DVD.

"Smashed." *Buffy the Vampire Slayer*. Director Turi Meyer. Writer Drew Z. Greenburg. 2001. 20th Century Fox, 2004. DVD.

Stevenson, Gregory. *Televised Morality: The Case of* Buffy the Vampire Slayer. New York: Hamilton, 2003. Print.

"Storyteller." *Buffy the Vampire Slayer*. Director Marita Grabiak. Writer Jane Espenson. 2003. 20th Century Fox, 2004. DVD.

"Surprise." *Buffy the Vampire Slayer*. Director Michael Lange. Writer Marti Noxon. 1998. 20th Century Fox, 2002. DVD.

Symonds, Gwyn. "'Solving Problems with Sharp Objects': Female Empowerment, Sex and Violence in *Buffy the Vampire Slayer*." *Slayage: The Online International Journal of Buffy Studies* 3.3–4 (2004): n. pag. Web. 5 Sept. 2009.

Tabron, Judith L. "Girl on Girl Politics: Willow/Tara and New Approaches to Media Fandom." *Slayage: The Online International Journal of Buffy Studies* 4.1–2 (2004): n. pag. Web. 19 Sept. 2009.

"Tabula Rasa." *Buffy the Vampire Slayer*. Director David Grossman. Writer Rebecca Rand Kirshner. 2001. 20th Century Fox, 2004. DVD.

Tjardes, Sue. "'If You're Not Enjoying It, You're Doing Something Wrong': Textual and Viewer Constructions of Faith, the Vampire Slayer." *Athena's Daughters: Television's New Women Warriors*. Ed. Frances Dearly and Kathleen Kennedy. Syracuse: Syracuse University Press, 2003. 66–77. Print.

"Tough Love." *Buffy the Vampire Slayer*. Director David Grossman. Writer Rebecca Rand Kirshner. 2001. 20th Century Fox, 2003. DVD.

"Triangle." *Buffy the Vampire Slayer*. Director Christopher Hibler. Writer Jane Espenson. 2001. 20th Century Fox, 2003. DVD.

"Where the Wild Things Are." *Buffy the Vampire Slayer*. Director David Solomon. Writer Tracey Forbes. 2000. 20th Century Fox, 2003. DVD.

"Who Are You?" *Buffy the Vampire Slayer*. Director and Writer Joss Whedon. 2000. 20th Century Fox, 2003. DVD.

"Wolves at the Gate, Part One." Executive Producer Joss Whedon. Script Drew Goddard.

Pencils Georges Jeanty. Inks Andy Owens. Colors Michelle Madsen. Letters Richard Starkings and Comicraft's Jimmy. Milwaukie, OR: Dark Horse, Mar. 2008. Print. Vol. 12 of *Buffy the Vampire Slayer Season Eight.*
"Wolves at the Gate, Part Two." Executive Producer Joss Whedon. Script Drew Goddard. Pencils Georges Jeanty. Inks Andy Owens. Colors Michelle Madsen. Letters Richard Starkings and Comicraft's Jimmy. Milwaukie, OR: Dark Horse, Apr. 2008. Print. Vol. 13 of *Buffy the Vampire Slayer Season Eight.*
"The Zeppo." *Buffy the Vampire Slayer.* Director James Whitmore Jr. Writer Dan Vebber. 1999. 20th Century Fox, 2003. DVD.

Images of Paraphilia in the Whedonverse

DON TRESCA

Introduction

The universe of Joss Whedon is one remarkably similar to our own. The cities of the world are all still present and at the exact same spots on the map. The same movie stars and politicians exist at the same level of popularity. Barack Obama is still the President, as Echo tells us in "Omega" (*Dollhouse*). But there is another darker level to the Whedonverse — a universe of black magic and sinister science, of cannibalistic humans and soul-devouring demons, of evil mind-controlling corporations and corrupted governments making secret pacts with the forces of darkness. Both God and Satan have abandoned this place, replaced by the Powers That Be and the Senior Partners, neither of which, most of the time, seem to have the best interests of humanity on their minds. While the vast majority of people remain ignorant of the evil monsters in their midst, there are heroes among them, individuals who battle for power and control, who struggle against the tide, threatening to overwhelm the universe. But even these heroes are tainted by the darkness, and nowhere is this infection more apparent than in one of the basic of human needs: sex. Sex in the Whedonverse has become transgressive and perverted, not just by the corruption of the universe but by the constant war for dominance and power. Normative sexuality is not an option; the fabric of the Whedonverse rejects it, destroys it, frequently before it even has a chance to blossom. The only way to sustain a sexual relationship in the Whedonverse is to kink it, and even that is no guarantee.

The technical term for a perverted, transgressive sexual practice is *paraphilia*. The standard definition of paraphilia is "sexual arousal in response to objects or situations not part of normal arousal activity patterns" (Aggrawal 10), and an activity in which the paraphile's personal sexual pleasure is paramount. The partner's sexual pleasure is of no concern to the paraphile, and any pleasure the partner does derive from the act may be counter to the paraphile's desire (Benvenudo 61–62). Many psychologists disagree on what mental condition causes people to engage in paraphiliac activities. Most see it as a manifestation of narcissistic personality disorder (Halberstadt 15) or as a method of escaping the emotional trauma of rejection (Cantor, et al. 538) by denying the ability of the partner to reject, either by making the partner an unwilling victim (sexual sadism), a subordinate victim (pedophilia), or a victim unable to deny consent (necrophilia, zoophilia). Within the Whedonverse, numerous characters participate (to varying degrees) in these paraphiliac activities. Although there are well over 500 known paraphilias, I will examine the manifestation of only a few of them within the Whedonverse and will conclude with an examination of a few sexual practices which, while not technically paraphilias, are still considered by many to be sexually taboo.

Pedophilia/Ephebophilia/Incest

One of the most insidious of the paraphilias, pedophilia, is the sexual desire for children, in particular prepubescent children typically under the age of twelve. Although pedophilia is used generically by most people to refer to any individual with sexual desire for anyone under the age of consent (18), the technical term for the paraphilia of sexual desires for adolescents and teenagers is Ephebophilia. Although, due to television standards and public moral values, the issue of true pedophilia is not frequently addressed in the Whedonverse (although there are exceptions as detailed below), ephebophilia is not only openly discussed, but becomes a major plot point in one of the most significant storylines in the Whedonverse, the relationship between Angel and Buffy. The issue of incest, on the other hand, is particularly difficult to address since incest is not, technically, a paraphilia (because incest can be practiced by two consenting adults). Many psychologists choose to lump incest in with pedophilia frequently since many cases of pedophilia do involve child sexual abuse at the hands of family members (Aggrawal 319).

Although there are no real instances of pedophilia imagery or language in Buffy, ephebophilia is addressed rather frequently, especially in relation to the Angel/Buffy relationship. Although the show seems at times to condone this particular paraphilia, a detailed reading of ephebophilia within *Buffy* suggests the opposite. As early as "Teacher's Pet," the viewers are shown the dangers of adults who sexually prey on young teenagers. Natalie French (in "Teacher's Pet"), Malcolm/Moloch (in "I Robot, You Jane"), and the college frat boys (in "Reptile Boy") are all shown as sexual predators, victimizing underage teenagers for their own nefarious purposes. In each case, one of the Scooby Gang falls into the predator's snare despite the efforts of their friend to warn them away from the potentially dangerous situation. These teens see sexual and emotional intimacy as a doorway to adulthood, a means of gaining personal power (Montgomery 158), but soon discover that they have been tricked and manipulated by ephebophiliac adults into making rash decisions (Cocca 33) that nearly cost them their innocence and their lives.

Despite the somewhat creepy ephebophiliac undertones, the early relationship of Angel and Buffy is largely couched in romantic terms. The show takes great steps to demonstrate that Buffy is a willing participant in the romantic encounters and that Angel is portrayed as loving and caring. Time is taken to establish the relationship, showing that, despite the age difference between the two of them, Buffy is clearly not being victimized and that Angel is a figure worthy of Buffy's love, not just a sexual predator attempting to curry sexual favors from an underage girl. All of this changes, however, after the first time they have sex (in "Innocence"). Angel transforms from the "Prince Charming catering to a young girl's fantasies" (Jowett, *Sex* 154) to Angelus, the dangerous older boyfriend. Angelus' actions become more aligned with the stereotypical ephebophile sexual degenerate. He no longer couches the meaning behind their sexual encounter in romantic terms, instead reducing it to a conquest, altering Buffy from a unique individual with whom he was in love to just a body with whom he had sex (Yong 13). The storyline is reconstructed from a grand romantic love story to "a standard cautionary tale directed at young women regarding the dangers of sleeping with the wrong sort of man" (Yong 24).

Likewise, in early Season Two, Spike's interactions with the (at the time) underage Buffy are highly sexually charged (foreshadowing their future sexual relationship). He refers to her with a variety of pet names, the kinds usually restricted for lovers ("pet," "love," "cutie"), and many of the fight scenes between the two take on a sexual flavor (as in "School Hard"). He even voyeuristically spies on her, videotaping her fights with other vampires. Given what we learn about Spike's predilection for sadomasochistic sexual encounters, it is not hard to see these fight videotapes he makes of Buffy as a form of pornography.

Despite all of the dangers each of the Scooby Gang has faced confronting these sexual predators, as they become adults themselves, they find that they are succumbing to the same urges. This appears to be a metaphor for the tendency of victims of sexual predators to become sexual predators later in life.

The main difference here is that the heroes maintain their desires as fantasies (unless magically manipulated), but it is still somewhat disturbing that many of these scenes are played for laughs rather than as the seriously dangerous scenarios they have the potential of becoming. In "Him," both Xander and Willow become sexually aroused by watching a teenage girl dancing provocatively on the dance floor at the Bronze (Xander even stresses his adult status in relation to the girl by commenting, "Daddy like"). The humor of the scene comes from the reactions of the characters (particularly Xander) at the discovery that the young girl they have been ogling at is, in fact, Buffy's sister, Dawn. Later, in the same episode, Buffy, Willow, and Anya all find themselves (due to the influence of a magically enchanted letterman's jacket) sexually attracted to R.J., a teenage boy at Dawn's school, where Buffy works as a guidance counselor. The lengths to which the three of them go to "prove" their devotion to R.J. provide many of the episode's laughs (although the humor is somewhat undercut by the near tragedy of Dawn's suicide attempt because she too is in love with R.J. and does not believe she can compete with Buffy for his affections). In a later humorous scene in the episode "Dirty Girls," Xander has a highly erotic dream about some of the Potentials. The scene demonstrates the depth of Xander's ephebophiliac desires for the girls. He imagines them in a variety of sexual scenarios, including same-sex couplings. However, the scene ends with Xander waking to the messy, noisy real world where he must deal with the ugly reality of a clogged toilet and a teenage girl wracked with stomach flu. By contrast, the darkest and most horrifying image of ephebophilia within the Scooby Gang itself occurs in "Two to Go" when Willow, twisted by grief and dark magic, engages in a sexual come-on to Dawn, the girl to whom she was a de-facto parent (along with Tara) after Joyce and Buffy's death. This scene shows the ultimate true evil of the sexual predator, that even those people who we trust the most can become monsters when overcome by their sexual excesses.

Pedophilia imagery appears with more frequency in the more "adult" worlds of *Angel* and *Dollhouse*. The first true pedophile character within the Whedonverse is Marcus, the torture vampire from "In the Dark" (*Angel*), whom Spike describes as "liking kids, to eat ... and other nasty things." Marcus represents a true monster, a sexual predator that can appear anywhere and anytime (when Marcus gains the Gem of Amara, he becomes indestructible and gains the ability to walk in the sunlight — suggesting that, unidentified, pedophiles are essentially unstoppable, which makes them deeply dangerous). However, once the pedophile is exposed, his power is removed, and the threat he represents can be nullified (as Angel does by taking the Gem of Amara back and killing Marcus). Marcus, as a vampire, represents the sexual perversity of pedophilia run amok. Other vampires within the *Angel* storyline share this perversity, although in much more metaphoric terms. Both of the major female vampires, Darla and Drusilla, are presented as focusing, at different times, on primarily child victims (Darla in "Offspring" and Drusilla in "Destiny"). Again, this demonstrates the deep corruption of the pedophiliac desire. Women, as mother figures, are deemed the ones most suitable for protecting children, yet the female vampires are the ones that primarily choose child victims. It is also Darla who attempts to corrupt Angel back to his evil ways by offering him an infant (in "Darla") to feed off of (a metaphorical sexual penetration). Unlike Darla, Angel refuses and runs off with the child to protect it from Darla's sexual appetites. Darla even plays off the image of pedophilia when luring victims. Her Catholic schoolgirl dress (in "Welcome to the Hellmouth," *Buffy*) is designed to highlight her feigned innocence and inexperience and "transform" her into a child to better seduce and then ambush sexually deviant men. Drusilla is also coded as very child-like with her baby doll dresses and her penchant for playing with dolls. Unlike Darla's schoolgirl persona, which is largely affected (and becomes quickly abandoned after her "resurrection" in "To Shanshu in L.A." (*Angel*) since, as Spike tells Faith, "schoolgirls are old hat" ("Dirty Girls," *Buffy*), Drusilla's childlike demeanor is largely as a result of her very underdeveloped maturity level at the time that Angelus sired her (in "Lie to Me," *Buffy*). Clearly, the connection between childhood/adolescence, vampirism, and sexuality for the two female vampires are very close indeed.

One of the strongest uses of pedophilia as metaphor for corruption occurs in "Smile Time" (*Angel*). As the child sits in front of the television during the teaser, one of the puppets addresses him directly from the screen once he is alone. The puppet tells him that he knows what to do and that "Smile Time" isn't free. The puppet's tone becomes insistent and demanding: "Now get over here and touch it." The little boy walks over and places his hands on the television. The puppet immediately begins to moan and tells the boy, "That's it, Tommy. Touch it. That's it … oh, yeah. Good boy, Tommy." The boy collapses unconscious, and the puppet resumes its normal behavior. The metaphor for sexual abuse at the hands of a seemingly innocent and trusted figure is clearly conveyed here. It is a deeply disturbing beginning to an otherwise humorous episode (Abbott 7–8).

Pedophilia in the world of *Angel* is seen as so corrupting in fact that the mere allegation of the paraphilia can be used to destroy someone's reputation (something that is just as true in the real world as it is in the Whedonverse).

In "Power Play," the evil Senator Drucker wishes to partake of Wolfram and Hart's services to discredit her political rival in an upcoming election through the planting of false stories (and, perhaps, false evidence) that he is a pedophile. The fact that he is not a pedophile is immaterial as long as people "believe that he is." The power of belief to influence and corrupt thoughts relating to such sexual deviancy is so strong that it outweighs even the truth.

In *Dollhouse*, the few references to pedophiles represent the corruption of the society as a whole. In "Ghost," Echo discovers that the kidnapped little girl whose release she has been assigned to negotiate has been taken by the same man who abducted the woman whose memories Echo has when she was a child. The man, called the Ghost, was a pedophile that molested and tortured the girl for weeks before she was able to escape. Although Echo is called off of the case due to her personality breakdown at realizing who the kidnapper is, she refuses to allow the Ghost to do to this little girl what was done to her. This episode represents a classic power play between the pedophile and his victim. Pedophiles typically focus on children because they are easy to dominate and manipulate; the pedophile has power over the child simply by virtue of his status as an adult figure. Echo, in this episode, realizes that she must remove that power by challenging the pedophile that victimized her (or the woman whose personality she has been downloaded with). Such an action threatens her, by going "off mission," she may face severe consequences, but as Whedon would say, the ability to challenge the power of the monsters of the world and defeat them is worth any risk.

The incest taboo, sexual relations between family members, is considered by many psychologists as a subset of pedophilia (Aggrawal 319) mainly due to the fact that many victims of incest are children being sexually abused by adult family members (such as a parent or uncle/aunt). The primary example of this type of incestuous relationship is one between Bethany Chalk and her father as detailed in "Untouched" (*Angel*). This episode focuses almost exclusively on the adult trauma of survivors of childhood sexual abuse and incest. Bethany exhibits many of the classic signs of this disorder (as related by Gobert 16–33), such as letting her emotions (particularly fear) get so out of control that she smashes two would-be rapists into an alley wall with a garbage dumpster and then drives a metal rebar through Angel when he is trying to help her and taking no aggressive actions against her; sexual dysfunction (attempting to relate to Angel on a sexual level rather than an emotional or intellectual one), and compulsive social interactions (in which the victim will be so starved for proper and positive emotional attention that she will cling to any person who gives her even the smallest amount of good will and attention, allowing her to be easily manipulated by those individuals like Lilah who do not have her best interest truly at heart, only their own selfish motivations). As Cordelia tells Wesley, when it comes to childhood incest, "There's not enough yuck in the world" (in "Untouched").

Necrophilia

One of the most disturbing paraphilias, necrophilia (sexual attraction to the dead) is also one of the least understood. Due to the nature of the condition, very few necrophiles willingly admit they suffer from it. Also, since its victims are in no condition to report the abuse, it often goes unnoticed and undiagnosed. Rosman and Resnick developed an empirical model to get a deeper understanding of the psychological events that could lead to necrophilia. According to their research, necrophilia typically develops in an individual with poor self-esteem, perhaps due in part to a significant loss. Frequently, the necrophile is fearful of the dead and transforms that fear (by means of reaction formation) into an erotic desire for the dead (161).

Necrophilia in the Whedonverse differs sharply from the condition as it exists in the real world. The dead in the Whedonverse are not inanimate corpses but walking and talking individuals capable of complete interaction with the living. Ironically, as Aggrawal states, although necrophilia is frequently associated with vampirism in the literature, a necrophile can be seen as the very opposite of the vampire. While the vampire is generally a dead person disturbing the living, a necrophile is a living person disturbing the dead (294). Even those individuals permanently dead (as opposed to animated undead) can still communicate to the living either as ghosts (Joyce in "Bring on the Night," *Buffy* or Darla in "Inside Out," *Angel*) or through conduits such as mediums (in "Hell Bound," *Angel*) or the First Evil (in "Amends," *Buffy* and throughout Buffy Season Seven — however, the contact to the dead via the First is a bit more problematic since it is actually the First being communicated with through the image, memories, and personality of the deceased). Therefore, necrophilia in the Whedonverse is more likely to be consensual. An argument could even be made that certain types of necrophilia in the Whedonverse would not be classified as paraphilic because it would not match the accepted definition due to its consensual and mutual enjoyment natures.

The most prevalent necrophile in the Whedonverse is Buffy herself. As Spike tells her, she is "in love with death" ("Fool for Love"). In the course of seven seasons, Buffy has had two dead lovers, Angel and Spike. Her status as the Slayer guarantees her a life of seeming solitude. Although she has her watcher and her friends, any boy with whom she has a romantic relationship would be placed in incredible danger and a target for quick death (which Owen Thurman almost finds out firsthand in "Never Kill a Boy on the First Date"). After the failure of her relationship with Owen, Buffy begins a relationship with Angel. Even after she finds out he is a vampire in "Angel," she continues the relationship with him. Through him, she displaces a great deal of her fear and hatred of the undead into a romantic desire. However, the corruption inherent in her necrophiliac desire comes to a head in "Innocence" when she and Angel consummate their relationship, and he goes from being a romantic hero to an evil monster. Buffy then pays the price for her perverted desire through the death of Jenny Calendar, the torture of Giles, and the near destruction of the world via Acathla by Angelus. In the end, she is forced to destroy the object of her desire for the greater good — the ultimate cost for her perversion.

In Season Three, Angel returns from the Hell dimension Buffy sent him to at the end of the previous season, and they begin their relationship anew, but Angel himself comes to realize that he and Buffy have no future together due to their unnatural love. Buffy denies her desires for a time and begins a romance with a "normal" man, Riley Finn. However, as with many individuals with paraphilias, she cannot long control her deviant sexual urges (Malin and Saleh 26) and finds herself drifting away from Riley emotionally. As Spike tells Riley, Buffy "needs some monster in her man" ("Into the Woods"). Eventually, Riley realizes that she will never love him the way he wants her to, and he leaves Sunnydale behind.

During Season Six, Buffy finds herself back in the world after sacrificing herself to save the world from Glory. She believes she came back to life (resurrected due to the spell cast by Willow, Tara, Xander, and Anya) "wrong" ("Dead Things"). Her loss of the peace and tranquility of Heaven drives her into the arms of Spike, another vampire, in an effort to "feel" ("Once More with Feeling"). Buffy, however, does not begin her sexual relationship with Spike until "Smashed" when she discovers that the chip that prevents him from harming humans no longer works for her. This now means that in the heat of their violent sex, they are both easy to kill, each knowing the "little death" of orgasm can, at any moment, change from metaphor to reality, and the fact that the sex is so violent simulates this (Crusie 92). Buffy's erotic desire for death (here symbolized by her desire for the undead Spike) moves from sub-textual conjecture to textual reality (Kromer 13). Like many paraphiles who feel isolated from the world around them (Benvenudo 63), Buffy states many times throughout the series how she is ultimately alone, even when surrounded by friends and allies, in her duties as a Slayer. As in her relationship with Angel, her necrophiliac desires corrupt here as well, leading to violent sadomasochistic sex, fractionalization of the close-knit ties between the Scooby Gang, and the attempted rape of Buffy by Spike. However, unlike the earlier vampire relationship, here a good outcome does emerge: Spike is so horrified at his rape attempt and so enamored with Buffy that he journeys around the world to obtain his soul and become the true champion that Buffy deserves.

The members of the Sunset Club in "Lie to Me" can also be coded as necrophiles. Although Ford has very specific reasons why he wants to be turned into a vampire (he suffers from a fatal brain tumor), the rest of the Sunset Club (exemplified primarily by Chanterelle and Diego) have a highly exaggerated notion of vampires as tragic Romantic heroes,[1] an image the show both disavows (through its portrayal of vampires as soulless monsters) and strangely endorses (through romanticized portrayals of vampires such as Angel, Spike, and James from "Heartthrob," *Angel*). Angel, attempting to talk the Sunset Club members out of their idealized notions of vampirism, is ironic since he himself represents the very notion of the vampire they aspire to be. Angel knows, however, that his situation is unique (at the time). The Sunset Club members are undeterred though, having been educated on the notions of vampires in Anne Rice novels (an image Whedon ridicules in episodes such as "School Hard" (*Buffy*) and "Origin" (*Angel*). It is only when they are confronted with the true nature of vampiric evil (represented by Spike and Drusilla) that the Sunset Club members' romanticized idealisms are shattered.

Like Buffy, Cordelia also suffers from low self-esteem due to loss, a clear sign of necrophiliac tendencies. At the start of *Angel*, Cordelia has lost nearly everything: her wealth, her social status, her loyal circle of friends. She comes to Los Angeles to get work as an actress but finds that, while her beauty made her a "queen" in Sunnydale, in Los Angeles, she is only one of a multitude of beautiful young women trying to break into the acting business, and she suffers from a severe lack of acting talent. Angel is the first familiar, friendly face she sees in the crowd, and, after he saves her life (in "City of") from the vampire Russell Winters (whose opposing name to Summers shows just how far Angel and Cordelia have gone from the world of teenage Sunnydale to adult Los Angeles), she agrees to join his cause to protect the innocent from the forces of darkness in the big city. Although their relationship begins platonically, it is not long before Cordelia and Angel begin to realize they have romantic feelings for one another. Cordelia is even allowed the opportunity in "Birthday" to become part-demon which, as a consequence, removes some of the paraphiliac barrier between the two of them. Cordelia continues to live in denial of her own desires and begins a relationship with an Angel substitute, Groosalug, who, like Angel, is a handsome champion for good. She even gives Groosalug some of Angel's clothes to wear, enhancing the similarity between the two. Groosalug soon realizes Cordelia's true feelings for Angel and leaves. With the path finally clear for their relationship, Cordelia makes a move and invites Angel to a secret, romantic rendezvous. However, as always occurs in the Whedonverse, the natural order of things seems to abhor romantic desire of any type and conspires at that moment to deny Angel and Cordelia their chance at love, almost as if nature (or the divine itself—in the form of the Powers That Be) balk at the inherent corruption of the love between a living woman and a vampire. Cordelia is immediately ascended into a higher plane to take her place among the higher beings while Angel (as if to insure that the two characters are kept as far away from each other as possible) is sunk into the deep sea by the betrayal of his son, Connor, in "Tomorrow."

Zoophilia

Zoophilia is defined as the sexual attraction of a human being for an animal. The specific type of animal varies based on the individual zoophile, with some being attracted to animals in general and some only to a specific type or breed of animal. For many zoophiles, their particular "perversion" is a lifestyle choice, not a sexual deviancy, equating it commonly to homosexuality. Many consider themselves to be in loving relationships with their animal "partners," and consider those whose sexual activities with animals are harmful or deadly to the animal (such as humans having sex with smaller animals or violently raping or abusing animals during sex) as practitioners of "bestiality," a violent form of sexual abuse which is differentiated from zoophilia (Melloy 13). Many psychologists and animal health experts disagree, however, arguing that, unlike homosexuality which involves two adult consenting partners who are involved equally in the relationship, zoophilia is more fundamentally aligned with pedophilia, in which the two partners are "unequal" with one partner (the paraphile) dominant over the other (Melloy 14). Criminologist Piers Bierne takes this comparison a step further, arguing that sexual contact with domesticated animals is inherently abusive because those creatures, like children, are "completely dependent on us for food, for water, for shelter, and for affection" (as quoted in Melloy 16).

Like necrophilia, zoophilia in the Whedonverse is different from zoophilia in the "real world." The "animals" with which the humans in the shows have sexual contact are not true animals (they are most typically werewolves (humans with animal-like characteristics that have the ability to transform into animals during certain times of the month — the nights before, during, and after a full moon); therefore, they have the ability to consent or deny sexual contact just as easily as a regular human (at least when they are in their human form). True zoophilia would be incredibly difficult to either show (or even suggest) on network television (or in a theatrical film — movies like *Clerks 2* notwithstanding). Therefore, almost more than any other paraphilia, the image of zoophilia in the Whedonverse is couched in metaphoric value.

The werewolf, in legend, literature, and film, is primarily viewed as a metaphor for the dark animalistic nature of sexual desire, that which gets first awakened in the human mind during puberty; therefore, the transformation of the body from human to wolf mirrors the transformation the body undergoes during puberty (voice deepens, hair growth, etc.). In the Whedonverse, there are three primary werewolf characters: Oz, Veruca, and Nina. Although each of them only fully transforms into the "wolf" three nights a month (which, in another connection to sexual maturity, correlates to the human menstrual cycle — as Willow alludes in "Phases"), which seems to suggest the dominance of their human side, Veruca tells Oz, "You're a wolf all the time, and this human face is just your disguise ("Wild at Heart"). Therefore, if the werewolf is a wolf all the time (an idea which is also suggested by Oz's ability to use his enhanced animal senses even during times when he is human, as in "Lovers Walk" and "New Moon Rising," when Willow (for Oz) and Angel (for Nina) make love to the werewolf character, they are engaging very much in a form of zoophilia. However, the true nature of zoophiliac desire is best symbolized in the character of Veruca. Veruca is able to use her natural "animal magnetism" to seemingly mesmerize not only Oz, a fellow wolf, but also normal humans like Xander and Giles. This seems to suggest that zoophilia is a "natural" impulse that draws in humans due to the influence of the animal; however, the viewers soon discover that Veruca's clear target for her seductive influence is Oz alone, and the humans, although enamored by her, are not irresistibly drawn to her sexually. But the fact that they are able to be drawn into her seductive influence suggests a bit of zoophilia in every man (an inherent nature of the sexual corruptness in the Whedonverse).

There are a few references to more literal and traditional, interpretations of the zoophile within the Whedonverse. Vamp Willow, in both "The Wish" and "Dopplegangland," shows definite signs of suffering from what Aggrawal calls Class I Zoophilia, which he defines as human/animal role-playing, a frequent component of BDSM, in which the submissive partner is reduced to animal status as a symbol of the other partner's authority and dominance (265). Frequently referred to among BDSM aficionados as "puppy play" or "pony play," Vamp Willow refers to this zoophiliac activity when she tortures Angel in "The Wish," referring to him as the "puppy." Later, in "Dopplegangland," she wistfully reminisces about her home dimension where there are "humans in chains that we ride like ponies." "Apocalypse Nowish" (*Angel*) includes a brief and comical scene with a zoophiliac element when Lorne, talking with a potential client on the phone about the snakes the individual has coming out of a bodily orifice (which orifice is never made clear), asks if the snakes "got up there themselves, or is this a thing?" He quickly makes clear to the person that he is "not judging" (since such bizarre sexual transgressions are a natural part of the Whedonverse).

The final incidence of zoophilia I wish to explore is a little less obvious than the others at first glance. In "The Target" (*Dollhouse*), Echo is assigned to act as the girlfriend of Richard, a nature-lover who regales her with his stories of hunting and living off the land. After he has made love to her, he immediately grows cold and distant (shades of Angel's transformation to Angelus after sex with Buffy in "Innocence," *Buffy*) and announces he is going to use her as his prey in his hunt. Anna Pickard, in her analysis of this episode, states that, while the reasons why Richard wants to hunt human quarry are not fully explained, there is definitely "a sense of arousal about the possibility of hunting the ultimate prey" which she likens to "the man secretly lusting after boning a stag," but she understands "why they might not want to expand upon that concept" (Pickard 5). However, while the writers do not expand upon the idea of Richard being a zoophile who transfers his sexual aggression onto Echo in the episode, the fact that the subtext is there to be explored offers the transgressive interpretation.

BDSM

In the Whedonverse, the forces of both good and evil are seen as taking equally aggressive and dominant stances in their neverending war. In fact, good, in the traditions of heroic storytelling, always triumphs over evil in the end, establishing good's dominance on the battlefield. However, in the sexual arena, things are a bit more complicated. Within the realm of BDSM (Bondage/Domination/Sadism/Masochism), evil tends to take the role of the sadistic, dominant force while good is relegated to the submissive position. However, as the Whedonverse develops into a more complex system, the roles of good and evil in the BDSM matrix become far less distinct.

In the early seasons of *Buffy*, BDSM was the exclusive purview of evil, in particular the vampires. Initially, the vampires were seen as almost purely masochistic. Darla's comment in "Angel" (*Buffy*) to Angel that, "You're hurting me. That's good, too" was the first ever indication of any kind of sadomasochistic desire in the series. It was quickly followed, in the same episode, by Angel's smile after he kisses Buffy despite the fact that her cross has burned a scar into his chest. Both of these scenes indicate not only can vampires tolerate a great deal of pain, but they seem to enjoy it as well. Darla continued as a masochistic character throughout her subsequent appearances on *Angel*.[2] She tells Angel that he's "hurting me. I like it" (in "Dear Boy"). However, even her masochism has limits, as indicated in "Quickening." When Darla complains about her labor pains, Angel tells her, "You like pain," to which she responds, "Not like this."

The enjoyment of pain, as well as an equal enjoyment of the infliction of pain, is developed further in *Buffy* Season Two with the introduction of Spike and Drusilla. In "School Hard," Giles informs the Scoobies that Spike is also known as William the Bloody, and that he took great pleasure in torturing victims with his preferred instruments, railroad spikes, through which he received his nickname. Drusilla's desires, however, run more toward the masochistic side (although she does sadistically torture Angel in "What's My Line, Part 2"). Drusilla taunts Angel in "Lie to Me" by reminding him of how he used to "hurt" her. Spike speaks of Drusilla's masochistic side in "Lovers Walk" when he tells Buffy and Angel that he is going to torture Drusilla "until she likes me again." In "Reunion" (*Angel*), when Angel discovers Drusilla and Darla in Holland Manners' wine cellar with the Wolfram and Hart lawyers, Drusilla hisses at him and does her erotic dance, holding her arms above her head as if handcuffed, purring, "Spank us til Tuesday. We promise to be bad if you do."

Although he is coded as a hero in both series, Angel has not always been so, as Buffy learns through the Watcher's Journals and straight from Angel himself: "For a hundred years I offered an ugly death to everyone I met. And I did it with a song in my heart" ("Angel"). He further admits to Buffy that it was he who sired Drusilla, but not before he drove her insane with "every mental torture ... I could devise" ("Lie to Me"). Later, after Angel's transformation into Angelus, Buffy gets to experience those mental tortures firsthand, as well as learning of the graphic physical torture Angelus is capable of inflicting in the name of passion, everything from murdering Willow's goldfish, to snapping Jenny Calendar's neck (in "Passion"), to his brutalizing of Giles to gain the secret of releasing Acathla (in "Becoming, Part 2"). Although

Angelus is clearly a sadist, he does have the occasional bout of masochism as well, as when he tells Faith in "Release" (*Angel*), "That hurt, baby, and I liked it!"

The only other character more horrifying in her use of sadistic torture than Angelus is Faith, and only because she is both a human with a soul and a Slayer. When the Scoobies first meet Faith, they learn how the violence of slaying vampires awakens Faith's baser appetites, "Isn't it crazy how slaying just makes you hungry and horny?" ("Faith, Hope & Trick"). Later, as she journeys closer towards evil, her sexuality grows darker and more sadistic. In "Consequences," when Xander comes to her to offer help in dealing with the murder of the deputy mayor, Faith attacks him, making sexually suggestive statements and choking him. Fortunately, he is rescued by Angel. When Angel later questions her about the incident, Faith claims it was consensual, to which Angel responds that Xander must have forgotten the safety word (indicating Angel's knowledge of the language of the BDSM culture). Faith's response ("Safety words are for wimps") indicates her break with the ethics of BDSM (as well as the ethics of the Whedonverse as a whole). Like Angelus and Spike before her, Faith's interest is in sadism for her own sexual satisfaction and with no concern for the welfare or enjoyment of her partner. The ethics of the Whedonverse condones consensual sadomasochism as a viable sexual choice but actively condemns sadism by restricting its use to only the most evil of characters. Ironically, the three characters most known for their sadism (Angelus, Spike, Faith) are each ultimately redeemed. After redemption, both Spike (with Buffy throughout Season Six) and Faith (as evidence of her conversation with Spike in "Dirty Girls") reaffirm the ethics of consensual sadomasochistic sexual practice over pure sexual sadism.[3]

Prior to her redemption, however, Faith gets one final opportunity to exercise her sadistic impulses by completing what she began with Xander through the brutal torture of Wesley in "Five by Five" (*Angel*). By the end of this episode though, we learn that Faith's motivation for her sadism has been drastically altered. Instead of an act of sexual self-pleasure, this sadism is seen as a cry for help, a desperate ploy to do something so unspeakable that Angel will kill her. This continues the path of self-loathing that began in "Who Are You?" Angel refuses to kill her, however, choosing instead to lead her to the path of redemption.

Starting in Season Four of *Buffy*, we begin to see the signs of BDSM infiltrating the forces of good as well. The first couple to acknowledge such behaviors is Xander and Anya who admit to spanking (in "The I in Team") during sex. Also, in "Hush," after witnessing Xander beating on Spike for mistakenly believing he had fed off of Anya, Anya gets so sexually excited by it that she immediately propositions Xander with a crude hand gesture much to the consternation of everyone else present. During their last sexual encounter prior to the final battle with the First, both Xander and Anya lament that Buffy has removed Spike's chains from the basement walls (in "Storyteller").

The penchant for BDSM among the heroes soon spreads to the others as well. While Riley rejects Faith's offer (while she is in Buffy's body) for BDSM sex in "Who Are You," Buffy off-handedly states that she is going to "punish" Riley for eating a Twinkie with his lunch in "The I in Team" to which Willow laments that "Everyone is getting spanked but me," evidence of her own desire for BDSM sex, a desire suggested by its manifestation in her alternative self, Vamp Willow, in "The Wish" and "Dopplegangland." Willow does eventually achieve this desire herself, however, but not until after she devolves into her evil self at which point she admits to "getting wood" from the violence she perpetrates against Warren, Andrew, and Jonathan in "Two to Go."

The ultimate expression of BDSM sexuality in *Buffy* comes from the Buffy/Spike relationship. While Buffy initially rejects Spike's romantic advances, she does admit some of her actions may lead him on, "I do beat him up a lot. For Spike, that's like third base" ("Crush"). After Spike discovers in "Smashed" that he can harm Buffy without activating his chip, he confronts her, leading to a fight which culminates in sex so violent they literally knock a building down. Dawn Heinecken states that it is significant that Buffy and Spike do not begin a sexual relationship until after the discovery that he can harm her, which "implies that, in order to be sexually viable, men need to be violent and able to dominate their women" (22). Buffy and Spike's sexual acts become more transgressive and tied to BDSM. Spike tells Buffy that she makes it "hurt in all the wrong places" (in "Dead Things") and that the two of them have done things together that "I can't even spell" (in "End of Days"). Buffy, for her part, "likes men that hurt" her (in "Never Leave Me") and can never seem to escape the "sexual violence" (in "Conversations with Dead People") inherent in her relationships. Her sudden desire for Spike and their increasingly violent sex worries Buffy to the point where she seeks help from Tara in "Dead Things" to determine if she "came back wrong" after being resurrected from death in "Bargaining, Part 1." When Tara assures her that there is nothing wrong with her, Buffy breaks down since she now knows the truth, that she has entered this relationship of her own free will (in a desperate effort to "feel" something, as stated in "Once More with Feeling") and that she is truly an individual capable of these perverted sexual feelings (Symonds 20). Her decision thereafter to deny herself these desires and return to a "normal" existence leads to dire consequences: Spike's attempted rape of Buffy (in a desperate attempt to get her to acknowledge her love for him and her own paraphiliac desires) and the restoration of Spike's soul.

The *Dollhouse* episode "A Spy in the House of Love" opens with Echo dressed in dominatrix garb and extolling the virtues of the BDSM lifestyle:

> Everyone thinks it's about the pain. It's not about the pain. It's about the trust. Handing yourself fully and completely over to another human being. There's nothing else more beautiful than letting go like that.

Echo's handler, Langdon, believes "that kind of trust always leads to pain." Langdon's words seem to echo Whedon's philosophy in this regard because we see many instances throughout the Whedonverse of this kind of trust leading to pain and betrayal (such as Xander and Anya in "Hells Bells" and Spike and Buffy in "Seeing Red"). Later, Langdon and Saunders continue the discussion of the value of "shameful" sexual impulses, which Langdon finds debilitating, perverted, and dangerous. Saunders concurs with the dangerous aspect since the Actives could get into deadly situations by being programmed to "trust" the wrong kind of client too much, which is why she claims the Actives are never sent on missions as submissives.[4] This conversation reveals just how flawed the Dollhouse system is and how little the Dollhouse can do if a bad situation spirals out of control. This idea is further enhanced in "Omega" when Alpha and Whiskey (under the effects of defective and paranoid implanted personalities) evade the Dollhouse handlers and agents and horribly torture the client in an effort to discover who is following them and why.

Homosexuality

Homosexuality at one time was considered a paraphilia simply by virtue of the fact that it was a sexual behavior practiced by a minority of people and involved sexual activities which most heterosexuals would not consider erotic. However, with recent changes to paraphilia definitions (in regards to considering paraphilias to be sexual acts in which only the paraphile derives erotic pleasure from the act), homosexuality (since it involves two consenting adult partners who both gain sexual pleasure from the act) has been removed from the list of paraphilias. However, this does not discount the fact that many in today's society still consider homosexuality a taboo topic and an "abnormal" sexual activity.

In the Whedonverse, Whedon and his Mutant Enemy writers maintain a fairly ambivalent stance towards homosexual relationships, as if they are unwilling to fully commit a major character to a completely gay lifestyle. Although Willow and Tara are thoroughly dedicated to one another throughout their relationship, Willow's commitment to a lesbian identity is much less secure. Even in relation to her doppelganger, Vamp Willow, Willow cannot fully come out and state that she is lesbian, qualifying only that she is "*kinda* gay" (emphasis mine). Even after she comes out and begins a relationship with Tara, Willow never identifies herself as "lesbian" at any time in the series. The closest she ever comes is in "Checkpoint" when she conditionally declares herself and Tara as "lesbian-gay *type* lovers" (emphasis mine). This identification of lesbianism as the "type" of relationship she is in rather than as an integral part of her self (as it is with many gay and lesbian individuals) is underscored further by her comment to Anya in "Triangle" that she is "gay *now*" (emphasis mine), reiterating that she is gay at the present time but has not always been so and (by assumption) may not be again in the future. Willow's commitment to her lesbianism is so weak that she does not even consider changing R.J. into a female in "Him" until Anya points out to her that she is supposed to be gay.

Willow's reluctance to admit to her own sexual orientation represents the problematic relationship Whedon's shows have had with their homosexual characters. The narcissism some see as an inherent part of homosexuality (Mendlesohn 58) is symbolized by Vamp Willow's sexual desire for Willow in "Dopplegangland" and Willow's relationship with Tara, whom Farah Mendlesohn found "superficially much like Willow" (58). Other critics appreciated that Whedon attempted to make lesbianism more a force for good than evil. However, for some, the relating of lesbianism to magic and witchcraft was an issue. For Edwina Bartlem, "The depiction of lesbian sex as a form of magic, situates it as being beyond the material world, outside the physical body, and beyond reality. This approach insinuates that lesbian desire and sexuality are anomalies that exist beyond the normal world, beyond representation on mainstream television and beyond the understanding of most viewers.... By assertively associating the lesbian characters with magic and witchcraft, the show still aligns lesbianism with supernatural powers, moral deviance, and unnatural desires" (22, 28). Alissa Wilts also states, "To associate lesbians with witchcraft still leaves them aligned with unstable, otherworldly powers. To relate lesbian sexuality to powers that cannot be understood by general society is to leave room for lesbianism to be interpreted by the *Buffy* audience as something that is unnatural, unfamiliar, scary, and possibly evil" (48). However, from Season Six onward, a radical shift took place in which lesbianism was displaced from its metaphoric connection to magic and witchcraft. As magic and witchcraft became more closely associated with issues of drug addiction, lesbianism became normalized, taken out of the realm of the supernatural, until in "Seeing Red," the show introduced its first lesbian sex scene and, with its subsequent dialogue, stripped away all its metaphoric pretense, "I forgot how good this could feel. Us, together, without the magic" (Willow to Tara). Unfortunately, immediately thereafter, Tara is killed by Warren's stray bullet and Willow, grieving and vengeful, turns evil, introducing yet another dark lesbian connotation to the series (Wilts 50).

Unlike Willow and other than Tara, the only unequivocally gay character in the Whedonverse is Larry, who comes out to Xander in "Phases" and is fully out and comfortable with his gay identity by "Earshot" with even "my grandmother setting me up with guys." But Larry is ultimately a relatively minor character who only appears in one other episode, "The Wish," before he is dispatched during Graduation Day.[5]

The sexual orientation of many other characters is left deliberately vague and undefined. Andrew is coded as gay through his numerous comments regarding his attraction to Warren (in "Seeing Red"), Spike (in "Entropy" and "Damage," *Angel*), and Xander (in "Storyteller"); however, this gay identification is constantly being undercut by his blatant homophobia in "Life Serial," his desire for sex with Katrina in "Dead Things," and his date with two beautiful women in "The Girl in Question" (*Angel*).[6]

Lorne is another character whose sexuality is kept indeterminate. His flamboyant dress, physical mannerisms, and choice of "I Will Survive" as opening performance seems to code him gay. He calls Angel by all manner of sexualized pet names: "sweetie" in "Happy Anniversary"; "gorgeous" in "Over the Rainbow"; and "Angelcakes" in "Unleashed," and, at one point, even asks Angel out on a date to attend an Elton John concert in "Belonging." However, Lorne also admits to being "in love with" Fred in "A Hole in the World,"[7] suggesting a possibility of bisexuality or perhaps even heterosexuality (with the gay coding detailed above as part of his "entertainer" persona).

Even many of the heterosexual characters in the Whedonverse engage in "same sex" liaisons or fantasies from time to time. Spike, for example, tells Illyria in "Power Play" that he and Angel have never been intimate "except that one time." Although the "one time" is left deliberately unexplored, the subtext of an Angel/Spike sexual relationship has been suggested on several occasions (Spike referring to himself as Angel's "date" in "Just Rewards," and the highly homoerotic conversation between the two in "Destiny": "Don't mistake me. I do love the ladies. It's just lately I've been wondering what it'd be like to share the slaughter of innocents with another man. Don't think that makes me some kind of a deviant, hmm? Do you?"). Spike's and Angel's vampire lovers, Drusilla and Darla, have also always had a relationship that suggested lesbianism, but nowhere is that subtext more evident than in the flashback scene in "The Girl in Question" in which Angel and Spike discover that Darla and Drusilla have had sex with the Immortal. Not only have the two female vampires had sex with him but they did so "concurrently" (which they have never done with Angel and/or Spike). Then they go off to share a bath together "to leave the boys to weep in private." Drusilla then asks if Darla will hold her head underwater (a comment containing within it the subtextual possibility of oral sex), and Darla responds, "If you like."

During *Buffy* Season Eight, Whedon generated a great deal of controversy by having Buffy engage in a lesbian fling with fellow slayer, Satsu in "Wolves at the Gate, part one." Many fans thought the relationship was nothing more than a marketing ploy designed to sell more comic books. While Whedon denied such allegations, claiming that the Buffy/Satsu relationship was a natural advancement of the storyline, critics like Stephen Krensky felt the storyline "is just the latest installment of [a comic] pushing the envelope. It disappoints me if the only reason they do it is because they're looking for new wrinkles to just have something to write about" (quoted in Friedman 23). Such is not the first time that Whedon has run into controversy of this nature. Many critics admonished him in the early days of the Willow/Tara relationship as using it for nothing more than publicity and a ratings bump, so much so that Whedon used that controversy, metatextually, in the *Angel* episode "Blood Money," when a reporter asks a television star at a fundraiser: "Serena, I have to know. This thing with making your character gay, is that, like, all about ratings because I just don't get it?" Whedon seems to suggest here that the fact that the reporter doesn't "get it" says perhaps more about the reporter's own feelings about homosexuality than it does about the storyline itself.

Other predominantly male heterosexual characters also have their moments of homosexual fantasies within the Whedonverse. Xander, for example, makes two different comments about Riley which suggest he has some (for him) less than appropriate feelings. In "Goodbye, Iowa," when Xander gets his first glimpse of the massive and impressive Initiative complex beneath UC Sunnydale, he tells Buffy that he now completely understands her adoration of the military organization and asks, "Can I have sex with Riley too?" Later, in "As You Were," Xander's admiration for Riley reaches such a level that Anya asks him, "If you like Riley Finn so much, why don't you marry him?" to which Xander responds, "He's taken," suggesting that perhaps if Riley wasn't "taken," then he might just consider Anya's statement.

The "transgressive" nature of homosexuality becomes so prevalent that many heterosexual characters are mistakenly believed to be gay. In the Whedonverse, there is so little stigma attached to homosexuality that such characters neither take offense nor necessarily always correct when others make such assumptions. In "Phases," Xander's questioning of Larry (whom he suspects of being a werewolf) creates the assumption on Larry's part that Xander has discovered his secret (that he is gay) and that Xander is gay as well. Although Xander tries desperately to point out that he is not gay, he does not do so in any outraged fashion and, ultimately, never does correct Larry to the point that Larry still believes Xander is gay during their second conversation in "Earshot." In "Expecting" (*Angel*), Cordelia's friends assume Angel and Wesley are gay which, rather than offending Angel, causes him to suggest that such a belief "adds mystery" when it comes to women.[8] Nandi believes Mal to be "shy" (gay) in "Heart of Gold" (*Firefly*) because he does not seem to have any desire for any of the prostitutes in the brothel. Mal does not act offended in any way at the accusation, but merely states that he is into "women folk" but that he is choosing to focus on the task at hand rather than on anything sexual. Willow's assumption in "Orpheus" (*Angel*) that Fred is gay and coming on to her (to the point where she feels the need to tell Fred she's seeing someone), which seems to puzzle Fred (although she does not seek to correct Willow), is an even further example of Willow's lack of complete involvement in the lesbian lifestyle. Kennedy, in "The Killer in Me," seems to sense immediately that Willow is gay (to which Willow responds by asking if Kennedy has "special lesbidar"). The (mostly mythological) belief that gays and lesbians have the ability to recognize each other on sight is typically seen as an innate ability of people with that sexual orientation. The fact that Willow's "gaydar" is flawed to the point of believing that Fred is a lesbian (as flawed as the "gaydar" employed by heterosexual and clueless Cordelia, who believes Harmony is a lesbian when she comes on to her in "Disharmony" (*Angel*) and almost seems relieved to discover that she is actually only a vampire) indicates that her lesbianism may not be as much a part of her self as she believes.

Prostitution

The issue of prostitution as a paraphiliac activity has been a source of controversy among researchers and psychologists for years. While many claim prostitution cannot be paraphiliac because it adheres (for the most part) to standard, traditional sexual practices, on the other hand, others comment that prostitution should be considered paraphiliac because it involves an uneven power exchange, being as it is based on an economic transaction. Such scholars indicate that prostitutes are forced by financial necessity to consent to sexual encounters rather than by sexual desire. The interest of the consumer (the "john") centers around his own sexual satisfaction, and he has no real concern for the sexual pleasure of the prostitute (Benvenuto 61). Further, Eve Pendleton argues for prostitution as a paraphilia, claiming it "has the goal of proliferating sexual deviance" (as quoted in Amy-Chinn, 7).

Ironically, many feel the power exchange in prostitution is based on the illusion of control. The economics of the situation would suggest the client is in the power position. He is, after all, the one paying for the services and would, therefore, seemingly control the transaction based on his amount of payment. However, as many sex workers state (and Whedon himself suggests in his works), the prostitute is actually the one who controls the power, not the client.

The two primary examples of prostitution within the Whedonverse are Inara in *Firefly/Serenity* and the Actives of *Dollhouse*. Inara is seemingly the ultimate empowered prostitute. The role of the prostitute (or "companion," as they are called in the future) in the *Firefly/Serenity* version of the Whedonverse is much more controlled yet respected and honored than in the present day. Like all of the favored "companions," Inara alone controls who she will accept or reject as a client (as seen in "Shindig"). Inara is extremely well-educated and conducts elaborate rituals within her profession which makes clear, despite the condemnation of the Magistrate in "Jaynestown" and Mal (in numerous episodes), her work is about much more than just sex, and the rules and order surrounding it are ways to ensure the companion stays in total power and control of the situation.

However, in many ways, Inara is a symbol of the illusion of power associated with organized prostitution. Starletharlot argues that Inara is a slave, "owned" by the Alliance through the requirement of registration: "Registration is also a practice that submits the whore's body to ownership by another: they are not our bodies to do with as we please, they belong to the governing body, who demands compliance to standards set often without our input and consultation" (20). The constrictions placed on her to submit to extensive yearly medical examinations (in "Ariel") and her inability to express her love to Mal are just two primary examples of the ways in which Inara's power is restricted or denied. Whedon uses Inara to convey the idea of the ways in which we submit to slavery of our own free will and how those who enslave us use methods of deception to make us believe we are freely making our own choices (this is also a central tenet of both *Dollhouse* and Season Five of *Angel*).

In "Shindig," Mal and Inara argue at the ball over his concept of his illegal, but "honest," work as a smuggler versus her legal, but dishonest, work as a Companion. His opinion is that her job is based upon "lying": the lie of love, of emotional attachment, of perfect companionship. Mal's description of Inara's work is also the perfect definition of the Dollhouse, an organization founded on lies and deceptions. The Dollhouse management denies its foundation of prostitution, but since many of the assignments shown concern sex or some sort of paraphiliac desire, such as in "A Spy in the House of Love," such denial does not hold much assurance. The Dollhouse clients believe they have all the control because they alone between themselves and the Actives know the situation is not real and they have created the scenario under which the Actives participate. However, frequently, the Actives may deviate from the plan which causes the potential loss of control. Richard tries to hunt and kill Echo in "The Target"; however, despite the fact that she is programmed simply as a helpless sex doll/victim, she is ultimately able to seize the power and control away from him and use it against him. And, in "Omega," we witness Alpha and Whiskey using a client's fantasy against him, showing just how little power and control the client has (or, for that matter, how little control the Dollhouse itself has).

Once again, Riley's relationship with the vampire prostitutes in "Shadow" (*Buffy*) demonstrates the lack of power controlled by the client in such situations. Initially, it appears that Riley does have the power here. He is able to take control of the encounter and ends up staking the vampire prostitute in a mock sexual climax. However, soon, in "Into the Woods," the addiction to the vampire prostitute bites grabs hold of Riley to such an extent that he relinquishes what power he had to the prostitutes, a dangerous proposition as Giles makes clear earlier in the episode regarding the inherent danger of the activity to the humans involved. The prostitutes also serve to corrupt the only purely non-transgressive sexual relationship in the entire series,[9] that of Riley and Buffy. Riley is so uninterested in deviant sexual behavior that he rejects Faith's offer (while in Buffy's body) of sadomasochistic sex in "Who Are You?" in favor of a standard, purely romantic sexual encounter (one which shocks Faith with its untainted emotion). While other characters in the Whedonverse have shared pure, non-transgressive romantic desires (such as Giles and Jenny Calendar, Joyce and Brian in "I

Was Made to Love You" and "The Body," and Fred and Wesley), none of those relationships are sexually consummated and each ends with the death of the female partner. Some critics have suggested that one of the reasons fans never took a liking to Riley's character in Buffy was because he was too nice, "not interesting enough to compete for attention in the dark world of the Buffy-verse" (Stokes 9). When Riley eventually did visit the vampire prostitutes in an effort to become darker and "absorb" a little of Buffy's necrophiliac tendencies, the move was seen as out of character and a desperate ploy to add some darkness to Riley's character. When fans rejected the new direction, Whedon had no alternative other than to send Riley off on a South American helicopter ride.

One of the ultimate negative ramifications of prostitution is the tendency for men to treat the women as property, commodities whose only value is their material or sexual worth. Jayne in *Firefly*, for example, treats Saffron in this manner in "Our Mrs. Reynolds," offering Mal his prized possession, a gun named Vera, in exchange for her. Mal, whose personal code of ethics prohibits the notion that one person can be owned by another regardless of who or what they are, reacts with indignation at Jayne's suggestion, just as later he will react with similar outrage in "Heart of Gold" at the idea that Burgess has the sole rights to his son simply because his mother is a prostitute at the local brothel. Because of this personal code, it is very likely (though never directly stated) that he chooses to protect River from the forces of the Alliance in *Firefly* and *Serenity* (even going so far as to threaten to kill Jayne in "Ariel" for attempting to deliver Simon and River into the hands of the alliance) because of the suggestion that River is viewed by the Alliance as a piece of property they own rather than as an actual living person (Jowett, "Back" 103).

In Whedon's essay on the death of Dua Khalil,[10] "Let's Watch a Girl Get Beaten to Death," he makes the connection between Khalil's death and the rise of "torture porn" horror films, especially in terms of the treatment of murder (of women in particular) as spectacle and why "the act of being a free, attractive, self-assertive woman is punishable by torture and death" (Whedon). Khalil was treated by the men of her society as a piece of property belonging to her family, not as an independent woman. According to the customs of her Middle-Eastern culture, Khalil did not, therefore, own her own body; instead, she was subject to the mandates of the men in her family. Her desires, beliefs, and dreams did not matter if they conflicted with the latter (Buckman 4). Like Khalil and the murdered women in "torture porn" (as well as the various characters within *Firefly* as detailed above), Penny in *Dr. Hor-*

rible is treated as an object, a commodity. Her very name suggests a monetary value. In the internet film, Penny becomes less a person (the media cannot even be bothered to remember her name — at her death, the headline reads, "Country Mourns Whats-Her-Name") than she becomes an "object for the exchange of desire and a means to the construction of masculinity between Horrible and Hammer" (Buckman 4). Unlike other female characters in the Whedonverse, such as Inara and Echo, both of whom refuse to allow themselves to be treated as objects despite their profession, Penny is ultimately destroyed (as Khalil was destroyed) by men who sought to own and control her. The sexual competition between Hammer and Horrible reduces Penny to a mere pawn in their corrupt game of machismo.

Conclusion

On the *Serenity* commentary, Whedon argues that we cannot control others' behaviors but adds a claim that "sin is just how people are ... all of those things we take as faults are also the source of pleasure and decency" (as quoted in Greene 91). Ultimately, the world we look at in the Whedonverse is a reflection of our own, both for good and bad. Sexuality is a source of great pleasure to the world and fills the world with love and happiness. But, like nearly everything else, sexuality has its dark side. Whedon, by holding up a mirror to the world, forces us to take stock of what we are really doing to ourselves, our world, our universe. The deeper we sink into depravity and sin, the darker we become. Sin is really just what we are, but that does not mean that our sins should define us. If we allow that, then just as in the Whedonverse, uncorrupted love, for us, may soon be nothing but a distant, happy memory.

Notes

1. However, as his conversation with Spike in that same episode makes clear, Ford shares at least some of their clichéd notions about how vampires should act.

2. The audience is able to eventually see some of that mental torture in episodes such as "Dear Boy."

3. Only Angel never engages in any sort of consensual masochistic sex after his redemption, no doubt due to the restrictions of his gypsy curse.

4. This does not prevent dangerous trust issues from arising, however, in episodes like "The Target" and "Omega."

5. Larry is mentioned one final time in "Smashed," but here he only serves as the punchline of a joke.

6. Whedon claims in the DVD commentary that he wanted Andrew to leave on his date with a beautiful woman on one arm and a handsome man on the other to accentuate Andrew's bisexuality, but the network refused to go along with the idea.

7. While it is possible that Lorne means that he loves Fred as a sister or as a friend, the line reading and context of the scene certainly indicates that he is referring to love in the romantic sense.

8. Despite his attitude in this scene, Angel definitely has had his moments of homophobia. He briefly considers joining to a gym in "Judgment" until Cordelia reminds him that it would require showering naked with other men. Later, in "Couplet," Angel gets somewhat insulted that one of the demon prostitutes assumes that he and Groosalug are "together" and makes it abundantly clear that they are not a couple.

9. Prostitutes in the nineteenth-century were frequently equated with vampires because both were considered evil predators who infiltrated, infected, and contaminated the public body with their bad blood and who sexually corrupted and transformed innocents (Diehl 41).

10. Dua Khalil was a seventeen-year-old Kurdish girl of the Yazidi religion. Authorities believe she was killed due to the mistaken impression that she had converted to or married into the Muslim faith since she was seen in the company of a Sunni Muslim man. Up to 1,000 men participated in her stoning, which was captured on cellphone video and transmitted worldwide via the You Tube video sharing website (Buckman 1–2).

Works Cited

Abbott, Stacey. "Kicking Ass and Singing 'Mandy': A Vampire in L.A." *Reading* Angel. Ed. Stacey Abbott. New York: I.B. Tauris, 2005. 1–13.

Aggrawal, Anil. *Forensic and Medico-Legal Aspects of Sexual Crimes and Unusual Sexual Practices*. New York: CRC, 2008.

Amy-Chinn, Dee. "'Tis Pity She's a Whore: Postfeminist Prostitution in Joss Whedon's *Firefly*." *Feminist Media Studies* 6 (2), June 2006. 175–190.

Bartlem, Edwina. "Coming Out on a Hell Mouth." *Refractory* (March 6, 2003). 32 paragraphs. http://www.refractory.unimelb.edu.au/refractory/journalissues/index.htm. All textual references to this work in this essay are by paragraph number.

Beirne, Rebecca. "Queering the Slayer-Text: Reading Possibilities in *Buffy the Vampire Slayer*. *Refractory* (February 3, 2004). 20 paragraphs. http://www.refractory. unimelb. edu.au/refractory/journalissues/index.htm. All textual references to this work in this essay are by paragraph number.

Benvenuto, Sergio. "Perversion and Charity: An Ethical Approach." *Perversion: Psychoanalytic Perspectives — Perspectives on Psychoanalysis*. Ed. Dany Nobus and Lisa Downing. New York: Karnac Books, 2006. 59–73.

Buckman, Alyson. "'Go Ahead! Run Away! Say It Was Horrible!': *Dr. Horrible* and the Murder of Dua Khalil. 1–12. http:// whedongeek1.livejournal.com/673.html.

Cantor, James M., Ray Blanchard, and Howard Barbaree. "Sexual Disorders." *Oxford Textbook of Psychopathology*. Ed. Paul H. Blaney and Theodore Millon. New York: Oxford University Press, 2009. 527–550.

Cocca, Carolyn. "'First Word 'Jail,' Second Word 'Bait": Adolescent Sexuality, Feminist

Theories, and *Buffy the Vampire Slayer.*" *Slayage* 10. 39 paragraphs. http://www.slayage. tv/essays/slayage10/cocca.html. All textual references to this work in this essay are by paragraph number.

Crusie, Jennifer. "Dating Death." *Seven Seasons of* Buffy. Ed. Glenn Yeffeth. Dallas: Benbella Books, 2003. 85–96.

Diehl, Laura. "Why Drusilla's More Interesting Than Buffy." *Slayage* 13–14. 49 paragraphs. http://www.slayage.tv/essays/slayage13_14/Diehl.html. All textual references to this work in this essay are by paragraph number.

Friedman, Emily. "Buffy's Romp: Marketing Ploy or Part of the Plot?" 26 paragraphs. http:// abcnews.go.com/Entertainment/story?id=4396156&page=1. All textual references to this work in this essay are by paragraph number.

Gobert, Sharon H. *Relationship and Personality Issues in Adult Female Survivors of Childhood Incest: A Case Study.* University of Wisconsin Research Paper, December 2002. http:// www.uwstout.edu/lib/thesis/2002/2002goberts.pdf

Greene, Eric. "The Good Book." *Serenity Found.* Ed. Jane Espenson and Leah Wilson. Dallas: Benbella Books, 2007. 79–93.

Halberstadt-Freud, Hendrika C. *Freud, Proust, Perversion, and Love.* Amsterdam: Swets & Zeitlinger, 1991.

Hall, Jasmine Young. "Im/Material Girl: Abjection, Penetration, and the Postmodern Body on *Buffy the Vampire Slayer.*" Paper given at the 2004 *Slayage* Conference, Nashville, TN, May 28–30. http:// slayageonline.com/ SCBtVS_Archive/Talks/Hall.pdf. All textual references to this work in this essay are by paragraph number.

Heinecken, Dawn. "Fan Readings of Sex and Violence on *Buffy the Vampire Slayer.*" *Slayage* 11–12. 42 paragraphs. http://www.slayage.tv/essays/slayage11_12/Heinecken.html. All textual references to this work in this essay are by paragraph number.

Jowett, Lorna. "Back to the Future: Retrofuturism, Cyberpunk, and Humanity in *Firefly* and *Serenity.*" *Investigating* Firefly *and* Serenity: *Science Fiction on the Frontier.* Ed. Rhonda V. Wilcox and Tanya R. Cochran. London: I.B. Tauris, 2008. 19–30.

_____. *Sex and the Slayer: A Gender Studies Primer for the* Buffy *Fan.* Middletown, CT: Wesleyan University Press, 2005.

Kromer, Kelly. "Silence as Symptom: A Psychoanalytic Reading of 'Hush.'" *Slayage* 19. 14 paragraphs. http://http://www.slayage.tv/essays/slayage19/Kromer.html. All textual references to this work in this essay are by paragraph number.

Malin, H. Martin, and Fabian M. Saleh. "Paraphilias: Clinical and Forensic Considerations." *Psychiatric Times* website. April 15, 2007. 29 paragraphs. http://www.psychiatrictimes.com/display/article/10168/55266. All textual references to this work in this essay are by paragraph number.

Melloy, Kilian. "Bestiality: The Next Wave in Sexual Freedom." Edge Publications website. 45 paragraphs. http://www.edgeboston.com/index.php?ch=topics&tag_id=369. All textual references to this work in this essay are by paragraph number.

Mendlesohn, Farah. "Surpassing the Love of Vampires; or Why (and How) a Queer Reading of the Buffy/Willow Relationship is Denied." *Fighting the Forces: What's at Stake in* Buffy the Vampire Slayer. Ed. Rhonda V. Wilcox and David Lavery. New York: Rowman & Littlefield, 2002. 45–60.

Montgomery, Carla. "Innocence." *Seven Seasons of* Buffy. Ed. Glenn Yeffeth. Dallas: Benbella Books, 2003. 152–158.

Nevitt, Lucy, and Andy William Smith. "'Family Blood is Always the Sweetest': The Gothic Transgressions of Angel/Angelus." *Refractory* (March 18, 2005). 36 paragraphs. http://www.refractory.unimelb.edu.au/refractory/journalissues/ index.htm. All textual references to this work in this essay are by paragraph number.
Pickard, Anna. "*Dollhouse*, Season One, Episode Two: 'The Target.'" Guardian website (May 27, 2009). 23 paragraphs. *http://www.guardian.co.uk/culture/tvandradioblog/2 009/may/27/*whedon-dollhouse-episode-two. All textual references to this work in this essay are by paragraph number.
Rosman, Jonathan P. and Phillip J. Resnick. "Sexual Attraction to Corpses: A Psychiatric Review of Necrophilia." *Bulletin of the American Academy of Psychiatry and the Law* 17 (1989): 153–163.
Starletharlot. "More Than Just a Whore: Sex Work, *Firefly*, and Audience Engagement." Whore to Culture website (February 21, 2009). 41 paragraphs. http://whoretoculture. net/2009/02/21/more-than-just-a-whore-sex-work-firefly-and-audience-engagement/. All textual references to this work in this essay are by paragraph number.
Stokes, Jenny. "'Who Died and Made You John Wayne?' or, Why Riley Finn Could Never Be a Scoobie." *Slayage*. 1–26. http://slayageonline.com/SCBtVS_Archive/Talks/Stokes. pdf.
Symonds, Gwyn. "'Solving Problems with Sharp Objects': Female Empowerment, Sex, and Violence in *Buffy the Vampire Slayer*." *Slayage* 11–12. 30 paragraphs. http://www. slayage.tv/essays/slayage11_12/Symonds.html. All textual references to this work in this essay are by paragraph number.
Whedon, Joss. "Let's Watch a Girl Get Beaten to Death." *Whedonesque* (May 20, 2007). http://www.whedonesque.com.
Wilts, Alissa. "Evil, Skanky, and Kinda Gay: Lesbian Images and Issues." Buffy *Goes Dark: Essays on the Final Two Seasons of* Buffy the Vampire Slayer *on Television* Ed. Lynne Y. Edwards, Elizabeth L. Rambo, and James B. South. Jefferson, NC: McFarland, 2009. 41–56.

Losing It

The Construction of Virginity
in *Buffy the Vampire Slayer*

SARA SWAIN

"But sexual interc — What you're talking about, well — and I'm actually turning into a woman as I say this — but it's about expressing something. And accepting consequences."

— Xander, "Harsh Light of Day"

Introduction

No chronicle of adolescence would be complete without exploring the tumultuous territory of sexual awakening. First coitus "is widely perceived as one of the most significant turning points in sexual life," Laura Carpenter remarks.[1] For this reason, sexual initiation has often been a wellspring for the pop cultural imaginary, particularly in those narratives that play out on the murky mire of adolescence. *Buffy the Vampire Slayer* is no exception. In fact, Whedon goes so far as to make the circumstances of his main character's sexual initiation the centerpiece of the entire series:

> "Surprise" and "Innocence" represent the mission statement of the show more than any other shows we've done because they operate on both a mythic level and a very personal level. On a mythic level, it's the hero's journey. She loses this very important person to her.... Angel goes bad and now she has to fight him.... But on a personal level, this is the show about, "I slept with someone and now he doesn't call me anymore."[2]

"Young people construct their identity as sexual beings in part through virginity loss," Carpenter adds, "but in the contemporary U.S., the meaning of virginity loss is ambiguous, as is the meaning of sex."[3] As one writer exclaims, "People have been talking authoritatively about virginity for thousands of years, yet we don't even have a working medical definition for it!"[4] The fact that the term is so ambiguous, and its meaning so contextual and inconsistent, prompts Jessica Valenti to suggest that the term is a myth; a social construction.[5] Clearly, virginity loss is much more than just a bodily experience, it is also a highly discursive event where gender dynamics are dramatized and sexual identities are played out. Fraught with dramatic significance to be sure, the first sexual experiences of the core characters in *Buffy the Vampire Slayer* are also critical moments from which we can glean a better understanding of the show's larger constructions of sexuality, gender, and identity.

Buffy

> "So, what I'm wondering is, does this always happen? Sleep with a guy and he goes all evil?"
>
> — Buffy, "Harsh Light of Day"

Buffy's foray into sexual intimacy is one of the more indelible "first times" ever committed to the screen. The passionate, devastating affair unfolds on the night of her seventeenth birthday when the star-crossed lovers finally consummate their love, in the unforgettable two-part episode "Surprise"/"Innocence." Up until this moment, Buffy and Angel are committed and in love. They also share a mutual attraction, which has been building for nearly two seasons. This turning point in their relationship is anything but unexpected. Buffy even openly confesses to Willow, early on in "Surprise," that despite harboring some reservations about giving into her desires, she is ready to have sex with Angel. And yet despite the planning and the deliberation, it all goes shockingly, terribly awry.

"Surprise" opens in the oneiric territory of Buffy's unconscious. In her dream, Buffy wakes up, roused from her sleep by thirst. She grabs a cup from her bedside table, only to realize it is empty. She slips out of bed and makes her way to the bathroom, presumably to get some water. Unbeknownst to Buffy, Drusilla is following closely behind her. Buffy opens the door, only to find herself at the Bronze. She saunters around the club, which is full of young couples dancing, talking, and flirting. Meanwhile Willow sits with a monkey and welcomes her with a smile and wave. Moving through the crowd, Buffy spots Joyce, who states with concern, "Are you sure you're ready, Buffy?" Her words strike with incredible portent, which is underscored by the sound of breaking glass as Joyce drops her plate. Joyce disappears, and Buffy turns to catch a glimpse of Angel. Just as they begin to walk towards each other, Drusilla appears behind Angel holding a stake. Buffy yelps in fear, but it is too late and Drusilla stakes Angel. Buffy reaches for his hand, only to have him turn to dust right before her very eyes. She wakes up with a start, realizing it was a dream but visibly shaken nonetheless.

Clearly, the dream sequence foreshadows Angel's demise and Buffy's feelings of helplessness to stop it. But the dream also intimates, as some have suggested, Buffy's own sexual awakening.[6] Drusilla's presence in the dream is then merely symbolic; she stands in as Buffy's dark double, a corporeal representation of Buffy's unrestrained sexual desire which is now astir within her. Furthermore, that Angel dies by Drusilla's hand insinuates that Buffy's newly emerging sexual drive is somehow implicated in his annihilation. And of course it is; Buffy's actions near the end of the episode bring Angel a moment of pure, unadulterated happiness, thereby breaking his curse, and tearing his soul from his body once again.

Thus, after an eventful evening full of drama and danger, Buffy and Angel find themselves alone in Angel's apartment. Desire dangles in the air between them as they desperately confess their love for one another. They kiss tenderly, then hungrily. Before they fall into their furtive embrace, Angel hesitates, whispering that maybe they should stop. But Buffy coaxes him to keep kissing her. They fall to the bed just as the scene dissolves into a close-up of the two lovers sleeping peacefully in a satisfied, post-coital state. Suddenly, Angel awakes in a panic. He stumbles outside, grasping as he clutches the cold wet ground. He cries out for Buffy, who is still fast asleep. She is completely unaware that his soul is about to escape the bounds of his body, and dissipate into ominous night.

In the morning, Buffy wakes up alone in Angel's bed, puzzled and worried about his unexplained disappearance. She leaves and returns to the scene of their recent lovemaking later that evening. There, much to her relief, she finds Angel and embraces him. He sarcastically dismisses her feelings, and makes biting comments about her sexual inexperience. "Did I do something wrong?" she asks timidly, flinching with shame, as her eyes well up with tears. Rather than console her, he denigrates her and then leaves, patronizing her with a promise of a phone call. Devastated and confused, Buffy returns home, curls up on her bed and cries inconsolably.

Buffy's emotional pain opens up a new, previously unseen side of her character. She's a basket case: insecure, anxious, and fearful; she is also ashamed and deeply distraught. In losing her virginity to Angel, she has also lost her self-respect and her personal integrity — at least temporarily. She loses the love of her life, but she does not lose herself. She emerges from the whole ordeal, hurt but healing, and even somewhat stronger than she used to be. She fell in love and made herself vulnerable so she could let Angel into her life. Being betrayed by him, while devastating, forces her to make one of the most difficult decisions she has faced in her life so far: to kill the man she loves, to sacrifice her personal feelings for the sake of her duty as a Slayer and the greater good. In fact, in an evocative inversion of the traditional tropes of virginity loss, it is Angel who has lost something: his purity. He has lost his soul, his innocence, and his inherent goodness; now, he reverts to his depraved demon ways. And Buffy, realizing what she has inadvertently taken from Angel, feels the loss in every fiber of her broken being.

Upon noticing that "Surprise"/"Innocence" are directly preceded by "Bad Eggs," Gregory Stevenson remarks that "it is interesting that [an] episode about teenage sexual *responsibility* occurs immediately before the two episodes in which Buffy learns the consequences of sexual *irresponsibility* by sleeping with Angel."[7] Stevenson insinuates that Buffy is being irresponsible, and thus the consequences of her actions are a well-deserved punishment. But the truth of the matter is that Buffy is not irresponsible. To the contrary: Buffy is very responsible, and this is in part what makes the whole ordeal so tragic. Buffy "made a carefully thought-out decision to have sex for her first time with her steady boyfriend, within the context of their loving relationship," Micol Ostow remarks, and yet Angel still "reverts back into his evil vampire self, and for the duration of the season he slowly, and cruelly stalks her."[8] Buffy could not have foreseen the consequences of her actions. She nevertheless made a choice based on the best of her ability and the most of her knowledge. She was everything she was supposed to be: responsible, considerate, and cautious — only to have every girl's worst fear come true, "that the boy will cease to value the girl after sex and that the act itself will be much less important to him than to her."[9]

"With all sorts of hormones surging through your bodies, compelling you to action, it is often difficult to remember, there are negative consequences to having sex," Mr. Whitmore reminds the class in the episode "Bad Eggs." He emphasizes that, "among teens, unwanted pregnancy is the number one negative consequence of sexual activity." To remedy this, the class is instructed to adopt an egg and care for it as if it were a baby. This is a means of teaching students about the pressure and responsibility that comes with parenthood, in order to motivate them to prevent unwanted pregnancy. Parents, teachers, and public health officials are constantly briefing teenagers about the risky nature of sexual activity, warning them constantly that they must protect themselves. Meanwhile, religious groups harp on them about the virtues of virginity, the risks of eternal damnation. And rather than contribute to the cacophony of authority figures telling adolescents what they should and should not do, Whedon shows instead, with great deftness, the emotional risks and complications associated with having sex by inviting his viewers to feel the emotional stakes of physical intimacy.

We can take the necessary measures to protect ourselves against unwanted pregnancy or sexually transmitted infections, but no matter how careful we are with our feelings, we cannot preempt the emotional consequences of sexual activity. In this sense, having sex is always a gamble. Its unpredictability is part of the fun, but it is also part of the pain. As Stevenson remarks, the show goes to "great length to emphasize the emotional horror that can arise out of sexual relationships. This grows out of a view that sex is a powerful force ruled by powerful passions and therefore can be potentially dangerous and damaging."[10] Sex is risky not only because it has very immediate physical consequences, but also because it unleashes such powerful feelings that are the enemy of logic and personal responsibility.

Buffy's first sexual encounter unleashes Angelus and ushers in the Big Bad of the season. It is a heavy burden for Buffy to bear, for Angelus will be responsible for many terrible things: he will break Buffy's heart; he will kill Jenny Calendar; sadistically torture Giles; and open up a hole in the world. This cataclysm is a direct result of her decision to have sex with Angel. This initiation is formative in her sexual development, and effects her romantic relationships throughout the remaining seasons. As a slayer, she must always have her guard up; she has to be ready to fight at all times. But in order to be romantically intimate with someone, she has to relinquish her armor and allow herself to be vulnerable. She allows herself to be vulnerable with Angel, and she pays dearly for it. Thereafter, Buffy has trust and commitment issues. She isolates herself in an attempt to protect herself, sometimes at the cost of being emotionally distant and inaccessible. This ultimately dooms her relationship with Riley. She continues to forsake her own personal desires for the safety of her friends, family, and community. She secretly fears the havoc her desires may unleash if she expresses them, so she represses them. But they return in other ways, like in her relationship with Spike towards the end of the series.

Xander

> "I'm 17; looking at linoleum makes me want to have sex."
> — Xander, "Innocence"

Xander's virginity has been a source of contention for him as early as the episode "Teacher's Pet." We see that, for him, sexual experience, or at least perceived sexual experience, is a sign of masculine adequacy. Of course this anxiety is rendered comical in the episode, as Blayne and Xander both compete for dominance through exaggeration and deceit. This undermines the authority of the notion that virginity is a stigma. It is strictly the way in which Xander measures his own self-worth. He hesitates to reveal his virginity to Miss French when she asks, and he is embarrassed at the end of the episode when his true status of "virgin" is revealed to the gang. There is little mention of his virginity thereafter, but by the time he falls into bed with Faith, he readily volunteers his status, revealing to her that he has never been "up" with people. This is a sure sign that Xander, despite being riddled with nervous energy and insecurity, has in some sense come to term with himself and his inability to conform to the benchmarks of conventional masculinity.

In the intervening time, he has also experienced his first romantic relationship with Cordelia and even had a brief fling with Willow, two encounters that reaffirm his sexual desirability and adequacy. But because he lacks any special skills, he does not feel as though he is an integral part of the group. This is something he struggles with from the very beginning, and continues to wrestle with until the end of the series. It never fully goes away, but it is alleviated somewhat by the events in "The Zeppo," particularly his brief fling with Faith. As one critic remarks, while sex leaves Buffy "weakened, responsible for the destruction unleashed upon the world," sex enables Xander to "face his crisis head-on, giving him the power to redeem himself and contain a similar type of destruction."[11] He argues that Buffy is punished for having sex, while Xander is rewarded. But simply because Xander's first sexual experience is situated within an episode where he also happens to restore his integrity does not necessarily mean his experience is one of positive reinforcement.

Xander's first sexual encounter transpires near the end of "The Zeppo." His tryst with Faith is by no means the episode's highlight. It is an integral part of the action to be sure, but it is upstaged by Xander's incredible act of bravery at the end of the episode, where he takes on Jack O'Toole, forces him to disassemble a bomb with nothing but his calm resolve. The bomb very nearly detonates, and it is Xander who stops it from blowing up the school, thus saving the lives of his best friends.

The episode openly deals with Xander's anxieties and insecurities — not about his perceived masculinity so much as his very self-worth. These insecurities are not without warrant; after all, as we see in this episode particularly, Xander is not often taken seriously. The episode features Xander undergoing various humiliations: he nearly gets himself killed in the episode's teaser; he proves his lack of physical coordination when he fails in a game of catch; he is nearly assaulted by the school bully, O'Toole; and is then called out by Cordelia as an ineffectual loser.

Xander then sets out on a quest to find his "cool." This quest takes him on an odd adventure where he gets involved with Jack O'Toole and his zombie entourage. Desperate to kill him and make him part of their group, Xander flees. He comes upon Faith fighting a demon from the Sisterhood of Jhe in the middle of the street. He rescues her, and they take refuge in Faith's seedy motel room. Faith, aroused by all the fighting and looking for some satiation, seduces Xander, who is willing but visibly nervous. They kiss, and they embrace. Faith hurls him onto her bed, straddles him, and reassures him that she will "steer him around the curves." The scene fades out, only to fade back into a shot of their bodies writhing underneath the bed sheets, an image that is reflected in the turned-off television set that sits at the front of the room. The scene dissolves once again into a shot of Xander and Faith lying side by side, looking into each other's eyes. The tenderness of this moment is quickly interrupted by an abrupt cut to a shot of Faith forcing a naked Xander out the door with his clothes in hand. He is not visibly upset by this premature ejection, though he is most likely in shock. He revels instead in the strangeness of the evening and the novelty of the fact that he has finally had sex.

Returning to his car, he realizes that O'Toole and his gang are planning to make a bomb. Fuelled by his recently lost virginity, and perhaps his realization that he is the only person who can stop them, Xander decides to track them down and save the day. And he does of course, though his friends are none the wiser. Thus, Xander's virginity loss, coupled with his ability to competently save lives — and be brave in a crisis — all reassure him that he is indeed a valuable and contributing member of the Scooby gang. While he never shares the details of his adventure, or the particulars of his heroism, at the end of "The Zeppo," he becomes impervious to Cordelia's disparaging words, walking away confidently, with a secret smile on his face. It seems he only needed to prove to himself that he was capable of something great.

But Xander's experience with Faith is more than just a means for Xander to get rid of his virginity once and for all. He hints in the later episode, "Consequences," that this experience with Faith meant more to him than he let on. When Faith accidentally kills the mayor's assistant, Xander volunteers to talk to her about it. He feels that because they have slept together, they share a special, intimate connection. While he is not particularly sentimental about it, he nevertheless respects the relationship they had, particularly since it was such a pivotal moment in his sexual development. When he does go to see her back in her motel room, she turns on him. She flings him on the bed once more, in a murderous inverse of their coital scene. She holds him down on the bed, this time choking him. His body writhes once again; as Xander fights for his life, Angel steps in and saves him. Xander realizes then that his experience with Faith meant absolutely nothing to her. She used him and genuinely felt nothing for him. Any boost in confidence he gained from his experience with Faith is now decidedly marred. He learns about the emotional and physical consequences of sex, which explains why he is much more reticent to have sex with Anya when she propositions him in "Harsh Light of Day."

Xander's experience with Faith is part of a formative pattern in Xander's romantic relationships. All his relationships involve powerful, dominating females who aggressively pursue him, boss him around, and too often try to hurt him (emotionally and physically). From Miss French in "Teacher's Pet" to Ampata in "Inca Mummy Girl," to Cordelia, Faith, Anya, and finally Lissa from the episode "First Date." Admittedly Xander is fairly indiscriminate when it comes to the women he gets involved with — he admits on more than one occasion that he is always ready for sex, or at least thinking about it. He is rarely an active sexual agent, while the women he gets involved with generally are. His most serious relationship with Anya begins with her aggressive pursuit of him. Though he is reticent at first, he responds to her advances and he gradually learns to love her. Meanwhile, the only girl Xander ever pursues is Buffy, but she never returns his feelings. Outside of Buffy, the women in his life have always pursued him. That his romantic *modus operandi* is to settle for less and respond to the demands of others suggests that he can never fully be satisfied in his romantic relationships. He never actively seeks out what it is he wants, a pattern that begins early in the development of his sexual maturity.

Willow

> "Well, we're alone, and we're both mature younger people and so we could ... I'm ready to ... with you ... we could do that thing."
>
> — Willow, "Amends"

Willow's sexual initiation occurs with Oz in the episode "Graduation Day, Part 1." This critical moment in their relationship had been building for some time. Willow had previously offered herself to Oz in the episode "Amends," staging an elaborate seduction scene in her living room, care of Barry White and candlelight. She explains that she wants to be with him first, a grand gesture to show him that he is special to her, and a means for them to share something new together. He patiently refuses her advances, wanting to wait until they both *need* for it to happen, and not *want* it to happen for a particular reason. And so when they do finally consummate their love, it is not for a reason, it is because they need to express their love in a new, more intimate way.

Willow and Oz are in Willow's bedroom researching potential spells to stop the Mayor's looming ascension. They are discussing the imminent danger and the possibility that they may not live through graduation. Oz comforts Willow, they kiss, and the scene fades to black. It fades back in to reveal the couple, beaming and satisfied, in a post-coital embrace. Their afterglow is, however, interrupted by a crisis. They must put their personal feelings aside to help Buffy with an injured Angel.

This is without a doubt the most positive sexual initiation experience of the entire trio. The only consequence of their lovemaking is that their relationship is further cemented, and they both feel ecstatic. This new level of physical intimacy is merely a manifestation of their already close emotional bond. Willow reveals that their sexual encounter is in fact, the best night of her life. It is a reaffirming experience for both of them, and there are no disastrous consequences. It is a pivotal moment in their relationship and in Willow's sexual development. And for all its importance, the event itself is overshadowed by the impending apocalypse, nestled in nicely with the themes associated with graduation: transformation, ascendance, and becoming.

In her relationship with Oz, Willow proves to be very generous and loyal, regardless of a momentary lapse with Xander. Though their relationship inevitably ends, and Willow's sexual orientation eventually shifts in Season Four, the positive and affirming nature of her first sexual experience sets Willow up as a fiercely devoted lover, who is generous with her feelings and can flourish in long-term relationships, something she later proves in her involvements with Tara and Kennedy.

While sexual content is fairly prevalent in the later seasons of *Buffy*, the first three seasons of the show are relatively chaste. The sexual initiations of its core characters make up the bulk of the sexual content during the high school years. These moments of sexual initiation are, however, relayed with incredible modesty and restraint. Whatever the reason, sexual imagery, as Anthony Enns suggests, "has always been a contested marked boundary of representation of what may be represented and what may not."[12] Both Buffy's and Angel's, and Willow's and Oz's lovemaking are merely suggested by an on screen kiss that is immediately followed by a dissolve. The act itself is never fully represented; it happens somewhere off screen. While Buffy and Angel's encounter is later relayed in flashbacks, it takes the form of abstract close-ups, where we see only furtive fragments of skin on skin, "the joy of transcendent love — only after it is gone."[13] Xander's and Faith's encounter by contrast, is visually represented, albeit at a distance. They kiss, and the scene dissolves into a shot of their rhythmically rocking bodies reflected in a turned off television screen.

The decision to represent Xander's first time, while leaving Buffy's and Willow's to the imagination may be incidental, but it produces a compelling case for the meaning of love and sex in the Buffyverse. When Buffy and Willow have sex for the first time with their respective partners, they are in love. Their sexual encounters are extensions and expressions of that love. Love is a phenomenon that pushes the boundaries of representation, for its mysterious ineffability makes it impossible to convey accurately. The ellipses that bookend both Buffy's encounter with Angel, and Willow's with Oz, cloak their sexual activity in secrecy, stimulating narrative desire and thus granting the invisible act more power. Xander's sex with Faith by contrast, is casual. They are having sex, something that can be simulated and represented with greater ease. But this does not necessarily make it less complicated or risky.

As Joss Whedon admits, "I don't want to make a reactionary statement. I don't want to say, 'Never have sex.' I don't want to say, 'Quick, go have it now.' I want to say, 'Some people have it. Everybody thinks about it. Here's how we deal with it.'"[14] Sex in Sunnydale is risky. But rather than preach about the dangers of unprotected sex and promiscuity, Whedon insinuates that risk is a necessary part of every relationship — sexual or otherwise. Life is not a safe place, but sometimes the risks are worth taking. Without risks, nothing is at stake, and therefore nothing is important. Risks are what elevate the significance of the choices we make. Whether they are the right choices or the wrong ones is often beside the point; what matters most is that we take responsibility for the consequences.

Notes

1. Laura M. Carpenter, "The Ambiguity of 'Having Sex': The Subjective Experience of Virginity Loss in the United States," *Journal of Sex Research* 38. 2 (May 2001): 127.

2. Joss Whedon, "Innocence" Interview, "*Buffy the Vampire Slayer*: The Complete Second Season," DVD, 20th Century Fox, 2002.

3. Carpenter, 137.

4. Hanne Blank, qtd. in Jessical Valenti, *The Purity Myth: How America's Obsession With Virginity is Hurting Young Women* (Berkeley: Seal, 2009), 20.

5. Jessica Valenti, 20.

6. For more in depth readings of this sequence see Rhonda Wilcox, *Why Buffy Matters: The Art of* Buffy the Vampire Slayer (New York: I.B. Tauris, 2005); and Melanie Wilson, "Buffy's Dream in 'Surprise,'" *Buffy Meets the Academy: Essays on the Episodes and Scripts as Texts*, ed. Kevin K. Durand (Jefferson, NC: McFarland, 2009), 125–130.

7. Gregory Stevenson, *Televised Morality: The Case of* Buffy the Vampire Slayer (Lanham, MD: Hamilton, 2003), 191.

8. M. Ostow, "Why I Love Buffy," *Sojourner: The Women's Forum*, 24.3 (1998): 20.

9. Christine Jarvis, "School is Hell: Gendered Fears in Teenage Horror," *Educational Studies* 27 (2001): 262.

10. Stevenson, 193.

11. Marc Camron, "The Importance of Being the Zeppo: Xander, Gender Identity and Hybridity in 'Buffy the Vampire Slayer," *Slayage: The Online International Journal of Buffy Studies*, 23, 2007, 8 June 2009. <http://slayageonline.com/essays/slayage23/Camron.htm>

12. Anthony Enns, "Sexual Imagery and the Space of Love," *Sexual Rhetoric: Media Perspectives on Sexuality, Gender, and Identity*, eds. Meta G. Carstarphen and Susan C. Zavoina (Westport, CT: Greenwood, 1999), 257–268.

13. Wilcox, 125.

14. Qtd. in James L. Longworth, Jr., *TV Creators: Conversations With America's Top Producers of Television Drama, Volume Two* (Syracuse: Syracuse University Press, 2002), 214.

Works Cited

Camron, Marc. "The Importance of Being the Zeppo: Xander, Gender Identity and Hybridity in *Buffy the Vampire Slayer*." *Slayage: The Online International Journal of Buffy Studies*. Eds. Rhonda Wilcox and David Lavery. 23, 2007. 8 June 2009. <http://slayageonline.com/essays/slayage23/Camron.htm>.

Carpenter, Laura M. "The Ambiguity of 'Having Sex': The Subjective Experience of Virginity Loss in the United States." *Journal of Sex Research* 38.2 (2001): 127–39. Print.

Enns, Anthony. "Sexual Imagery and the Space of Love," *Sexual Rhetoric: Media Perspectives on Sexuality, Gender, and Identity*. Eds. Meta G. Carstarphen and Susan C. Zavoina. Westport, CT: Greenwood, 1999. 257–268.

Jarvis, Christine. "School is Hell: Gendered Fears in Teenage Horror." *Educational Studies* 27.3 (2001): 257–67. Print.

Longworth, Jr., James L. *TV Creators: Conversations With America's Top Producers of Television Drama, Volume Two.* Syracuse: Syracuse University Press, 2002. 214.

Ostow, M. "Why I Love Buffy." *Sojourner: The Women's Forum* 24.3 (1998): 20–35. Print.

Stevenson, Gregory. *Televised Morality: The Case of* Buffy the Vampire Slayer. Lanham, MD: Hamilton, 2003. 191. Print.

Valenti, Jessica. *The Purity Myth: How America's Obsession With Virginity is Hurting Young Women* Berkeley: Seal, 2009.

Whedon, Joss. "Innocence" Interview. Buffy the Vampire Slayer: *The Complete Second Season*. DVD. 20th Century Fox, 2002.
Wilcox, Rhonda. *Why Buffy Matters: The Art of* Buffy the Vampire Slayer. New York: I.B. Tauris, 2005.
Wilson, Melanie. "Buffy's Dream in 'Surprise.'" *Buffy Meets the Academy: Essays on the Episodes and Scripts as Texts*. Ed. Kevin K. Durand. Jefferson, NC: McFarland, 2009. 125–130.

Nothing Left but Skin and Cartilage

The Body and Toxic Masculinity

RACHEL LURIA

Since the show *Buffy the Vampire Slayer* is clearly committed to upending gender stereotypes, it is surprising to find it rife with so many of them. The jock, the frat boy, the bully, and the hood are all "types" found in the Buffyverse. And while we also get feminine gender stereotypes, such as the cheerleader and homecoming queen, these stereotypes are almost always lampooned and deflated in ways that the male stereotypes are not. These labels come preloaded with certain expectations and the show does little to challenge that. In fact, at first glance, the show — with few exceptions — seems to be committed to reaffirming those expectations. All of these male villains on *Buffy* fit neatly into their stereotyped labels: As we learn in "Reptile Boy," frat boys really do drink to excess, manipulate and objectify women, and crave money and power above all things. "The Zeppo" shows us that the school thug/bully really is dangerous, unhinged, destructive, and happy to use physical intimidation to terrify and control others. He delights in violence. His rough exterior doesn't belie some childhood trauma or emotional insecurity. Rather, his rough exterior conceals an even rougher, and sometimes rotting, interior. In "Go Fish," we find that the school jock is also as aggressive, competitive, and entitled as the stereotype tells us he would be. If he seems at all sensitive or thoughtful, it is just a ruse to lure female victims into a vulnerable position. It would seem, then, that *Buffy* holds these stereotypes to be true and inflexible. How progressive, then, is the show's gender politics if it cannot imagine a world in which men are not more than simple stereotypes?

In "It's About Power: Gender Dynamics in *Buffy the Vampire Slayer*," the author questions the show's feminist position and notes that, rather than advocating equality between the sexes, the show seems to advocate a view that holds women as *superior* to men — that any wrongdoing on the part of a woman is, in fact, a response to abuse by men and therefore not the woman's fault. There does seem to be something very compelling about this reading of the show. While it is true that nearly every character on the show at least flirts with evil — if not indulging in outright acts of villainy and violence — there is a gendered difference. It seems in the world of *Buffy*, women *go* bad while men *are* bad. I would argue, though, that while the show does hold something of an essentialist view of masculinity, it at the same time critiques that essentialist position. Through its treatment of the body, the show complicates masculinity and its manifestations.

The series presents a variety of types and reveals how a particular version of masculinity — one that embraces aggression and dominance over healthier alternatives — leads to violence against the self and others. The use of the body and its transformations both reaffirms and challenges the stability and essentialism of these stereotypical roles: if it is the body itself (and not simply some behavior) that must change, then these traits must be at the core of who these men are. Aggression is as essential to their being as their very flesh. Yet, at the same time, if these bodies can change, how stable and essential are the identities that go with them?

Buffy makes cunning use of these identities to offer an examination and critique of masculinity. While the list of male characters who either struggle with or succumb to the caustic grip of toxic masculinity is nearly endless — from the Mayor's transformation into a pure demon to Riley's use of government steroids to Spike and his chip — I am going to focus on three early episodes and their exploration of toxic masculinity and the body. I will examine the episodes "Go Fish," "Reptile Boy," and "The Zeppo." The male characters in these episodes not only fit the stereotype of their particular role (jock, frat boy, and thug respectively), but they also fit a larger stereotype of masculinity. All of these men and boys behave in a manner consistent with common cultural standards of idealized masculinity — strong, tough, aggressive, dominant, and unhindered by messy emotions — though something in each of their cases pushes them beyond acceptable and into toxic masculinity. These men and boys take "normal" masculine qualities to unnatural extremes. No longer are they paragons of masculinity, they are now cautionary tales of toxicity. The show uses these characters to examine the costs of toxic masculinity.

Though many scholars have studied masculinity and offered definitions of the term toxic masculinity, psychologist Terry Kupers offers a practical, working definition: "Toxic masculinity involves the need to aggressively compete and dominate others and encompasses the most problematic proclivities in men.... Toxic masculinity is the constellation of socially regressive male traits that serve to foster domination, the devaluation of women, homophobia, and wanton violence" (713, 714). In the show, jocks, bullies, and power-hungry frat boys are used to represent this particular type of masculinity and the violent toll it takes on their own bodies and the bodies of others.

Before looking closely at these characters and their episodes, however, it will be useful to pause for a moment and consider what the show offers as healthy masculinity — though even these "healthy" masculine identities are fraught. In the world of the show, it seems, the behaviors of toxic men display something essential and true to all men — even those who fall outside the rigidly drawn lines of a stereotype. Though there are variations in roles for the men in the *Buffy* universe, what Lorna Jowett calls in her book *Sex and the Slayer* "old masculinity" and "new masculinity," there seems to be pronounced commonalities among these roles. So, then, what is the difference between toxic masculinity and healthy masculinity — or "old" and "new?"

Jowett says, "In simple terms old masculinity is macho, violent, strong, and monstrous [...] new masculinity is 'feminized,' passive, emotional, weak, and human" (95). She also points out that many men in Buffy display both kinds of masculinity, taking on something of a "split personality." In fact, split personalities and doubles abound in *Buffy the Vampire Slayer*. For example, Willow meets her vampire doppelganger and Buffy meets her robot twin. However, these doubles differ along gender lines: women find their double in a different body, while men find their double housed within their own body. Both Giles and Ripper inhabit the same body. Angel and Angelus too must share a body. As must Oz share a body with his dark self— the wolf.

By placing the alternate, evil split personality within the same body, it suggests that there is something essentially dangerous about men. One wonders then how "new" is this masculinity, if it is never entirely separated from the "old" even in the likes of Giles, Xander, and Oz? It seems that even the best and healthiest of men in the *Buffy* universe are still marked by and susceptible to displays of old, or toxic, masculinity. They may use humor and emotion as a primary resource, as characters like Xander and Giles do, but they also can, and do, employ force, aggression, and dominance whenever necessary. And unlike the women of the Buffyverse, these competing identities must inhabit the same body. While no one on *Buffy* is immune to the allure of violence and aggression (we see most, if not all, the characters on the show grapple with darker impulses), there is a difference that splits along gender lines: as I noted earlier, women, it seems, *go* bad while men *are* bad.

If this is true, one must ask what it is that enables characters like Giles, Xander, Angel, and Oz to all serve as the show's healthy versions of masculinity — they are, after all, always used as the counterpoint to the toxic villains and literally save the world time and again from these villains. Certainly, it isn't their unblemished pasts and essentially passive and nurturing natures. Not one of these characters is free from a violent past or exempt from the use of violence and aggression. As Jowett observes, for some men, this past manifests as a suppressed, though easily accessed, alternate personality as it does for Giles/Ripper and Angel/Angelus. For others, it is an essential element of their character, though one not often acknowledged. Xander, after all, had something in his character that the hyena spirits of "The Pack" recognized and responded to. And the framing of the shot when Xander is first possessed by the hyena spirit, with him at the center of the screen and the rest of the pack flanking him in subordinate positions, suggests that Xander is the pack leader — the most hyena-like of them all. It is as if, as Faith says, "all men are beasts" ("Beauty and the Beasts"), even the beloved Xander. If this is true, and it certainly seems to be, at least in Sunnydale, then what is it that makes Xander, Giles, Angel, and Oz not only different, but likable heroes whom the audience roots for? I think by looking closely at the three representative episodes, the reasons — what Giles and company do differently — will become clear.

In "Go Fish," the boys of the swim team are willing to go to any lengths to achieve physical dominance. Their competitive drive makes them willing to subject their bodies to unhealthy toxins — both literal and metaphorical — that while enhancing their speed and endurance, rob them of their very humanity and turn them into murderous monsters. By soaking in the steam room and then by eating their coach, they literally ingest something toxic which then causes them to shed their human exterior, leaving nothing but skin and cartilage behind. They are now awesome swimmers, sure, but monsters none-the-less. They may have finally achieved the ultimate goal of any athlete — unbeatable physical prowess — but the cost is their humanity and their position in human society. The episode ends with the transformed swimmers — who look something like the monster from the black lagoon — returning "home" to the ocean.

Interestingly, the fact that the episode figures "home" in this way suggests that this transformation may not have been a change at all but rather a *revelation* of their natural state. Maybe the monster beneath the human exterior was the true face all along, their true essential nature, and giving in to their toxic masculinity simply unleashed what had always been there. By refusing to suppress their aggressive and competitive tendencies so that they may win more swim meets — a goal that theoretically serves the betterment of the school, but actually only enhances the privileges and reputation of the individual athlete — makes the jocks shed any pretense of humanity and returns them to their true home, alienated from "normal" human society. By connecting this revelation to the ingestion of a drug, the show literalizes and highlights the danger and toxicity of revealing, rather than suppressing, their true nature.

Similarly, the frat boys in "Reptile Boy" who consume alcohol to excess and harm their bodies through ritual scarification, also allow toxic masculinity to reveal their true nature and alienate them from "normal" society. In service of their demon patron, the men use swords to ritually mark their bodies. This flesh sacrifice — along with the sacrifice of unsuspecting young girls whom the frat boys feed to the demon — buys the men power, privilege, and financial success. As the body count rises, so do their stock portfolios. Some of their displays of overt hostility towards women are fairly run-of-the mill and what we would expect from any frat party — the use of female drag as a hazing device, for example, or even the slipping of mickies into girls' drinks — but these frat boys go a step further. By murdering young girls, they go beyond any degree of acceptable macho behavior and land firmly in the realm of toxic masculinity.

Here, however, the show cleverly undermines the masculinity of these characters and, once again, challenges the very position it seems to take. The ritual performed on the frat boys' own bodies makes them both passive and penetrable — and therefore feminine. So, even as they attempt to dominate and embrace a toxic masculinity, they are thwarted. By indulging in violence, misogyny, and domination, these boys actually destabilize their identities — ironically undermining the very masculine identity they are attempting to secure — and scar their bodies, allowing their crimes to mark them forever. And it seems the more toxic the man — or the more willing he is to harm others in service of his own gain and the more venomous he is towards women — the more marked his body. Tom, the seemingly nice one, the one to look out for, is also the most marked. When Buffy has defeated Tom, the other fraternity brothers, and their demon, the boys are all left physically scarred and on the fringes of society: they are now known criminals and their wealth evaporates as their businesses collapse.

It is worth noting here that, like the jocks of the swim team, the fraternity "brothers" should, in theory, be working as a community and serving a communal purpose. In fact, however, each member of the fraternity serves only himself and his own individual desires. Like the single, phallic demon whom they worship, their desire for wealth and privilege eclipses everything else. Yes, they are members of a community, but they are each only concerned with their own personal gain. Rather than serving a greater good and fostering true brotherhood, membership in the fraternity is simply a tool to be wielded against those who stand between them and their desires — even if that someone happens to be a drugged, teenage girl. The scars on their bodies will be a permanent testament to their toxic masculinity and their aggressive, ruthless pursuit of wealth, power, and privilege — and also a testament to their failure.

Toxic masculinity's cost to the body is dramatized again in the episode entitled "The Zeppo." In this episode, we meet Jack, a classic tough-guy hood. He steals cars, vandalizes property, carries a knife, and is generally violent and intimidating. He is bad to the bone and, this being *Buffy the Vampire Slayer*, we find that we can take this phrase quite literally: even Jack's flesh and bones have gone bad as he is now actually a reanimated corpse. His body bears the marks of his violent and toxic character in the form of the bullet wounds that took his life. Jack's buddies have also sacrificed their human lives for afterlives as the definitive lawless thugs. Their bodies must also account for their enthusiastic embrace of toxic masculinity — each of their bodies is marked as dead and they are each in various states of decay. Again, like the jocks, they have achieved the ultimate goal for their type, but there is a cost. They have defied not just the laws of man but the laws of nature, and they have paid a price. Their bodies are destroyed, marked forever as "other," and they could never again return to a society of humans, even if they hadn't all been re-killed and/or eaten.

Though the reanimated corpses of "The Zeppo" form a gang and do seem to have more genuine loyalty and affection for each other than the fraternity brothers do, their community is no less problematic than the frat boys' or the swim team's. This gang is motivated by a desire to spend time together, but that time is spent in the destruction and vandalizing of the larger Sunnydale community. Ultimately, these boys represent the pinnacle of toxic masculinity: their aggression and violence destroys the community and literally rots their bodies.

For the men in these examples, letting their unsavory tendencies run amuck has serious costs — they didn't control their aggressive nature so they paid the price as did their victims. The hazards of letting one's aggression and need for dominance run wild, the show warns, are devastating and irreversible. The toxicity of this brand of masculinity burned their very flesh and marks them forever as outside "normal" society. And that is the difference between these men and the healthier versions of masculinity: these men did not even attempt to control their nature, in fact they sought ways to enhance and unleash that nature, and they did not work in the service of a greater good. They worked selfishly, rather than communally. A willingness to suppress aggression — unless justified — and to work cooperatively is what seems to separate the toxic from the acceptable. There is never an absence of aggression, only the suppression of it.

Often, the characters of *Buffy* will, themselves, acknowledge this very phenomenon. Not only does Faith call men beasts, but so do Giles and Angel. In "The Pack," when Buffy tells Giles of Xander's various misdeeds — picking on Willow and acting aggressively, for example — Giles is unsurprised. He says to Buffy, "It's devastating. He's turned into a sixteen-year-old boy. Testosterone is a great equalizer. It turns all men into morons." So Xander's cruelty towards women and his aggression is normal and unsurprising, not because he is the individual that he is, but because he is becoming a man.

In "Amends," Angel worries that he will lose control and commit violence. The problem, he says, is not his demon nature, but his human one. He tells Buffy, "It's not the demon in me that needs to be killed, it's the man." If even our supposedly good guys acknowledge and accept violent, toxic behavior in men, then it seems the show is taking a certain essentialist stance — there is something essentially dangerous about being a man. It seems the best a man can hope for is to manage and control those elements, though that is always a precarious position to be in: several times throughout the series we see how easy it is to lose that control. Angel becomes Angelus, Giles becomes Ripper, Oz succumbs to the allure of Veruca. Even good men are always at risk of losing control.

Examples of men who struggle with or succumb to toxicity abound in this show but even a partial list gives an idea of how predominate this topic is within the show's narrative. The already referenced characters represent a tiny fraction of the characters used to explore this topic, the list could go on and on: there is no man on this show who is free from toxic influence, either by choice or involuntary circumstance. There are only men who choose to resist this influence, who find other means of expressing their manhood besides violence (though they may employ violence when justified, as Giles does against Ethan Rayne and Ben). Though this may seem that the show accepts that men are essentially "doomed to badness," in each of these cases, the show offers an escape, a way to break free from a toxic nature and subvert stereotypes, even if many, if not most men, can't or won't make the choice necessary to escape.

While the show accepts the inevitability of certain toxic qualities and the fragility of any resistant position, it also uses its stable of healthier male characters to exemplify and advocate for a more cooperative and less damaging brand of masculinity — no matter how difficult the struggle to maintain control, these men do always recommit to that struggle after any slip. They commit and recommit to a version of masculinity that works cooperatively within a group, serves a greater good, and doesn't commit violence against women. Through these characters and their struggles, the show seems to support the same version of masculinity that scholar R.W. Connell advocates: masculinity that "sacrifices on behalf of others," (quoted in Martin and Connell).

In the cases of the types like jocks and bullies, because they willingly subject themselves to toxic masculine roles, their bodies are totally destroyed or permanently transformed. For the men who don't deliberately court the toxicity, and therefore stand a chance of redemption, the transformations are temporary or reversible. The permanent scarring of the frat boys, the reanimated corpses of the thugs, and the shedding of the skin for the swim team, for example, versus Giles' marked body — a tattoo, which could be removed — Oz's part-time wolfness, and Angel's resoulment. As the actions of the characters and the subsequent consequences suggest, context and intention matter: you may use violence, even kill a person (as Giles does and Oz does — though he was a wolf at the time) so long as you are serving some sincerely greater good, like saving the world. Though you may never be without toxic tendencies, if you resist and suppress those tendencies, then you can be redeemed and your body won't be permanently scarred or destroyed.

In the end, it seems that *Buffy* uses transformations of the body to express an understanding of men and masculinity: yes, there is something essentially dangerous about being a man that can never be fully excised from a man's character. But a man can suppress that toxic nature and rely on cooperative, and therefore healthy, behaviors. A man's saving grace is his willingness to fight his aggressive, dominant nature and work as a true team.

Just as the use of the body both essentializes and problematizes masculinity, the show's particular use of the body offers a further critique. By doing violence to men's bodies as well as their female victims, the show illustrates the toxicity of masculinity and questions its stability — this identity causes harm and can be harmed. With the exception of Jack, who lived on the fringes of society even before his transformation — though as a "rebel" he exudes a certain measure of "cool" that gives him elevated status — all the toxic men are "winners." Either they literally win contests, as the swim team does, or they inhabit the upper echelons of privileged society, as the frat boys do. Despite their status, however, each of these men are taken down and defeated both by their own actions and through the intervention of nontoxic characters like Giles, Xander, and Oz. By offering these characters as healthy alternatives and having them win out over their toxic adversaries, the show challenges the stability and primacy of the dominating, aggressive, and toxic masculinities. Through the specific examples discussed in detail, and the myriad of others that could be cited, *Buffy* shows that the toxic body is flexible and vulnerable, thereby critiquing the very essentialist position it often seems to take. There may be no "new" masculinity — you can't ever truly shake the toxic qualities essential to being a man — but you can subvert them and use them towards a positive, communal goal.

Works Cited

Connell, R.W. *Masculinities.* Berkeley: University of California Press, 1995.
"It's About Power: Gender Dynamics in Buffy the Vampire Slayer." *All About Spike* November 2002. 27 August 2009 <http://www.allaboutspike.com/gender.html>
Jowett, Lorna. *Sex and the Slayer: A Gender Studies Primer for the Buffy Fan.* Middletown, CT: Wesleyan University Press, 2005.
Kupers, Terry. "Toxic Masculinity as a Barrier to Mental Health Treatment in Prison." *Journal of Clinical Psychology* 61.6 (2005): 713–724.
Martin, Patricia Yancey. "Review: Why Can't a Man be More Like a Woman? Reflections on Connell's Masculinities." *Gender and Society* 12.4 (1998):472–474.

Virtually a Femme Fatale
The Case of *Buffy*'s Faith

PNINA MOLDOVANO

Introduction

A stereotypical femme fatale, as portrayed in popular Western culture, is a smooth, sophisticated, white lady dressed to kill who is without doubt a villainess. This lady-in-leather is an innovation of white, male hegemony. She serves as an object, not a subject, of lust, and as such she carries power but does not execute it. Such are fem-vamps on *Buffy*: they serve as fetishized objects which are doomed to be slayed by Buffy, who symbolizes the white patriarch, the one responsible for their construction. Faith, in contrast, is an agentive subject who verbally expresses the enjoyment, the empowerment she finds in being a slayer. Because she is a person (not a vampire, a demon, a witch or a goddess), she may actually be someone we know, hence she materializes the mythical femme fatale. Since on *Buffy*, violence and power are many times linked together and may take different forms: slaying, biting, casting a spell, and other more familiar shapes, what is crucial is whether females on *Buffy* are able to fully articulate their power, and in that (aggressive) sexuality, and find pleasure in it. I will examine what it means for a female to be sexually powerful on *Buffy*, while exploring her overall performance. To me, a non-stereotypical femme fatale is one who, despite heteronormative restrictions on behavior and speakability, verbally expresses her desire. She is one who fulfills *her* desire and no one else's. Such is the case of Faith; such is not the case of Vamp Willow.[1]

Doane claims in the introduction to her *Femmes Fatales* that "the femme fatale is a clear indication of the extent of fears and anxieties prompted by shifts in the understanding of sexual difference in the late nineteenth century ... the feminine body is insistently allegorized and mythified as excess in art, literature, philosophy..." (1–2). The standard femme fatale, represented as a mythical creature, finds a body in the cinema (and consequently, as technology advanced, in in-color television), where "she persistently appears ... in a number of reincarnations: the vamp of the Scandinavian and American silent films, the *diva* of the Italian film, the femme fatale of film noir of the 1940s" (2, Doane's emphasis). Such is the female vampire on *Buffy*; such is not Faith. That the femme fatale emerges out of and keeps constituting fears involves "a desperate reassertion of control on the part of the threatened male subject ... [she is] a symptom of male fears about feminism" (2–3).

Slayees

Buffy's fem-vamps are creatures dressed in black who employ their great appetite onto their methods of seduction, which means that they hunt and shag the same: for the fem-vamp, S/M is the answer to all sorts of desires. Many times, fictional femmes fatales have supernatural powers which refine their fantastic, mysterious character (Doane). Female vampires' allure encompasses such powers which are their strategy to captivate their victims, the victim being the white Western male or the phallus, which are synonymous in hegemonic discourse. The male fears his mistress who makes him weak and thus a candidate for emasculation. In the best case, she will bite it/him (also known as CBT — cock and balls torture); in the worst case, she will feed on it/him. But a stereotypical femme fatale is the heteronormative woman's worst nightmare and greatest fantasy as well. In this case, the fem-vamp represents everything the every-day woman suppresses: omnipotence, omnisexuality. The heteronormative woman treats the fem-vamp with caution, when she says, as I often hear in Hebrew: "im *haiti* lesbit, *haiti* osa ota" ("if I *were* a lesbian, I *would* do her"), "her" being the hegemonic femme fatale or the fem-vamp. Of course, the speaker is not a lesbian, as she urgently stresses; thus, the use of the subjunctive: "if I were," but obviously I'm not. The subjunctive mood introduces possible, alternative worlds, unlike this world, where the heteronormative woman dumps her secretive fantasy. The female vampire stays there; in fact she can only exist *there*.

Following Doane (2), the fem-vamp is "not the subject of power but its *carrier*" (Doane's emphasis). In other words, she is *his* dangerous woman, not her own, fulfilling his infatuation with his own phallus (Hart 1994). On *Buffy*, stereotypical femme fatales are slayees. This has several implications. Firstly, on *Buffy*, slayers are stronger than vampires, so every stereotypical femme fatale can be beaten by Faith, a non-stereotypical femme fatale. It is as if fact succeeds in eluding the myth. But since, on *Buffy*, no woman ever articulates her sexual desire (without any guilt, remorse or awkwardness) as fem-vamps do, except for Faith,[2] who is not approved by Buffy's imperative, female sexual agency, who is wiped out all together. Secondly, vampires are Buffy's victims, victims of the patriarch who plant the seeds of their construction as mythical objects and hence deprives them of their agency. Thirdly, when fem-vamps are killed, so are any remnants of their once human, non-articulated sexually violent agency. And though the vampire version is an object of power (not a subject), the person she once was, is arguably a subject. Yet, the person, as is demonstrated below, can only express her sexual agency *when she is a vampire*: the before person is not necessarily any sort of a femme fatale. This means that on *Buffy* femme fatales are phantasms: either they are vampires which are paradoxically doomed to death despite never having been construed as subjects[3] that can be foreclosed, or they are "bad" girls who must correct their ways if they wish to remain subjects, namely shed their femme fatale identity, which amounts to silencing any sexual agency.

Willow

Vampire Willow is an interesting case because she is constantly compared to her human version. She is viewed as her shadow, alter-ego (Jowett). She is first introduced in the episode entitled 'The Wish," where an alternate universe is introduced, one in which Buffy had never arrived in Sunnydale. In such a world, vampires take over Sunnydale, as there is no one to stop them. Xander and Willow turn into vampires and lovers that are led by the first season's villain, The Master. Vamp Willow reappears in the episode "Doppelgangland," only this time she intrudes this reality and we find two Willows: the human and the non-human version.

Willow and her vampire version cannot be more distinctly marked. One is shy, a "doormat person," as Willow calls herself on that same episode; the other, is confident and into "a leather thing," as Buffy comments on the vampire version of Willow. Unequivocally, helpful, submissive Willow cannot be a dominatrix. She jokes when Buffy raises the possibility: "It was exactly you, Will, every detail. Except for your not being a dominatrix. As far as we know," to which Willow responds, cynically: "Oh, right. Me and Oz play 'Mistress of Pain' every night." Giles furrows his eyebrows. "Did anyone else just go to a scary visual place?" says Xander. Buffy confirms. Is this world's Willow perverse? Only as a mythical creature can she perform her sexuality, name the unnamed, and say: "No. This is a dumb world. In my world there are people in chains, and we can ride them like ponies."

Willow is appalled by her vampire twin: "That's me as a vampire? I'm so evil and ... skanky. And I think I'm kinda gay." Buffy calms her down by indicating that there is no correlation between the vampire and the person she once was. Angel wants to correct this, but redraws. Vampire Willow is everything Willow is not at the time she emerges. The two Willows perform differently, and in Butler's terms, it is this performativity which materializes, or gives ontological credibility, as it were, to different identities (*Gender Trouble*).

Butler adopts Austin's idea of performative utterances and takes it one step forward. In his 1955 *How to Do Things with Words*, Austin proposes that language is not only descriptive but performative as well. A quintessential example would be "I name this ship Queen Elizabeth," where the person uttering this sentence is not describing an event in the world, but is actually performing the naming itself. Thus, we construct realities simply by the use of language. Butler broadens Austin's theory and applies it to politics and gender identities.

According to Butler, then, one's identity is construed performatively "by the very 'expressions' that are said to be its results" (*Gender Trouble* 25). By performativity, she means "acts, gestures, enactments [such that] the essence or identity that they otherwise purport to express are *fabrications* manufactured and sustained through corporeal signs and other discursive means" (136, Butler's emphasis). Performativity, then, by definition, is dynamic (non-static), hence it includes bodily movements, part of which is language. What it does *not* include is mere appearance or linguistic structures viewed in isolation. Crucially, it is what one says, how she says it, to whom and in what circumstances which construct, endlessly, one's identity.

Willow's speech is hesitant, sloppy, snuffy, and puffy. Many times, she says the wrong thing at the wrong time which is later followed by an "oops," but Willow is forgiven and her slips of the tongue quickly turn into a joke rather than an insult. Her fluffy clothes, academic achievements, and (a)-sexuality characterize her as "good" and this is validated via her speech. Vampire Willow, who wears a binding leather suit with cleavage, who wears red lipstick and heavy makeup, speaks slowly, quietly, and softly. Vampire Willow's speech is mellow, almost metric, giving a sense of control: every word is weighed in and every sentence, even if pertains to a request, is in essence a command. Her character coined the phrase "bored now." Her speech, her seductive bodily movements: when she seduces Sandy, a girl she sees at the Bronze, and bites her, or when she finds Willow and licks her neck, these construct her identity. It is not what she wears or what she looks like: when the Scoobies catch her and lock her up in the library, she and Willow change

clothes and Willow pretends to be the vampire while the vampire pretends
to be Willow. Vampire Willow manages to fool Cordelia, but Willow does
not fool Anya or the other vampires at the Bronze. Alyson Hannigan draws
the distinction: even when they masquerade as each other, the dissonance is
carried through in their speech and gestures. In other words, whether an ego
or an alter-ego, there are two performances to two variant I's which in *Buffy*'s
terms contradict one another: either you are human or non-human, "good"
or "evil," dominant or submissive — pick one.

One Willow, the more aggressive one, cannot exist in this world: she
does not abide to Buffy's imperative because "her initiation of the seduction
set her apart from 'normal' women" (Hart 10). In the introduction to her *Fatal
Women* (1994), Hart claims that the symbolic Order (or male, white hegemony) cannot conceive of female aggression; therefore, it represents the woman
who kills as a man, "not-woman." Thus, aggressive women (hetero or homo)
are marked as Other, as criminals, and cannot form subjects of desire, or put
differently, cannot be agents of aggressive lust. If you desire, you must be a
man; otherwise, you're a pathological pervert. According to Hart, then, a
non-stereotypical femme fatale, in my terms, cannot exist in the symbolic
Order. If a woman initiates sex, and/or if she is an S/M mistress she is an
offender, a deviant, an invert, a felonious crazy, if not "truly" a man.

At the end of "Dopplegangland," the Scoobies perform a spell and Vampire Willow returns to her reality where she is immediately killed: no way
will she ever come back. But she does come back (Hello, Dark Willow!): even
on the expense of one body, her performance is diverse, illuminating Willow's sexual agency. Dark Willow is a blunt manifestation of the violent side
of Willow. *Buffy*'s apparent dichotomy is not sustained. But even before the
Goth version of Willow emerges, though redhead, Willow is far from being
any sort of a femme fatale; as time passes, her androgynous appearance is feminized and her neutralized sexuality (even when she's the girlfriend of a werewolf, Oz) (Jowett) becomes more settled and is articulated when Willow falls
in love with Tara (Season Four) and when she has a sexual relationship with
Kennedy (Season Seven). Willow announces she's gay, and though she chooses
the less fixed, less sexually charged term "gay" in her careless speech, she
notices April the fembot's attractiveness ("I Was Made to Love You"): "Oh,
not me, I, I was just saying, a pretty girl like that, there's always someone
lurking around, looking for some action." Eventually, she accidentally emits
this: "this goes beyond anything I've ever done. It's a total loss of control, and
not in a nice, wholesome, my girlfriend has a pierced tongue kind of way"
("Chosen"). Yet, what her speech signifies is clad in awkwardness.

Masson and Ruddell each separately analyzes Willow's speech and the effect it has on the construction of her identity. Masson observes Willow's technique to elicit response by using questions. To her, "rhetorical questions, in particular, have value, not only as 'persuasive devices,' but also in their 'communicative effect' ... for Willow, [they serve as] ... a source of effective rhetorical power in her relationships"; thus, Willow's speech can be analyzed as powerful. Sure it can. But Willow's speech, however it is viewed, *is* distinct from Vamp Willow and Dark Willow's speech. Even though Vamp Willow uses questions as a rhetorical tool as well ("Questions? Comments?"), Vamp Willow's questions are uttered with no hesitation, no breaks, and sometimes they are indirect commands. For example, when she encounters this world's Willow, she asks her, while licking her neck: "What do you say? Want to be bad?" This last question is by no means open for negotiation: if Willow refuses to be vamped, Vamp Willow is going to leave her dead. Willow's speech is also very distinct from Faith's speech. As mentioned above, Willow's sexual speech is only accidental; whereas, Faith's speech is always intentional: Faith deliberately asks Buffy if slaying makes her feel hungry and horny, leaving Buffy, Willow, and everyone else appalled ("Faith, Hope, and Trick").

Ruddell, adopting Austin's speech act theory, sees Willow's language as constructing Willow's (split)-identity. The magic language itself signifies Willow's transition into a self-confident, powerful witch/person. Ruddell claims that "Willow's use of magical speech differs dramatically from her usual hesitancy in speech." Ruddell and I share the view that "the difference between Willow and Vampire Willow can therefore be identified through the differences in how the two use speech." However, my innovation is in claiming that Willow's confident, magical or non-magical, powerful speech is censored by Buffy. "Bored now" can never be uttered by "old, plain" Willow. Dark Willow is a junkie that is eventually redeemed; Vamp Willow is banned from ever entering this reality. Thus, Willow cannot be a sexually violent agent (as constructed via her alter-personalities' speech) in heteronormative Sunnydale. In Sunnydale, Willow can either continue being hesitant, red-haired Willow (and not assert her violent self), or she can be White Willow (a fantastic, a-sexual ideal).

Call gives Willow as an example of one who "is inherently kinky," who fulfills *her* wish in "The Wish" and "Doppelgangland" to be "generally sadistic ... [but also] ... very switchy." Furthermore, he takes the character of Willow and her transition as proof that *Buffy* is tolerant towards myriad sexualities. He recognizes the heteronormative constraints imposed on the producers of

Buffy and applauds them for trying to represent BDSM in an encouraging manner. Applause perhaps is in place, but in his interpretation Call ignores the vampire/human insisted on dichotomy on *Buffy* and the *modes* in which articulations of kink take place. He seems to forget that sadistic/switchy Willow is blocked from ever entering this reality; that when Willow says "I am the magic" ("Conversations with Dead People"), she says it reluctantly reflecting upon the previous season when her power nearly brought the world to its end; that on the last episode of *Buffy* her redemption raises an ideal, and as such Willow is no longer a subject of desire; and finally, that whenever she is "just" Willow, her BDSM driven speech comes out as humorous and juvenile: "everyone's getting spanked but me" ("Goodbye, Iowa"). As Call puts it: "Willow wants out of the closet"; but she can't be, not under *Buffy*'s ethics.

Alexander, with whom Call corresponds, takes the Buffyverse canon to be femdom oriented, contrary to De Sade's patriarchy: "In the kinky register of the Buffyverse canon the show's queer and feminist sensibilities stage and eroticize the bodies of the tortured and dominated as almost exclusively male, whilst positioning participating women almost exclusively on top." As evidence, she takes Vamp Willow, who finds pleasure in torturing Angel in "The Wish," Faith, who is on top of Xander in "Consequences," and even Buffy, who beats Spike a lot in "Crush." To her, these women celebrate their aggressive sexualities. *Buffy*, as any polymorphous narrative, is open for interpretation. Yet, given Alexander's argumentation, there still remains the question of what it means for a female to be domineering in *Buffy*'s world. Though the author recognizes that "vampire narratives 'have always been used as a vehicle for more or less encoded articulations of sexuality and desire'" (Jones in Alexander), she disregards the lineation of the dominatrix who, as a vampire, is destined to be slayed by the in denial, agonized Buffy who does not forget to ban top-switchy, having fun Faith. Wearing leather or vinyl and/or torturing another male/female do not cut it. To take Alexander's example, if in De Sade's patriarchy dominatrices occupied brothels or hanged on rich men's arms, in *Buffy*'s hegemony they occupy tombs or jails (unless they make amends: are vanillized/ensouled).

Assuming a category of a femme fatale that male hegemony preserves as static, I argue that Faith's performance challenges *such* a discourse. Though in reality no category is static, and every identity is forever construed through bodily movements, surely I need to start with something. I need to start with something, even if this something is not a predetermined original, but in itself a copy (of a copy of a copy, etc.). As Butler says, "Gay is to straight not as copy is to original, but, rather, as copy is to copy" (*Gender Trouble* 31).

Butler's critique of gender formation can be expanded on to *any sort of identity*, including a femme fatale identity/label. Thus, given a copy of a stereotypical femme fatale, which has been kept static and objective by the symbolic Order, to me, a non-stereotypical, actual femme fatale, is an agentive subject who articulates her sexual desire and finds pleasure in violence. Language-use, as part of performativity, constitutes subjects: "acting one's place in language continues the subject viability..." (*Gender Trouble* 136). "The performance ... is one of the influential rituals by which subjects are formed and reformulated" ("Implicit Censorship" 160).

An *agentive* subject, to Butler, is one who "given the rules governing signification" (*Gender Trouble* 145), the social rules of speakability ("Implicit Censorship" 1997), explores new possibilities, subverts repetition (the continuous permissible expressions used) and practices variation. Simply put, this means that if you don't articulate your desire, your aggressiveness, in your own words, in your own acts, despite hegemonic bars on what can and can't be said, you are not an agentive subject of desire. "Real," everyday women, just like Faith, the human slayer in *Buffy*'s world, that express sexual aggressiveness and act upon it must be agentive subjects. Stereotypical femme fatales are no subjects, no agents, because it is not *their* desire which they perform.

Vamp Willow, regardless of her S/M role, is only *allegedly* powerful. Faith is more rebellious. Whether a top or a bottom between the sheets, contrary to Willow, Faith's speech constructs a self-assured subject who maintains her agency under her terms. Faith intentionally and straightforwardly expresses her sexuality. She does so at the cost of being stigmatized as a villainess. However, since losing Buffy is nothing a human desires, Faith eventually pays for her sins, dismisses her leather jacket, and fights alongside Buffy against the First Evil (Season Seven). And yet, in jeans, she's still a sexually charged agent who prefers to be on top.

Sprach Faith

Faith's agentive, aggressive language include: "I see, I want, I take," which she tells Xander in bed ("Consequences"), along with "I can make you scream ... I can make you die"; and "want, take, have," which she says when she steals weapons from a store ("Bad Girls"). She surprises everyone around, when she confidently asks her fellow slayer, "Isn't it crazy how slaying just always makes you hungry and horny?" Buffy, who doesn't know how to respond to that, says, "Well, sometimes I crave a non-fat yogurt afterwards." Xander immediately starts liking Faith.

Kirchner, who analyzes *Slayer Slang*, admits that each character on *Buffy* has his/her unique speech and that the speech used signifies extra-linguistic, social properties. Faith is the only character on *Buffy* to use the phrase "five by five." "Five by five" is originally a radio communication signal that means "I understand you perfectly."[4] Right after the body swap, Faith-as-Buffy signals to the audience/viewer that she is performing as Buffy by uttering this phrase ("This Year's Girl"). Faith usually uses it as an answer to questions such as "what's up?" or "how have you been doing?" In that same episode, when Buffy and Faith meet again, Buffy asks Faith, "Are you alright?" Faith replies, "Five by five. It's that thing about a coma. Wake up all rested and rejuvenated. And ready for payback." Willow notes that no one knows what "five by five" means. She mocks Faith by re-interpreting Faith's speech: "Ooh, check me out, I'm wicked cool, I'm five by five." Tara asks, "Five by five? Five what by five what?" Willow answers, "See, that's the thing. No one knows. Buffy can handle Faith and you're plenty safe with me." Willow associates the empty phrase "five-by-five" with Faith's uninterpretability, while reassuring Tara, herself, and the viewer that Buffy can handle this uncontrollable, ambiguous girl.

Faith is also the only one to refer to Buffy as "B." When they first meet, Faith borrows Buffy's stake and kills a vampire: "Thanks, B. Couldn't have done without you" ("Faith, Hope, and Trick"). Her being the only character on the show to call Buffy "B symbolizes their relationship. Firstly, it positions Faith in a place no one else, however close to Buffy, occupies — after all she and Buffy are the only two slayers — but aside from this, it materializes, as it were, her position as a phantasm that keeps hunting Buffy even when dormant. "B" is the linguistic handcuffs.[5] Secondly, being a "happy, rogue"[6] slayer with a sense of fun, she is likely to come up with a nickname for her (non)-associate in crime. Nicknames mark intimacy. Buffy rejects this intimacy right away when she says resentfully stressing the "F": "Why are your lips still moving, F?"

In that same episode, Faith uses the phrase "a hoot and a half," referring to Willow and Xander, signifying how great it must be to have them as friends and indirectly signifying how she is missing that. Kirchner notes that "Faith's inability to use other slang terms in the same way as Buffy, Willow, and Xander is symptomatic of her failure really to become part of the Scooby Gang." Faith's speech departs from hegemonic speech.

Faith's general use of truncation ("rough sitch" for "rough situation"; "fam" for "family"), Standard American Slang ("later," "a hoot and a half") and her own idiolect ("five by five") signifies her alien, working-class status.

Her rough, pushing, grunting body language sets her as queer in Stallings's terms.

Stallings analyzes Lil' Kim's song lyrics and overall performance. She argues that her use of strong language and provocative outfits signify resistance. To her, Lil' Kim sings about unorthodox, aggressive sex and by so doing, empowers the black female. The author identifies her as queer because she goes through transgression and because her sexual habits are not exactly heteronormative. By the same token, Faith's aggressive sexual habits and body language signify opposition to Buffy's white, upper-class, lady-like mannerism and sex. If Lil' Kim unnames the black bitch, then Faith unnames the stereotypical femme fatale. Unnaming the stereotypical femme fatale means obscuring moral and gender boundaries/categories, eliminating passivity, and connoting the name "femme fatale" with agentive sexuality or self-sexual fulfillment. Faith uses both her body and her speech to do so.

Meet the Slayers

Faith's opposition to Buffy, who represents the dominant culture, is set right from the start. Buffy is hyperfeminine. She has straight, up to the shoulders, blond hair, she has blue eyes, she wears colorful dresses, makeup and nail polish, she even has matching shoes and bags. Buffy stays with her mother, Joyce, who works in an art gallery, and it has been suggested that Buffy and her close friends are all white folks who come from middle-class families, except for Xander (Jowett). Faith, however, has long, straight, dark hair, brown eyes, her outfit includes black leather pants and jacket and cleavage. She does not wear high heels, but she does wear red lipstick. The character of Faith (portrayed by Eliza Dushku who is of Albanian descent) is not white, and it is implied that Faith comes from an abusive, working-class family. Faith does not go to school and throughout her appearance on *Buffy* does not have a long-lasting watcher.

Buffy is an agent who is *limited* by *her own* set of moral/behavioral codes; Faith refuses to obey Buffy's norms. She's an agent who *follows her own* rules. Her speech, behavior, and looks do not only distance her from "normality" (hence Buffy), but help draw the contours of her own category/identity: a tenable femme fatale

Buffy sleeps with a vampire (Season Two), drops out of college (Season Five), neglects her younger sister (who first appears in Season Five), yet she's still a "good" girl (Jowett). Circumstances benefit with Buffy: she drops out of college because her mother dies and she now needs to look after her sister; she sleeps with Angel during the second season, but that's okay because he's an ensouled vampire; and she struggles with her attraction to Spike, the redeemed vampire that still lacks a soul, and after practicing S/M with him, during Season Six, she feels ashamed and expresses remorse. All this represents Buffy as moral. Yes, she's "only human" and so she makes mistakes, but she has a good sense of judgment, she can tell "right" from "wrong" and she tries to correct her ways.

Though she's an average American teenager/student/young woman (she's not too brainy — that's Willow's job; she's not too funny — that's Xander's job; she's not too pretty — that's Cordelia's job) because she is a responsible person who does not exploit her power, she deserves the title "superhero," which she undertakes when rediscovering her slaying powers, after Willow cast a spell which erased the Scoobies' memories, Buffy says: "I'm like a superhero or something" ("Tabula Rasa").

A superhero is an ideal: someone who is above human. Buffy is somebody to look up to not just because she has powers other humans lack but because she is not intoxicated by them, namely because she carries her job (of slaying) responsibly. Faith can never be a superhero because she's preoccupied with the material instead of the ideal: she cares about the mundane: food, sex, or what can be summed up as fun. Buffy is earthly, so to speak, when she has an exam, when she has a job interview or when she waits for her mother to come out of surgery. Buffy can never *enjoy* the mundane the way Faith does. Only a conformist, like Buffy, can be a superhero, and one who challenges norms by speaking and playing dirty, like Faith, can never be an ideal. Because Faith dares to enjoy her power, because she likes killing, and because she admittedly practices S/M (she asks Xander if he prefers "kinks or vanilla") she is a villainess, or in other words, a femme fatale. And the terms "superhero" and "femme fatale" are cultural antonyms.

Faith and Buffy strike up a friendship. At first, Buffy likes the idea of having another slayer friend, and Faith likes the idea of belonging: of being part of a group of family and friends. Faith encourages Buffy to ditch school, go out, have fun. In the episode entitled "Bad Girls," the two slayers' fun goes too far when Faith accidentally slays a human. Presumably, Faith does not take responsibility for killing an innocent man and shows no remorse. She betrays Buffy when she tells Giles that Buffy did the killing, and Giles who trusts Buffy labels Faith as unstable and dangerous. Naming Faith unstable is another characteristic of a prototypical femme fatale: stereotypically, femme fatales' mental power drives them to insanity (Hart). Clearly, circumstances do not benefit with Faith; they benefit only with those who accept

Buffy's ethical imperative. If Faith's sexual liberty was not enough to label her a villainess, her being a murderer and a traitor supposedly leave no doubt. Faith collaborates with the mayor of Sunnydale, Wilkins, the villain of the season, while pretending to be friends with Buffy.

Faith's ethics do not match Buffy's; however, Faith does experience a range of emotions atypical of the fem-vamp, or stereotypical femme fatale, such as compassion, love, and remorse. Faith *does* regret having killed a human. In the rush of slaying some attacking vampires, she accidentally stakes a human. She is in a state of shock, mumbling: "I didn't ... I didn't know. I didn't know." She is shaking, and Buffy has to take control over the situation. Later, in her motel room, Faith is shown scrubbing her shirt, trying to take the blood off. Buffy tries to get her to talk about it, to face the consequences, but Faith remains quiet. Buffy tells her that "[she] can shut off all the emotions that [she] want[s]. But eventually, they're gonna find a body." Faith appears to be cold and calculative when she tells Buffy that she got rid of the body and that she does not care. But Faith had to try and convince herself of that first. Washing the blood off the shirt is a weak metaphor to washing off her guilt. The point is that *guilt was and is there*.

Reed claims that only when she's "back stage," a term he borrows from dramaturgy, not having to give a "front stage" performance of a slayer, does Faith reveal her vulnerable side. Reed claims that "Faith tends to gravitate towards people who use the nuturant parent model of communication with her [which includes empathy and responsibility].... [Such people] are well received by her while those who attempt to use their authority with her are rejected ... which in turn leads to her giving people her allegiance, no matter if they are good or evil." This explains Faith and Wilkins's father-daughter relationship: Faith allies with the evil mayor because he speaks softly to her, referring to her as his daughter, by which he wins Faith's loyalty and obedience: "They can't all turn out like my girl Faith," Wilkins says tenderly to Faith ("Enemies"). Their interactions indoors, in his office, or in her new apartment provided by Wilkins, show a girlish, soft Faith: this is a "back stage" performance, which according to Reed, is made possible because Faith interacts with a person she does not feel she has to impress or look superstrong in front of. Faith's lack of a stable home and watcher's neglect draw her to a loving authority figure. When confronted with Buffy in her motel room after the accidental killing, Faith puts on her "front stage" performance, thus putting on a tough exterior. Faith does not expose her vulnerability, her regret, to Buffy, since Buffy performs as a strict authority figure. Buffy demands intimacy — in itself contradictory — and this backfires her. Faith does not appreciate being bossed around, which explains why in the next season, she criticizes Buffy's overt conceit: "you're still the same better-than-thou Buffy" ("This Year's Girl").

Richardson and Rabb apply Sartre's existentialist philosophy in analyzing the character of Faith. Under their interpretation of Sartre, "the Look of the Other," or an "Outside View," limits freedom and thus relieves us from responsibility. After the contingent slayage of a human, Buffy projects her feeling dirty onto Faith whom she views as a criminal. These outside views: criminal, dirty, shameful, according to Sartre, restrict Faith's freedom and responsibility. Faith does not find compassion and approval in Buffy, but is judged to be a criminal. Thus, she decides to act out the role and joins Wilkins. This correlates with Reed's theory, under which Faith's behavior is much dependent on the response, or the Look, she is getting from other people. In Buffy's eyes, she is "bad"; therefore, she lavishes her "I don't care" image in front of her. To Wilkins she is "...a powerful girl...." Taking the father role, he tells her, "I think of what you've done, what I know you will do; no father could be prouder" ("Graduation Day, Part 1"). The mayor's reinforcement shuts out Faith's guilt and she is willing to take orders from someone who loves her and views her as powerful. The mayor gives her a sense of family, something she does not get from the Scoobies.

Ultimately, Buffy wins her battle against the evil mayor when she threatens him with the dagger he gave Faith as a present with which Buffy stabs (but does not kill) Faith. Being stabbed by her own dagger, Richardson and Rabb argue that Faith's own consciousness turns against itself, pulling out a bunch of guilt, resulted from Buffy's (the one who sticks the knife) outside look. The authors claim that when Faith says to Buffy "you killed me," she finally acknowledges, to herself, that killing a human is wrong. In their words: "Buffy, in taking Faith's dagger, a dagger functioning like a relic, which is possessed by Faith's spirit, is in effect taking Faith herself, possessing Faith. She then makes Faith conscious of herself, and reflexively conscious of her concealed guilt and remorse, by returning the dagger to her in the most forceful way possible, by stabbing her, making it a part of her, thus revealing to her the gut-wrenching guilt from which she has been fleeing."

Buffy serves as an emissary, articulating the voice of the just. Here we see a radical attempt of imposing her orthodox morality onto someone who dares to resist. Buffy is an emissary of the patriarchy whose binary system of values labels Faith "the human monster." Unless she accommodates herself to the majority, she is dead. As demonstrated above, Faith is no monster and not exactly a villainess. Her sexually violent appetite does not have to be reduced to being a lunatic criminal (Hart). But it is typical of non-white, formerly abused working-class women to fall for "the bad side," as *Buffy* reminds us; presenting her as a powerful woman is left at the hands of a villain.

Buffy and Faith's relationship is multilayered. Faith cares for Buffy. Buffy cares and is allured to Faith. Their relationship hints on lesbianism, where the lesbian part functions as subtext.[7] When Angel pretends to be Angelus and collaborates with Faith in her attempt to kill Buffy, Faith ties Buffy up and threatens her with her knife. Being this close to Buffy, yet so far away, Faith is able to reveal her abusive past: "...mom was so busy, you know, enjoying the drinking and passing out parts of life..." ("Enemies"). She signifies how oppositional she and Buffy are and leaves no doubt as to which side of the creek each belongs to. While remaining tied up, Faith comes closer to her. She might have kissed her at this point, but Faith (and the production team) have to restrain themselves because Buffy (and WB)[8] are the enemy. The lesbian trail remains a subtext for numerous reasons, one of which being what Hart calls "a secret that must be withheld from its potential practitioners"(4). Buffy, a white, middle-class woman is a potential practitioner. Because it is a secret, yet a threat, it is settled as subtext. Faith, a working-class American of Albanian descent that is infected by the "disease," is the prophecy of Hart's suspicion, with regard to the prohibition of lesbianism, that "the displacement of deviant sexuality onto these "other" women [women of color and working-class women] would spread into the worlds where [white men] desired to keep their white wives and daughters"(4). Later, Angel reveals his plan and Faith tries to escape. The Scoobies burst in; Buffy and Faith fight. At a certain point during the battle, Faith tells Buffy: "What are you gonna do, B, kill me? You become me. You're not ready for that." Buffy remains silent, as she is not willing to admit to being influenced by Faith. Faith grabs Buffy's neck and kisses her on the forehead — she's being affectionate towards her rival who she can't kiss on the mouth. Buffy's only reference to their ambiguous relationship is when she tells Spike, after having spent the night together, "I am tired of defensiveness and weird, mixed signals. You know, I have Faith for that" ("End of Days").

In "Graduation Day, Part 1," when Buffy finds Faith in Faith's apartment, the two face each other for one last battle (of Season Three, that is). Buffy wants to feed Faith to Angel, who is hurt. Here, too, dark-haired, leather pants Faith fights her blonde, girlie sister, Buffy. "You told me I was just like you. That I was holding it in," Buffy says to Faith. They are facing each other. "Ready to cut loose?" asks Faith. "Try me," replies Buffy. Faith, with a content smile on her face, says: "Okay, then. Give us a kiss." Buffy punches her in the jaw. Buffy kicks her and to prevent Faith from escaping, while being on the terrace, she handcuffs their hands together.

This picture of Buffy and Faith handcuffed to each other resembles the picture of the two protagonists in the film *Bound*: two female lovers working together to cheat the mafia. When they are caught, the viewer sees them tied together in ropes, lying on the ground. One of them, the femme, is the girlfriend of one of the mafia members; the butch is an ex-con on redemption. This film takes *Thelma & Louise* one step further with respect to women's bonding/bondage: it is the case that two women form a relationship that binds them together, yet sets them free, for which they are willing to risk their lives. When they are on the porch, handcuffed to each other, Buffy risks her own life, if Faith chooses to jump off the roof. These handcuffs are symbolic of Faith and Buffy's relationship: being used both to enforce the law and as a kinky sexual tool, their relationship is bound to move between the moral and immoral, the platonic and the sexual, never really taking a side. Faith releases her hand. Buffy stabs her. They look stunned. "You did it ... you killed me," says Faith. Only she didn't: "Still won't help your boy, though. Shoulda been there, B, quite a ride." Faith jumps off the terrace, landing on a bed of a moving truck. Faith knows Buffy does not have the courage to join her, so Faith's only choice is to escape. Buffy does not immediately chase her. She sees the truck driving away when looking down. Faith does not kill Buffy and Buffy lets her go. Eventually, Faith is hurt and is in a coma ("Graduation Day, Part 2"). Buffy, who is also in the hospital, and the mayor, the only two people that care, pay a visit to her bed. Buffy, Faith, and the viewer know Faith lands on solid grounds — she's going to wake up, some day, in Season Four. Contrary to a stereotypical femme fatale, Faith executes power, which means that she is destined to open her eyes again.

Switching

On first inspection, it seems that Buffy's remark "I'm the one getting single-white-femaled here" ("Faith, Hope, and Trick") foreshadows the events of Season Four. It looks as if Faith's wish to be Buffy is actualized. After last season's events, her only way to penetrate Buffy's Sunnydale is by becoming Buffy. But, I think things are more complex, and I claim that the body swap does not signify Faith's wish to be Buffy. I read this switch as a mockery performance, where the masquerade is ontologically realized as the performer, Faith, is able to actually "wear" the body of the ridiculed, Buffy.

Barrett analyzes the performance of black drag queens. Contrary to the view that sees their performance as symbolizing their aspiration to be white, Barrett, who carefully examines their language use and signification during their performances, reveals that by imitating a stereotypical white, middle-class lady, the drag queens make fun of the image they portray and by so doing express their resistance to white hegemony. The very idea of drag is mockery and resistance. A drag queen would not impersonate a female rocker, for example. Faith's imitation of Buffy is complete, in a sense that no drag queen can ever accomplish.[9]

Yes, as a consequence, Buffy gets to "dress up" as Faith as well; however, she does so to her regret. Buffy does not mimic Faith's performance — does not ridicule it — in fact she reluctantly takes it on, trying later to escape from the police and get her body back because in her logic, the swap act is wrong. Buffy cannot contradict herself and mock the very same Order she so passionately preserves, nor does she have the guts to tease the oppressed group of which Faith is a member.

Buffy's world seems ludicrous in Faith's eyes. Faith-as-Buffy is shown bathing.[10] Following my line of thought here, it is stereotypical of white, middle-class women to take bubble baths and caress their over-indulged bodies. In the following act, Faith-as-Buffy is looking in the mirror making faces: she wrinkles her nose, pulls her eyebrows back, pulls her upper lip back to see her teeth and sticks her tongue out. Indeed, she's missing a clown's hat. These bodily maneuvers construct Faith's identity as Buffy (Butler "Implicit Censorship") who is clearly ridiculed. Faith-as-Buffy expresses her resistance, performatively, through language as well (Butler *Gender Trouble*) when in that moment she mimics Buffy's speech. Looking at the mirror, impersonating Buffy, she says: "Why, yes, I would be Buffy. May I help you?" ("Who Are You?"). Faith's normal speech does not make use of the higher register modal "may" or of this typical, white syntax; white, college girl, Buffy, just might. By using an over the top sentence construction and immediately afterwards repeating Buffy's name, Faith, the performer, signifies how silly and phony Buffy's speech and thus entire performance is. This becomes clearer when her following act is "you can't do that. It's wrong," while shaking her finger to her mirror-image. "You can't do that because it's naughty." And then repeating it twice, loudly and softly: "Because it's wrong." Faith-as-Buffy, while staring at the Buffy body in the mirror, repeating these lines, mocks Buffy's arrogance and ethics. Faith mimics what she conceives to be Buffy's articulations of what can and cannot be done, can and cannot be said. Her intonation and body language expose the absurd in Buffy's or *Buffy*'s ethical imperative and codes of behavior.

Faith-as-Buffy chooses to wear black leather pants and red lipstick. This is how Faith typically dresses; not Buffy. This enables the performer to highlight a dormant side to her object of mimicry. Buffy cannot do that which is naughty "because it's wrong" and she has to maintain her "good," responsible slayer image. By dressing Buffy's body in leather, Faith enforces a different ethics upon her — that which Buffy is afraid of practicing — let alone when Faith-as-Buffy comes on to Spike, the vampire Buffy supposedly hates but secretly lusts or when she wishes to practice unorthodox sex with Buffy's boyfriend.

At the Bronze, Faith-as-Buffy meets Spike who's not very kind to the slayer (Buffy). "You know why I really hate you, Summers," asks Spike. Faith-as-Buffy replies: "'Cause I'm a stuck-up tight-ass with no sense of fun?" This is one of the few moments when the performer reveals her resentment towards the impersonated: this is Faith's speech, not Buffy's. Faith-as-Buffy then continues: "I could have anything. Anyone. Even you, Spike. I could ride you at a gallop until your legs buckled and your eyes rolled up. I've got muscles you've never even dreamed of. I could squeeze you until you popped like warm champagne, and you'd beg me to hurt you just a little bit more. And you know why I don't? Because it's wrong." Here, Faith frees Buffy's deepest, "darkest" desires. Faith is the only human female who can articulate her aggressive sexuality, and by taking Buffy's body along for the ride, she condemns Buffy's ethics and enables her to be a subject of desire. The same is with Buffy's boyfriend. Faith-as-Buffy enters Riley's room and jumps all over him, telling him that the Faith situation has been taken care of. Riley says he would have liked to meet Faith. Faith-as-Buffy responds: "Oh, you wouldn't have liked Faith. She's not proper and joyless, like a girl should be. She has a tendency to give in to her animal instincts." Here too, Faith-as-Buffy is being sarcastic, ridiculing the entire stereotypical "good" girl image. Faith has a tendency to be a sexual creature, and we all know how wrong that is. Faith remarks, "...What nasty little desire have you been itching to try out? Am I a bad girl? Do you wanna hurt me?" Heteronormative Riley knows nothing about playing: "...I don't wanna play"; he and Buffy are used to love making, and *Buffy* reassures Faith and the viewer that the two contrast.

The performer is still performing in the symbolic Order; thus, Faith cannot have heteronormative Buffy do S/M, even though the white, middle-class woman fantasizes it. Instead, the performer must drop her act. It is as if a white woman in the audience stops the black drag's performance because she's offended. The performer must apologize, explain herself, redeem herself. This is why when Riley tells Faith-as-Buffy that he loves her, she is upset and responds with "this is meaningless." According to *Buffy*'s rules, "bad" girl Faith, who stole Buffy's body, has to face up to her deeds and embrace hegemonic ethics. This is made clear when Faith-as-Buffy admits to Buffy's own words that being a slayer is not like being a killer. When Faith and Buffy fight each other at the church, Buffy-as-Faith tells Faith-as-Buffy: "You can't win this." Faith-as-Buffy tells her to shut up, sits on top of her, punching her, saying: "You're nothing. Disgusting. Murderous bitch." Faith-as-Buffy stares at *her* face when she calls Buffy-as-Faith a "disgusting, murderous bitch." This is the black drag's apology to the white gentle soul in the audience. Faith and the drag should be on the verge of redemption.

Virtually Fatal Faith

A redeemed Faith appears on the last season of *Buffy*. Buffy thanks Faith for coming to help her fight against the First Evil. In response to Faith claiming that there is supposed to be only one slayer and this is why they never got along, Buffy remarks, "Also, you went evil and were killing people" ("Dirty Girls"). Faith's response, "Good point. Also a factor," marks a turning point in Buffy and Faith's relationship; Faith admits her wrong deeds, thus validating Buffy's superiority. This time Faith cooperates with Buffy and is reluctant to take the leader's position when the Potentials eliminate Buffy as their leader and prefer non-patronizing, attentive Faith who also knows how to show them a good time. Though she is redeemed, *Buffy* keeps reminding us that the leader is the patriarch, Buffy, and not the underdog, Faith: Faith leads the group into a trap causing the injury of some Potentials.

Faith, admitting to being "an ex-con who didn't finish high school" ("Chosen"), another subtextual class reference, especially to Robin Wood, current principal of Sunnydale High, is the ultimate subservience. Jowett argues that by sleeping with Principal Wood, who jokingly points at her not "out of the world" performance between the sheets, thus trying to eliminate her notable femme-fatalist characteristic, she finally gets the redemption she wants and needs. After all, she has had non-violent sex with a "good" guy who reassures her that there are decent guys out there in the world. However, true to her character, Faith does not tolerate Wood's insult and starts unbuckling her belt, saying "we're going again, baby. You're gonna learn a little respect here, pal." Both Faith and Principal Wood survive their last battle.

Faith's appearance on the last season does not include black leather. Her hair is slightly brighter and her lips are not rouged. Her body language includes less grunting, though she is still far from being stigmatized as a "delicate lady." Her speech is more sensible and much less violent. Her only reference to S/M is when she sees Spike handcuffed in the basement and Spike exclaims that it is not what it looks like. Faith tells him that after her long incarceration, she "[is] thinking about looking up the guy with the bull-whip" ("Dirty Girls"). Spike laughs and tells her the school girl play is old news and Faith makes sure her position is clear: "Just don't forget who's on top." This last line signifies Faith's holding on to her true self. She keeps holding her head high, despite her endorsement of Buffy's set of morals. Yes, she fights with "the good guys" now, but she's still fighting, and she's still taking pleasure in it. Faith reminds herself and the viewer that her sexually aggressive nature is very much there and will probably manifest itself again in the future.

Conclusion

Male fear is responsible for creating and reviving the myth of a stereotypical femme fatale. What remains of this myth and in fact subverts it is female aggressive sexual agency. Following Butler's identity-through-performance, a female performs her non-stereotypical, agentive, femme fatale identity by adhering to language. The character of Faith on *Buffy* serves as an example of a non-stereotypical femme fatale. An examination of the Buffyverse reveals Faith's unique speech, bodily movements, and appearance, which together form her femme fatale identity. Because she is a human who verbally expresses sexually aggressive agency, within white, male hegemony represented by the female character of Buffy, she is able to materialize the mythical, stereotypical femme fatale. The world of Buffy mirrors real world's politics, where female vampires are symbolic of the off-screen world's idealizations of a "true" femme fatale, marking her intangibility and passivity. Functioning as a tangible femme fatale, on the other hand, is nearly impossible both in the off-screen and in the on-screen world, since female sexual agency is foreclosed by hegemonic ethics. This explains why the character of Faith is eventually redeemed. The character of Faith, much as any woman out there, must learn how to navigate her desire within patriarchal frontiers.

Notes

1. Faith's appearance on *Angel* will not be considered here. Nor will be any unaired episodes of *Buffy*, i.e., the Season Eight comics.
2. And to some extent so does Kennedy, who comes on to Willow, but since Kennedy is a Potential who becomes a slayer on the very last episode of *Buffy*, she has no opportu-

nity to express [sexual] pleasure she may find in slaying and in her mate. Anya very often articulates her sexual appetite when she says that she and Xander are about to have sex. But her speech always comes off as inappropriate and socially awkward, marking her alien nature (diverging between being and not being a vengeance demon, Anya or Anyanka). Jowett observes that the character of Anya "is used as a device to make our [*Buffy*'s] world seem strange ... [her] comic function is as the butt of jokes, not ... the scathing wit" (33).

3. Willow is a special case. Other vampires on *Buffy* perform *as* vampires (objects) and any human remnant (subjectivity/agency) is a dream or a memory (of the person the vampire once was). Ensouled vampires like Angel turn "good," in Buffy or *Buffy*'s terms, and as a consequence do not express their violent sexuality.

4. <http://en.wikipedia.org/wiki/Five_by_five>

5. See Bi-Slaying sub-section.

6. Part of the title of K. Schudt, "Also Sprach Faith: The Problem of the Happy Rogue Vampire Slayer." *Buffy the Vampire Slayer and Philosophy: Fear and Trembling in Sunnydale,* ed. J. B. South (Chicago: Open Court, 2003). 20–34.

7. The actresses themselves are fully aware of the subtext: "Actress Eliza Dushku (Faith on *Buffy*) has admitted that she deliberately encouraged the sexual undercurrent between her character and Sarah Michelle Gellar's during her stint on *Buffy*." <http://www.afterellen.com/archive/ellen/TV/lesbianactionhero.html>. In addition, I say that Buffy could not have engaged in girl-on-girl action, especially with a leather-pants gal, and keep her "good" girl image.

8. While *Buffy* aired on the WB network, Joss Whedon was forbidden to display a kiss between two women. Later, when the show moved to UPN, Willow, who was categorized as gay, was shown kissing other women and more. <http://www.whedon.info/article.php3?id_article=17567>. Thus, the subtext becomes a text but with different characters. See endnote 8.

9. Transsexuals/transgenders do not imitate. When a person changes her/his sex and/or gender, the change takes place within and becomes part of the symbolic Order — the person embraces a new identity which s/he previously sought, not mocked.

10. This scene can be analyzed as Faith trying to unite with Buffy in a way uncanny under *Buffy*'s restrictions. Perhaps, had it been possible, Whedon would have shown a masturbation scene instead.

Works Cited

Alexander, J. "A Vampire is Being Beaten: De Sade through the Looking Glass in *Buffy* and *Angel*." *Slayage* 15 (2004). Ed. D. Lavery and R.V. Wilcox. <http://slayageonline.com/essays/slayage15/Alexander.htm>

Austin, J.L. *How to Do Things with Words: The William James Lectures Delivered at Harvard University in 1955.* Ed. J.O. Umson and M. Sabisa. Oxford: Clarendon, 1955.

Barrett, Rusty. "Supermodels of the World Unite! Political Economy and the Language of Performance among African American Drag Queens." *The Language and Sexuality Reader.* Ed. D. Cameron and D. Kulik. New York and London: Routledge, 1995.

Buffy, the Vampire Slayer (WB: 1997–2001, UPN: 2001–2003). Creator Joss Whedon.

Bound (Dino De Laurentiis Company/ Spelling Films, 1996). Directors Andy and Larry Wachowski, 109 min.

Butler, Judith. *Gender Trouble: Feminism and the Subversion of Identity*. New York: Routledge, 1990.

_____. "Implicit Censorship." *Excitable Speech*. New York: Routledge, 1997. 127–163.

Call, L. "Sounds like Kinky Business to Me: Subtextual and Textual Representations of Erotic Power in the Buffyverse." *Slayage* 24 (2007). Ed. D. Lavery and R.V. Wilcox <http://slayageonline.com/PDF/Call.pdf>

Doane, Mary Ann. *Femmes Fatales: Feminism, Film, Theory, Psychoanalysis*. New York: Routledge, 1991.

Hart, Lynda. *Fatal Women: Lesbian Sexuality and the Mark of Aggression*. Princton: Princeton University Press,1994.

Jones, D. *Horror: A Thematic History in Fiction and Film*. Oxford: Oxford University Press, 2002.

Jowett, Lorna. *Sex and the Slayer: A Gender Studies Primer for the Buffy Fan*. Middletown, CT: Wesleyan University Press. 2005.

Kirchner, J. S. "And in some Language That's English?: Slayer Slang and Artificial Computer Generation." *Slayage* 20 (2006). Ed. D. Lavery and R.V. Wilcox. <http://slayage online.com/PDF/Kirchner.pdf>

Masson, C. "'Is that Just a Comforting Way of not Answering the Question?': Willow, Questions and Affective Response in *Buffy the Vampire Slayer*." *Slayage* 20 (2006). Ed. D. Lavery and R.V. Wilcox. < http://slayageonline.com/PDF/Masson.pdf>

Reed, E. "The Case for Faith: The Rogue Vampire Slayer's Search for Identity." *Watcher Junior* 3 (2006). Ed. L. Edwards. <http://www.watcherjunior.tv/03/reed.php>

Richardson, J. M., and J. D, Rabb. "Buffy, Faith and Bad Faith: Choosing to be the Chosen One." *Slayage* 23 (2007). Ed. D. Lavery and R.V. Wilcox. <http://slayageonline. com/essays/slayage23/Richardson_Rabb.htm>

Ruddell, C. "'I am the Law' 'I am the Magics': Speech, Power and the Split Identity of Willow in *Buffy the Vampire Slayer*." *Slayage* 20 (2006). Ed. D. Lavery and R.V. Wilcox. <http://slayageonline.com/PDF/Ruddell.pdf>

Stallings, L.H. "Representin' for the Bitches: Queen B(?) in Hip-Hop Culture." *Mutha is Half a Word: Intersections of Folklore, Vernacular, Myth and Queerness in Black Female Culture*. Columbus: Ohio State University Press, 2007.

Schudt, K. "Also Sprach Faith: The Problem of the Happy Rogue Vampire Slayer." *Buffy the Vampire Slayer and Philosophy: Fear and Trembling in Sunnydale*. Ed. J. B. South. Chicago: Open Court, 2003. 20–34.

Thelma and Louise (MGM/ Pathé Entertainment/ Percy Main/ Star Partners III Ltd., 1991). Dir. Ridley Scott, 129 min.

The Role of Masculinity and Femininity in Buffy the Vampire Slayer

JESSICA PRICE

In every aspect of *Buffy*, there is a theme of completeness. Buffy was not a complete person until she accepted her duties as The Slayer, vampires are not complete because they lack souls, and the primary characters of *Buffy* are not complete without a significant other. These significant others complete the masculine/feminine binary that seems to be imperative for *Buffy*. Through the manipulation done by the show's runners and writers, "...the terms that make up one's own gender are, from the start, outside oneself, beyond oneself in a sociality that has no single author" (Butler 1). The characters in *Buffy* react to the societal need (for masculinity or femininity) by other characters. The dismissal of or tension present in characters of related gender performances could easily be a reflectance in the characters' inability to transform oneself into the person needed to meet the need of the other character. My discussion is based around the fact that gender and sex are two different identities. It is unreasonable to believe we can classify everyone into a sex binary of male/female just as much as it is impossible to control the gender construction to woman/man. "The simple belief in 'only two' [sexes] is not an experiential given but a normative social construction" which opens up the discussion for a spectrum of gender identities (Bing and Bergvall 496). Gendered traits are influenced by all the socially constructed aspects of our lives with masculine and feminine identities on the two ends of the spectrum. All the characters in *Buffy* are situated in various places on the scale based on a host of non–sex based traits: "...[A]lthough we seem to have a difficult time defining masculinity, as a society we have little trouble in recognizing it..." (Halberstam 1). We can debate the existence of a masculinity/femininity dichotomy, but as a society, the traits associated with these identities are identified clearly. "...[F]eminist scholars pointed out in the 1960s and 1970s that feminine and masculine behaviors were prescriptively divided into two mutually exclusive sets which do not necessarily correspond to female and male...," a concept which is the bedrock to my analysis of the Buffyverse (Bing and Bergvall 496). My discussion will refer to "masculine" and "feminine" as representing the primary gender performance (respecting the spectrum) of each character and refer to stereotypical Western society's concepts of the two. In the Buffyverse, all of the secondary characters exist in relation to the primary characters. The secondary characters are only there to further the primary characters, affecting them positively or negatively, but never existing on their own. Once the characters no longer have impact on the primary characters, they leave Sunnydale (or are killed off before they can have a life separate from the primary characters).[1]

In Lorna Jowett's gender study of Buffy, she argues for the masculinity of the male characters and the femininity of the female characters, taking in all aspects of the character's personalities (social forces, "callings," abilities, language, etc). "...[G]ender is fixed through opposition: [Buffy] must be feminine because her partners are masculine; if they are not masculine, she need not be feminine" (Jowett 65–6). My reading of her work deduces that the men are masculine because they fight, but even though the women fight, they are feminine based on the way they are dressed (societal expectations). Jowett's work is instrumental in the study of gender in *Buffy*, and I hope to take the ideas behind femininity and masculinity in *Buffy* one step further. Using her analysis as a jumping off point, I hope to illustrate how *Buffy* actually promotes a challenge to the traditional gender expectations in relation to a character's sex. The opposition of genders helps to make the audience stop and think about what they are watching. Even as stereotypes persist (the traits of femininity, the traits of masculinity), the show sends a message of "be who you are," showing that it's okay for girls to have masculine traits and boys to act feminine.

Buffy, Willow, Xander, and Giles make up the primary characters of *Buffy the Vampire Slayer*. While Buffy *is* the "main character" of the show, Xander, Willow, and Giles help to carry it and exist (however loosely) separate from her. They are the outcasts of Sunnydale High School (at the start of the show)[2] and that rejection from the "in-crowd" is what brings them together. A plot point of the show is that the role of The Slayer is traditionally performed alone. Since Buffy is, by far, not the first Slayer, it's obvious that something did not work during the reign of the other women. All Slayers are all granted "Slayer powers" and trained by members of the Watcher's

Council (and most, not including Buffy, were taught with the Slayer Handbook),[3] the conclusion is made that the demand by the Council to be secretive and fight alone is what led to their deaths. Buffy's friends are a large part of her power[4] and prove their worth during the trials of the finale ("Chosen"). Buffy is able to challenge death *because* of her friends.[5]

With each pairing on *Buffy*, friendship or romantic, there is a masculine person and a feminine person. To play with gender, *Buffy* tends to switch-up the traditional gender/sex binary, creating masculine women and feminine men, particularly within the primary characters. This is not to say that each character is one hundred percent masculine or feminine, but that their dominate gender challenges society's expectations. Buffy, by virtue of being a vampire slayer, is exceptionally strong and a skillful fighter. She is outspoken, confident, and her attitude demands respect, all traits stereotypically reserved for men. On top of this, she craves the idea of being treated "like a girl" and wears very feminine clothing. For the first five seasons there seems to be a clear distinction between "day Buffy" (school girl, more feminine) and "night Buffy" (Slayer, masculine). After Season Five, though, the line between these two parts of her life becomes blurred and she is almost exclusively Buffy the Vampire Slayer, leader of a group fighting evil at all times. This is also the time when Buffy no longer attends school (as a student), offering a debate as to whether or not the school setting and societal pressures is the reason for Buffy's push for the life of a "girl." After leaving college, her tirades about not having a normal life and wanting normalcy in general cease. Does her exclusive identity as Vampire Slayer come from the rejection of her school identity?

Willow begins the show as an awkward teenager, picked on by the popular students (mainly Cordelia and her followers, the Cordettes). "She is intellectual and enjoys study, valuing academic success and thus identifying with 'masculine' rationality and status" (Jowett 37). She does not identify with the traditionally feminine roles and physical characteristics (designer clothing, makeup, etc.) and Buffy does not attempt to change that, allowing Willow to befriend her. She interacts on a heterosocial level (unlike the Cordettes and the Basketball team, each relying on homosocial interactions), her only friends being Xander and (Mr.) Giles until Buffy arrives in Sunnydale. Even when the friendship with Buffy began to strengthen she did not abandon her other friends, instead aiding in the formation of a powerful (heterosocial) group. As the show progresses, she becomes a powerful member of the Scooby Gang[6] and acts as leader in numerous situations (most notably the summer after Buffy dies in "The Gift").[7] "This leadership position allows Willow to display behavior and skills traditionally coded masculine. Just as two male heroes might compete for leadership, tension arises between Willow and Buffy" (Jowett 38). This tension Jowett mentions is attributed to the fact that Willow and Buffy are both coded as masculine, disrupting the masculine/feminine binary *Buffy* tries to adhere to. That being said, the fluidity of gender comes into play as Willow takes a back-seat to Buffy's masculinity — when Willow challenges her, it results in conflict.

Xander was Willow's best friend growing up, also an outcast at Sunnydale High. He is sensitive and witty and any attempt at performing masculinity is awkward and seems out of character. This permits the audience to read him as feminine. This is toyed with on the show as he is mistaken for gay a handful of times.[8] Xander tries to overcompensate with material objects like driving his uncle's car in "The Zeppo,"[9] although he has more moments of taking the "damsel" role, like arming himself with lousy weapons or needing to be rescued.[10] One of the most important aspects of his character is the fact that he has no superpowers. When everyone turned into their costumes on Halloween, he became a soldier (hypermasculine), but even that was far from the (superhuman) powers his friends have on a daily basis ("Halloween"). His role in the group (aside from window-fixer in the later seasons thanks to his construction jobs) is The Heart. In "Grave," Willow's grief-stricken attempt to destroy the world is averted by Xander, who stops her after a speech about their friendship and telling her he loves her, a nonviolent/feminine response to conflict. In a conversation with Dawn, Buffy's sister and one of only two other major character with no superpowers,[11] he talks about the difficulty of watching everyone around him grow stronger and Dawn suggests that his power is "seeing, knowing" ("Potential").[12] Irony takes hold when, only six episodes later, Caleb (Season Seven's "bad guy") grabs Xander during a fight and gouges out his left eye ("Dirty Girls"). Caleb is a self-proclaimed minister who spends much of his time on screen talking about religion and quoting the Bible. In the ancient Egyptian tradition, the left eye represents the moon[13] ("Eye"). I would say that Caleb choosing to gouge Xander's left eye was not accidental. Genesis 1:16 of the Bible says, "God made two great lights — the greater light to govern the day and the lesser light to govern the night." This could easily be translated into the sun being masculine and the moon being feminine (out of the stereotype of femininity being "lesser" than masculinity). I believe Caleb chose the left eye in an attempt to return Xander to his "proper" role of masculinity, as implied by Caleb's misogynistic reading of The Bible.

Giles' background in ancient/strange artifacts and his social awkwardness makes him an outcast with other teachers, but fits in well with Buffy, Willow, and Xander. Giles was Buffy's Watcher after she moved to Sunnydale and is an instrumental part of the Scooby Gang. He transforms from strict instructor to loving parental figure throughout the years. His father-like love for Buffy and his willingness to ignore everything he is told by the Council for her adds to the feminine qualities of parental protector. He does become the surrogate father to Buffy, Willow, and Xander and eventually gives them space to be on their own, returning briefly to help save the world. He is closest to Buffy and Willow, their masculine qualities complementing his femininity. While he and Xander are close, it is not on the same level.[14] Jowett points out that "three of the four Scooby meeting places are 'his' (the library ... his home ... and The Magic Box)" (128–9), which could be seen as the feminine action of providing a home (literally and figuratively). His masculine traits are filtered through his alter ego, Ripper, from his earlier years. This is very similar to Angel's Angelus (discussed later), the difference being Ripper does not have quite the same violent streak. Ripper could not exist within the Scooby Gang because of the clash between him and Buffy. Giles' femininity, along with Xander's, helps to balance the primary Scooby Gang.

Every single secondary character on the show is directly involved with a primary character, never another secondary character. Even in group scenes, if they split up to do something, it almost never ends up that secondary characters are exclusively together. It's as though the primary characters have to chaperone the secondary characters. Angel, Riley, Spike, Faith, Dawn, Joyce Summers, Oz, Tara, Cordelia, Anya, Wesley, and Miss Calander have all been part of a pair with primary character. Angel, Riley, and Spike all dated Buffy, Faith's existence on the show was dictated by Buffy's death and her motivation is centered exclusively around her jealousy of Buffy, Dawn is Buffy's younger sister, Joyce is Buffy's (and Dawn's) mom, Oz and Tara dated Willow, Cordelia and Anya dated Xander, Wesley was Faith's Watcher and Buffy's Watcher as well as Giles' colleague, and Miss Calander and Giles were a couple. All of the secondary characters embody the opposite gender characteristics from the primary character they are paired up with. For the purposes of this paper, I will focus on Angel, Riley, and Spike, who all represent very important and different gender interactions, as well as Tara, being Willow's significant other and subsequently half of the first lesbian couple on *Buffy*.

Angel, Riley, and Spike are quite different from one another. The only way a relationship on *Buffy* can be sustained in any way is if the two characters maintain the gender performance binary. Angel is soft-spoken and romantic, both traits normally used to describe women. It is David Boreanaz's performance in the episode "I Only Have Eyes for You" in Season Two that sent Whedon to work on creating a spin-off for Angel ("Interview"). In the episode, Buffy and Angel/Angelus are possessed by the spirits of star-crossed lovers, only the spirit of the man entered Buffy's body, while the women's spirit took over Angel's body. It was Boreanaz's ability to act in such a feminine way that sparked the idea for his own show. If this idea of men as feminine wasn't such an important aspect of the Whedonverse, why would acting feminine be grounds for a new TV show? Whedon clearly respects and encourages the disruption of society's gender expectations. When Angel loses his soul and Angelus returns, he is violent and cruel, the opposite of Angel. This coincides with Buffy and Angel consummating their relationship and Angel experiencing one moment of true happiness (thus, the loss of his soul). When they see each other for the first time after having sex, Buffy does not realize Angel has changed, but his flippant remarks and brushing off their time together plays off the stereotype of the masculine man leaving the feminine woman after sex ("Innocence"). The relationship with Buffy could never work with Angelus, not only because he is "evil," but because he embodies stereotypical masculinity, clashing with Buffy's established role. When he regains his soul, he is able to submit to his role as feminine. When he does leave, he doesn't directly say goodbye, instead passively walking away from Buffy and Sunnydale, believing his leaving will give her the chance at a "real life" ("Graduation Day, Part 2"). This self-sacrificial moment parallels the idea that women should be self-sacrificing for their families.

At the beginning of their relationship, Riley seems like he could be the perfect match for Buffy, providing evidence for a nurturing man who enjoys picnics and helping the campus gay and lesbian organization hang banners. When it is revealed that he works for a government agency called The Initiative, created to fight and capture vampires, demons, and the like, Riley's feminine nature begins to disappear. "Riley is traditional and conservative and displays all the characteristics of a tough guy. His early interactions with Buffy demonstrate that he wants to protect her" (Jowett 103). This masculine trait of needing to protect can't sit well with Buffy, the woman who, by fate, does the protecting. Where the other men in her life have protected/saved her on occasions, they are able to return to her the role of protector at the end of the day. Riley likes his strength (even though it is created within him by The Initiative) and feels losing it "[would] emasculate him" (Jowett 104–5). He challenges Buffy, constantly trying to be better, stronger, faster than she is, but is constantly "beaten by a girl." Being unable to let go of his masculinity, Buffy and Riley's relationship falls apart dramatically. Expecting to have a stereotypical feminine lover in Buffy, Riley is upset by her absence (between dealing with her mother's sudden illness and dealing with Glory the God) and acts out. Buffy is taken to where Riley is being bitten by a female vampire (representative of prostitution and addiction [Jowett 106]) and she ends the relationship. Riley going to a prostitute is an extreme move to assert his masculinity.

Spike is the most feminine of Buffy's lover's. Before he became a vampire, he was William, a poet in love with a woman named Cecily, for which he was teased mercilessly. The vampire, Drusilla, sired him and they became lovers and traveled the world for many years. During his relationship with Drusilla, he was very loving and cared for her while she was ill. These emotions aren't supposed to live within a vampire, but Spike could not rid himself of his need to care for his loved one, a trait associated with the role of caretaker, one of which is connected to femininity. When he is injured and put into a wheelchair, it closely coincided with Angel's turn to Angelus and this helped to reinforce Spike's femininity (helplessness) and Angelus' masculinity (dominance). Through a dozen wheelchair jokes made by Angelus, the sexual innuendos would put into question Spike's manhood when it came to Dru, Angel clearly flirting with her and trying to assert his manhood ("I Only Have Eyes for You"). Spike is forced, due to his lack of mobility, to be passive. Since he cannot challenge Angelus in any "masculine way," he has no other choice than to watch Angelus flirt with his lover. When Spike does get out of the chair and goes to Buffy to propose a deal to stop Angelus from destroying the world, his one requirement is that Drusilla lives ("Becoming, Part 2"). This is not a "masculine" act of protecting Drusilla, but rather the "feminine" act of loving her so much he can't leave her behind, Spike not wanting to be alone. Spike was captured by The Initiative in Season Four and a chip was put into his brain to cause severe neurological pain if he tried to harm a human, rendering him more-or-less "flaccid" ("Something Blue"). This castration does not allow him to act out any masculine tendencies he may have (except fighting against other demons, which separates him from the "boys club" of the demon world) and this permits him to enter into the Scooby Gang. He even plays the part of babysitter to Dawn and becomes someone she feels safe with (a feminine attribute). His role as protector to Dawn is more along the lines of feminine than Buffy's complementary role as protector. They can both fight, but Buffy is the first one to run out into the fight, while Spike is relegated to the living room playing cards with Dawn. As he sings to Buffy in the musical episode, "You know, you've got a willin' slave..." he indicates his ability to pass up the masculine energy to be with her ("Once More with Feeling"). During their numerous borderline-S/M sex rendezvous, he ends up falling in love with her while she denies any affection toward him, but rather that he makes her feel dirty ("Dead Things"). This is similar to Buffy's post-sex moment with Angel(us), using the same attitudes but flipping the gender roles. Where Angelus is masculine and clashes with Buffy's masculinity, Spike remains feminine after sex (through his hyper-masculine attitude post-coital) and is denied the love and affection he desires from the masculine character. That Buffy and Spike retain the masculine/feminine binary is what permits the relationship to continue. It is obvious that Buffy feels something for him, even if it's not quite love, but her masculine call to duty keeps her from returning the gesture. Spike's sacrifice at the end of the final episode finds him the self-sacrificing lamb ("Chosen").

Tara breaks the mold created by this mostly heterosexist show's man/feminine, woman/masculine binaries. She is introduced to the show in Season Four as painfully shy, she and Willow meeting at a UC Sunnydale campus Wicca group ("Hush"). "...Battis suggests that Willow's rejection of the university Wicca group implies that she has 'no particular desire for feminine empowerment through Wicca'" (Jowett 38). Tara, on the other hand, only leaves the group to be with Willow. The group members know her name and seem to know how shy she is to speak (illustrated by their over emphasis to quiet everyone down so she can speak), which can mean that she was a regular at the meetings, not completely casting away the "feminine empowerment." Their friendship blossomed and they fell in love. By nature of the show, Tara represents femininity to Willow's masculinity. Tara's femininity is emphasized in the dream-based episode "Restless." At the start of Willow's dream, Willow is seen writing in Greek on Tara's naked back. This is translated as being part of Sappho's poem "Ode to Aphrodite."[15] It is also important to note Willow's choice of Sappho's poem. "Ode to Aphrodite" was Sappho's first complete poem, just as Willow and Tara's relationship is the first "complete," non-dysfunctional relationship on *Buffy*. This being an invocation to Aphrodite, Tara represents Aphrodite and Willow represents Sappho. "Homer identifies Aphrodite as a 'feminine' goddess, weak, *analkis*, unsuited to take part in male warfare. Her appropriate sphere ... is to seduce weak women" (Winkler qtd. Abelove et al. 582). Tara represents femininity from Aphrodite and is Willow's seductress. It is the combination of Tara's magics and Willow's power that gives Willow the confidence to become the Wicca that allows for her high standing within the Gang and her eventual downfall as she begins to abuse magic and then attempts to destroy the world in her grief over Tara's death ("Entropy"; "Seeing Red"; "Grave"). Willow's representation of Sappho allows her to enter the "male warfare" (in *Buffy*, the "Slayer warfare") as she mirrors Sappho's leadership.[16]

Tara is a powerful witch, although her power is strongest while paired up with Willow.[17] Often times watching Dawn was left to Spike, but Tara was also frequently left at home to watch over the youngest member of the Scooby Gang. It's no coincidence that they both represent the feminine. Tara expresses her concern to Willow regarding her growing use/abuse of magic and Willow simply brushes off her concerns and actually does a spell to make her forget their fight ("All the Way"). In this instance, magic is used to represent addiction, which Willow cannot accept, causing Tara to leave. Between their break up and reunion, Tara continues to visit the house, but mainly for Dawn's sake, continuing to be a mother figure to her.[18]

One of the problematic things with the way *Buffy* presents gender is the static nature of it. While fluidity exists, if a character floats too far away from the show's gender prescription, they are no longer allowed to be part of the Scooby Gang (i.e., Riley). At first, it seems that *Buffy* allows its characters to live without the constraints of gender, allowing them to transgress their sex roles, but the restriction does exist. On the outside, the characters are expected to dress and socially act like their expected gender, but I find that the gender of *Buffy* is based on the essence/actions of the characters which does not always match their presented sex. While the world outside of *Buffy* focuses on man/woman binaries, *Buffy* is more concerned with the pairings of masculine/feminine (regardless of sex).

Notes

1. Cordelia moved to L.A. and teamed up with Angel on *Angel*; Anya is killed off when it starts to look like a story between her and Andrew could develop (neither character being primary); Faith ended up in a coma (on *Buffy*), then jail (on *Angel*), then returned to *Buffy* all to fit the stories of the primary characters of both shows (*A* "City of...," "Chosen," "Graduation Day, Part 2," *A* "Sanctuary," "Dirty Girls," respectively).

2. Willow and Xander become outcasts as they move up through the same school system their whole lives, Buffy is shunned for hanging out with Willow and Xander, and Giles is not popular with the other teachers and staff.

3. BUFFY: "Wait. Handbook? What handbook? How come I don't have a handbook?" [...]
   GILES: "After meeting you, Buffy, I realized that, uh, the handbook would be of no use in your case" ["What's My Line," Part 2.]

4. This is taken literally in Season Four's "Primeval" when a spell is used to grant Buffy superpowers to defeat Adam (Giles as the mind, Willow as the spirit, and Xander as the heart).

5. Buffy died twice throughout the seven seasons. Both times she was brought back: the first time by Xander performing CPR ("Prophecy Girl"), the second time Willow led the group in a resurrection spell ("Bargaining, Part 1").

6. The Scooby Gang is a reference to the Scooby Doo group of friends who fight crime. On *Buffy*, the Scooby Gang consists of anyone who joins the primary characters in saving the world.

7. XANDER: "Excuse me? Who made you the boss of the group?"
ANYA: "You did."
TARA: "You said Willow should be boss."
ANYA: "And then you said 'let's vote,' and it was unanimous..."
TARA: "...and then you made her this little plaque that said 'Boss of Us,' you put little sparkles on it..." ["Bargaining, Part 1].

8. Larry (stereotypical jock) is gay and thinks Xander is struggling with coming out and tries to talk to Xander about how to do it ("Graduation Day, Part 1").

9. BUFFY: "Is this a Penis metaphor?"

10. XANDER: "Calvary's here. Calvary's a guy with a big rock, but it's here" ("Becoming, Part 2").

11. Joyce Summers has no superpowers

12. D'HOFFRYN (re: Xander): "And the young man, he sees with the eyeballs of love" ("Selfless").

13. The right eye represents the sun.

14. GILES: "It's a trick. They get inside my head, make me see things I want."
XANDER: "Then why would they make you see me?"
GILES: [pause] "You're right. Let's go"
["Becoming," Part 2].

15. See Battis 19, Mendlesohn in Wilcox and Lavery 59, and Pateman 129–131 for further analysis of Willow's dream.

16. Sappho in poetry, Willow in magic.

17. The stereotype mentioned before of the feminine person needing the masculine person to complete them.

18. After Joyce's death, Willow and Tara move into her room and become surrogate mothers to Dawn, although Tara tended to be the more feminine (comforting, passive protecting) while Willow continued to be the more masculine one (scolding, controlling).

Episodes

"Bargaining, Part 1." *Buffy the Vampire Slayer.* UPN. 2 October 2001.
"Becoming, Part 2." *Buffy the Vampire Slayer.* WB. 19 May 1998.
"Chosen." *Buffy the Vampire Slayer.* UPN. 20 May 2003.
"City Of..." *Angel.* WB. 5 October 1999.
"Dead Things." *Buffy the Vampire Slayer.* UPN. 5 February 2002.
"Dirty Girls." *Buffy the Vampire Slayer.* UPN. 15 April 2003.
"The Gift." *Buffy the Vampire Slayer.* WB. 22 May 2001.
"Graduation Day, Part 1." *Buffy the Vampire Slayer.* WB. 18 May 1999.
"Graduation Day, Part 2." *Buffy the Vampire Slayer.* WB. 13 July 1999.

"Grave." *Buffy the Vampire Slayer.* UPN. 21 May 2002.
"Halloween." *Buffy the Vampire Slayer.* WB. 27 October 1997.
"Hush." *Buffy the Vampire Slayer.* WB. 3 November 1999.
"I Only Have Eyes for You." *Buffy the Vampire Slayer.* WB. 3 March 1998.
"Once More with Feeling." *Buffy the Vampire Slayer.* UPN. 06 November 2001.
"Prophecy Girl." *Buffy the Vampire Slayer.* WB. 2 June 1997.
"Potential." *Buffy the Vampire Slayer.* UPN. 21 January 2003.
"Primeval." *Buffy the Vampire Slayer.* WB. 16 May 2000.
"Restless." *Buffy the Vampire Slayer.* WB. 23 May 2000.
"Sanctuary." *Angel.* WB. 2 May 2000.
"Something Blue." *Buffy the Vampire Slayer.* WB. 30 November 1999.
"What's My Line, Part 2." *Buffy the Vampire Slayer.* WB. 24 November 1997.
"The Zeppo." *Buffy the Vampire Slayer.* WB. 26 January 1999.

Works Cited

Battis, Jes. "'She's Not All Grown Yet': Willow As Hybrid/Hero in Buffy the Vampire Slayer." *Slayage: the Online International Journal of Buffy Studies* 8 (2003).
Bing, Janet M. and Victoria L. Bergvall. "The Question of Questions: Beyond Binary Thinking." <http://www.uvm.edu/~jadickin/bingandbergvall.pdf>. 13 September 2009.
Butler, Judith. *Undoing Gender.* New York: Routledge, 2004.
Genesis 1:16. "New International Version." 2007. <http://www.biblegateway.com/passage/?search=Gen%201:16&version=31;>. 6 June 2007.
Eye of Horus. <http://www.themystica.com/mystica/articles/e/eye_of_horus.html>. 5 June 2007.
Halberstam, Judith. *Female Masculinity.* Durham: Duke University Press, 1998.
Interview with Joss Whedon. "I Only Have Eyes for You." *Buffy the Vampire Slayer.* Buffy & Angel Chronicles Gift Set VHS. 1997
Jowett, Lorna. *Sex and the Slayer: A Gender Studies Primer for the Buffy Fan.* Middletown, CT: Wesleyan University Press, 2005.
Mendlesohn, Farah. "Surpassing the Love of Vampires; or, Why (and How) a Queer Reading of the Buffy/Willow Relationship Is Denied." *Fighting the Forces.* Ed. Rhonda V. Wilcox and David Lavery. Lanham, MD: Rowman & Littlefield, 2002. 45–60.
Pateman, Matthew. *The Aesthetics of Culture in* Buffy the Vampire Slayer. Jefferson, NC: McFarland, 2006.
Winkler, John J. "Double Consciousness in Sappho's Lyrics." *The Lesbian and Gay Studies Reader.* Ed. Henry Abelove et al. New York: Routledge, 1993. 577–594.

Exploitation of Bodies and Minds in Season One of Dollhouse

CATHERINE COKER

"You make people different. You can make me help."—Echo, "A Spy in the House of Love"

"When you hear the words 'doll house' you probably think of little girls playing 'tea party.' But for some people in Los Angeles, those words have a different meaning. A darker meaning."
— Reporter, "Man on the Street"

Introduction

Dollhouse has become Joss Whedon's most controversial work yet, with many fans, viewers, and critics troubled by the images and aspects of human trafficking and prostitution depicted on the show. Female characters are regularly menaced and abused, often sexually, both within and without the confines of the Dollhouse and the assignations it arranges. This chapter will focus on how the Dolls, both male and female, are programmed in both body and mind to be the toys and the tools of the people who will use them. In particular, the show depicts people's attitudes towards the Dolls as objects or pets rather than as human beings. Reactions to the show from viewers and critics focus on this aspect, inviting a reading of Whedon, the writers, and the camera as being exploitive, rather than the show being a story of exploitation.

What is the Dollhouse?

"The Dollhouse. It's pink and it opens up and there's teeny furniture, and you put the boy doll on top of the girl doll and we learn about urges."
— Joel Mynor, "Man on the Street"

In 2008, many months prior to the show's first airing, the geek news website *i09* reported on the appearance of several script pages from *Dollhouse* with the headline "Joss Whedon is Even Creepier Than We Thought."[1] The script pages were released as "casting sides," the pages sent to casting agencies. The script detailed the major plot points of the new pilot for the show entitled "Ghost." The story focuses on the kidnapping of a child, with the Doll Echo first as a "hot date" for a wealthy playboy and then a hostage negotiator; Echo's new identity of Ellie Penn, a kidnap-victim-and-sex-abuse survivor, and the botched negotiation and rescue of the child. The *i09* piece focused on the transition of "sex kitten to survivor" and the author's fretting that the show may be "a little too weird for most viewers."

Dollhouse is very different from Whedon's prior works: it's darker, more serious, less fantastical. For those reasons, many of the narrative themes we have seen before seem imminently more shocking: when Ted hits Buffy in Season Two of *Buffy the Vampire Slayer*, we aren't concerned for Buffy's safety because we know she will meet a show of violence with superior force. This is not true with *Dollhouse* because the only superpowers the Dolls have are, quite literally, their brains. When Echo is struck and bloodied, she is not going to heal rapidly, and she may or may not be programmed with fighting skills. The Dollhouse maintains an infirmary and medical staff on their premises and engagements where Dolls may be physically harmed are (ostensibly) either refused or made prohibitively expensive. The Dolls' handlers remain nearby in case an emergency extraction from a dodgy situation is called for.

"We are pimps and killers, but in a philanthropic sort of way," Boyd Langton states in the episode "A Spy in the House of Love." Boyd is a former cop and Echo's handler. The term "handler" acts as a title for the people who shepherd the Dolls from base to assignment and back; its use invites the connotation of both animal training and political machinations. Throughout the show, we see his clear affection for Echo in particular and his desire to protect the Dolls in general. In many ways, he is the moral compass of the show — a moral compass who nonetheless aids in the prostitution of a woman he clearly has fatherly feelings for, uses violence as an interrogation method and a deterrent, and whose position is probably cloaked in a dubious past.

The Dollhouse is a shadowy organization, global in scope, rich in means and resources. The Dolls are its business but not its purpose, or so we are told. Above all, the Dollhouse will remind viewers of the Wolfram & Hart offices from *Angel* as the morally ambiguous characters inhabit a gorgeously appointed, vaguely Asian-influenced condo-spa and office high-rise. It acts at once as a womb and a fortress: inside of the Dollhouse, the Dolls are "protected." The Dolls themselves, female and male, are beautiful adult bodies with the functional minds of children. They don't have names, but NATO-style phonetic alphabet appellations: Echo, Sierra, Victor, November, Tango, etc. Handlers and staff are instructed to be polite and pleasant, but not to become overly close with their charges. "They're like pets," says Laurence Dominic, the head of security, in the episode "Needs." "If your child starts talking for the first time, you feel proud. If your dog does, you freak the hell out."

The Dollhouse can also be viewed as a microcosm for society itself. As children, we are programmed with gender expectations, sexual mores, and the thousands of other bits of cultural coding that we take for granted every day. A Doll in the "tabula rasa" state has what appears to be the mind of a child; they roam throughout the Dollhouse between activity rooms, gyms, and cafeteria at will with a minimum of scheduling, though it appears everyone goes to sleep at the same time and wakes up at the same time. When a Doll is imprinted, they are programmed with the adult persona and skills that the client desires. People with the minds of children and the bodies of supermodels leave themselves open to exploitation, despite the care most of the staff lavish on them. Thus, we find by the sixth episode that one of the handlers has been serially raping his charge, Echo's friend, Sierra. The handler is eliminated hastily and Sierra's mind wiped of the horrible memories as much as possible. Though the erasure of these particular memories is a kindness, the concept of calculatedly expunging memories and experiences can quickly fall into a morally gray area — and so of course it does.

"Everything is not as it seems," Adelle DeWitt states in the first line of the show. She coerces Caroline, a troubled woman on the run, to sign away her life for five years by becoming a Doll. After the time period is up, she will have a clean record and an expanded bank account. In return, she is possessed body and mind by the Dollhouse as Echo. Though the use of the NATO alphabet was mentioned earlier, the name also has mythological connotations traced back to the Greek myth of Echo and Narcissus: the story of a woman who is punished with the loss of self and the man she loves who loves only himself. We as the audience are quickly set up to not only question everything we see, but seemingly to watch a woman's life be dissolved on a weekly basis.

Broken Women

In "Gray Hour," Echo is imprinted with a persona called Taffy, a quick-witted thief who is hired along with three men to steal artwork. At first dubious of her abilities, the men quickly become appreciative and admiring of

Taffy's talents, with the ring-leader even asking her out for a date once the theft is completed. Moments later, however, an implanted signal in a phone call erases the imprinted Taffy, leaving a bewildered Echo in her place. Echo doesn't know anything about lock-breaking, security side-stepping, or high tech gadgetry; they are now locked in the vault that they have broken into. Her former admirers are frustrated and impatient now that she is "useless" and unable to get them to safety; the man who had moments before been asking her out even striking her in frustration, declaring that she is now "a talking cucumber." At first bewildered by this abuse, Echo eventually fights back and escapes with an injured comrade whom she says is broken. "I'm not broken," she greets Boyd; this phrase becomes a trope that will appear throughout the series.

The phrase "broken woman" in American culture symbolizes an abuse or rape victim, often mentally incapacitated from trauma. River Tam of the stripped amygdala is perhaps Whedon's most famous example of this type of character. In the television show *Firefly* and follow-up feature film *Serenity*, River's story chronicles a girl genius who is abused by the government. In the *Firefly* episode "Ariel," her brother Simon describes what doctors did to her:

> They opened up her skull ... and then they cut into her brain. [...] The only reason to make an incision in someone's brain is to lobotomize them — you go in to remove damaged tissue. Why someone would cut into a healthy brain.... They did it over and over.

River's first appearance to the crew is curled up in a box, nude and fetal. She is often depicted as childlike, though she is supposed to be aged sixteen. Her eventual recovery is presented as the ultimate will-to-power to save her family and friends from death at the hands of the cannibalistic Reavers.

When Echo declares that she is not broken, she is emphasizing her wholeness in mind as well as her physical body. She is no longer a toy to be made or broken at someone else's will. Her very being — mind and body — is consistently at stake when she is in or outside the Dollhouse. She is menaced within the Dollhouse itself by Laurence Dominic — who maintains that she is a danger and should be sent to the Attic where she will be completely erased — and outside the Dollhouse by abusive clients. Most disturbingly, it appears that a high percentage of engagements involve significant physical threat — enough that one has to wonder how many Dolls survive to be freed after their five year contract is up. In addition, though there are numerous male Dolls, the females as programmed objects face a higher level of implicit social violence.

Though DeWitt and others maintain that the Dolls are there by choice, we also eventually find out that that is not the case. Caroline, and later a student named Sam Jennings, are coerced by DeWitt into becoming Dolls to escape legal ramifications. In addition, Sierra was a woman named Priya who was effectively sold to the Dollhouse by a client through a combination of money and blackmail. We also find out this happened because she refused to have sex with the man, and that as a Doll she is regularly imprinted to have sex with him on their assignations together. In that case, we can be sure that the Dolls are definitely programmed into performing acts their real selves could never have agreed to, thus presuming that the contracts would be sufficiently vague on services rendered to be barely legal, if they are legal at all. As Ballard later states in "Briar Rose," "there is no provision for consensual slavery. It is wrong. You know it's wrong."

The slavery angle is later explicit when Alpha interrogates Dr. Saunders, asking about when he was first brought to her as a new Doll. This scene is fraught with sexual tension, with the implication being that on some level Saunders has used or engaged Alpha sexually. We later find out through flashbacks that during the time Alpha was in the Dollhouse, Dr. Saunders was an older, male doctor, and that the woman we know as "Claire Saunders" was then herself a Doll called Whiskey. When the original Saunders was murdered by Alpha, his imprint was (presumably) placed in the Doll that has been physically scarred. Was Alpha abused by the doctor? If so, this is a recounting of male rape, a topic that is virtually invisible in our culture. Its placement here is a marker on how abuse reflects on both genders.

The new Dr. Saunders, called Claire, now never leaves the Dollhouse. Previously, Whiskey had been the most popular Doll in the Dollhouse; with the loss of her beauty, she is relegated to mending the other Dolls. Though it is clear that she knows she was once a Doll, it is unclear what has happened to "Claire's" memories of her former life. However, her bitterness implies a loss of freedom and choice. When Victor is attacked by Alpha, he asks Saunders how he can "be his best" now that he too is scarred. She replies:

> You can't be your best. Your best is past, a past you can't even remember. You're ugly now. You're disgusting. All you're good for now is pity. And for that, you're gonna have to look somewhere else.[2]

Saunders is brutal but accurate in her assessment. Victor's assignments were most often sexual in nature. With his beauty marred, he is like Whiskey. However, as a large male, he can still complete his contract with missions that involve force. The term "broken man" implies a spiritual rather than a physical loss, and it is noticeable that the word "broken" is never used by Victor or by those around him. The loss of looks does not affect males in the body trade as much as it does females.

The Dollhouse as Our House and the Language of Control

"There is an amazing amount of unbelievable shit happening to women all over the world every single day. A lot to cull from—and to fight against."

—Joss Whedon[3]

Catharine A. MacKinnon reflects on the Universal Declaration of Human Rights: "In 1948, it told the world what a person, as a person, is entitled to. It has been fifty years. Are women human yet?"[4] She comments on each article of the Declaration, noting that across the world, many women are not yet free, not yet educated, not yet protected from genital mutilation and rape. The very language of the document is inclusive to men (repeated male pronouns and possessives: him and his; "brotherhood") but exclusive to women.

The Dollhouse terminology emphasizes the aspects of play: the Dolls serve at others' pleasures. Much of the time it seems as though most assignations are strictly recreational, particularly sexual. They are "pets," to use Dominic's terminology. They are not friends, coworkers, or colleagues, not even human: they are pets. They are "trained" through the imprinting process; they are punished through removal to the Attic (it is unclear whether the death is physical or metaphorical) and rewarded with freedom after their five year contract is up. In the mean time, they have no rights and no choice; they are objects.

The use of language is important in the dehumanization of a person. In our society, women are dehumanized with words like "bitch," "cow," "cunt," "babe" or "baby," etc. The terms consistently emphasize sexual and mental reduction. In *Dollhouse*, the codification for Dolls is similar. "Somebody put her tiny little thinking cap on," Topher says derisively in "A Spy in the House of Love" when Echo makes an observation to him. Though Topher doesn't physically abuse any of the Dolls—in fact he himself is viewed as nearly asexual—his treatment of all women leaves much to be desired. He regularly sends his coworker, Ivy, to fetch him juice boxes and snacks instead of treating her like a colleague. He is also a social misfit who, seemingly, regularly imprints himself on Dolls in order to have social contact.

Ballard's language is just as reductive. At first he seems to be the hero in this story, though he gradually emerges as a man who is just as reductive in his view of the Dolls as others. For example, when he goes to a colleague at the FBI and describes the evidence he has found thus far, Ballard still refers to "his neighbor" as a "a Doll," yet Loomis replies, "I was gonna go with victim." Though his vocabulary is outwardly the terms of a man obsessed with his mission, internally it invites a different reading. As we will later see, his investigation of the Dollhouse is more about his ego than it is the desire to correct a wrong.

Echo & Narcissus

> "I think your fantasy is about my Rebecca. [...] But then, the brave little FBI agent whisked her away from the cash-wielding losers and restored her true identity. And, she fell in love with him."
> — Joel Mynor, "Man on the Street"

The two main protagonists of the show are Echo and Paul Ballard. With the conscious naming of Echo and an explicit theme on desire, however, there are obvious connections to the classical myth of Echo and Narcissus. Psychoanalytic readings of Ovid's text have produced many studies focusing on the effects of narcissistic disorders, nihilism, and self-destruction. A translation of the poem[5] reads of Narcissus "'Can her boy live long / With such perfect beauty?' The seer replied: / 'Yes, unless he learns to know himself.'" When he is first introduced, Ballard seems to be an FBI agent who genuinely wants to save people from the Dollhouse. Though he is continuously mocked by his colleagues, he alone follows leads and trails to the organization that viewers know is real, and thus seems to be the obvious hero of the story.

As the show continues, however, it begins to paint a darker picture. Ballard is at first coldly oblivious to his neighbor, Mellie, who clearly has a crush on him. Later they embark on a tentative romance, only for it to be revealed that Mellie is really November, a Doll that has been programmed explicitly for Ballard to fall in love with so he will be thrown off the track of his quest. Ballard's desires to protect have left him vulnerable to manipulation by the Dollhouse. Later Mellie/November declares to Ballard, "I will give you what you need, and let you take it from me. If you want to give back, give back, but it doesn't have to mean anything." Ballard makes love to Mellie violently; the expression on his face throughout is dark, sinister, and almost hateful. The man who had in the beginning been the heroic figure is now diminished to being little more than a client himself. Clearly filled with self-loathing afterward, he finally manipulates Mellie into an emotional breakdown — and when the handlers come to pick her up, he follows her to the Dollhouse.

Ballard's primary drive to discover the Dollhouse is ostensibly to save

"Caroline," the real identity of the woman we know as Echo. His encounters allow him to build a vision of himself as a savior. What is happening internally is best expressed through a psychoanalytic reading of the myth by Maryanne Hannan (though I have changed the genders of the pronouns used):

> She is his fantasy, and having her will bring him success and happiness he wants. He has seen her, and created in her an image that satisfies his own purposes. The more he sees her, the more convinced he is that she is indeed who he wants her to be. He is more concerned with her appearance, her *corpus*, than with who she is; he knows her not at all. He becomes obsessed with his fantasy of her and pursues her relentlessly until he has the opportunity to enact his fantasy.[6]

When Ballard reaches the Dollhouse and faces the pods that house the Dolls, his expression is one of sorrow as he views the sleeping November, and one of joy when he wakes "Caroline." Unfortunately, Echo has no idea of who he is and is frightened. When given the choice of going with Boyd, who she knows and trusts, and the stranger, she chooses Boyd. Ballard is left alone, beaten.

Ultimately, Ballard joins the Dollhouse as a "contractor." Narcissism is destructive, a kind of nihilism. Ballard is becoming the thing he hates — much like Angel when he goes to Wolfram and Hart. Angel mortgages his soul to save his son; Ballard does so to save Mellie, whom Adelle releases from her contract as payment to Ballard for his services. It remains to be seen whether this act will be one of redemption or final dissolution.

Saving Hazel

> "The technology my mother created has been used by R Corp. to create Dollhouses all over the world. My mother was against that project. And that's what got her killed. Mom wanted to brainwash me to make me better. Dollhouses mold people into something they're not and they sell them for profit. Everybody does it. Brainwashing people into obedient little consumers who think they're influencing the world by voting for the least bad choice every four years. Everyone has a right to their own personality. Without you, I would've been just another broken Doll. And who knows, maybe there are others like me.... Are you one? You've helped me so far, and I'll probably ask for your help again. Together, we must take down R. Corp. and the Dollhouse.... They must go down. Identity wants to be free."
>
> — Transmission 51, February 28, 2009

For three weeks in February 2009, Fox implemented a viral ARG, or Alternative Reality Game, entitled "Saving Hazel." The game was accessed through a website called R Prime Lab.[7] The game consisted of "transmissions," short videos of a few minutes each, that began with a young African American woman named Hazel locked in a room and begging for help. Players could make short videos of themselves and submit them to the website for other players and for Hazel to view. Players could also chat with one another separately. In this way, the game continued and the story opened up to viewers.

The story goes like this: Hazel has been looking for her mother, Andrea Rose. She is locked in what appears to be a small office or lab that appears to be in a moving vehicle, possibly a ship or a van. She and the players discover how to use EWEN and CAMERON, the chair and imprinting devices seen on the show, as well as three "wedges" (the disk drives that hold imprints) containing the imprints of Andrea Rose, Christopher Brink, and Eduard Bertucci. Hazel imprints herself with Andrea Rose, while viewers pretended to be Topher. "Andrea Rose" then leaves a video for Hazel to destroy the lab and get out. We also find that this woman is responsible for removing parts of Hazel's personality that she found distasteful and placing them on a wedge. We also find out that Bertucci has a dying daughter he wants to imprint on another body so she will live; that Hazel was herself a project as a child code-named "Foxtrot," and that Bertucci killed Andrea Rose before a R. Corp. security suit killed Bertucci. Once the Andrea Rose imprint has worn out — apparently these only last for about twenty-four hours — Hazel imprints her other personality on herself and essentially re-integrates her mind. She has now solved the mystery of her mother and has the knowledge of how to leave the lab. At the end of her final transmission, we see her stepping out into light with a drawn gun, expression guarded, curious, and ready for anything.

This rendition of a young woman's quest for an identity may remind viewers of a sped-up version of *Buffy the Vampire Slayer*. The story of Buffy Summers is also about the reclamation of power and identity. The final season depicts Buffy's search for the origins of Slayer powers; the conclusion of the show, "Chosen," shows her decision to share the power she holds with all women who have the potential to be Slayers. By broadcasting her search and ultimately freeing herself, Hazel is also sharing the power she has now earned — the power of living her true identity — with those who would do the same. That this story is presented as a game invites users to view the concept of constructed identity as a mind-experiment before concluding as a declaration, even a dare, for others to do the same.

This viral gameplay that encourages participation in the show's universe as well as a critique of the show's universe adds a valuable dimension to the story. It accepts a critical view within the universe itself that remains objective by virtue of not involving weekly characters we are familiar with, and by making the participating players and viewers characters as well. When Hazel declares that culture brainwashes people into thoughtless consumers, we face the fact that *we* are the consumers, and thus question ourselves as viewers. When she encourages us to free ourselves, we begin to question ourselves, and take on an active role rather than a passive role.

Foxploitation

"So let's make Friday night our little date night."—Eliza Dushku, promotional advertisement for *Dollhouse*

Given the early critiques of *Dollhouse* by both critics and viewers, most of which concentrated on the repugnance they felt for the human trafficking and body exploitation on the show, the FOX network's advertisements were bewildering. During the first half of the season, the show followed *The Sarah Connor Chronicles*, which starred Whedon alum Summer Glau as the new Terminator robot. Promotionals[8] featured Glau and Dushku inviting a (presumably) male audience to spend their Friday evening with "girls like us, who can be everything you want — smart but stylish, and strong enough to throw a car." "There are benefits to being the ultimate female genius/detective/lover/killer/sex object," Dushku coos in one ad. "Girls have to look good, be good, and save the world," she simpers in another.

Throughout the run of the series, a male announcer declared that the show would return in sixty or ninety seconds while a camera slowly panned over a wet and nearly nude Dushku's body. She lies on her stomach, her head bent down and slightly looking up as she faces the camera. Her expression is unreadable but the entire pose is explicitly submissive. It must be noted here that Eliza Dushku is the producer with Whedon as the executive producer of the show, but what hand if any they had in this marketing decision is unknown as of this writing. Mary Ann Doane describes the stripping of a female body as the female body becoming the property of the patriarchy. She asks in her essay on filming the female body,[9] "what is left after the stripping, the uncoding, the deconstruction? For an uncoded body is clearly an impossibility." This image of Dushku, and the aforementioned ads, are clearly coded specifically to the male viewers: watch us. Buy things. Our words may be about power but our exposed bodies are here for your delectation.

What are we then to make of a show about the conspicuous consumption of human bodies that invites us ourselves to consume those bodies?

Commentary at the progressive political blog *The Daily Kos* discussed the ramifications of *Dollhouse* as meta-fiction, or about a show within a show:

> It's not about guys with a brain washing machine who can make some-one behave how they want. It's about what it means that guys with a brain washing machine use that device to satisfy shallow, mostly sexual, fantasies.... Whedon is reflecting on what it means to *have a television show*. The brain washing device is an analog for television that's as old as the medium. Give someone a chance to build a whole program ... and what will they make? Mostly characters that ... define some "dream girl / dream boy" who meets their needs and has no internal demands. Easy sex, eye candy, and no commitments....[10]

Another blog post at *Tiger Beatdown* explored the possibility of one of the characters as a stand-in for Whedon himself:

> Because then, there's Topher, the programmer, who is responsible for constructing the artificial personalities ... who is a dorky blonde guy just like Whedon ... who we are encouraged to dislike more than almost any-one else in the series. What you hear, when you hear Topher speaking about how difficult it is to construct a believable personality, how achieve-ment is fueled by lack and he gave her asthma because that made her a more complete person ... is noted feminist auteur Joss Whedon reflect-ing on his life's work — hiring gorgeous women and making them into who he wants them to be — and saying that sometimes, he feels kind of icky about it.[11]

This reading of Whedon as a self-aware insertion is both plausible and invit-ing, possibly to the point of excluding all other readings. It makes sense on both the level of storytelling and on the level of critique — a critique that comes from "inside." However, if we go back to the concept of the Dollhouse as our house, it speaks also to Whedon's own radical feminist credo: it is the Man within society who programs women, and by doing so, sets them up to succeed or fail. And of course, we then go back to Fox, who many have claimed have set *Dollhouse* to fail by interfering in the methodology of episodes that remind many of the cancelled *Firefly*. As of this writing, however, *Doll-house* has been renewed for a second season, though the final episode is not set to be aired and will only be available on DVD — a DVD that now, many people must buy in order to get the whole story.

Conclusions

> "Nobody has everything they want. It's a survival pattern. You get what you want, you want something else. If you have everything, you want

something else. Something more extreme. Something more specific. Something perfect."

— Paul Ballard, "Ghost"

Dollhouse is in many ways Whedon's most provocative piece of work yet. It repels viewers far more than it attracts them by virtue of its subject matter. Fans of the show are sometimes labeled "Whedon apologists" for consuming media that feeds on such outrageous content. However, the show can be read as Whedon's newest manifesto: one must forge an identity before one can take on society. His previous attempt, *Buffy the Vampire Slayer*, was more palatable to viewers because of its fantastic nature and its humor, though that show too was at its strongest in declaring its feminist ethics. The feminist ethos of *Dollhouse* is a thorough explication of what makes society an enemy of women, and how women can fight society and hopefully make it better.

Most recently, Whedon was criticized by bloggers for facetiously using the phrase "hot chick" during his acceptance of the 2009 Bradbury Award for screenwriting.[12] Many posters decried his hypocrisy and sexism, though a minority pointed out that since in that same speech he was claiming to come from the future and was using the phrase "fi sci" in place of "sci fi" he probably shouldn't be taken seriously. This eagerness to criticize within his own fanbase speaks to a conflict in fandom that's not just about a television show, but how we feel about feminism. Many claim that we are now in a post-feminist era and that women's rights no longer need to be championed; many argue just the opposite. Whedon has made it clear that he believes women's rights are an ongoing issue. That he specifically and constantly introduces these dialogues into his work make it a valuable part of the media debate, no matter how viewers may feel about it.

Notes

1. Anders. Date accessed: 4/20/2009.
2. Minear.
3. Rosenberg. Date accessed: 5/4/2009.
4. Mackinnon, pp. 41–43.
5. Hughes, p. 69.
6. Hannan, p. 564.
7. The transmissions are archived at <http://www.rprimelab.com/>. Date accessed: 4/27/2009.
8. A video of four such clips strung together is available online through YouTube. <http://www.youtube.com/watch?v=snLEZoMmop4>. Date accessed: 4/27/2009.
9. Doane, p. 281.

10. Posted by Devilstower on April 25, 2009. "We Interrupt This Channel..." <http://www.dailykos.com/storyonly/2009/4/25/724353/-We-interrupt-this-channel...>. Date accessed: 4/27/2009.

11. Posted by Sady at Tiger Beatdown on April 20, 2009. "Dollhouse, Joss Whedon, and the Strange and Difficult Path of Feminist Dudes: Some Thoughts." < http://tiger-beatdown.blogspot.com/2009/04/dollhouse-joss-whedon-and-strange-and.html >. Date accessed: 4/27/2009.

12. Posted by Lauredhel at Hoyden about Town on April 28, 2009. "Cos Chicks Shouldn't Dig SF! Especially Hot Ones!" < http://viv.id.au/blog/20090428.4685/cos-chick s-shouldnt-dig-sf-especially-hot-ones/> . Date accessed: 5/27/2009.

Works Cited

Anders, Charlie Jane. "Joss Whedon is Even Creepier Than We Thought." <http://io9.com/5034351/joss-whedons-dollhouse-is-even-creepier-than-you-thought>.

Bellomo, Tracy. "Needs." *Dollhouse*. Dir. Félix Enríquez Alcalá. Original airdate: April 3, 2009.

Clambliss, Andrew. "Haunted." *Dollhouse*. Dir. David Solomon. Original airdate: April 25, 2009.

Doane, Mary Ann. "Woman's Stake: Filming the Female Body." *Feminism and Film Theory*. Ed. Constance Penley. New York: Routledge, 1988. 216–228.

Espenson, Jane. "Briar Rose." *Dollhouse*. Dir. Dwight H. Little. Original airdate: May 1, 2009.

Fain, Sarah. "Gray Hour." *Dollhouse*. Dir. Rod Hardy. Original airdate: March 6, 2009.

Hannan, Maryanne. "Ovid's Myth of Narcissus and Echo." *Psychoanalytic Review* 79(4): 555–575.

Hughes, Ted, trans. *Tales from Ovid*. New York: Farrar, Straus and Giroux, 1997.

Mackinnon, Catharine A. *Are Women Human? And Other International Dialogues*. Cambridge, MA: Belknap Press of Harvard University Press, 2006.

Minear, Tim. "Omega." *Dollhouse*. Dir. Tim Minear. Original airdate: May 8, 2009.

Molina, Jose. "Ariel." *Firefly*. Dir. Allan Kroeka. Original airdate: November 15, 2002.

Rosenberg, Alyssa. "Joss Whedon and the Real Girl." *The Atlantic*. March 20, 2009. <http://www.theatlantic.com/doc/print/200903u/joss-whedon>.

Whedon, Joss. "Chosen." *Buffy the Vampire Slayer*. Original airdate: May 20, 2003.

_____. "Ghost." *Dollhouse*. Director Joss Whedon. Original airdate: February 13, 2009.

_____."Man on the Street." *Dollhouse*. Director David Straiton. Original airdate: March 20, 2009.

_____."A Spy in the House of Love." *Dollhouse*. Director David Solomon. Original airdate: April 10, 2009.

The Companion as a Doll
The Female Enigma in
Firefly and *Dollhouse*

NICHOLAS GRECO

"Like a man with the bright-eyed euphoria of narrowly escaped death, DOLLHOUSE is coming back from a hilariously unexpected non-cancellation with a verve, a joy and a visceral excitement that borders on manic. We're psyched. This is the show we want to make. The twisty lives of the Dollhouse peeps are truckin' along, and ECHO (Eliza Dushku) is going through one of her fresher Hells."

— Letter from Joss Whedon to members
of the press, dated 1 September 2009

"When Firefly *got the axe, I went into a state of denial so huge it may very well cause a movie."*

— Joss Whedon, in an email
dated 14 February 2004

The cancellation of *Firefly* did not spell the end for the character of Inara Serra, a Companion, a kind of prostitute (so much more than this, actually). She went on to appear in the movie that Whedon threatened would come about from his denial of the cancellation. Even so, she remains a mystery, an enigmatic figure that continues to live on (as a *twisty* life) as Echo in *Dollhouse*. This paper explores the transplantation and translation of the Companion character as a gendered and sexualized enigma in two of Whedon's television series, *Firefly* and *Dollhouse*. Roland Barthes' analysis of *Sarrasine* by Honoré de Balzac is especially helpful in order to more deeply understand the functioning of the female enigma character.

In *Firefly*, the Companion is a high-class, hired "companion," basically a prostitute. In the case of Inara, the viewers know of a backstory that remains hidden, a story which suggests that Inara was forced to leave from where she came. The transplantation and translation of this character occurs in another of Whedon's properties, the television series *Dollhouse*. In *Dollhouse*, the "doll" character is a high-class, hired "companion," basically a prostitute, although a "doll" can take on many roles beside those involving sexual behaviour. In the case of Echo/Caroline, the main protagonist, the viewer also knows of a backstory which remains hidden, a story which suggests that Caroline was forced to become a "doll." It is not that she is necessarily in that role against her will; the suggestion in the show is that she has made her own choice, although her choices were extremely limited. There is a lingering question which hangs beneath the surface of this present analysis: how is the notion of free will and choice expressed in terms of gender and sexuality as presented in these series?

Inara and Echo are both female sexual characters with enigmatic backstories which arguably string the viewer along in order to gain knowledge of that backstory. In the enigmatic backstory for Inara Serra from *Firefly*, the viewer learns that, at the time of the events in the series, she has left a high-profile position at the Companion House on the planet Sihnon for some unknown reason. There are some clues in the series that point to further mysteries in her backstory: she reaches for a syringe in the pilot episode when the Reavers are almost upon the ship; in the episode "Out of Gas," she is speaking to the resident doctor Simon Tam and responds to his statement, "I don't want to die [on this ship]" with "I don't want to die at all." Another hint to this enigmatic backstory, though perhaps more suspect, surfaces when Nandi, Inara's friend in the episode "Heart of Gold," comments that Inara hadn't aged a day since they last met, leading some fans of the series to conclude that Inara is using some sort of medication or narcotic to maintain her youthful appearance, or that she is much older than she seems. During a panel at the science-fiction/comic convention *Dragon*Con* in 2008, Morena Baccarin confirmed that Inara was dying in the series. What any of these elements of a backstory had to do with the character's departure from Sihnon and her position there is another part of the mystery.[1]

Caroline/Echo, the central character in Whedon's *Dollhouse* series, has an enigmatic backstory as well, which is slowly revealed as the first season continues. Caroline is highly encouraged to become a "doll" or "active" after discovering that a corporation was using a university laboratory not only to conduct unethical experiments on animals, but also on human infants. The Rossum Corporation, the company behind the lab, is also responsible for the Dollhouse. They apprehend Caroline after her discovery and, after powerful persuasion, Caroline accepts to enter the Dollhouse, and to become employed as a "doll," for five years. Caroline makes her own choice, but it appears that her range of available choices was quite limited. Her free will was not exactly free; she suggests that she does not have a choice. She does, explicitly, accept the role as a "doll," prostituting her body to any paying client for any need. Exploring Inara as a Companion, Andrew Aberdein writes:

> In our world, prostitution is not a source of high status. That is not to say there are no high-status prostitutes; clearly they exist. They may even owe their status to their profession (for example, if they have made a lot of money or have influential clients) but their status would be even higher if, all other things being equal, they were not prostitutes. Hence prostitution appears inseparable from shame [63].

Aberdein makes the point that, in the universe of *Firefly* (the "'verse"), things are different: prostitutes are *Companions*, an order of educated and influential practitioners of various, say, social arts, a vocation which covers more than simply carnal and sexual activities.

In a similar way, so is the role of the "doll," a fictional figure placed within a present reality. A "doll" can be educated or influential, and can do much more than simply engage with a client physically. And, while notions of prostitution and human trafficking are hinted at in the world of *Dollhouse*, the "vocation" of the "dolls" (a vocation that they are "called to," for whatever nefarious reason) is also separated from shame. In fact, the "doll" does not experience shame; the "doll" does his job, whatever that might entail, because he thinks (knows, feels) that this is what he is supposed to do. For a "doll," there is no other option.

For Caroline, in *Dollhouse*, there seems that there is no other option but to become a "doll." The shame of prostitution, if such shame exists in this context, is overpowered by the shame (or consequences) of whatever has happened in Caroline's life that has put her in the situation of needing to make that choice (or non-choice, perhaps). She has seen too much, she knows too much, and she has lost too much.[2]

One way to conceptualize the two characters as enigmatic is to observe them as exotic Others, as characters that one cannot know fully because they are intrinsically and culturally different. This difference manifests itself in the asian-ness of Inara and, in a way, a similar asian-ness is injected into Echo because of her surroundings in the Dollhouse. Furthermore, Echo is an Other because she is not like the viewer: she can be anyone except her true self.

In discussing the character of Inara, one might start with the question posed (and answered) by Rebecca M. Brown: "What does that melding [of China and the U.S.] (and the other exoticizing/Asian elements in the show) tell us about the construction of the Other from the margin?" (par. 16). She suggests that the show and film serve to normalize the Asian elements which appear there, while "the hub of all Asian elements within the show is the interior of Inara's shuttle and the persona of Inara herself" (pars. 18–19). Brown continues:

> While on the one hand the history of the courtesan is a long and varied one, marking a space of power for women, the representation of the courtesan for Orientalizing discourse plays up the *mysterious* sexuality attainable only to the few who "penetrate" the "veil" of the Middle East.... These elements present a vision of the "East" that reinforces its exotic and erotic aspects [pars. 22–23, emphasis added].

Though Brown suggests that Inara and other "Eastern" elements in the show serve to realign the notion of Orientalism "from Europe to the margins," to "the roots of modernity firmly within the (formerly) colonized world," the Orientalizing discourse still manages to instill an exoticism and, in fact, a mystery particularly in terms of sexuality. There is an unknown *something* attainable only to the few who manage to properly (and completely) engage with Inara Serra.

Similar visions of the "East" can be located in *Dollhouse*: the tea that Adelle DeWitt serves Echo in the pilot episode "Ghost" and Sam Jennings in "Echoes," the yoga, tai chi, and calligraphy that is practiced by the actives in the Dollhouse, as well as Echo's unveiling from beneath a kimono in the opening credits of the show. Even the motorcycle ride in Chinatown in the pilot episode seems to contribute to the asian, if not slightly inauthentic, sense of asian-ness (Otherness) in the show.

Barthes' S/Z

Roland Barthes describes various methods and tools for delaying the revelation of truth in discussing Balzac's *Sarrasine*. Barthes demonstrates, through what he calls "dilatory morphemes," how the enigma in the story is set up and maintained. The various tools that he describes can be recognized when dealing with both Inara and Echo as female enigmata.

Barthes identifies a point in the narrative where a character provides an answer to one of the central questions of the story up to this point. Yet, this answer is only partial: "The truth is submerged in a list whose parataxis sweeps it along, hides it, holds it back, and finally does not reveal it at all."[3] Barthes calls this example of "ineffective solving" an "equivocation" (38). That term also suggests the use of ambiguity to conceal truth or to avoid commitment. Barthes characterizes the equivocation further by stating that it is a "mixture of truth and snare which frequently, while focusing on the enigma, helps to thicken it." For Barthes, the snare is "a kind of deliberate evasion of the truth" (75). He suggests that the snare, "the feint, the misleading answer, the lie," is the main type of delay (32). Barthes calls the snare and the equivocation "dilatory morphemes," part of his "hermeneutic code" (75). In addition to the snare and the equivocation there are the partial answer, the suspended answer, and jamming, all working to "*arrest* the enigma, to keep it open."[4] The partial answer "only exacerbates the expectation of the truth" (75–76). The suspended (or avoided) answer occurs when the narrative itself delays the solving of an enigma; Barthes, in the context of his analysis of *Sarrasine*, describes it as follows: "had the discourse not moved the two speakers off to a secluded sofa, we would have quickly learned the answer to the enigma." Barthes adds that, if the mystery had been solved (in this case, revealing the source of the Lanty fortune), "there would have been no story to tell" (31). Jamming refers to an "acknowledgment of insolubility" (76). Barthes suggests that jamming occurs when "the discourse declares the enigma it proposed to be unresolved" (Barthes quotes from *Sarrasine* to illustrate an instance of jamming: "Was it affection or fear? Those in society were unable to discover any clue to help them solve this problem") (46–47).

Barthes also links desire to the process of discovering truth: "truth predicates an incomplete subject, based on expectation and desire for its imminent closure" (76). Thus, Barthes proposes the "hermeneutic sentence." He explains:

> The proposition of truth is a "well-made" sentence; it contains a subject (theme of the enigma), a statement of the question (formulation of the enigma), its question mark (proposal of the enigma), various subordinate and interpolated clauses and catalyses (delays in the answer), all of which precede the ultimate predicate (disclosure) [84].

His suggestion is that any enigma could be inserted into this structure of "sentence." Similarly, Barthes contends that an enigma is like a *fugue*:

> both contain a *subject*, subject to an *exposition*, a *development* (embodied in the retards, ambiguities, and diversions by which the discourse prolongs a mystery), a *stretto* (a tightened section where scraps of answers rapidly come and go), and a *conclusion* [29].

Barthes also considers the narrative to be like the "gradual order of melody" in a *fugue*, polyphonic, with various "voices" occurring at the same time. Barthes goes as far as setting up a kind of musical table, with rows of music notes indicating "events" which occur throughout the narrative, divided temporally into columns. Therefore, like music, "the classic text ... is actually tabular (and not linear), but its tabularity is vectorized, it follows a logico-temporal order" (30). For Barthes, the "classic text" is one which can be read but not written, as opposed to "what can be written (rewritten) today"; he calls the "classic text" a "readerly text," while the other is called a "writerly text" (4).

In a similar way, the discourse which surrounds the mediated enigma is tabular, with various "streams" or "voices" constructing the celebrity's persona. Discourse provides fragments of truth, which in turn allow for the delay of answers to enigmas by the emergence of various "dilatory morphemes," in order to keep the question at the forefront of the persona. Without such "incomplete truth" with regard to the persona, there is no desire for closure, and thus no desire for sustained attention. There is the desire to *know* and *know completely*.[5]

Another way that Barthes identifies the construction of the enigma is in terms of power. The enigma fascinates and spellbinds; Barthes formulates these elements as seduction on the part of the enigma and pleasure for the audience, for lack of a more elegant term. Power over an audience is not something that can be documented in interviews, at least explicitly, but it can be implicit in the discourse. For Barthes, in the narrative that he uses as a case study, Sarrasine is, in a sense, both freed and captured when he hears the music, *in anticipation of* the entrance of La Zambinella, the object of his desire. Barthes states, "The first (sensual) pleasure is initiatory: it serves as a basis for memory, repetition, ritual: afterwards, everything is organized to recapture this *first time*." This statement suggests that there is a certain power at work, which demands from Sarrasine to continue to be exposed to the enigma; the audience is seduced by the enigma, compelling the audience to repeat the experience. The pleasure of such an experience is evident in the returning of the audience to experience it again. Barthes suggests that the pleasure can come from simple proximity to the desired object: "Proximity to the stage, and thus to the desired object, serves as a (fortuitous) point of departure for a series of hallucinatory feelings which will lead Sarrasine to solitary pleasure" (108). Later, Barthes suggests, "The proximity of La Zambinella ... is of an hallucinatory order: it is an abolition of the Wall [of Reality], identification with the object; what is involved is an hallucinatory embrace." He also states, "La Zambinella's features are no longer described according to the aesthetic, rhetorical code, but according to the anatomical code (veins, planes, hair)" (118).

Similarly, in the pilot episode of *Dollhouse*, "Ghosts," Echo is shown dancing with her client, and the camera focuses particularly upon her, her legs, dress, and hair. In the episode "True Believer," Echo is imprinted with the personality — and physical deficiency — of a blind person. Perhaps to accentuate her blindness, the camera is often focused close on her face (perhaps to focus on her "blind" eyes). We can see the pores of her skin, and the various beauty marks that dot her face. Similarly, in *Firefly*, the camera focuses — even pauses — on the naked body of Inara bathing in her room. We see the details of her body in focus, a kind of proximity not possible in reality.

In the pilot episode of *Firefly*, "Serenity," we first encounter Inara with a client, and he laments that "the time went too quickly," suggesting also that the clock might have been sped up on purpose. The experience with Inara is over, and perhaps the client is experiencing the same emotion as Sarrasine after La Zambinella's performance: "Overcome by an inexplicable sadness, he sat down on the steps of a church. There, leaning back against a pillar, he fell into a confused meditation, as in a dream. He had been smitten by passion" (119).

Barthes' characterization of the relationship between a desired object and the one who desires it is a physical one: there exists an initial desiring, an embrace, a climax and subsequent fatigue and sadness. The desiring is established by a seduction; the seductive power of the enigma, as well as the draw that the enigma has on the desiring one, evoking sadness and eliciting the desire for more contact, imbues the desired object with a certain power. Barthes links seduction with intense pleasure, and thus an intense desire for repetition (111).

Even so, pleasure is fleeting for both parties; La Zambinella states, "For me, the world is a desert. I am an accursed creature, condemned to understand happiness, to feel it, to desire it, and, like many others, forced to see it flee from me continually" (161). Consider the assignments that Echo is hired for, in which she is programmed to love another truly and completely, not simply as something that is being required of her, but as actual and genuine feelings of happiness. These feelings of love are then wiped from her mind as she reenters the Dollhouse and the child-like state of the actives there.

Like Inara's client on the planet Persephone, in the pilot episode, Sarrasine experiences a similar, rather violent, sentiment. Time moved too quickly, perhaps by some kind of trickery:

> Sarrasine wanted to leap onto the stage and take possession of this woman: his strength, increased a hundredfold by a moral depression impossible to explain, since these phenomena occur in an area hidden from human observation, seemed to manifest itself with painful violence [116].

Thus, the enigma is seductive, and its mysteries are part of that seduction as well. Does the viewer, then, become pressed to violence over the seduction of the enigma? Does the character also have power over the viewer, as the viewer is overcome with desire?

The analysis here serves to show how the female enigmatic character functions in both the *Firefly* and *Dollhouse* worlds. Some critics, though, suggest that these characters are rendered powerless because of their position, and that these characters are situated at sites of unequal power relations:

> The Dollhouse is a giant metaphor, not only for rape culture, but for patriarchy and oppression at large: even the boy dolls are girls, stripped of agency or access to power and cast in pre-defined roles to fulfill the fantasies of the folks who are actually in charge [Doyle].

Similarly, Inara is simply a struggling figure whose path in life is unsure and difficult: "Inara herself seems to struggle with her life as a Companion, along with her unresolved feelings for Mal. This is presented as an either/or dichotomy.... As it is, we are left with the feeling that Inara can't establish a relationship with Mal because she works as a Companion" (Smith). These views might be true when one considers the context of the characters within the narrative in which they operate; they are placed in problematic situations, in contexts that are rife with questionable ethics. If one considers the characters from the point of view of the television audience, then these characters are in powerful positions, particularly for the reason of their enigmatic nature.

The viewer is caught by these characters, wanting to know more of them (and perhaps wanting to be known by them as well). In other words, the viewer desires these characters, and is strung along by them, continually desiring a complete picture of the character. The viewer wishes to uncover, to know all of Inara's and Echo's details; these characters have power over their viewers because of their mysteries remain as such. Until the viewer knows all that there is to know of the character, the character will continue to hold the desire of the viewer.

Notes

1. One need only search for "Inara Serra" on the various wiki sites to find this information: http://wikipedia.org; http://www.fireflywiki,org; and http://www.firefly.wikia.com. Baccarin's confession of Inara's backstory can be found on an amateur video of a *Dragon*Con* panel, available from http://www.youtube.com/watch?v=YTxGOi9coWQ; Internet; accessed 11 May 2009.

2. Her boyfriend was fatally wounded shortly after the discovery of the Rossum lab. It should be noted here that the following suggestion, that *Dollhouse* is simply a continued deconstruction, from *Firefly*, of the nature of prostitution, is not new. In an Internet post, dated 17 February 2009, "Abigail" writes: "I've been thinking some more about this show, and it occurs to me that the scepticism being voiced about the concept of actives is very familiar — the same doubts were raised at the idea of Companions in *Firefly*. In both cases Whedon takes a real-life fact — that the very rich will pay for exclusive, custom-made pleasures — and takes it to its (il)logical conclusion, so that we get custom-made playmates or hookers trained in languages and swordfighting. It's not an entirely unreasonable logical leap, but in both shows Whedon appears to be trying to deconstruct prostitution (Echo's first assignment in 'Ghost' is precisely the sort of job Inara used to do) by removing or ignoring its fundamental seediness, and I'm not sure that's possible" (available from http://vectoreditors.wordpress.com/2009/02/14/dollhouse-ghost/#comment-45844; Internet; accessed 10 August 2009).

3. The parataxis (referring to the placing of phrases in sequence without any indication as to their importance) to which Barthes is referring is as follows, from *Sarrasine*, "The beauty, the wit, the charms of these two children, came solely from their mother" (p. 38).

4. Barthes also adds the "false reply" to the hermeneutic code; the false reply differs from the snare because the former emerges from error rather than from a lie or the intention to mislead (p. 42).

5. Frederick Buechner writes, "Beneath the longing to possess and be possessed by the beauty of another sexually — to *know* in the biblical idiom — there lies the longing to know and be known by another fully and humanly" (*The Longing for Home: Recollections and Reflections* [New York: HarperSanFransisco, 1996], 23).

Works Cited

Aberdein, Andrew. "The Companions and Socrates: Is Inara a Hetaera?" *Investigating Firefly and Serenity: Science Fiction on the Frontier*. Edited by Rhonda V. Wilcox and Tanya R. Cochran. London: I.B. Tauris, 2008.
Barthes, Roland. *S/Z*. Translated by Richard Miller. New York: Hill and Wang, 1974.
Brown, Rebecca M. "Orientalism in *Firefly* and *Serenity*." *Slayage* 25 (Winter 2008). Available from http://slayageonline.com/essays/slayage25/Brown.htm. Accessed 2 September 2009.
Doyle, Sady. "Dollhouse, Joss Whedon, and the Strange and Difficult Path of Feminist Dudes: Some Thoughts." *Tiger Beatdown* (20 April 2009). Available from http://tiger-beatdown.blogspot.com/2009/04/dollhouse-joss-whedon-and-strange-and.html. Accessed 2 September 2009.
Smith, S. E. "Is Joss Whedon a Feminist? The Women of Firefly/Serenity." *This Ain't Livin'* (18 April 2009). Available from http://meloukhia.net/2009/04/is_joss_whedon_a_feminist_the_women_of_fireflyserenity.html. Accessed 2 September 2009.

Exploding Sexual Binaries
in Buffy *and* Angel

KATHRYN WEBER

"The world is not to be divided into sheep and goats. Not all things are black and white. It is a fundamental of taxonomy that nature rarely deals with discrete categories. Only the human mind invents categories and tries to force facts into separated pigeon-holes. The living world is a continuum in each and every one of its aspects. The sooner we learn this concerning human sexual behavior the sooner we shall reach a sound understanding of the realities of sex."

—The Institute for Sex Research, Indiana University,
Sexual Behavior in the Human Male

KENNEDY: *"How long have you known ... that you were gay?"*
WILLOW: *"Wait-that's easy? And you just assume that I'm-I'm gay? I mean, presume much?"*

—"The Killer in Me"[1]

For the casual viewer—or at least one who has watched enough of Season Four to understand Willow Rosenberg's changing relationship status—*Buffy the Vampire Slayer* appears to be a fairly traditional, though at least somewhat socially progressive, teen drama with a token gay character. Among the younger set, Buffy Summers and Xander Harris have their fair share of heterosexual relationships, as does watcher and librarian Rupert Giles and even Buffy's mother, Joyce Summers, among the older generation. Vampires Angel and Spike, too, participate in slightly exaggerated versions of heterosexual romance, each playing a slightly embellished yet different version of the "bad boy" all wrong for our heroine. Willow Rosenberg appears to be the only variant, dating and pining for (males) Xander and Oz in high school, yet falling for (females) Tara and Kennedy during her college years. If one reconciles Willow's more fluid sexual history by believing she has discovered her "true" sexual identity upon falling for Tara, then the television show itself appears to hold up the binary way in which many Americans classify the sexual orientations of others. That binary assumes that one is gay or straight, with heterosexuality as the norm and homosexuality as the variation.

But does this classification truly fit the way the world of Buffy, and later Angel, works? Although on the surface the characters of *Buffy the Vampire Slayer* and *Angel* appear to embrace heteronormativity and the exceptions hold to a binary concept of homosexual versus heterosexual with no options in between, a closer look elicits a slightly different interpretation. The sexual speech used by Willow, Xander, Spike, and Angel in particular in combination with show creator Joss Whedon's "Bring Your Own Subtext" policy reveals a greater amount of sexual fluidity exists in Sunnydale than one might expect from merely observing the on-screen pairings (Saxey 208). This interpretation exhibits more in common with Kinsey's scale of sexual preference than a strict binary of either gay or straight. The characters that exemplify this most show flexibility in other areas of their identities as well, perhaps allowing them to embrace a greater sexual variety without an internal inconsistency. Willow's evolving, and at times unstable, identity provides her with the opportunity to try on different aspects of herself in magic, in academics, and in the bedroom. Xander, Spike, and Angel on the other hand demonstrate inconsistent adherence to traditional gender norms, enabling them to inhabit or exhibit more traditionally feminine characteristics or points of view both linguistically and sexually. In a town where speaking Latin in front of the wrong book can set it aflame, might not sexual rhetoric be equally important in revealing the sexual desires and identities of its inhabitants as on-screen pairings?

Significant looks and language from Willow, Angel, Spike, and Xander occurring throughout the combined twelve seasons of the two series serve to expand the realm of sexual possibilities past the ones openly depicted on screen. In the pages that follow, I will outline these additional possibilities offered by the texts of *Buffy the Vampire Slayer* and *Angel*, and argue that their unstable or hybrid natures allow certain characters to evoke if not embrace a less conventional sexual nature. I will be using Alfred Kinsey's scale of sexual preference to quantify those variations.

Kinsey and Sexual Orientation

Although gay and lesbian identities were hardly seen as socially acceptable, by the time Alfred Kinsey began his study of human sexuality in the latter nineteen-thirties, they were seen as identities one might have in opposition to the more socially acceptable heterosexual identity. The binary between the two had become so strong that the public could not tolerate a middle ground. Heterosexuals were considered such when all of their sexual activities consisted of those with the opposite sex. On the other hand, an individual act of same-sex genital contact or other physical affection was enough to label a person as homosexual to the vast majority of American society, whether the rest of their sexual history consisted of heterosexual sexual acts or not (The Institute for Sex Research, Indiana University [1953]: 469).

With some exceptions, Americans still view sexuality as black and white. Yet Alfred Kinsey's scientific training, interviews with a large number of people about their sexual practices, and perhaps as well his sexual experiences both with men and women allowed him to develop an alternative framework for viewing sexual orientation. Kinsey's scale allows for the vast differences that tend to occur among such a large and diverse population of people, unlike the binary view of sexual orientation that gives people only two selections for their identities. The scale is a fairly simple construct that covers a wide variety of human sexual interactions or lack thereof. The categories involve classifications from entirely heterosexual at a zero rating, to entirely homosexual at a six rating, and X for asexual. The ratings take into account not only activity, but also psychosexual responses. This allows us to consider overt relationships, speech, and visible response when determining how a person or a character might rank on such a scale.

At first glance, it might be simple to place most *Buffy* and *Angel* characters on the scale. Willow would be a six for being a gay, as would Larry, Tara, and Kennedy and maybe Andrew or Lorne. The rest of the characters, since their dating relationships are strictly opposite sex, would rank a zero, right?

Among the characters the audience gets to know well, I'd argue that there are very few zeroes and very few sixes. This fits in well with the themes themselves in the series; *Buffy* confronts a universe increasingly filled with grays and *Angel* in many ways is about making meaning in a world of grays. Additionally, many of the characters of *Buffy*, the series in which I find a greater number of characters that exhibit sexual ambiguities, are also adolescents, a stage in life in which most people are still establishing their identities, sexual and otherwise. It is probably no coincidence then that Cordelia Chase, the character we get to see mature the furthest in the two series, as well as Rupert Giles, the oldest adult human character, seem to be the most solid in their sexual identities as well, with Cordelia presenting as a zero, or strictly heterosexual on the Kinsey scale, and Giles ranking one, or largely heterosexual, due mostly to his fondness for his Jonathan swimsuit calendar in "Superstar"[2] (4–17). Other sexually ambiguous characters tend to be demons or vampires, characters that are already placed outside the realm of normal human society and behaviors. Their very existence is already a challenge to the world they inhabit, so their tendency to defy sexual norms is not surprising.

In order to more fully examine these ideas, I will take a closer look at two human characters, Willow and Xander, as well as two vampire characters, Angel and Spike. Each of these characters show a greater range of possibility in the way they and others talk about their sexuality that allows the audience to contemplate complicated sexual identities for them. From Willow's varied dating history to Spike and Angel's ongoing sexual competition and unclear sexual past, each of these characters are not as committed to one side of the sexual binary as they might seem at first.

Willow

Willow is the most obvious example of sexual diversity, as she moves from strictly heterosexual to homosexual relationships during the course of *Buffy*'s run. This change at first appears to re-enforce the sexual binary as Lorna Jowett suggests; Willow identifies as heterosexual during the first three and one half seasons and then she identifies as gay for the rest of the series (Jowett 58). The change in Willow's sexual preference could be seen as a young woman embracing a new or latent facet of herself in college, yet a closer look at her language in concert with her actions shows that her sexual identity is a tad more complicated.

From early on in the series Willow has exhibited an ability to divorce physical qualities from romantic attachment. Her online romance in Season One's "I, Robot, You Jane" allows her to voice the feeling when asked about her online boyfriend's physical appearance that "that stuff doesn't matter when you really care about each other." Although that romance ends rather unsuccessfully, as the object of her affection is a robot inhabited by an ancient demon, it reveals Willow as a young woman who can see past physicality when contemplating romance and sexuality. Her openness is exhibited more fully when she chooses to engage in an ongoing dating relationship with Oz, who is not quite human. Despite the danger Oz's werewolf body plausibly represents, Willow only sees this as part of him and wants to continue dating. "I like you. You're nice, and you're funny. And you don't smoke," Willow says, explaining her choice to the surprised Oz ("Phases"). According to this statement, smoking status and sense of humor ranks lower on her list than species.

This openness is reduced in the future, as seen when Willow, under a spell, develops an obsession with a high school boy and decides she must transform him magically into a girl ("Him"). Although the obsession is magically induced, Willow still finds herself attracted to a male "essence" but her identity is less fluid than it had been at fifteen, and she cannot accept this attraction fully. Since all the women affected by this spell find themselves doing outlandish tasks to prove their love that rationality might convince them were unnecessary or unsafe, it is hard to know whether Willow's view of her own sexuality is actually rigid at this point in the series. It is, at least, until Willow once again defines her sexuality audibly.

Willow's conversations with Kennedy later in the same season push me to think that she does not entirely dismiss the possibility of future attractions or relationships based on gender alone. While the "how long have you known" exchange in "The Killer in Me" serves to show that Willow identifies as gay on at least some level, referencing her initial attraction to Tara and prefacing the beginning of a relationship with another woman, Kennedy, it also reveals that Willow considers her own sexual identity open to interpretation, and furthermore, she might possibly interpret it as not easily definable. Willow refuses to apply the label of lesbian or gay to herself in this conversation. When pushed to define herself, she infers that she has known for three years and that "it wasn't women, it was woman. Just one." This is a far cry from claiming strictly lesbian "street cred," something that even Willow admits that she does not have in Season Five's "Tough Love."

Anya also has suspicions that Willow's sexuality is not entirely lesbian. While Willow's relationship to Tara has been fairly well established at this point, Anya voices her lingering doubts that Willow might once again engage in a physical relationship with Xander as late as Season Five's "Triangle." Willow does deflect the suggestion by claiming to be "gay now," yet her first reaction to Anya's fear has nothing to do with her sexual orientation, rather, she says that she wouldn't do that again and that the situation of her physical involvement with Xander is definitively a part of the past. In addition to the order of her reasons, the temporality of them is also interesting. The statement that she is "gay now" has nothing altogether to do with her kissing transgressions with Xander in the past, but it might be equally surmised that it will not entirely determine her sexual choices in the future. She is "gay now" while she is in a relationship with Tara. This could allow her to be straight later, in a future relationship with a man.

This "gay now" attitude towards her sexuality exemplifies Willow's continual questioning and shifting of identities. Jowett notes that "her identity is exposed and unstable and fractured" more so than the identities of her peers on the series (Jowett 60). Buffy is always the Slayer, though she has to figure out exactly what that means, and Xander changes from poor student to highly capable carpenter, Willow bounces from "net girl" of Seasons One and Two, to nascent witch in Seasons Three through Five, to powerful witch and then supremely evil witch in Season Six, and supremely good witch in Season Seven. This does not even take into account the other roles Willow plays, such as band member's girlfriend in Seasons Two through Four, and Tara's girl-friend in Seasons Four through Six.

Willow defines herself through her relationships and through her power, though both of these tendencies seem to strengthen when she is unstable and weaken as she feels more comfortable both with her power and her romantic relationships near the end of the series. Willow's identity is at its most frac-tured when she can no longer claim her relationship with Tara or her magi-cal powers to define herself. Having given up magic and lost Tara in an accidental shooting, Willow cannot cope with her loss of both and her rage and grief redefine her, pushing her to attempt ending the world. Her loss of Tara and loss of control of her powers provide her with the opportunity to reconstruct a new more stable self out of the ashes. Indeed, the Willow of Season Seven does not seem as likely to label herself as Kennedy's girlfriend as eagerly as she laid claim to having a "boyfriend in the band" in Season Two's "Bewitched, Bothered and Bewildered."

Xander

The problems Xander has in establishing an adult identity are different degrees of the ones that Willow is faced with while establishing hers. Like Willow, he defines himself through his relationships and his power, but he does so in a distinctly masculine way. Instead of concern about magical pow-ers, Xander has fears about his lack of career and monetary success, particu-larly in Season Four and early Season Five. He also faces anxiety over his sexual virility, particularly when he is not in a relationship. These anxieties are traditionally associated with masculinity, and it is easy to focus entirely on that aspect of why Xander has those particular fears. However, Xander's dream in "Restless" depict his fears as being much more a function of his fam-ily and class background than of his gender. Many of Xander's concerns come back to the suspicion that he cannot escape his working class family roots and find a way out of his parents' basement, literally and figuratively. Though these fears subside when he finds increasing success through his job as a carpenter and a position in management within the construction business at which he works, they never disappear entirely, and are a large part of why he leaves Anya at the altar.

Xander's fears about his sexual virility may constrain him from acting on same-sex desires, but they do not stop him from voicing them, though often in a roundabout way. Xander's romantic feelings for Buffy in early seasons place him at odds with Angel because he considers them to be in competition for Buffy's affections, particularly in Season One. In fact, the first time Xander meets Angel his reaction shows equal measures of contempt and attraction. "He's a very attractive man. How come that never came up?" Xander grouses in "Teacher's Pet." Xander's jealousy also rears its head when Willow begins to date Oz in Season Two. "I just don't trust Oz with her. I mean, he's a senior. He's attractive. Okay, maybe not to me" ("Phases"). Once again, Xander evaluates his competition's sexual attractiveness, but qualifies it this time by saying he may not find him personally attractive. Although "not to me" removes some of the power of the statement, Xander's continuing evaluations of the desirability of male characters on the series moves my focus more to the "maybe."

A number of those statements appear to be meant for comic effect. After visiting the Initiative, the large demon-killing military installation under the ground of the University of California-Sunnydale campus, Xander remarks on the attractiveness of Buffy's love interest, though his statement has more to do with his judgment of Riley's power in relation to the Initiative than it does to his physical body. "Can I have sex with Riley too?" he asks upon seeing the massive Initiative compound ("Goodbye, Iowa"). Although it is presented as a joke, it is part of a long line of jokes about Xander finding other men attractive. Xander's obsession with Jonathan in the alternate reality of "Superstar" is also played for laughs and furthers this comic theme. Xander owns posters, comic books, and all manners of Jonathan memorabilia, seen on display in his living space. Yet this is not only hero worship. Both Xander and Anya are turned on enough by Jonathan's performance at the Bronze to inspire them to leave the Bronze to engage in sex. Anya initiates it, but Xander's open-mouthed gaping at Jonathan while he hits the high notes in his trumpet solo establish that it is not just she that has been sexually titillated by Jonathan's stage persona. The more these jokes are repeated, particularly about different men, Xander undermines his own status as a zero on Kinsey's scale, and it appears he is much more likely a two, heterosexual with a fair amount of response to the same sex.

As Xander's sexual experience and monetary and career successes strengthen his confidence, he becomes less likely to qualify his statements about male characters by joking or explaining he is not actually attracted to them. Late in Season Five, after he sees a robot–Buffy he believes is the actual Buffy engaging in sex acts with Spike, he admits that while he is unhappy about Buffy and Spike's apparent sexual relationship, "It's understandable. Spike is strong, and mysterious, and sort of compact but well-muscled" ("Intervention"). This comment is a bit more graphic than his jealous remark about Angel's attractiveness and more thought-out than his joke about wanting to sleep with Riley. He mentions both aspects of Spike's persona, his mysteriousness and possibly the strength of his personality, as well as his physical body, his smaller stature but still muscular physique, when explaining Spike's particular brand of sexual charm. Even Buffy's reaction to Xander's comment reveals that she too finds Xander's evaluation of Spike a little too detailed. "I'm not having sex with Spike. But I'm starting to think you might be." Buffy likely does not believe that Xander is sleeping with Spike, but the way in which he describes Spike may just make her, and the audience, wonder whether or not he has thought about it.

Another element to consider when regarding Xander's sexuality is his well established role as a "demon-magnet" when it comes to love. The first times his attractions are reciprocated onscreen include a near-mating with a giant praying mantis woman, and a flirtation and dance date with an Incan mummy who appears as an attractive young woman ("Teacher's Pet" and "Inca Mummy Girl"). Even Anya, with whom he has his longest-running relationship and to whom he proposes marriage, is a former vengeance demon. Although it might be less indicative of Xander's tastes if he did not find them attractive and demon women merely tended to fall for him, before he knows about their evil status he finds the demon women who like him desirable as well. This happens enough times that he and Willow even have a secret code so that he can text her for help when his date is a demon ("First Date"). The desire of these demon women for Xander does put him at risk often enough that at one time he even jokingly considers becoming gay. Although this does not establish any same-sex dating or romantic activity on Xander's part, when one considers that many of the women and girls he has dated are presently or formerly non-human, it furthers the idea that he (as well as Willow and Buffy) is willing to embrace sexualities that do not restrict a person to activity merely with a human of a particular sex. Justine Larbalestier too notes that this kind of sex, at the very least sex between human and vampire or between two vampires might be considered to be unnatural by some, since it cannot result in the production of a child (Larbalestier 196). Yet Buffy, Xander, and Willow do not uphold this ethos, and so residents of the Whedon-verse may consider the possibility of sex with friendly vampires, werewolves, and former demons in Buffy's words "a valid life choice" ("The Prom") much as those of us in the real world might consider humans of the same sex.

Angel and Spike

It is hard to consider the sexualities of Spike and Angel without referencing the other. Liam and William, as they were known in their human days, often seem like two halves of the same whole. One is light, the other dark. One is intellectual, the other mostly impulse. They are both objects of Buffy's affection and desire, both sexually involved with Drusilla, both feminized by a number of means, both come to be ensouled, though by different processes. The relationship they share is fraught with tension and jealousy as much as grudging affection and homoeroticism. Although the audience is not sure what has occurred between Angel and Spike throughout their centuries long relationship, it seems clear that it is not entirely uncomplicated by sex.

One aspect of them both that makes their sexuality more inscrutable is the feminization their characters face throughout the two series, though notably more so on *Buffy*. As romantic objects of the titular character, Angel and Spike suffer the kind of marginalization that is more common to women in television and the movies, that of being the "love interest." Both Angel and Spike's bodies are displayed as "objects to be looked at and desired" (Jowett 163). Their shirts come off for any variety of reasons, their bodies are penetrated with "sexy wounds" ("The Initiative") and the results of those wounds are prominently displayed visually. While this is a convention that usually concerns women, particularly in horror, in *Buffy* and *Angel*, it is male bodies that are fetishized. Appearing as love interests also restricts our view of these characters, though Spike suffers this less due to the variety of roles he does serve in the narrative before becoming enamored of Buffy in Season Five. It is hard to determine what Angel desires for himself in *Buffy* other than Buffy herself, and it takes his own series for us to learn more about his desire for a soul and his sexual desires that do not involve slayers.

Spike is more open with his desires for Drusilla, Harmony, Buffy, and violence (and likely in some combination) but even he is not able to voice the variety of his feelings about Angel until they meet again in Los Angeles while he is busy trying to be worthy of Buffy's love or at the very least her bed, barring his response to Buffy's idea in "Chosen" that he and Angel should wrestle over their mutual affection for her to determine the winner. Meant in jest, Buffy nonetheless sexualizes the comment by suggesting that "there could be oils of some kind involved." His reply is equally telling. "No problem at this end." He hardly bats an eye. Spike is ready to compete for Buffy; or at least, Spike is ready to "rassle it out" with Angel.

Another visual theme that feminizes Angel and Spike consists of their repeated physical penetration by female and male characters. Buffy penetrates Angel with a sword, sending him to hell in "Becoming, Part 2." Buffy stakes Spike while he is wearing an invincibility ring and he asks for more in "The Harsh Light of Day." Riley penetrates Spike with a plastic stake in "Into the Woods." Angel's body is symbolically penetrated by possession by a female ghost, and by an elderly man ("I Only Have Eyes for You" *Buffy* and "Carpe Noctem" *Angel*).[3] Spike even shows a sexual desire for penetration, making it a part of his fantasies about Buffy and his sexual role playing with Harmony. Significantly, both Angel and Spike are created by female penetration which they invite if not desire while they are human men, by Darla and Drusilla, respectively.

The feminizations of being objectified and penetrated are not their only feminine ways. Their vampire condition leaves them masculine and yet not a man at the same time, creating them as an "other" that is usually the experience of women or minorities. This hybrid nature allows them to embrace characteristics that are generally associated more with femininity that leak into the realm of sexuality. Spike plays a "passive role as a sex toy" in Season Six, and also displays "a 'feminine' way of being attuned to situations, relationships, and underlying emotions" (Jowett 161, 163). Angel's overly problematic sexuality also marks him as feminine; the fear over what might happen if his sexuality is unleashed is never entirely sublimated despite his prolonged bouts of celibacy, and it conflates easily with the long-standing male fear of an uninhibited female sexuality. Although that fear is more concerned with a gypsy curse that will rid Angel of his soul upon finding true happiness instead of the fear of what may happen when women feel free to engage in sex freely outside of marriage, both are concerned with the havoc that will be released on the world if the status quo is disrupted.

While the sexual desires mentioned thus far concerning Spike and Angel may mark them as not quite *straight* straight, as Larbalestier would say, due to their kinkiness, most of them are still heterosexual in nature (Larbalestier 201). It is in relation to each other and in relation to violence that Spike and Angel most often verbally position themselves as having some measure of homosexual desire. This is not surprising. Vampire sex is often portrayed as a violent act, as much pain as pleasure. Angel does not openly engage in sado-masochistic sex while possessing a soul, but even he admits at the beginning of a good fight that "I have no problem spanking men" ("Conviction" *Angel*). Because the opponent that Angel is facing has been established earlier in the episode as a recreational spanker, this statement is obviously a double entendre. The presently celibate Angel must get his jollies fighting evil and he will enjoy beating Spanky to a pulp just as much if not more than beating a female evildoer, since his sense of chivalry might keep him from fighting a human woman. Spike has no curse restraining his sexuality and so directs his violence equally at his opponents and the objects of his sexual interest; Buffy realizes this when she discovers Spike's romantic/sexual feelings for her. She is understandably concerned that their constant fighting has encouraged these feelings. Yet the only being Spike seems to be happier to fight over the course of the two series than Buffy is his "Yoda," Angel, and Angel seems equally satisfied to be fighting him. Not five minutes after his appearance in Angel's office in "Just Rewards," Spike is ready to fight Angel; in fact it is the first physical act he tries after his resurrection. It is also when he discovers his lack of corporeality, but that does not negate his attempt to knock Angel out.

Once Spike realizes he can't leave Los Angeles, he decides to follow Angel around as his own personal tormentor, and also due in no small part to the jealousy and desire he feels for Angel and his life. Spike wants Angel's chair, his job, his destiny, and to be the only vampire with a soul that Buffy loves, as Spike continually states. "You and me together again," Spike muses merrily as he settles in for a drive with Angel. It's a line he repeats when he and Angel commiserate over a shared fate, as they both mostly believe that they are doomed for hell.

Their relationship is a complicated one. They are old soldiers, together fighting the forces of evil, and sharing a long history of fighting as soldiers of evil together. At the end of *Angel*, when he proposes the suicide mission of destroying the Black Thorn, Spike is the first to volunteer. Shoulder to shoulder, he is ready to go with him to their spot in hell. They are brothers, with Spike as the younger, continually looking for approval while nonetheless attempting to hide his need for it. The glee on his face in "Hell Bound" when Angel tells him that "there was one thing about you" that he appreciated is short lived but apparent. They are an old (unhappily) married couple who know each other so well that they are rehashing all the same fights and demonstrating they still know how to press all the right buttons. One could almost imagine Spike in a flowered house dress, haranguing Angel about why he doesn't take him out to nice places any more. This dynamic between them comes out in the competition, back-biting, and nagging they continually aim at one another, as well as the disappointment they sometimes exhibit over one another's choices. Spike is not just Angel's conscience, but his little brother, and he cannot hide his disillusionment about his elder brother's choices whether they consist of mooning over the Slayer in *Buffy* or to lead an evil law firm in *Angel*.

Yet they are more than soldiers, brothers, and old marrieds. The tension between them could also be read as sexual, and the bantering in the conversation quoted above could alternatively be read to represent a couple in a romantic comedy. They bicker and claim to hate each other, but every fan of romantic comedy knows the two characters who act as if they cannot stand one another likely will end up together by the final frame. The desire behind this friction is possibly the most obvious early in their relationship. From the first time that they meet, they have a special bond. "Another rooster in the hen house?" Angelus muses ("Destiny" *Angel*). But he is not angry; in fact he is excited about the prospect. "Don't mistake me, I do love the ladies. It's just lately I've been wondering what it'd be like to share the slaughter of innocence with another man. Don't think that makes me some kind of a deviant, do you?" This entire speech is delivered with innuendo and homoerotic overtones. Angelus pauses significantly after saying "what it'd be like," implying that it's not just sharing slaughter that he's looking to share with the newly vamped William. The question about being a deviant is also superfluous as well. Of course they are deviants; they are vampires. They feel each other out during this meeting, each displaying their capacity for enduring pain by sticking his hand in the sunlight and letting it burn, first Angel, and then William eagerly copies him.

The sexual nature of Angel and Spike's connection crackles more strongly when both are evil; this could possibly be because without souls they would be open to a greater level of sexual "deviance" and in part because Angelus' sexuality is freer and less problematic than that of Angel. When Angelus is striking fear in the hearts of the Scoobies of Sunnydale during Season Two, he mocks Spike in his wheel-chair, seduces and tortures Drusilla, and offers Spike advice. "Be thinking of you," he says to Spike when he leaves to unleash destruction on the Sunnydale mall, and pats him somewhere on the back, or maybe the butt. It is not a traditional come on, but it is an insult meant to wound Spike coupled with suggestiveness, much like their original meeting. Once again, Angelus is also sexually involved with Drusilla, and daring Spike to try and do something about it. Angel even uses this jealousy to his advantage when he is being held captive by Spike and Drusilla. "The way she just now.... I can tell when she's not being satisfied" ("What's My ..., Part 2"). This time, the taunt is being used as a distraction, but when Angel uses the jealousy to inflict pain, he does so with the knowledge that, for vampires, pain and pleasure are close relations. "Maybe you two don't have the fire we had," Angel adds. The obvious reading is that Spike and Drusilla are not as passionate in their lovemaking as Angel and Drusilla are, but an equally correct conclusion to draw in this context could be that he is referring to Spike and Angel when he says "we." Perhaps he is referring to "that once" when they were intimate, referred to by Spike in "Power Play," a statement Illyria interprets as a joke despite the even tone and lack of characteristic swagger with which he surrenders the information. It is far from definite that Spike and Angel, or Spike and Angelus, have seriously been or will be intimate in the physical sense of the word, but it seems that one can hardly make the obvious assumptions about what has gone on or might go on between them. They can easily be placed at a five on the Kinsey scale, if not a four.

Conclusion

With an auteur who tells the audience that there is something more to the text than there seems, and that they should bring their own ideas, interpretations, and inferences to the places between the lines of the scripts, *Buffy* and *Angel* are rife with subtext the authors are giving us permission to puzzle out. Since *Buffy* and *Angel* are so much about relationships, much of this subtext concerns how the characters feel about one another from disgust to platonic love to lust.

"You think you know what you are, what's to come," the guise of Tara tells Buffy in her dream in "Restless," and we suppose that what we see shows us all there is to know about Willow's coming out in college, Xander's virile heterosexuality established through his long-term romance with Anya, and Spike and Angel's ongoing rivalry. Like Kennedy, we are presuming based on surface perceptions. Until we consider the language the characters use with and about one another more clearly, as well as their reactions to this language, we haven't even begun. Each of the characters mentioned shows a considerably less binary view of their sexual wants and needs, a view that Kinsey's scale makes clear in which straight and gay is just a start.

Notes

1. Unless otherwise noted, episodes referred to throughout the essay are from the series *Buffy the Vampire Slayer*. Episodes from Angel will be prefaced with that series' title.

2. As the texts of the comic books add to each series, it is possible that this too will change. Originally, I had planned to put Buffy herself in this category as well, but after reading *Wolves at the Gate* and discovering her sexual relationship with a fellow slayer, I had to adjust my assessment. Her own discussions about that affair, though, lead me to believe that Buffy would probably still consider herself a five, or a heterosexual with some homosexual activities in her past.

3. One interesting thing to note about this is that Xander is also possessed by a spirit; that of the hyenas, feminizing him as well. When viewed in total, it is almost always the feminized males or the female characters that face some sort of bodily displacement, possession, or demon pregnancy in the two series with the exception of Giles, whose transformation into a demon in "A New Man" is less a feminization through possession or pregnancy than an outward sign of the identity crisis and displacement he feels while without a paying job in Season Four.

Works Cited

Goddard, Drew. "Wolves at the Gate." *Buffy the Vampire Slayer, Season Eight.* Dark Horse Comics, 2008.

Jowett, Lorna. *Sex and the Slayer: A Gender Studies Primer for the Buffy Fan.* Middletown, CT: Wesleyan University Press, 2005.

Larbalestier, Justine. "The only thing better than killing a Slayer." Roz Kaveney, *Reading the Vampire Slayer: The New, Updated, Unofficial Guide to Buffy and Angel.* London: I. B. Tauris, 2004. 195–219.

Saxey, Esther. "Staking a Claim: The Series and Its Fanfiction." Roz Kaveney, *Reading the Vampire Slayer.* London: I. B. Tauris, 2001. 187–210.

The Institute for Sex Research, Indiana University. *Sexual Behavior in the Human Female.* Philadephia: W. B. Saunders, 1953.

_____. *Sexual Behavior in the Human Female.* Philadelphia: W. B. Saunders, 1948.

About the Contributors

Alyson R. Buckman is an associate professor of humanities and religious studies at California State University, Sacramento, where she teaches courses on film, popular culture, and American culture. Her work has appeared in journals and anthologies such as *Slayage, Modern Fiction Studies, Exchanges, FEMSPEC, The Journal of American Culture, Screwball Television: Critical Perspectives on the Gilmore Girls* (Syracuse University Press, 2010), and *Investigating* Firefly *and* Serenity*: Science Fiction on the Frontier* (I. B. Tauris, 2008).

Tamy Burnett holds a Ph.D. in English literature from the University of Nebraska, Lincoln, where she is currently a lecturer. Her primary research interests are American popular culture and literature, particularly in relation to issues of gender, sexuality, race/ethnicity, socio-economic class, and (dis)ability studies. She is co-editor of *The Literary* Angel (forthcoming, McFarland) with AmiJo Comeford.

Lewis Call is an assistant professor of history at California Polytechnic State University, San Luis Obispo. He is the author of *Postmodern Anarchism* (Lexington, 2002) and he has also written extensively about alternative sexualities, especially kink. His article about representations of erotic power in the Buffyverse won the 2008 Mr. Pointy award for best article in the field of Buffy studies.

Catherine Coker is an assistant professor of library science at Texas A&M University and the coordinator of research services at Cushing Memorial Library and Archives. Her research focuses on women in science fiction and fantasy. Her articles have been published in *Foundation* and *College and Research Libraries*, among other journals.

Hélène Frohard-Dourlent is a graduate student in sociology at the University of British Columbia in Canada. Her research interests are in qualitative research that focuses on gender, sexuality, education, cultural representations and the negotiation of privileged and minority identities.

Nicholas Greco is an assistant professor of communications and media at Providence College in Otterburne, Manitoba. His doctoral dissertation explored the enigmatic star image and the nature of fan desire in the case of British singer Morrissey. He is a founding fellow of the Canadian Institute for the Study of Pop Culture & Religion.

Rachel Luria is a writing instructor at Florida Atlantic University's Wilkes Honors College. She has an M.F.A. from the University of South Carolina and an M.A. in American studies from the University of Maryland. In addition to her creative work, she is currently co-editing a volume on Neil Gaiman and philosophy.

ordovano earned a B.A. degree in English linguistics and philosophy from _Hebrew_ University of Jerusalem. She is currently working on a M.A. thesis in linguistics and is a teaching assistant in the Hebrew University's Generative Linguistics department.

Todd Parks currently attends Marshall University in Huntington, West Virginia. He received his bachelor's degree in secondary education with specializations in English and Spanish. He is currently working on a double master's degree in English and leadership studies.

Patricia Pender is a postdoctoral research fellow in the School of Humanities and Social Science at the University of Newcastle, Australia. She has previously published essays on Buffy in _Fighting the Forces_ (2002), _Third Wave Feminisms and Postfeminisms_ (2004/2007) and _Slayage: The International Online Journal of Buffy Studies_ (2006).

Jessica Price holds a B.A. in women's studies and is currently working on an M.A. in women's, gender, and sexuality studies from the University of Cincinnati. She aspires to work with the LGBTQ community, specifically with relation to the representation of LGBTQ identities within popular culture.

Sara Swain is a Ph.D. student in the Joint Program in Communication and Culture at York and Ryerson Universities in Toronto. She holds a B.A. (Hons.) in English literature from Memorial University and an M.A. in film studies from Concordia University. She has presented several papers, including work on David Lynch's _Wild at Heart_ and the role of cell phones in contemporary thrillers, at the Film Studies Association of Canada.

Don Tresca lives in Sacramento, California, with his wife and daughter. He received his M.A. in English from California State University, Sacramento, in 1995. He is currently working on his doctoral dissertation on modern horror literature and a book on horror pseudo-documentaries.

Erin B. Waggoner is an adjunct professor of English composition. She holds a bachelor's degree from Morehead State University, and an M.A. from Marshall University. She has attended and presented papers or facilitated presentations at several conferences, including the Pop Culture of the South, Southwest/Texas Pop Culture, Watson Conference, and SAMLA. Her creative works can be found in _HLLQ (Harrington Lesbian Literary Quarterly)_ and Marshall University's _Et Cetera_, where she served as editor in chief for the 2008–2009 edition.

Kathryn Weber holds an M.A. in history and an M.A.T. in secondary social studies from Washington University and a B.A. in history and politics & law from Webster University. At the University of Missouri, St. Louis, she created and moderated an honors seminar on "Women in Popular Culture: From Flappers to _Buffy the Vampire Slayer_."

Index